Killing for Profit

Killing for Profit

Exposing the Illegal Rhino Horn Trade

Julian Rademeyer

Published by Zebra Press
an imprint of Random House Struik (Pty) Ltd
Company Reg. No. 1966/003153/07
Wembley Square, First Floor, Solan Road, Gardens, Cape Town, 8001
PO Box 1144, Cape Town, 8000, South Africa

www.zebrapress.co.za

First published 2012
Reprinted in December 2012 (twice) and 2013

5 7 9 10 8 6 4

PUBLISHER: Marlene Fryer
EDITOR: Ronel Richter-Herbert
PROOFREADER: Jane Housdon
COVER DESIGNER: Michiel Botha
TEXT DESIGNER: Monique Oberholzer
INDEXER: Cliff Perusset
TYPESETTER: Catherine Coetzer

Set in 10.5 pt on 15 pt Minion

Printed and bound by Interpak Books, Pietermaritzburg

ISBN: 978 1 77022 334 9 (print)
ISBN: 978 1 77022 335 6 (ePub)
ISBN: 978 1 77022 336 3 (PDF)

Contents

For Trish, without whom this book could never have been written

Introduction

The Lao People's Democratic Republic, December 2011

The sun is setting on a sweltering winter's day in the Laotian capital, Vientiane. Across a sea of concrete lies the sickly grey Mekong River and, beyond that, a mess of cellphone towers and radio antennas. I climb the stairs of a seedy riverfront bar that reeks of stale cigarettes and alcohol, order an ice-cold quart of Beerlao Lager and find a window seat.

In the far corner, two sweaty tourists play a game of pool with a bar girl wearing impossibly tight white shorts and a fake smile. The place is starting to fill up with the late-afternoon crowd.

Nine thousand kilometres from my home in South Africa, I'm nearing the end of a journey. My flight landed a few hours ago. In my backpack is a photograph, an address and the name of a company. In a folder on my laptop are scanned pages of documents detailing illegal shipments of tons of monkeys, snakes, pangolins, ivory tusks, lion bones and rhino horns. Somewhere out there is the man I'm looking for; the kingpin of an international wildlife-trafficking syndicate. I just have to find him.

Three years ago, I could not have imagined being in that bar or writing this book or quitting my job to do so. Nor could I have imagined where this journey would take me, or the depths of the greed, folly, corruption and depravity that I would encounter.

––––––––––

Rhinos are unique creatures. They're a link to a distant prehistoric past, a precious relic of our long-dead history. Ian Player will never forget his first sighting. It was sixty years ago. He was a young game ranger of twenty-five on an anti-poaching patrol. 'It was a misty morning,' he recalled recently. 'I was looking into a patch of bush when two white rhino came looming out of the mist, with steam rising from their flanks and their backs, and hundreds of stable flies hovering above them. Something within me was deeply touched by this primeval scene, and I had an intuitive flash that somehow my life would be bound up with these great prehistoric animals. There was sacredness about their presence …'

Along with a pioneering wildlife veterinarian, Dr Toni Harthoorn, Player is one of the men credited with saving the southern white rhino from extinction. In the 1960s, the few remaining southern white rhino were confined to the Hluhluwe-iMfolozi Game Reserve in South Africa's Natal province (later KwaZulu-Natal). Between 1961 and 1972, more than 1 100 rhinos were translocated from there to national parks, private reserves and zoos across Africa, Europe, the United Kingdom, Canada and the United States in what was called Operation Rhino. Today, as a result of that intervention and the involvement of commercial game farmers, the number of southern white rhinos has increased tenfold, from just 1 800 in 1968 to nearly 19 000 today. Ninety-five per cent of them are found in South Africa. It is the country's greatest conservation success story. And one that is dangerously close to being unravelled.

While rhino population growth rates in South Africa still exceed the rate at which the animals are being poached, the 'tipping point' is drawing nearer. As I write this, towards the end of 2012, more than 400 rhinos have been killed for their horns this year alone, and projections suggest that as many as 550 could fall victim to poachers' guns by the year's end. Since 2008, without fail, a grim new poaching record has been set every year. If the number of killings continues to rise unabated, it is only a matter of time before the tipping point is reached. And, as was seen in the 1960s, 1970s and 1980s, the results will be devastating. The black rhino population, Africa's other species of rhinoceros, was decimated – cut down from an estimated 100 000 in 1960 to barely 2 400 in 1995. Today their position is dire and, unlike white rhinos, which are considered 'near threatened', they remain on the 'critically endangered' list.

'Rhino have a particularly plaintive cry,' Player wrote, 'which once heard is never forgotten. The screams of agony from rhino that have had their horns chopped off while still alive should reach out into the hearts of all of us.'

When I first read his words, I had no idea what he meant. Months later I heard those terrible dying cries for the first time. And they have stayed with me ever since.

———————

Perhaps the greatest irony is that rhinos are being killed for the very things that evolved to offer them a means of defence. On the black markets of Southeast Asia, rhino horn is worth more per kilogram than gold, cocaine, platinum or heroin. It is a product that people are prepared to kill and die for. In Vietnam, it has become a party drug for the wealthy and a panacea for the very sick. And yet, it offers no real scientific benefits. Its value is artificial, founded on myth and propagated by greed.

But the prices keep rising and the syndicates and the market keep evolving. Since 2009, nearly fifty rhino horns have been stolen in brazen museum robberies, break-ins and smash-and-grabs across Europe. Many of the thefts have been linked to the Rathkeale Rovers, an Irish gang also implicated in robbery, money-laundering, drug dealing, airport heists and trading in counterfeit goods. Even the Russian mob is said to have stolen a mummified woolly rhino, excavated from a Siberian glacier, for its horns. And in the United States, antique dealers and even a rodeo cowboy have pleaded guilty to conspiring to traffic rhino horn trophies that they had bought on auctions across the country. There have been attempted armed robberies of government stockpiles in South Africa. In some instances, cash-in-transit gangs and 'ATM bombers' have turned to rhino poaching because of the low risk involved. Poachers have grown steadily more sophisticated. Some use helicopters and veterinary sedatives. Others have amassed arsenals of weaponry. They are adept at corrupting officialdom and subverting the very regulations meant to protect the animals. And all the while, poachers are being killed and rhinos shot on a scale not seen since the 'Zambezi Valley war' of the 1980s.

In South Africa, a bitter debate is raging over calls for the legalisation of the trade in rhino horn as a last-ditch effort to save the animals. In China, rhinos sold by South Africa to a Chinese pharmaceutical company are penned up in a breeding farm where they regularly have their horns harvested with a purpose-built 'self-suction living rhinoceros horn-scraping tool'. The company, Long Hui Pharmaceutical, is reportedly pressing local government for permission to legally sell horn it has so far gathered under the auspices of 'scientific research'.

———

I have never considered myself a 'conservationist' or an 'environmentalist'. But like many city-bound South Africans, I have something of a yearning for the escapism offered by the bush; for that magical illusion of the wild. It is something that most of us in South Africa take for granted.

For close on twenty years, my work as a journalist has led me to focus on people. Rarely have I written about the environment. I've written about crime and courts, rape and murder, politics and corruption, war, unrest and famine, atrocities and human rights abuses. I've even 'paparazzied' a 'celebrity' or two. I've done stories I'm proud of and many that I would rather forget. There was a time when I thought I'd seen it all, when I sometimes arrogantly believed that nothing could shock or surprise me any more. And then this came along. A story that has angered and gripped me; a story that epitomises the rot that is steadily permeating the heart of South African society. But also a story of a handful of dedicated cops, prosecutors, conservationists and game farmers who, despite minimal resources and overwhelming odds, are trying to fight back.

I didn't set out to investigate rhino poaching. In a way, I stumbled on the story. I'd seen the articles in the papers, read the angry comments, heard the cries of outrage, followed the reports of a rhino shot here, a poacher killed there, and learnt of the nameless arrests. But I hadn't taken much note. At the time I was mired in a seemingly endless pursuit of corrupt politicians, trying to find 'quick hits' that would guarantee page leads and a nice performance review.

Then, quite by chance, I came across the story of a South African, a farm attack and rifles being smuggled across the border into Zimbabwe to be used to kill rhinos for their horns. I was intrigued. I wanted to know more. And so I dug. And the more I dug, the more I unearthed, and the more horrified I became. Horrified at the tales of ruthless criminal enterprise on a scale that I could not have imagined.

What follows is the true story of poachers, killers, pimps, soldiers, generals, assassins, mercenaries, con men, prostitutes, gunrunners, game farmers, corrupt politicians, diplomats and scoundrels. It is also the story of one of South Africa's most precious assets: an animal that has been around for fifty million years. This is the rhinos' last stand. One that, tragically, they may not survive.

Website: www.killingforprofit.com
Facebook: facebook.com/KillingForProfit
Twitter: @julianrademeyer

1

Crooks' Corner

3 August 2009, Southern Zimbabwe
Blood seeps through the dark-green fabric of Hardlife's anorak. At first, the scouts think he is dead. Only when they are about thirty metres away from him do they see movement.

Hardlife looks up at the two men standing over him. Brown boots. Olive-drab uniforms. One of them is holding a rifle. He asks the men for a cigarette. 'You shouldn't smoke,' someone says. Hardlife insists. There's a pack in his trouser pocket. They light the cigarette for him.

A hundred metres away, across a stream, a body is sprawled in the brush. Life Mbedzi is dead. A .303 rifle, the stock bloodied and smeared with finger-prints, lies nearby. It is fitted with a battered scope and a custom-made silencer.

The men had crossed the fence line into the Bubye Valley Conservancy the previous night under a full moon. There were three of them: Hardlife Nkomo, Life Mbedzi and Never Ndlovu. They carried packs, tinned food, two .303 rifles, including the one with the silencer, a handheld spotlight and an axe. They set up camp and slept fitfully until first light.

Game scouts discovered the remnants of their campfire shortly after 9 a.m. The ash and cinders had been covered up, but were still warm. An empty tin of baked beans was found hidden nearby.

Some distance from the camp, the scouts came across the scuffed boot prints of three men and the spoor of two adult rhino and a calf. It made their task a little easier. Poachers rarely deviate from spoor once they're on it.

For six hours the scouts followed the tracks, moving quietly and steadily, careful not to miss any signs. Finally, they came across fresh spoor. Two 'stop groups' were quickly deployed to cut ahead and set up ambush positions.

They didn't have long to wait. Fifteen minutes later, three figures emerged from the scrub and thorn trees. They walked slowly. A hundred metres ... fifty metres ... twenty-five metres. Then a shout tore through the silence. Startled, the poachers took flight. They ran hard, headlong into the scouts.

Life fired blindly at them with the silenced rifle. The scouts returned fire. Hardlife dropped like a stone. Life and Never sprinted across a narrow stream, the scouts following close behind. Suddenly Life stopped in his tracks, swung around and fired another shot. An instant later, he was dead, struck by a scout's bullet. Never Ndlovu kept running.

The 340 000-hectare Bubye Valley Conservancy is one of the last strongholds of Zimbabwe's embattled rhino population. More than 80 per cent of the country's rhinos are now situated on a handful of private conservancies in the country's south-eastern Lowveld.

In 1970 there were an estimated 65 000 black rhino across Africa. By the 1980s, most had been slaughtered by poachers. Today, only 5 000 remain. In Zimbabwe, there are just over 400.

In recent years, Zimbabwe has experienced some of the worst levels of rhino poaching since the 1980s. The killings have been fuelled by Zimbabwe's ongoing political and economic turmoil, large-scale illegal hunting by ruthless South African safari operators, and growing demand for rhino horn on the black markets of Southeast Asia.

In 2000, President Robert Mugabe's government began a 'fast-track' land-resettlement programme that saw hundreds of predominantly white-owned farms seized by squatters and independence 'war veterans' determined to reclaim land they said had been 'stolen by settlers'. The seizures – which Mugabe repeatedly claimed were intended to benefit the 'poor, landless masses' – were often accompanied by violence and used to intimidate and attack political opponents of the ruling ZANU-PF party.

Mugabe and his allies reportedly seized nearly half the country's commercial farms for themselves and their cronies. Wildlife conservancies and plantations were parcelled off to a 'well-connected elite', with devastating results.

Agricultural production reportedly fell by as much as 70 per cent over the course of a decade, with production losses estimated at nearly R100 billion (about $12 billion). By 2002 it was conservatively estimated that game worth R330 million (about $40 million) had been lost since the start of the farm invasions. Some conservancies had lost up to 60 per cent of their animals. In places, poachers tore down game fences and used the wire to make hundreds of snares.

A US embassy assessment in 2003 attributed the dramatic escalation in poaching to widespread hunger, land seizures, and 'the general breakdown of law and order'. Some 'commercial operators' had also taken advantage of the 'relative chaos by marketing "bush meat" and smuggling rhino horn'.

Some South African hunters and safari operators had also been quick to cash in. 'A lot of South Africans thought Zimbabwe was going to the dogs, and their attitude was, "Let's get in and get our cut,"' says Blondie Leathem, Bubye's general manager.

In the Gwaai Valley Conservancy, near the Hwange National Park in western Zimbabwe, South African hunters were accused of 'shooting whole herds of animals'. Describing the carnage, a conservationist I interviewed said: 'Gwaai was destroyed early on. There were a lot of South African hunters involved in raping that place – just shooting entire herds of zebra and wildebeest.'

Zimbabwean rhino specialist, Raoul du Toit – the man credited with driving the formation of the conservancies in the early 1990s – said that while 'impoverished Zimbabweans may claim that they are driven to poaching in order to feed themselves, relatively wealthy sports hunters from South Africa have no such excuse – their unethical behaviour is driven by financial interests and thrill-seeking'.

There were other elements involved, too. US diplomatic cables warned of 'heavily armed "military" personnel' linked to incidents of rhino poaching. A 2009 cable from the Harare embassy reported on 'persistent rumours that senior government officials may be involved in poaching and smuggling'. The cable's author noted that journalists and conservationists had been 'warned not to investigate too deeply'.

————

Hardlife takes a drag on the cigarette and coughs. He speaks slowly, weakened by shock and loss of blood. The silenced .303 had been given to them by a South African, he tells his interrogators. A 'heavy white man' called Johannes. He said the gang had previously supplied him with zebra skins and rhino horns. He had arranged to collect them at 8 p.m. that night at a spot along the tar road near the conservancy, about sixty kilometres north of the Zimbabwean border post at Beitbridge. The gang would leave a tree branch in the road to signal that all was safe.

————

At least 123 rhinos were poached in Zimbabwe in 2008 – the highest number recorded since 1987 and nearly three times the number killed in 2007. The Bubiana Conservancy, just to the north of the Bubye Valley, bore the brunt of the initial attacks. One of Bubiana's scouts was killed; another was wounded. By the end of 2008, seventy-one rhinos had been shot in the Lowveld conservancies.

In one incident, a group of Zimbabwe National Parks (Zimparks) rangers and rhino monitors surprised a gang of poachers who were resting among the granite boulders of a *koppie*. Two rangers and a poacher simultaneously opened fire with AK-47s, spraying the hillside with bullets. They were only about seven metres apart, but in the chaos most of the shots went wide. One of the poachers was hit in the arm. Somehow, the rangers escaped unscathed. Nineteen spent cartridge casings were later picked up at the scene.

The carnage in Bubiana peaked in June 2008. Over the next six months, nearly fifty black rhino were poached. In the first five months of 2009, a further twenty-four were killed. The remaining rhinos – twenty-two in all – were translocated to Bubye in May 2009. Teams of scouts, veterinarians and conservationists worked frantically to move the survivors. But the slaughter continued to the very end. At night, as Bubiana's last rhinos were trucked out of the conservancy, the sound of automatic rifle fire could be heard rolling off the hills.

The Bubye Valley Conservancy escaped the initial surge relatively unscathed, losing only five rhinos in 2008. That changed abruptly in 2009, as Bubiana's rhino population teetered on the brink of extinction. Bubye's scouts, caught up in the desperate rescue efforts, had taken their eyes off their 'own backyard' just long enough for the poachers to gain a foothold. By the time they managed to bring the situation back under control, Bubye had lost thirty-eight rhinos. The deaths of only four rhinos could be attributed in 2009 to 'natural mortalities'.

Two very distinct groups of poachers emerged amid the bloodshed in the Lowveld. There were the Harare-based gangs, armed with AK-47s and axes. Many appeared to be serving, or former, soldiers, as their tactics betrayed their military training. Some also carried army equipment and clothing. They were aggressive and quick to open fire when confronted by the scouts, whom they often outgunned and outnumbered. Once they tracked a rhino, they made little or no effort to hide its killing. The rattle of AK-47 fire could be heard kilometres away, reverberating off the rocks and valleys. The poachers would hit hard and fast, mowing the animals down with sustained bursts of fire, often aiming at their legs to cripple them before they moved in for the kill. The horns were hurriedly hacked off with axes, leaving behind a bloody mess of mangled flesh, bone and cartilage.

The other poachers were local, drawn from nearby villages and towns. Dubbed the 'zebra gangs', they had cut their teeth on hunting game and bush meat, but by 2003 were smuggling hundreds of salted zebra skins across the border into South Africa. Unlike the Harare-based gunmen, they used hunting rifles and bush knives and were subtler, more proficient killers.

Their signature was their knife-work, a skill they had acquired skinning the zebras they had poached. Some were said to be able to skin an entire zebra carcass in just five minutes. Unlike the 'AK gangs', they didn't waste time hacking off the horn and chopping through bone. A rhino's horns, unlike those of an antelope, do not have a solid bone core. The horn develops from a dome-shaped growth plate that sits above layers of bone and cartilage. It is a bit like a fingernail. Someone skilled with a knife will cut around the seam at the base of a horn, insert the blade under the edges and then essentially pry it loose.

The zebra gangs' weapons of choice were .303s and .458s – standard hunting rifles. It made the killings harder to detect. From a distance, a single shot – and usually that was all that was required – could easily be confused for a legitimate trophy hunt, an elephant snapping a branch or the crack of a whip.

But there was another significant factor that set them apart from the Harare crime syndicates. The zebra gangs were armed, funded and directed by South Africans – a group that would eventually become known in the press as the 'Musina Mafia'.

There are no ambulances in Beitbridge, and the police station at Makado, ninety kilometres to the north, has no patrol cars at its disposal. If a poacher is arrested, shot or killed, a Bubye staffer has to drive to Makado, collect a policeman and return with him to the conservancy. Only then can the suspect be transported to the police cells, the hospital in Beitbridge or the government mortuary.

The task of getting Hardlife to hospital falls to the co-ordinator of a rhino monitoring project at Bubye. The poacher is bundled into the back of a Toyota Land Cruiser. A Makado cop comes along for the ride.

Hours later – satisfied that he is not likely to die or escape from the hospital – the pair head back to Makado. Night has fallen. Somewhere near the conservancy scouts and cops are lying in ambush for a heavy-set South African called Johannes. Others are keeping an eye on the road.

A bakkie tears through the darkness towards the border. The fat man behind the wheel has his foot hard on the accelerator. It is a dangerous road, narrow and jagged along the edges where the tar has crumbled away. At night, cattle and goats roam freely across it. The man barely notices the Toyota Land

Cruiser heading in the opposite direction. As he passes it, he flicks his lights on high, blinding the occupants. Then he's gone, his tail lights a red blur in the blackness. He doesn't see it, but the Land Cruiser brakes sharply, does a U-turn and speeds after him.

———————

The immigration hall at Beitbridge is still teeming with people trying to cross the border into South Africa before it gets too late. The fat man hurries inside. Somehow, he manages to force his way to the front of a queue. He is sweating heavily. A Zimbabwean immigration officer stamps his passport and waves him along. He is almost through the door when the cop and the Bubye staffer run inside and confront him.

They don't need to look at his passport to know who he is. The conservancy's anti-poaching unit has had a file on him for years. His name is Jan Johannes George Roos, but he calls himself Johan. He's forty-two, divorced, and lives with his father in Musina, an uninspiring border town eighteen kilometres away in South Africa. He has lived there most of his life.

It was 1985 and Roos was nineteen when he fell foul of the law for the first time. A magistrate found him guilty of illegal hunting and contravening South Africa's nature conservation regulations, and he was given a suspended sentence. Two weeks later, in a separate case, he was convicted of poaching 'endangered wild animals'. He was sentenced to 'six strokes with a light cane'. After that, he appeared to remain out of trouble until 1988, when he was arrested again and found guilty of stealing livestock. He was fined R1 000. Five years later he was back in the dock, on charges related to illegal hunting. But he managed to avoid prison and was sentenced to a year's correctional supervision.

Blondie Leathem, the Bubye Conservancy's general manager, recalls catching Roos shooting game along the tar road from Beitbridge to Bulawayo in early 1995. 'That fat-arsed bastard was *klapping* animals with three locals and selling the meat in Beitbridge,' he says. 'I had him on the ground with an FN [rifle] at his head, and he kept whining, "*Ag, meneer, meneer, ek is jammer. Meneer, asseblief, ek het 'n klein kind. Ek sal dit nooit weer doen nie.*" (Sir, sir, I'm sorry. Sir, please, I have a small child. I'll never do it again.) Sometimes I wonder if I shouldn't have pulled the trigger. It would have saved us a helluva lot of trouble.'

Records indicate that Roos worked for a construction company in Musina as a foreman for a couple of years until 2002. Then, in October 2003, he and one of his friends were caught illegally hunting game on a farm across the road from Bubye. The farm had been seized by squatters during the 2000 land invasions. A case was opened with Beitbridge police, but neither Roos nor his friend was ever prosecuted.

The Bubye file states that 'informants have consistently identified Roos as the buyer of zebra hides and as the supplier of .30-calibre bullets to poachers for them to hunt zebras for him'. In 2006, a group of poachers caught laying snares for zebra in the Bubiana Conservancy named Roos as one of the 'buyers'. There were also allegations linking him to the poaching of giraffe and zebra on the Nuanetsi Game Ranch, 120 kilometres north-east of Beitbridge.

'There are places that once had 400 or 500 zebra,' says Leathem. 'Today there are none left. The sheer quantity of hides going across the border from 2000 onwards into South Africa was staggering, but the South African authorities didn't do much [about] it. The border is so porous and the level of corruption at Beitbridge so great that the poachers were just sending skins across all the time.'

Gradually, the zebra gangs began turning their attention to rhinos.

Outside the immigration hall, Roos's passport – black and blue with entry and exit stamps for Zimbabwe and South Africa – is taken away. Fifty-seven out of fifty-nine pages of the passport have entries on them, revealing that between March 2007 and July 2009, Roos had travelled to Zimbabwe 226 times – an average of two crossings a week.

In the parking lot, police find his bakkie, a battered gold 1987 Nissan Safari, registration number DZZ 615 N. It matches the description Hardlife had given them – it is also the same bakkie that Roos was driving in October 2003 when he was caught shooting game on the property opposite Bubye.

Oddly, an identical registration number had previously been recorded for a brown Volkswagen Caravelle, which Zimbabwe Republic Police (ZRP) had stopped at a roadblock in July 2003. The occupants – a dozen South Africans, including four teenagers – had been accused of illegally hunting hippo, crocodile and elephant on a farm that had been seized by 'war veterans' in the West Nicholson area. There were claims that one of the South Africans had also shot a black rhino in the Bubiana Conservancy a month earlier. Police confiscated close to 400 kilograms of meat. The South Africans denied any wrongdoing and claimed they belonged to a Christian organisation. The eight adults spent a night in police holding cells in West Nicholson, were questioned and then released without charge after a senior government official 'pressurised' the cops into dropping the case.

Roos is taken to the Makado police station, where he'll spend the night in a lice-infested cell. His cellphone is confiscated after he is seen hurriedly sending an SMS. In Afrikaans, the text message reads: 'Clean the laundry'. When questioned about it, he claims the recipient is his 'garden boy' in South Africa, a man who investigators know had previously accompanied him on trips to Zimbabwe.

All other messages stored in the cellphone's inbox and outbox appear to have been deleted. But fragments of SMSes can still be extracted from the delivery reports sent to the phone, which indicate when messages are successfully delivered. Copies of some SMSes are also found in the phone's draft folder.

For instance, there's a message sent to a contact called 'Fish' a day before the Bubye shooting. 'I will buy 7 items this evening ...' it reads. Two hours later, there's a message to another contact, identified as Ian: 'Don't forget to bring me that [sic] 10 items ...' And there is a record of a call to a number saved as 'New Mbedzi'. In fact, half a dozen numbers stored on the phone are for 'Mbedzi'. Investigators write them down as they scroll through the contact list. Two other entries pique their interest: one for 'Freedom', and another for 'Teacher number 2'. The numbers are later linked to two known poachers: Freedom Chiradza and Rodgers 'Teacher' Mukwena.

————

The tiny village of Mpande is situated about seventy kilometres east of Bubye in the so-called Siyoka Communal Lands. It is a hardscrabble place – a scattering of mud-walled houses, a liquor store and a spaza shop set in an arid wasteland of dry scrub and dust.

It was to Mpande that Roos went in about 2000, allegedly in search of zebra skin. 'The guys in the area recall him going there, sitting around drinking beer with the people, and then suddenly the villagers were buying cars and had money to spend,' Norman English, the head of anti-poaching at Bubye, says.

More than any other village, Mpande has been a thorn in the conservancy's side for close to a decade. Hardlife, Life and Never were all from there. So was Rodgers Mukwena – the man they called 'Teacher'. As you drive into the village, one house stands out among all the others. There's a stone wall around it. Although it is not a particularly prepossessing place, in Mpande's impoverished surroundings it signals money. It is the house Mukwena built, allegedly on the proceeds of zebra skin and rhino horn.

Mukwena was a teacher before he became a poacher. When Zimbabwe's economy collapsed in the late 1990s, he, like so many others, found himself trying to survive on a salary that amounted to little more than $100 a month. It wasn't long before he picked up a rifle.

'Mukwena's a bright guy,' English says. 'Unlike the others, he's done all right. The rest have come out of it with nothing. But he's got a couple of houses in Beitbridge that he rents out. By local standards, he's well off.'

In 2005 Mukwena was arrested in Mpande along with several other men. Two .303 hunting rifles – the serial numbers removed – were found, along with zebra and lion skins and pangolin scales. There were bags of skinning salt and brine bins in which to prepare the skins. Despite the evidence, the case never went to trial. There were suspicions that a cop, a prosecutor or even a magistrate had been paid off to quash the charges.

Mukwena was arrested again in February 2010, having been named in the confessions of five men caught trying to poach rhino in Bubye. They had been found with a silenced .303 rifle, which they had brought into Zimbabwe from South Africa. It was concealed in a secret compartment built into the tailgate of a Nissan bakkie. Unlike the silenced rifle found when Life was killed and Hardlife wounded, it wasn't particularly well made. 'It was just a tin can on the end of a barrel,' says English.

A search of Mukwena's house turned up one rhino horn. Mukwena claimed to have picked it up in the veld in the Bubiana Conservancy. Later he changed his story and the charge was shifted to his wife, who was alone inside the house when the horn was found. By then she was safe and sound in South Africa.

In September 2010, police confirmed that a .303 rifle, registered to Mukwena, had been modified to accommodate a silencer. Silencers are illegal in Zimbabwe. But by then Mukwena was also nowhere to be found. There were rumours that he had fled to South Africa and was hiding out in Musina with his wife.

————

4 August 2009

Roos is transferred to the Beitbridge police cells ahead of his first court appearance. He convinces a cop to let him use his cellphone to call his 'sick father'. The phone is taken away from him when someone spots him 'pushing way more buttons than required to simply phone his dad'.

A few messages appear to have been deleted. The cops leave the cellphone on. At 1 p.m. it beeps loudly. It is an SMS from 'Teacher number 2'. There is only one word: 'Boom'. Sixteen minutes later, there is another SMS, this one from 'Jonathan New 2'. 'When will we meet,' it reads. 'I hope to bring stuff.'

The case against Roos crumbles spectacularly quickly. Prior to his appearance in the local magistrate's court, an 'influential Beitbridge businessman' complains to senior court officials that his 'friend', Johan Roos, is being unfairly 'harassed' by the police. When the case is finally called, the prosecutor fails to make any mention of key evidence against Roos. The magistrate orders that Roos be released. Within a few hours he's across the border and over the bridge, safely back in South Africa.

Never Ndlovu is arrested five months after the shooting at Bubye. He appears in court and then disappears. Later he is sighted in Musina in South Africa. In April 2010, Hardlife Nkomo – by now fully recovered from his chest wound – is sentenced to six years in prison. The sentence is hailed by Vitalis Chadenga – the then acting director-general of the Parks and Wildlife

Management Authority – as a necessary deterrent that will 'help put the country's conservation efforts back on track'.

Roos's arrest and subsequent release go largely unnoticed but for an article in the *Zoutpansberger*, a tiny community newspaper in Limpopo province. It picks up on the story two weeks after the shooting. Roos's name, however, appears in only two paragraphs at the end of a brief article that quotes a Zimbabwe police spokesman, Chief Superintendent Hosiah Mukombero, who describes him as the 'brainpower behind the poaching syndicate'. Mukombero – either because he is misinformed or lying – claims that Roos is still in custody.

————

19 April 2010

For two days game scouts follow the tracks of two poachers deep inside Bubye. Finally, after a frustrating hunt, they find fresh spoor leading out of the conservancy towards the Beitbridge road. They radio ahead. Police set up a trap near the fence line in the general direction the spoor appears to be taking. At last two men emerge from the bushes. One is holding a rifle. They are quickly apprehended.

The 'shooter' is subsequently identified as Andrew 'British' Bvute, a government veterinary officer. He had previously admitted to poaching a rhino in Bubye, but somehow the case had gone nowhere. The second man – the tracker – is called Joseph Chiguba. He's from Beitbridge. Four other men, who had dropped the poachers off, are also arrested.

The weapon Bvute had been carrying is a .375-calibre hunting rifle with the serial number G1179783. The rifle has been fitted with a silencer. The lathe work appears to be identical to the silenced .303 found next to Life Mbedzi's body after the contact in Bubye.

Under interrogation, Bvute and his cohorts claim that Johan Roos had supplied them with the rifle and ammunition, along with instructions to shoot a rhino and bring out the horns. He had supposedly bragged that he had 'eight different gangs [of poachers] operating for him' in the area.

Bvute is later fined $100 for possession of an unlicensed firearm. The fact that the rifle was fitted with an illegal silencer is completely overlooked by the magistrate. The others are all acquitted.

_____

In April 2010, I drove to Beitbridge and then on to Bubye. I wanted to know more about Roos and the origin of the rifles and the silencers. A few months earlier I had joined a team of investigative journalists at South Africa's Media24 newspaper group. By chance, in the course of researching another story, I had stumbled across the article in the *Zoutpansberger* and the reference to Roos. The only other mention of his name that I could find when I Googled it was contained in a submission made by Zimbabwe to the Convention on International Trade in Endangered Species of Wild Fauna and Flora (CITES) about the status of the country's rhinos. The report gave basic details about the case, the shooting at Bubye and the discovery of the silenced .303. It was a detail that intrigued me. I had never before heard of silenced weapons being used to kill rhinos.

On my return to South Africa, I called up a law-enforcement contact and asked him whether he could find out anything about the .375 that had been found with Bvute. It was one of the few weapons to be recovered with an intact serial number. A few days later, he called back. 'The rifle was stolen in a farm attack near Musina,' he said. A case had been registered with the police. The complainant was a man named Faan Lemmer.

_____

The farmhouse smells of mildew and mothballs. 'They never open it up any more,' Faan Lemmer complains, motioning disdainfully at a servant in the kitchen. I follow him along a darkened passageway to his father's bedroom. Pink light streams through the curtains. The furnishings are spartan: a white dresser, a full-length mirror, seventies-style built-in cupboards and a space where a safe once stood. 'This is where it happened,' Lemmer says. 'My dad was sitting on this bed. The four *bliksems* were standing there in front of him, looking at me ... They didn't say a word.'

It was 8 May 2009. Two days later, the family fled the farm. Faan, sixty-seven, and his wife, Christi, sixty, lived in a flat behind the main farmhouse. They had moved there from Vryburg in South Africa's North West province five years earlier, following the death of Faan's mother. His father, Faan Snr, aged ninety, couldn't continue on his own – he'd lost most of his hearing and his eyesight was fading.

The old man had bought the 1300-hectare farm, called Nekel, in 1957 while working as an accountant for ISCOR, the state-owned steel company. A decade later he retired early and moved there to take up cattle farming.

Situated ninety kilometres west of Musina in Limpopo province, the farm is a stone's throw from the entrance to the Mapungubwe National Park, one of South Africa's most significant archaeological sites. The park is situated at the confluence of the Shashi and Limpopo Rivers, where the borders of South Africa, Zimbabwe and Botswana converge. A kilometre inland, rising above the southern bank of the Limpopo River, is Mapungubwe Hill, a natural citadel that once guarded the golden treasures of an Iron Age kingdom.

Its secrets were rediscovered in 1933, when a group of fortune seekers, pursuing tales of hidden riches, clambered up the narrow crevice that leads to the top. There they dug up a grave that had lain undisturbed for 700 years. Inside they found a skeleton, adorned with gold. The bones crumbled when they touched them. Near the skull, one of them found a delicate gold-foil rhinoceros, once a symbol of royalty, and today the site's best-known artefact.

In forty years, Lemmer Snr had never locked his doors. Violent crime was something that happened in the towns and cities. Out here, people felt safe. Of course, there were the occasional stock thefts and petty theft, but in more recent years, there had been a dramatic escalation in the illegal bush-meat trade and the poaching of game.

The most notorious poacher in the area was nicknamed 'Rasta'. For years he'd evaded capture. Although his snares were everywhere, few people had ever seen him. Those who had said he wore dreadlocks, carried a knife and an AK-47 assault rifle, and daubed himself with *muti*, a traditional potion designed to protect him. Some said he was a ghost. When Mapungubwe park rangers finally captured him, he reportedly asked them how they had tracked him – the *muti* was meant to conceal him. The conservative local newspaper approvingly reported that 'the ranger replied that *muti* does not work on a man of God'.

Faan and Christi walk me through the events of that Friday night in May. 'We were negligent, but after so many years, who would think to lock the doors?' he asks. He recalls that it was late – probably about 11 p.m. Christi was watching television, and he had just taken a shower. He stepped outside for a moment. He was only wearing shorts. It was a hot night. 'I saw that my dad's light was still burning. Normally he'd be having a kip by then. I went to the main house to have a look. The door was pulled shut, but as usual it wasn't locked.

'When I got to his room, there they stood. The four "gentlemen". I knew we were in big *kak*. What are three guys doing in another guy's bedroom at eleven at night?' Faan Snr was sitting on the side of the bed, looking up at the men. He seemed bewildered. Someone had struck him on the leg with a heavy object, perhaps an iron pipe. His deafness, it seemed, had been mistaken for defiance.

The men surrounded Faan. 'One of them took me by the arm and led me out of the house. They didn't say anything. *Jissus*, but when we got to the stoep, they *bliksemmed* me! I don't know what they hit me with. I remember three blows, and then I passed out. When I came to, I was sitting up and the blood was pouring off my head like water. For some reason I took my watch off and threw it into the darkness. Then one of the blacks tied my hands tightly behind my back. Two of them pulled me to my feet and marched me back to the house.'

He remembers the look of horror on his father's face and the old man's desperate question: 'Fanie, what's going on?' Afraid of what they might do if he spoke, Faan simply shrugged his shoulders. All the men, except one, spoke to him in English. From the accents, he thought they were Zimbabwean. The fourth man spoke Afrikaans. He was local. 'I know this place,' he told Faan. The men wanted money, and lots of it.

They dragged Faan to the flat. One of them had found Christi and was busying himself tying her wrists together. 'If you make a noise, we are going to kill you,' he said. Faan tried to reason with them. 'I voted for the ANC,' he lied.

'Fuck the ANC!' came the terse reply. Christi remembers that one of the men had red-painted fingernails. 'He had such cruel eyes,' she says. Another carried a hand-axe. 'That's probably what they hit me with,' Faan speculates. 'With the blunt side. If it was the sharp side, I'd be dead.'

For three hours, the men terrorised the family. They ransacked the flat, piling up their spoils: R14 000 in cash, a camera, a pair of binoculars, bottles of whisky and beer, biltong, chocolates, cold meats and clothes. They demanded the keys to the two gun safes in the farmhouse. 'If I hadn't given them the keys, the chances are slim that I'd still be alive,' Faan tells me. There was a small arsenal there for the taking: five hunting rifles and a 9mm pistol. One of the weapons was an old .375 Holland & Holland Magnum rifle that belonged to Faan's nephew, who had relocated to the United States.

Christi had somehow managed to hide a knife under a bowl of dog food in the flat and cut them loose once the men had gone. The robbers had taken their keys, including those for the two bakkies on the farm. 'We stayed inside until the farmworkers arrived at 7 a.m. We were too scared to go out. If they caught us, they'd kill us.'

Hours later, two of the suspects were arrested on a nearby farm after boasting to a farm labourer about the guns they had stolen. Three rifles were seized. The other weapons, including the .375, were nowhere to be found. The case was postponed six times between October 2009 and February 2011. On the seventh occasion, a Musina regional court magistrate scrapped it from the court roll and freed the suspects. The reason: a key witness – the farm labourer who had turned the men in – was not in court to testify and was unlikely to return. He had sent a message to the prosecutor. He was in Zimbabwe, he said, but had no way of coming back, because 'the Limpopo River is full'.

The Lemmers spent the Saturday night after the attack on the farm. They barely slept. The next day, they packed their bags. 'I decided, fuck it, we weren't going to stay here any more.' They moved to a house in Musina. Ironically, it is situated a few blocks from the house where Johan Roos and his father live. 'It was so nice here,' Christi tells me. 'We never thought something like this would happen. We hardly ever come here any more.'

The property is neglected. Game fences are in need of repair. In the bushes, there are mounting numbers of snares. Squatters are building wood and corrugated-iron shacks near a dip in the road below the farmhouse. 'They are probably family or connections of the workers,' Faan says. He no longer cares. 'Our policy, when we lived here, was that no other family members were allowed, not even children,' says Christi. 'We paid for electricity and food. Now everyone is squatting here and they come to me this morning to say they are short of bread, milk and coffee.'

Later, Faan loads up the workers in the back of the bakkie and heads out to inspect the farm. It is green and lush after recent rains. Grey storm clouds hang overhead. We stop and get out. There's a pungent smell of decay. The desiccated remains of a dead warthog lie caught in a snare under a bush. Further away is the skull of an impala, and another snare. 'The poachers are a bloody curse,' Faan remarks.

He drives me to a spot on the farm where the burnt-out remains of an old Mercedes-Benz had been found. 'We think it was poachers [who] were driving through long grass, [and when] the engine got hot, the grass caught fire. The car was completely burnt out. The poachers ran away.'

But there is no sign of the wreck when we get there. 'Where is it?' he snaps at one of the workers on the back of the bakkie. 'It's gone,' the man replies. 'The people from the scrapyard came and took it.' Faan is enraged. 'This is what happens if the farm owners aren't around.'

He jerks his thumb towards the back. 'They start to think that they are boss and do what they like.' He spits out orders at the men. His contempt is poisonous. For the most part, they ignore him, sniggering when his back is turned. He has no authority here any more. He'll be gone before nightfall, and it will be weeks before they have to endure him again.

———

Musina is an ugly place, tacky and cheap; a rough-and-ready border town that is not uncommonly referred to as South Africa's 'Wild West'. The Great North Road runs through the town to the border with Zimbabwe. It is rutted and potholed from the wheels of the thousands of trucks that pass through it every year.

Near the taxi rank, a faded mural blackened by exhaust smoke warns: 'Play it safe, AIDS kills'. It is plastered over with pamphlets for penis enlargements and 'Quick Same Day Abortions' by 'Dr Bob' that are supposedly '100% guaranteed and pain free'. Alongside it, another mural exhorts: 'Keep our country clean for the next generation'.

The shops in the main street have names like the Musina Cheap Price Shop and the Bargain Centre. There are countless cut-price dealers, informal traders and *spaza* shops. Fast-food outlets do a roaring trade in greasy fried chicken. You could say that Zimbabwe's economic catastrophe was a boon for Musina.

Johan Roos lives in Paul Mills Street, a few blocks from the Spur steak-house. The house is largely hidden from view by trees and thick foliage. There are two bakkies and a car parked in the driveway, but nobody is home. A domestic worker says the *baas* is away. She's not sure when he will be back.

On my return to Johannesburg, I dial his cellphone number, hoping we can arrange a meeting and that he'll be prepared to talk to me about Zimbabwe. There's no answer. Fifteen minutes later, at 3.33 p.m., while I'm on another call, someone leaves a voicemail on my phone. 'It is Johan speaking ... You can possibly just give me a call again so that I know who it is that is looking for me,' he says.

But when I call back, the phone is answered by another man. He identifies himself as Johan's brother, Pieter. I tell him about the message. 'I don't know about that,' he says. There's a pause. 'It was probably my friend. He's sitting in the bakkie.' He admits that it is Johan's phone, but claims Johan is in Swaziland.

I ask about the allegations levelled against his brother in Zimbabwe. 'It is just a story that is being spread,' he tells me. 'They held him completely unnecessarily. He was totally innocent. He had nothing with him. His name was mentioned by a black who stuffed up,' Pieter says. 'It was completely ridiculous. He did absolutely nothing and he had absolutely nothing with him [when they arrested him].'

I never do hear from Roos. Not even when one of Media24's papers, *Beeld*, leads with a story exposing the 'Musina Mafia' and the rifles smuggled across the border. Not long afterwards, Roos changes his cellphone number.

'If you want to know rage,' says Blondie Leathem, 'you have to see a rhino calf standing next to her decaying mother for three days in 40 °C heat, trying to suckle.' For thirty years, Leathem has been at the heart of Zimbabwe's bloody rhino wars, first in the Zambezi Valley and now in the Lowveld. It is a rage he knows all too well.

Zimbabwe escaped the initial poaching surge of the 1970s and early 1980s, which saw Africa's black rhinos reduced from roughly 65 000 in the late 1960s to just 15 000 in 1980. Ironically, the Rhodesian Bush War in the 1970s insulated the country's rhinos from the carnage elsewhere on the continent. It was a brief respite.

To Zimbabwe's north, across the Zambezi River, lies Zambia. In 1981, its national parks, particularly those in the Luangwa Valley, had an estimated 3000 black rhino. Six years later, there were fewer than 100. Zambia's economy had historically been based on copper, but when copper prices plummeted in the 1970s, so did its economy. By the 1980s the country was destitute, its currency almost worthless. Poaching surged, and one by one Zambia's wildlife sanctuaries were decimated.

By 1983, Zambian poachers were venturing across the river into Zimbabwe's northernmost parks. Fishermen and tourists began to report hearing unexplained volleys of shots. Four rhino carcasses were discovered after the 1983 rainy season. The skulls bore signs of having been hacked with machetes. The horns were gone.

Once it started, the killing was relentless. In 1984, twelve carcasses were found. In 1985, it was sixty-eight; in 1986, 149; in 1987, 170. In response, Zimbabwe's then prime minister, Robert Mugabe, approved a controversial 'shoot-on-sight' policy against poachers, known as Operation Stronghold. The man in charge was Glenn Tatham, the newly appointed chief warden of Zimparks. He didn't mince his words. 'Desperate situations require desperate measures,' he told a reporter from *Sports Illustrated*. 'We knew we had to take the guys on and fight fire with fire. Our objective is to save animals; it's not to kill people. But we cannot afford the possible loss of life among our men by letting them walk into gangs of armed criminals without having the option of shooting first.'

Blondie Leathem is a veteran of the Bush War and fought with the Rhodesian Light Infantry, an elite airborne commando unit known as 'The Saints' or 'The Incredibles'. He was badly wounded in combat, suffering a gunshot wound to the stomach and losing two fingers on his left hand. He spent a year recovering in hospital and then returned to the RLI. At the end of the war, when the unit was disbanded, he signed up with Zimparks, took a substantial cut in pay, and found himself in the middle of a new war.

By 1986, the number of incursions by armed poachers had risen to 150 a year. There were frantic efforts to move black rhinos out of the lower Zambezi Valley, the area closest to the border. Over the course of the next three years, 170 would be translocated to the relative safety of private lands in central and southern Zimbabawe.

In the Zambezi Valley, dozens of poachers were being killed. 'The poachers were coming across the river in dugouts. A lot of [them] had AK-47s. The fire-fights were usually over quickly. If you didn't get them down in the first couple of seconds, they were gone.'

'It got really ugly,' Leathem says. 'We had *carte blanche* and we hammered them, but it didn't help, of course. More guys just kept coming. We had one period where we killed ten guys in fourteen days. And then it went quiet. For three weeks there wasn't a single incursion. But after three weeks, they came back with a vengeance. It turned out, from our informant, that these *okes* had gone back to the middleman and said: "It's dangerous over there. We're not going back." The middleman then simply upped the price per kilogram from $300 to $800. Now, they had three times the number of guys prepared to come in and risk it.'

Zambia's capital, Lusaka, was a key hub in the international rhino horn and ivory trade. The police were easily corrupted and turned a blind eye to the traders. Leathem and his men ran their own groups of informants, but were careful not to pay them in cash and risk violating currency regulations. The Zambians were so poor that the informers routinely did their work for a few cigarettes, cooking oil, maize, cakes of soap and cheap digital watches.

Norman English was a senior ranger at the time. 'We got sorted properly there. I remember one day when I had six gangs in my area with an average of four to six guys in a gang. When you have fourteen scouts to take them on, you're not going to win. We lost 104 rhino in three years.'

In one incident in 1989, English's scouts found a gang of six in the Chizarira National Park. Once described as the black rhino's last Eden, it is a spectacularly beautiful landscape with deep gorges and panoramic views. A tour guide had taken a group of tourists up to a viewpoint overlooking a gorge. Three hundred metres below, he spotted a group of six men bathing in a river. On the bank were military backpacks and kit. He radioed English.

'It was a group of poachers,' English says. 'They felt so secure that they were bathing there in the middle of the day. We killed five and caught the last bugger. In their camp we found heavy weapons and thirty-two rhino horns.'

As the killings in the Zambezi Valley mounted, so did criticism of the operation, both within the Zimbabwean government and from human rights organisations abroad. Relations between Zimbabwean police, Central Intelligence Organisation operatives and the Zimparks rangers grew increasingly strained.

'It was a helluva thing being a white guy in charge of anti-poaching operations where you were shooting black *ouens*,' Leathem says. 'By the end of 1987, I had been locked up on three occasions by police. It was getting beyond a joke.' He was arrested for murder after a suspected poacher – the son of a senior Zambian police official – drowned in the Zambezi River. Later, Leathem was accused of being a South African spy. Glenn Tatham was also arrested and accused of murdering a poacher on an undercover operation. The cases were all eventually dismissed. Of the shootings, Leathem told a *Time* magazine reporter at the time: 'Trying to arrest a man with an AK-47 is like trying to grab a lion with your bare hands.'

By the end of the war in the Zambezi Valley in 1993, more than 170 poachers were dead. At least four Zimbabwe park rangers had lost their lives. And more than a thousand rhinos had been killed for their horns. The killing stopped, but only when there were no more rhinos left to kill.

By the mid-1990s, the surviving rhinos in Zimbabwe's parks along the border with Zambia had all been translocated to the Lowveld. Driven by Raoul du Toit, a conservationist and rhino specialist, a number of conservancies had been created as safe havens for the animals. They were on land that had previously been used for cattle ranching. But in the late 1980s and early 1990s, a series of crippling droughts hit the Lowveld. Coupled with decades of exploitative cattle farming and overgrazing, the impact was devastating.

Clive Stockil, later chairman of the Savé Valley Conservancy, said at the time that the cattle ranches 'were headed for an economic disaster, let alone an ecological disaster'.

'We saw soil erosion. We saw overgrazing. We saw the loss of perennial grasses. And we were forced, by the end of the 1980s, to sit down and really think about what our future was.' Encouraged by a feasibility study which concluded that conservancies, through tourism and hunting, could generate double the income of cattle ranching, many farmers began to embrace the idea.

Fences between farms were dropped and properties were linked into ever larger conservancies. Without them, Zimbabwe would have no black rhinos today.

'Killing poachers doesn't achieve anything,' Leathem says. 'There are so many poor guys out there and criminal elements that are prepared to take the risk to make quick bucks. No matter how many of them you shoot or arrest, you'll never stop it. The only way is to cull the market. You have got to get to the guys at the top.'

2

The Wiseguy

The obituary buried in the pages of the *Hartford Courant* on 27 July 2007 ran to barely a dozen lines. A dry, characterless assessment of a life lived, it recorded the sudden passing of John C. Lukman Jnr in Costa Rica on 7 July 2007 at the age of fifty-three.

Lukman, also known as 'Captain Jack', was a resident of Newington, Connecticut, for most of his life before moving to Central America in 2001, the obituary noted. He was survived by his father, three daughters and two granddaughters. 'He loved them dearly and will be missed by all.' A small gathering of remembrance was planned.

The only hint at Lukman's identity and life was included almost as an afterthought. 'He loved to travel and did so extensively in Africa and Central America.'

A year later, someone started digging for information. Logs of requests made to the Central Intelligence Agency under the Freedom of Information Act show that on 4 September 2008, the CIA received a request for access to files on John Charles Lukman Jnr. The identity of the applicant is not listed and there is no indication whether the files – if they exist – were ever released.

––––––––––

2 June 1988
Special Agent Rich Moulton checks the microphone taped to the centre of his chest and buttons up his shirt. He is used to wearing a wire. 'I have no chest hair left as a result,' he likes to joke. He has worked undercover for much of

the fourteen years he has spent with the US Fish and Wildlife Service (USFWS). In law-enforcement circles, he and his colleagues are sometimes disparagingly referred to as 'duck cops'. It is not something any of them pay much heed to.

Moulton has that rare, chameleon-like ability, so prized in undercover agents, of being able to become his cover story. It is a bit like being a method actor, only the stakes are far higher. Early in his career, Moulton hadn't thought he could cut it as an undercover operative. 'But the more comfortable you got, the more you realised that, hey, this is like being an actor. You just gotta remember the script.'

Once he posed as a wealthy collector to trap a New Yorker who was smuggling snow-leopard skins from Afghanistan and selling them for US$15 000 each. At the time there were fewer than 2 000 of the animals left in the world. Moulton swapped his jeans for suits and his wheels for a Corvette and an SUV. He pretended that another agent was his chauffeur.

Today, he's Rick Moore, a businessman who buys exotic animal trophies and resells them to home decorators. Moulton has code-named the sting 'Operation Wiseguy', a name he borrowed from a popular TV show. Moulton is a fan. Every Thursday night, he and millions of other viewers tune in to the improbable exploits of undercover agent Vinnie Terranova as he takes on the Mob. It is fantasy stuff, complete with gunfights, car chases and vehicles that invariably explode on impact. Even the stakeouts are exciting. There will be none of that today.

———————

The Berlin Diner is a nondescript little eatery in the small town of Berlin in Hartford County, Connecticut. It is a sleepy place with a population of around 16 000. In the street outside the diner, Bob Clifford, a special agent with the federal Bureau of Alcohol, Tobacco and Firearms (ATF), is sitting in a parked car, fiddling with a radio receiver and a sandwich. He stifles a yawn and shifts uncomfortably in his seat. It could be a long afternoon.

Moulton's sixth-floor office in downtown Hartford is run on a bare-bones budget and the kind of electronic surveillance equipment he needs for the sting isn't readily available. So he'd turned to the ATF. Clifford was assigned as back-up, and the suits approved access to the ATF's repository of gadgets. It would be good to work with a buddy. Rich and Bob went back a long way.

Clifford had been briefed about the case. Four months ago, a guy in Hartford had put out word that he had a stuffed leopard mount for sale. A sports hunter could legally own a leopard trophy, provided he'd taken the trouble to get the requisite permits and paperwork filled out. Selling the trophy, however, was a federal crime, prosecutable under the Lacey Act, America's oldest national wildlife statute, which made it illegal to import or export wildlife in violation of any federal, state, Indian or – significantly – foreign law.

Moulton had followed up the tip and called the seller. 'Hi. My name's Rick Moore,' he'd introduced himself, before going on to explain that he had a small decorating business and was looking for trophies. 'You the guy who's got the leopard for sale?'

'Yeah,' said the voice on the other end of the line. 'But I sold it.' The buyer had been a guy in New Jersey. He did, however, have a mounted leopard head for about 500 bucks, if 'Rick' was interested.

'I'll think it over,' Moulton said, and left his number. Later, the man called back and said he also had a leopard-skin rug for sale. 'How much?' Moulton asked.

'One thousand two hundred dollars'

'It's a deal,' Moulton said.

They met for the first time in a parking lot. Moulton was accompanied by another agent. Their target was a lean, bearded man in his mid-thirties with jet-black hair and wire-rimmed glasses. He was kitted out in a 'jungle outfit'. Khaki seemed to be his colour of choice. Perched on his head was a safari hat with a zebra-stripe band. He clutched a black elephant-skin bag. There and then Moulton decided on a nickname. From now on he'd call him 'Shaka', after the nineteenth-century Zulu king and warrior.

'I'm Rick,' Moulton said. 'This is my business associate,' he added, pointing at the other agent. Moulton handed over $500 in cash for the head, which they stashed in the boot of his car. He gave the man a cheque for $1200 for the rug, which would be delivered only once it had cleared. Warming to his

25

new client, Shaka boasted that he had contacts in South West Africa and Zimbabwe who could supply other trophies, including endangered species. Moulton decided to push him. 'What about rhino horn? Can you get it?' he asked.

'No dice, that's taboo,' Shaka said tersely. Normally, Moulton would end the case right there with a bust-and-buy. But something told him to hold back and let this one play itself out.

Their next meeting took place in another lot, outside a movie theatre. Shaka pulled up in a Land Rover with a personalised Connecticut licence plate that read 'ZAMBIA'. A bumper sticker proclaimed: 'I love Africa'. With him was his girlfriend, Mary Ann McAllister. 'Shaka', it seemed, had begun to trust his new friend, 'Rick'.

———

Clifford gets as comfortable as he can in his car. The meeting is set to take place any minute now. There is a burst of static as Moulton's shirt catches on the mike, then the audio returns to normal. You never know with these things. Sometimes there's interference with the signal. They'll only know when they play back the tapes. Hopefully it works today. The target is ready to deal. Inside the diner, Moulton shakes hands with the bearded man. 'Hi, John,' he says. Lukman smiles back.

———

Moulton doesn't really know what to make of Lukman. He's collected snippets here and there, gleaned what he can from official documents and listened attentively to Lukman's tales of derring-do.

He knows that, in 1976, Lukman – then twenty-two – had sued the CIA and its director, George H.W. Bush, for access to classified documents they had on him. In refusing a Freedom of Information Act request filed by Lukman, a CIA review committee said that the only document it had could not be released, as it was a 'classified document relating to our liaison contacts with a foreign government'. The 1972 file contained 'information pertaining to intelligence sources and methods which the director of Central Intelligence has the responsibility to protect'.

A report in the *Hartford Courant* quoted Lukman as saying that the only explanation he had for the existence of the document was his shortwave radio hobby. As a teenager, he had written to countries around the world requesting broadcasting schedules and 'cultural information'. Lukman argued that he was seeking a job with the US State Department and wanted to review the document in case he had to undergo a security-clearance interview. The article noted that Lukman, 'who hasn't any formal education beyond high school, said he has travelled in the southern and eastern regions of Africa and in Europe, Jamaica and Canada'.

Moulton quickly learns that Lukman is an incorrigible storyteller. Stroke his ego enough and he'll tell you everything – up to a point. He likes to impress and name-drops shamelessly. He claims his 'good friends' include senior Reagan White House officials and Ian Smith, the former prime minister of Rhodesia. The leopard mount he sold to the man in New Jersey was initially stored in the garage of Smith's Harare home, he later tells Moulton. Lukman also has ties to the Mozambican National Resistance (RENAMO), the Mozambican rebel movement established in the 1970s with the shadowy support of Zimbabwe's Central Intelligence Organisation (CIO). He's spent time with Jonas Savimbi, leader of the National Union for the Total Independence of Angola (UNITA), the South African and US proxy in the Cold War against the Soviets and the Cubans.

In fact, Lukman seems irresistibly drawn to all things military. He describes the editor of *Soldier of Fortune* magazine as a close friend. His acquaintances include several members of the Rhodesian Veterans' Association, and he once paid $5 000 for a leather-bound collector's edition of a book by military author Peter Stiff about the Selous Scouts, the notorious Rhodesian counter-insurgency unit.

Lukman's views of the African continent are rose-tinted and romanticised, his imagination fuelled by the exploits of big-game hunters and tales of mysterious warriors and ancient kingdoms. 'Africa is where my soul is,' he often says. He travels frequently to destinations there and also in South America. Once he dropped in on 'friends' stationed at the Ilopango Air Base in El Salvador – the launch pad for US military supplies to Nicaragua's murderous contra rebels. On another occasion, he turned up in Nicaragua. And then there are the frequent trips to Cuba. In those days, what American went in and out of Cuba so effortlessly? None that Moulton knew. For some time now, he's wondered about Lukman's background. Could he be CIA? The agency denies it.

————

Lukman and Moulton order lunch. Soup for Moulton, a submarine sandwich for Lukman. Moulton hands over $2 400 for a mounted cheetah head and a skin. They arrange for the goods to be shipped from South West Africa to a post office box Moulton has set up for the sting. The goods will be marked as 'curios'. Lukman assures him his contacts in South West Africa, a man named Marius and his wife Pat, are reliable.

The conversation drifts from illicit wildlife trophies to Lukman's adventures in Africa. Then, Lukman broaches a new subject. 'You know, Rick, I can get you machine guns,' he says abruptly. Moulton remains poker-faced. In the car outside, Clifford – who has just taken a bite of his sandwich – starts to choke.

In retrospect, Moulton isn't too surprised. Often wildlife crime investigations diverge into other areas: drugs, guns, money-laundering, you name it. Pablo Escobar, the violent Colombian drug lord, is known to have his own private menagerie of hippos, zebras, giraffes and rhinos at his sprawling estate near Medellin. It's a little narco-zoo, perfect for laundering drug money. In Florida, some of the biggest drug kingpins are avid collectors of reptiles and animal trophies. Increasingly, federal agents are seizing consignments of live reptiles stuffed with cocaine-filled condoms. When the condoms burst, the deaths are frightful. On other occasions they've found drugs stashed in polar bear hides. Rhino horn, reptiles, guns, drugs – they are all commodities to be bought and sold on the black market, and the smuggling routes are often the same.

'AKs are nice,' Lukman says. He claims that his contacts handle all the weapons with gloves to ensure that there are no telltale fingerprints for customs or the ATF to work with, should they intercept a shipment. 'They're brand new, ready to go,' he says.

Lukman boasts that not only can he get AKs, but he has access to Soviet fragmentation grenades and even landmines. He claims the weapons form part of stockpiles captured from Cuban soldiers in Angola by South African troops. He confides that a friend of his in Georgia – a member of the Rhodesian Veterans' Association – resells the arms. The profits from these spoils are then divided up between Lukman, his friend, and his South West African contacts, Marius and Pat.

'I'm not much into guns,' Moulton says. 'But my marine buddy Bob is.' It is a coded message to Clifford. ATF can take the guns from here. 'You tell your marine buddy that if he's interested in anything that is communist-bloc-orientated, there's nothing we can't get,' Lukman says.

Moulton arranges for Lukman to meet Bob. Clifford will be the ideal plant. He is a Vietnam veteran and a former marine. No acting required.

The meeting is delayed when Lukman is suddenly called to Washington. He's been invited to the White House, where UNITA leader Jonas Savimbi is on a charm offensive to secure US support for the movement. Moulton marvels at how Lukman has managed to get security clearance in only twenty-four hours.

'It makes you really wonder what's going on,' he confides to Jim Genco, the US prosecutor who will be handling the 'Wiseguy' case. Moulton notifies the Secret Service that a target of an investigation is going to be at the White House. They promise to keep an eye on him.

On his return to Connecticut, Lukman calls Moulton. 'Tell your marine buddy I have a few things that those pig-stickers attach to.' In military parlance, 'pig-stickers' are bayonets. The 'things they attach to' are evidently AK-47s.

July 1988

Lukman ushers Moulton and Clifford into his Newington condominium. It is crowded with the detritus of his travels. On a wall is a large map of Africa. There are wood carvings of animals, line drawings of warriors armed with spears and shields, and an elephant footstool. Rather bizarrely, there's a bayonet stuck into a wooden table. African masks stare blankly into space. In one corner is an autographed portrait of the bearded Savimbi wearing green army fatigues and a red beret. There is a UNITA flag and election posters for Smith's Rhodesian Front. A framed photograph shows Lukman posing alongside Smith. They have their arms around one another. Taking pride of place is a painting of Lukman – the great adventurer – in khaki shorts, jungle boots and a bush hat. He's staring into the middle distance, looking noble, like the explorers of old. The Victoria Falls thunder below him.

Lukman closes the blinds next to Moulton. He flips a switch in the corner of the room. Shadows dance up the walls as the white glare of a spotlight blinds the two agents. Without a word, Lukman turns and walks quickly to the kitchen. Blinking, Moulton looks at Clifford. This is odd. What's going on? They see Lukman reach up for something in the kitchen. When he turns around, there is an AK-47 in his hands. The 'pucker-factor', as Moulton likes to call it, goes way up. Lukman had said nothing about selling a gun today.

'Crap, he's figured out who we are,' Moulton thinks. Heart pounding, he feels a surge of panic, but keeps it in check. Neither he nor Clifford is carrying a weapon. If Lukman pulls the trigger, they'll be plugged full of lead and dead in a blood-spattered heap before the back-up team can crash through the doors. There's nothing they can do.

Lukman advances, the barrel pointed directly at them. He hands the gun to Moulton. There's an uncertain pause. Then the tension breaks. They breathe again. 'Look, Rick, I don't know him,' Lukman says, nodding at Clifford. 'I know you. I'll only sell it to you and you can give it to him.' It is a bizarre statement, given that Clifford is standing right there. No matter. The deal is still illegal. Moulton passes the AK to Bob, who does a quick field test. Satisfied, he gives Moulton the money, and Moulton hands it to Lukman.

'The AKs are from Marius,' Lukman says proudly, referring to his contact. He gestures at a photograph on a counter. It shows an army major in full battle dress. Marius, Lukman explains, has access to South African Defence Force (SADF) warehouses in South West Africa (later to become Namibia) that are 'loaded with Soviet and Cuban weapons' taken from Angola. Some of the weapons are being funnelled to RENAMO in Mozambique. In the garage of his home in South West Africa's capital, Windhoek, Marius has hoarded assault rifles, pistols and even landmines, and is doing a neat trade in 'war memorabilia' to US connections made through *Soldier of Fortune* magazine's classified ads.

While Lukman chats animatedly to Clifford, Moulton hastily jots down a name on the photograph: 'Marius Meiring'. It's another link in an ever-widening puzzle. He notices another photograph of Meiring on the wall. It's a family portrait of Marius, Pat and the kids. It strikes him as odd that Lukman – who is divorced and has kids of his own – would have a photograph of another man's family on his wall.

Lukman offers to give them the 'grand tour' of his home. He ushers them into the spare bedroom, which doubles as an office. On the wall hangs a map of Zimbabwe and a series of drawings of soldiers and warriors. There is a shortwave radio on the table. Moulton worries that it may pick up the wire. It would be a disaster if their voices suddenly come echoing back at them through the speakers.

Then Lukman does it again. Without warning, he stops talking, turns on his heel and walks away. They hear him return moments later. There is a pistol in his hand. It's a CZ 75, a semi-automatic 9mm Parabellum made in Czechoslovakia, and it is pointed right at them. The pucker-factor kicks in all over again. But Lukman's just showing off his stuff. There's no need to worry. They clinch the deal. Two thousand dollars for an AK. Clifford orders five more. He isn't interested in the CZ.

'I've just sold you a totally illegal weapon,' Lukman confides.

18 July 1988

Moulton's phone rings. He depresses the record button of a cassette player on his desk. There's a click and the reels begin to turn. It's Lukman. The wire gets it all. Lukman has a deep, booming voice that is beautiful to tape. 'He's in El Salvador. For the first time since he declared the subject taboo, he wants to talk about rhino horn. Marius Meiring, he says, has managed to get his hands on an 'unlimited supply' of horn. 'Marius was just in Angola and inspected the product, and there's plenty available,' Lukman says.

Somewhere on the South West African–Angolan border is a pit containing between forty and a hundred horns. The location is known to a group of San Bushmen, whose leader is apparently the uncle of an army tracker. Meiring has already secured one horn weighing in at about 3.6 kilograms and is storing it at his home for a rainy day.

Moulton tells Lukman that he has Asian clients in New York who are prepared to pay $58 000 for the horn in Meiring's garage, no questions asked. The men cut a deal. Moulton will give Lukman $30 000, which he will pay over to Meiring for the horn. The $28 000 profit will be split two ways, with Lukman getting $10 000 and Moulton $18 000.

———————

At first Pat Meiring is hesitant, asking Lukman how well he knows 'Rick' and if he trusts him. 'This is much bigger than the others,' she says. Lukman allays her fears.

Much later, Lukman is told to collect a package in Chicago. The courier is an SADF sergeant major, Waldemar Schutte, who is set to take part in a skydiving competition in Illinois. Federal agents, careful not to be spotted, shadow Lukman's every move as he flies to O'Hare Airport. There, he almost loses his nerve when he sees a heavy-set man matching Schutte's description being led away in handcuffs by customs officials. But the man had been aboard a flight from Brussels. Schutte is due from London.

When Schutte arrives, he clears customs without a hitch. The horn is transferred to Lukman's carry-on luggage. An envelope stuffed with $1 800, the courier fee, changes hands and Schutte disappears into the throng. Lukman heads back to Connecticut. As his bag passes through the baggage scanner, a security guard hits the stop button and examines the flickering image on his screen. 'Sir, what's in your bag?' he asks. Lukman goes cold. He can hear the blood pounding in his ears. His hands itch. 'It's buffalo horn,' he blurts out, hopefully. 'Mooo!' The guard laughs and lets him pass. Fear gives way to elation. There is a rush of adrenaline, not unlike a naughty schoolboy who has got away with mischief. 'I've done it!'

In the safety of his apartment, Lukman shows Moulton the horn. It's magnificent, curved and heavy. The horn's been stored long enough in the heat to dry out, so the telltale stench of rot from the base where it was hacked off is barely discernible. But Moulton won't be able to take possession of it just yet. First, Lukman has to go to South West Africa to deliver Meiring's $30 000 to him. He's arranged for a friend, Russell D. Beveridge Jnr, to keep the horn while he's away.

10 August 1988

Moulton drives Lukman to the airport for the connecting flight to JFK International Airport in New York City. On previous occasions they'd taken a left to the highway. Today, Lukman tells him to turn right. Moulton can't understand why, but he does so anyway. He glances in the rear-view mirror. The surveillance team should be behind them. But the streets are clear. Either they're doing the greatest job ever or he's going blind, Moulton thinks. Lukman wants to get some aspirin, so they turn off to find a pharmacy. 'Turn here, turn here, turn here, turn here,' Lukman directs him. They make four right-hand turns and drive slowly past a cluster of shops. There's no pharmacy. Lukman gives up his quest. 'Let's get going,' he tells Moulton.

Moulton later finds out that the surveillance team had decided to grab an early lunch at a Roy Rogers around the corner from Lukman's condo. They'd expected him and Moulton to follow their usual route, turning left past the restaurant. By the time they realised they'd lost their quarry, it was too late.

One follow-car had been cruising the streets and picked up Moulton and Lukman as they hit the road. But he was ATF and the guys stuffing their faces were customs. They used different radio frequencies and there was no way to call them in. The four right-turns unnerved the ATF agent. Internationally, that was the accepted signal if an undercover operative in a moving vehicle was in trouble. Moulton didn't know that, but fortunately the ATF agent held back.

Lukman is excited about his trip. He chatters away to 'Rick' as they walk through the airport. Moulton spies a young woman in customs uniform walking towards them. She's engrossed in a sheaf of papers. He knows her well. Lukman prods him in the ribs. 'That's the enemy,' he says with a wink, gesturing at the woman. 'Oh crap,' Moulton thinks. 'If she sees me, she'll probably come over and give me a big hug. My cover will be blown.' But luck is at hand. The woman turns into an office, her eyes never leaving the documents in her hand.

Hours later Lukman is winging his way over the Atlantic to Jan Smuts Airport in Johannesburg. From there, he'll catch a flight to Windhoek and Marius. Stashed in his luggage is $30 000 in cash that had been raised by Rick and his business associates. This is going to be a very profitable relationship. Marius will be happy.

Lukman has done his best to conceal the cash. Normally, anything over $10 000 has to be declared, but at JFK International, Lukman had signed a customs form stating that he was only carrying $2 000. The pencil-pushing losers would never find out. What Lukman doesn't know is that the airline officials who greeted him as he boarded the aircraft and asked if he'd filled in his declaration form were all undercover customs agents.

On his arrival in South West Africa, Marius and Pat welcome Lukman into their home as if he were the prodigal son. Over beers and *braaivleis*, he learns that the horns are hidden near Rundu, a dusty border town on the South West African–Angolan border. About 250 kilometres to its east lies Jamba, UNITA's headquarters, a reed-thatched rebel playground built with the help of the South Africans. The name means elephant. Marius claims that a group of soldiers went into Angola to bring out the horn.

Lukman's next stop is Zimbabwe. There he visits his 'old friend' Ian Smith, the sharp-tongued former Rhodesian prime minister, who had retired from politics the previous year. Lukman gives Smith a letter from a mutual buddy whose son is RENAMO's Washington representative. Lukman will later claim to know nothing about the contents of the letter.

'I didn't want to know. I just know Smith didn't trust his phones or mail because he lived next door to the Cuban Embassy, which could hear him taking a piss.' The Cubans had set up shop shortly after Smith grudgingly relinquished power to the black majority in 1979. Smith often used the embassy sign as a direction marker for visitors. 'At least they're good for something,' he would say bitterly.

Twelve days after setting foot on African soil, Lukman returns home. In a box on the aircraft is a leopard skin. It has been carefully folded inside a zebra hide to camouflage it from the beady eyes of customs officials. Smith, he tells Moulton, gave it to him to smuggle out of the country. He needs cash to attend a Rhodesian Veterans' Association meeting in Las Vegas, and Lukman has been entrusted with selling it. As a ruse to further distract customs agents from the contraband, Lukman is also carrying zebra meat. As expected, they confiscate that, but miss the leopard skin. Lukman sells the rug to Moulton and gives Smith $1000.

On 25 August, Moulton receives a package in the mail. The postmark is Windhoek. Inside are a buffalo-hide briefcase and a note. 'This is just a small token of our appreciation for your help in this last "deal", and we hope this is the start of a long and happy (and also profitable) relationship ...' It is addressed to 'Rick', and signed John, Marius and Pat.

Rick's clients now want twenty-five kilograms of horn. That works out to about eight horns. Lukman feverishly sets about raising funds for the venture. His girlfriend and two other Connecticut businessmen are persuaded to put up the cash. Then, in October, Lukman returns to Windhoek. He calls Moulton a few days later and says he has managed to get his hands on the requisite amount of horn. Then he changes his tune, claiming that things are too hot because of the Border War and the horns are 'across the river', in Angola; an apparent reference to the Okavango River, which flows past Rundu. His efforts to secure the horns have been unsuccessful. Finally, Lukman admits to Moulton that he only has a set of two horns and will be back in the States on 2 November.

The minute Lukman's aircraft touches down and he enters JFK International, federal agents are on his tail. They shadow him as he boards the connecting flight for the hour-long hop to Bradley Airport in Connecticut. There he collects his luggage, including a large box containing the rhino horn and some heavy wood carvings. Moulton and Lukman's girlfriend, Mary Ann McAllister are there to meet him. A surveillance van is parked near McAllister's car, cameras rolling behind tinted windows. The trio opens the trunk of the car and then loads the luggage. Lukman can't resist showing Moulton his prize. He unpacks the rhino horn. Lukman and McAllister are all smiles.

Moulton gives a signal, then rapidly turns on his heel and walks away into the fog and rain outside. Two cars screech to a halt. Someone shouts: 'Federal agents! You're under arrest.' Lukman is rooted to the spot. In a bar near the airport, Moulton later watches the evening news. He can't help but laugh. A CBS news crew had got wind of the Lukman case and had been allowed to film the take-down. He sees himself on the screen for a few seconds. His face has been fuzzed out, as agreed, to protect his identity. For a long a time afterwards, agents rib him and call him 'Electric Head'. They like to make fun of each other. It keeps you from getting too big for your britches.

Later, when agents tear through Lukman's luggage, they find a vinyl record he had brought back from his travels. The single is titled, 'Run Rhino Run'.

Guns & bullets & daggers & knives
Money & blood & horns & lies

Run rhino run …
Run away from the bullet & the gun
Run away with the wind
Run away from the dagger & the knife

Men with guns at sunset, with a thousand bullets, maybe more
The animal runs defencelessly, fear & death once more
Something breaks the silence, yes a bullet rips the air
The animal lies dying, does anybody care?

A day later, US prosecutors call a press conference. Soon the story is buzzing on the wires to newsrooms across the United States and South Africa.

7 November 1988
Dean Golembeski
Hartford, Conn (AP) – An international smuggling ring that relied on South African soldiers to kill endangered rhinoceroses in Angola has been cracked by US undercover agents with the indictments or arrests of six people …

In addition to smuggling black and white rhinoceros horn into the United States, the scheme also involved the illegal importation of seven AK-47 machine guns, cheetah skins and leopard skins, including one owned by former Rhodesian Prime Minister Ian Smith, authorities said.

Three Connecticut residents were arrested and the US government was seeking the extradition of three South Africans, including an army sergeant major in a parachute unit, who smuggled a rhinoceros horn into this country while attending a sky-diving event.

More arrests were possible from the undercover investigation that began in February, said US Attorney Stanley A. Twardy Jnr as he announced the arrests during a news conference.

Twardy said he had no idea how long the smugglers had been in business, nor was he able to say how many others did business with the group.

But those charged in the scheme indicated they had enough rhino horns to earn hundreds of thousands of dollars.

'This is something that is unique, at least in my experience,' Twardy said.

Events move quickly. There are fiery exchanges on diplomatic channels between Washington and Pretoria. The FBI, working with the state and justice departments, is negotiating with the South African authorities for the immediate extradition of Marius and Pat Meiring, along with Schutte. It's not going well. The South Africans are, as can be expected, enraged, defensive and obstructive. Perhaps *too* defensive.

————

The South Africans' sensitivity can be traced to an event that occurred four months before Lukman's arrest. On 14 July 1988, an American environmentalist, Craig van Note, presented a written statement to a US congressional committee. South Africa, he claimed, had become 'one of the largest wildlife outlaws in the world'.

'According to reliable sources in Africa, a massive smuggling ring has been operating for years, with the complicity of South African officials at the highest level of government and military, to funnel ivory and other contraband out of Africa.

'Jonas Savimbi and his UNITA rebel forces in Angola, largely supplied by South Africa, have ruthlessly liquidated perhaps 100 000 elephants to help finance the war. Most of the tusks have been carried out on South African air transports or trucks ... the South African staging post at Rundu in the Caprivi Strip warehouses the contraband. Tractor-trailers then transport the ivory across South West Africa to South Africa ... The South African military has cynically aided the virtual annihilation of the once-great elephant herds of Angola.' The rhino population had also been targeted, Van Note said.

South Africa demanded Van Note identify his sources and turn over evidence backing his claims. He refused. But the barrage of publicity unleashed by his revelations had done damage. Brigadier Ben de Wet Roos, who had commanded South African troops during the invasion of Angola in 1976, was hauled out of retirement to head a military board of inquiry. Its terms of reference are restricted to allegations of illegal trade in ivory. The hearings are held in secret and the final report classified and buried.

———————

On a chilly November day, a federal grand jury indicts eight people implicated in the 'Wiseguy' sting. Lukman, the ringleader, will be arraigned on seventeen charges, including counts of conspiracy to smuggle endangered species and AK-47s. He faces up to seventy-seven years in the slammer if convicted, the press tell their readers. He's out on a $227 000 bond, which was posted by his father. Russell Beveridge, thirty-three, the friend who was entrusted with the horn Lukman had fetched from Chicago, faces a twenty-one-year sentence. Mary Ann McAllister, also thirty-three, Lukman's girlfriend, is looking at eleven years in prison. Isaac Saada, fifty-two, the guy from New Jersey who had bought the stuffed leopard from Lukman in February, could go down for seven. Martin Sher, forty-three, is accused of conspiring to import and sell a leopard-skin rug. He's a bit-player. Six years.

And then there are the South Africans: Marius and Pat Meiring, and Sergeant Major Waldemar Schutte. For now, they're safe in South Africa. But, if they are ever extradited, the Meirings will face ten counts each and a possible fifty years in jail, along with $2.5 million in fines. Schutte is indicted on two counts, which carry a maximum ten-year jail term. In December, prosecutors charge two more people with aiding the conspiracy: Kenneth R. Hussey, fifty-one, and Joseph F. Riley, forty-one. Both had helped Lukman raise funds for his South West African adventure.

While the Americans gather their evidence in preparation for the case against Lukman, the SADF is hard at work covering its tracks. On 7 December 1988, a few weeks after the inquiry was announced, the public relations department issues a turgid press release. It is a whitewash. The Roos board of inquiry 'found there was no evidence to prove that the defence force was responsible for, or involved in, the killing of elephants ... The board also found that the figures given for the elephant population in Angola in Mr van Note's report could not be substantiated.'

It quotes 'leading conservationists', who place the elephant population at 'no more than 12 400'.

'We take exception to being regarded as the outlaws of the wildlife world, which indicates [Van Note's] obvious lack of knowledge regarding wildlife matters in South Africa.'

---

9 February 1989

Hussey is the first to take a plea, admitting his guilt and confessing to investing $25 000 in Lukman's scheme. He is later fined $2 500. Then Lukman falls on his sword. On 23 February 1989, he pleads guilty to four counts, including the sale of the stuffed leopard to Saada, the importation of an AK-47 and the smuggling of two rhino horns. As part of a plea deal, prosecutors ditch thirteen other charges. His girlfriend, McAllister, follows suit, admitting to her role in the shipment of a leopard skin. Two charges against her are dropped.

Then news breaks that South African authorities are willing to co-operate. Twardy is quoted as saying that they recently determined 'this is an extraditable case'. On 20 April, Lukman's attorney turns over a package to the ATF that had been posted in South West Africa. Inside are sixteen AK-47 magazines and two Soviet F-1 grenades.

It takes another four months before Lukman is sentenced. With barely concealed contempt, the judge describes Lukman as having been part of an 'international netherworld of marginal characters who deal in guns, join foreign armies and associate with mercenaries'. Lukman is sentenced to twenty-seven months in prison, fined $20 000 and ordered to spend three years under supervision by federal authorities after his release. Not quite seventy-seven years. The other accused are fined between $100 and $10 000 and released on probation. Mary Ann McAllister gets a year's probation and a $250 fine.

―――――

It is more than a year before the South Africans make a move on Meiring. By then he's left the SADF. On 19 March 1990, he and Pat are picked up by members of the police's fugitive tracing unit in Berea in central Johannesburg. Initial reports are scant on details. The Afrikaans daily newspaper, *Beeld*, states simply that the couple appeared briefly in the Johannesburg Magistrate's Court and describes the charges for which they are being sought in the US as 'related to ivory smuggling'. There is little information about the mysterious Sergeant Major Meiring.

―――――

Meiring, it later emerges, cut his teeth in combat with the Rhodesian African Rifles (RAR) in the 1970s as Ian Smith's regime fought an increasingly futile war against black liberation fighters. When black rule became inevitable, Meiring – like many other disgruntled members of his unit – crossed over to South Africa and joined the SADF.

There, according to military historian Peter Stiff, he assumed control of fifty former members of the RAR. The black soldiers were stationed at Gumbu Mine, a makeshift forward-operating base near the Zimbabwean border, seven kilometres north-east of Messina (later Musina), as it was known then. In August 1982, ironically on Friday the thirteenth, an assault force with men from Meiring's group crossed into Zimbabwe on a mission to destroy forty diesel locomotives that Robert Mugabe's ZANU-PF government had recently purchased. To ensure deniability for the South Africans, they were clad in old Rhodesian camouflage and carrying AK-47s, RPK machine guns, 60-mm mortars, RPG-7 rocket launchers, landmines, TNT and unmarked rat packs.

The mission was a disaster. Three ex-Rhodesian soldiers were killed in a contact with Zimbabwean National Army troops. The fifteen survivors cut and ran for the South African border, abandoning their kit and materiel. Mugabe said the incident was evidence of 'South Africa's programme of destabilisation'. SADF chief General Constand Viljoen denied any South African involvement, saying there were 'no operations authorised in Zimbabwe'.

Meiring was later absorbed into the SADF. Some US reports around the time of his arrest erroneously suggested that he had joined 32 Battalion, the notorious 'Buffalo Soldiers', and had risen through the ranks to become the 'second-highest ranking' 32 Battalion officer stationed in Namibia. There are no records of Meiring ever having served in 32 Battalion. The unit's founder, Colonel Jan Breytenbach, says he believes Meiring may have worked for Military Intelligence. It would have been 'impossible for him, as a major, to be the second-most senior guy. A general has a shithouse full of colonels under him, and that's before you even start getting to the majors.'

———

Initially, efforts to extradite the Meirings are a dismal failure. South African prosecutors fail 'within a reasonable time' to produce evidence to justify the extradition. The case is thrown out of court. The State launches a second extradition bid, but it will be seventeen long months before the end is in sight. On 18 May 1992, the US Department of the Interior and the USFWS issue a jubilant press release.

'In a landmark action, the US Fish and Wildlife Service, in conjunction with the Justice Department and other Federal Agencies, has obtained the extradition of an accused wildlife smuggler from South Africa, the first extradition ever from a foreign country on wildlife-related charges.

'Meiring is alleged to have used his official position … in South West Africa to acquire and transport rhinoceros horns, automatic weapons, and hand grenades, and smuggle them into the United States …'

USFWS director, John Turner, says, 'The extradition is a sure sign the world is becoming a riskier place for those who smuggle endangered species and other protected wildlife.'

Meiring is escorted aboard an aircraft at Jan Smuts Airport in Johannesburg and flown to the US. He is arraigned days later in a Hartford courtroom. He agrees to take a plea. In exchange, prosecutors won't push for the extradition of his wife, Pat, who is still in South Africa with their two children.

On 20 May 1992, Meiring pleads guilty to a charge of falsifying US customs documentation and admits to shipping three AK-47s to the US in packages marked 'wood carvings' and 'brass candlesticks'. The extradition treaty between South Africa and the US makes no provision for charges of smuggling as a prosecutable offence. Meiring is sentenced to eight months in prison. The judge gives credit to Meiring for time spent behind bars in South Africa and the US and, on 24 July 1992, he is released from prison and deported.

Moulton got to know him fairly well in the time he was in jail. 'He was a very nice gentleman,' he recalls years later. 'He did it, but as I understand it, in those days the military was quite underpaid. Just before he went back he asked me, "Rick, can you get me out of the prison and take me shopping? My children still think I'm on military manoeuvres." They were used to him going away for long periods of time and, whenever he went away, he'd bring back gifts for his kids.' Moulton couldn't allow it. Instead, he bought a few things out of his own pocket, including a Spider-man action figure, which he gave to Meiring.

'He had tears in his eyes. He took those back with him for the kids. I felt really sorry for the children, because they had nothing to do with this whole thing.'

When they parted company, Meiring extended an invitation: 'Rich, if you ever get to South Africa, find me and I'll have you over for dinner.' Moulton replied: 'Yeah, probably, but I don't think your wife would want me there.'

Lukman emerges from prison after nine months, supposedly a 'changed man'. He starts a company called African Investments Ltd, which he claims 'works on legitimate investments in Africa'. He tells journalist Edward R. Ricciuti: 'I'm sorry for my past transgressions. I regret them terribly.' Speaking to Steven Galster – at the time an investigator with the Washington-based sector of the Environmental Investigation Agency (EIA) – Lukman claims that the smuggling was not an isolated incident. He says it formed a 'major part of the covert war in Angola' and involved 'high-ranking South African officials'. And he makes the startling claim that 'the biggest traffickers of rhino horn in the area were Americans operating out of Kamina' – a reference to the abandoned Kamina Air Base in the then Zaire (now the Democratic Republic of Congo), where CIA operatives providing support for UNITA were stationed.

Lukman says a company called Southern Air Transport – once a CIA front company – regularly flew in and out of Kamina and Jamba carrying illicit cargoes of diamonds and rhino horn.

Lukman's claims may have some credence. Acquired by the CIA in 1960 and later sold to an aviation lawyer who had worked for the agency, Southern Air Transport had documented links with arms shipments to Panama and the contras in Nicaragua. In September 1987, the *New York Times* revealed details of secret airlifts of arms and materiel to Angola's UNITA rebels. The shipments had all been routed via Kamina.

———

Lukman vanishes into quiet obscurity and the case is quickly forgotten, consigned to collect dust in court and newspaper archives. Nothing further is heard of Meiring until May 2003, when a letter defending him is published on the website of the Australian newspaper *Green Left Weekly*. The writer identifies himself as Steve Thornton. He lives in Australia and describes himself as an 'extremely close friend of the Meiring family'. Meiring is dead, he writes, killed in a motor-vehicle accident shortly after his return to South Africa.

'He was a warm, compassionate and caring man ... Marius was entrapped ... Marius had obtained one rhino horn from a curio shop legally and was not a "supplier" of parts from endangered species. Knowing that this item was illegal in the USA, Marius had the package labelled differently. A few AK-47s were also mailed to the USA. Anyone doing a thorough investigation into Marius's affairs would realise that he could never have been a ringleader, nor play a major role in smuggling. His bank account would prove that.'

The true extent of Meiring's involvement in the smuggling of weapons and rhino horn will probably never be known. But the case shone an uncomfortable spotlight on a hidden corner of the SADF's war in Angola; one that the Defence Force was determined to keep secret.

* Acknowledgement is given to the following articles, which, along with an extensive interview with Rich Moulton, provided much of the basis for this chapter:
Ricciuti, Edward R. 'Guns 'n Roses'. *Wildlife Conservation* 95 (1), 1992
Galster, Steven R. 'The trail leads to South Africa'. *The Nation*, 15 February 1993

3

Apartheid's Secret

A twenty-three-year-old intelligence officer returns to base at Rundu in Namibia after an operation deep inside Angola. Des Burman is strung out and exhausted. A lieutenant in the SADF, he's been working closely with elements of Jonas Savimbi's UNITA movement as a military advisor. He's lost count of the number of 'contacts' he's been in lately. Things move fast on the ground. Burman and his teams are perpetually on the run, pursued and shot at by Cuban gunships. By now, the ops follow a familiar pattern: Get in, find the enemy, kill them, and get out in a cloud of dust and a whirr of rotor blades.

The frequent deployments take their toll. Burman needs a new rifle. If you're regularly dropped into combat by chopper, the solid stock of a standard-issue R1 is nothing but a hindrance. He's looking for a rifle with a folding stock. He dumps his pack and heads for the stores. The warehouse is chock-a-block with army-green packing cases.

He opens one, then another, and another. He's astonished by what he finds.

'Every single case was packed with ivory and rhino horn and game skins, including sable, roan antelope, leopard skins and lion skins. Boxes and heaps and heaps and heaps of it. I blew a fuse. I lost it completely. Nobody was mentally normal at that stage, but in my case, that was basically the straw that broke the camel's back.'

There must have been at least sixty crates, all labelled 'dental equipment' and marked for dispatch to Waterkloof Air Force Base near Pretoria.

In the 1970s and 1980s, Rundu is one of the SADF's main forward-operating bases. The administrative capital of the Okavango region, it's a large town by Namibian standards. Just to the north is the Okavango River and, across it, Angola.

When the Portuguese, who had colonised Angola for 400 years, hastily abandoned the country in 1975, conflict between the three main Angolan liberation movements – UNITA, the People's Movement for the Liberation of Angola (MPLA) and the National Liberation Front of Angola (FNLA) – escalated into bloody civil strife. Angola's tragedy lay in its riches – seemingly unlimited quantities of oil, diamonds and minerals. Everyone seemed to want a piece. In addition, the country formed part of the unhappy *cordon sanitaire* of buffer states that apartheid South Africa regarded as protection from 'hostile black Africa' and the ever-present threat of the communist *Rooi Gevaar*.

War turned Angola into a proxy battleground for the Cold War superpowers. Cuba and the Soviet Union threw their weight behind the MPLA. Along with Pretoria, Washington – in the guise of the US Central Intelligence Agency's shadow warriors – threw its weight behind UNITA and the FNLA. By the war's end, over 600 000 Angolans were dead and more than a million displaced.

Before the war, Rundu was a major trans-shipment point between Angola and Namibia. By 1979, the pont that once ferried cargo across the river is disabled and a chain with a no-entry sign bars the way to the access ramp. Sometimes at night, after bingeing on warm beer, callow South African *troepies* can be heard shouting insults at shadows across the river. 'Castro is a cunt,' is a particular favourite.

Rundu is a magnet for profiteers and smugglers. You can get anything, if you know the right people. Sometimes the only currency you need is cans of fish or what the soldiers call '*Owambo piele*' (Owambo penises): horrid tins of Vienna sausages in brine.

Sector 20 HQ is where the army brass sit in their cushy offices, shuffling paper and sending young men out to kill and die. Many of the officers are little more than 'civvies in uniform'. Somewhere along the line they get a degree and join the Defence Force. Before you know it, they have rank. They may have brains, but they are not fighters. Most never see battle, feel the fear, hear the screams, or smell the blood, rot and shit of the dead and dying.

Chief of Staff Intelligence, better known as CSI, has offices at the base in Rundu. They are at the pinnacle of wartime intelligence gathering, accountable directly to the chief of the Defence Force. In his current role, Burman reports to a CSI co-ordinator, Colonel Fred Oelschig. Oelschig's brother, Mo, also a colonel, heads up the Rundu office of CSI's Directorate of Special Tasks, which oversees logistical support to UNITA.

———

Burman storms out of the warehouse and heads for Fred Oelschig's office. He's apoplectic with rage. 'I lost my cool so badly with that arsehole that they thought I was suffering from battle fatigue,' he recalls thirty years later, his voice sharp with anger. 'What pissed me off the most was that some of these guys were sitting in the backline earning a bloody lot of money and I was on the front line, getting shot at. They were running a flourishing pipeline of exploited products and pocketing the money.'

Oelschig, convinced that Burman is going to 'hammer' him, backs up against a wall behind his desk. 'I'm going to take this to the press and expose the whole thing,' Burman threatens.

Two weeks later, he is on a *flossie* – an air force Hercules – back to South Africa. They say he's gone *bossies*, literally 'bush mad'. For the next four or five months, Burman is assigned to a desk in a secret CSI building in Pretoria. It is the 'seat of power in the intelligence sector', but all he does is one mind-numbing army course after another. 'Pathetic courses that meant jackshit to me ... I felt like I was an animal in a cage being watched.' When he is declared fit to return to combat, he is moved to a UNITA training camp in the Caprivi Strip, a narrow, 450-kilometre-long finger of land that extends from the north-eastern corner of Namibia, thrusting eastwards between Angola and Botswana to the Zambian border. He never sees the warehouses or their contents again.

———

There are other clues; hints that what Burman had seen in the warehouse is part of something far greater than he can imagine. In Jamba, UNITA's base in Cuando Cubango Province just north of the Caprivi, he comes across a factory churning out ivory carvings of 'outstanding quality'. He can't recall the exact date, but it must have been some time in 1982.

Then there are rumours about a shadowy South African Military Intelligence front company, Frama Intertrading. Run by two Portuguese–Angolans, José Francisco Lopes and Arlindo Maia, it is formally incorporated in 1980. An army general, Gerhardus Philippus Ortlepp du Preez, arranges for the company's bank account to be opened at a branch conveniently located near military headquarters in Poynton Building in central Pretoria. Du Preez and other SADF members have signing powers on the account, in addition to Lopes and Maia. The SADF supplies the start-up capital.

Maia is based in Johannesburg. Lopes, nicknamed Lobbs, is the man on the ground in Rundu. He's a sergeant major in the SADF, but earns far more than the average officer of his rank. Before the war, he lived in Angola. He and his family lost everything when they fled to Namibia, but he managed to wangle a pilot's job with CSI. A bad heart put paid to that, but they found other work for him. Lobbs has a sawmill in Rundu and another in a place called Buabuata. Within CSI, it is an open secret that Lobbs and Frama are a conduit for the SADF's covert supplies to UNITA. Standing orders prevent soldiers and police from searching the company's trucks that ply the road south carrying vast quantities of timber, primarily teak and kiaat. There are whispers that other contraband is hidden in the consignments.

In 1984, Burman – now a major – is running 'Delta teams' in the Okavango. They are small squads of five to seven men comprising a mixture of SADF Special Forces troops and Askaris – 'ex-terrorists' or *terrs* who have been 'turned' and are now fighting against their former comrades. Burman has informants feeding him information about '*terr*' movements in the Caprivi.

'They picked up info that poachers were working together with *terrs* that were supposedly coming across from Zambia, through Angola and into the Caprivi. We tracked them down, but we didn't find any *terrs*, just the poachers.'

One of the men has a rifle and a stash of ivory. He is a San Bushman. Burman drags the poachers and their ivory back to Rundu, where they are locked up. He is astonished by what happens next. 'I was told in no uncertain terms to release them all, because they were working for CSI and hunting for CSI.'

The rifle the poachers had been using is traced back to Colonel José d'Oliviera, a Portuguese Angolan working for CSI. D'Oliviera, Burman learns, flies the ivory to Windhoek in a private Cessna.

Before the war, the colonel worked in Angola for the *Polícia Internacional e de Defesa do Estado* (PIDE), the Portuguese secret police. They were notoriously brutal and excelled in the dark arts of torture. In the old days they were known for their hammer-and-tongs approach to inflicting pain. Prisoners would be whipped, burnt and electrocuted.

But by the 1960s and 1970s, with the help of a CIA instruction manual, PIDE officers in Portugal and its colonies had adopted subtler methods, perfecting techniques of sleep and sensory deprivation and 'positional torture', where prisoners would be made to stand or kneel in stress positions for hours, and sometimes days, at a time. The victims left with their bodies largely intact, but their minds broken. The rare cases that didn't crack or became too much of an inconvenience simply disappeared.

'D'Oliviera was useless and a thief of note,' Burman says. 'All of them, those Portuguese, were in cahoots right down the line.' D'Oliviera pulls Burman aside a few days later. 'Be careful, or something bad is going to happen to you,' he says. The emphasis is on the word 'bad'. The rest is left unspoken, but Burman gets the message. 'I could meet with an accident ... or get taken out somewhere on the highway, in an ambush, on the aeroplane. Whatever. I'd disappear.'

Some time later, D'Oliviera vanishes. It is said that he's gone AWOL. The Defence Force will eventually claim he's resigned. Burman hears he is in Lisbon, still working for CSI. It's deep-cover stuff. There are also rumours that police are investigating D'Oliviera in connection with the murder of four people in the Caprivi. One of them was the reputed 'contact man' at a De Beers mine for a diamond smuggler linked to the Rundu mafia. The man's car had been stopped at a roadblock by 'Angolans' dressed in police uniforms. He, his wife, daughter and a hitchhiker were all murdered, their throats slashed and the bodies dumped next to the side of the road.

Police tracked down the killers, who implicated D'Oliviera and a cop in the killings. But when police went looking for him, they were told he had disappeared.

Burman keeps his head down and his mouth shut, for now.

———————

In the mid-1970s, before joining CSI, Burman served in what would become the SADF's most decorated and most notorious unit: 32 Battalion. Known as the Buffalo Battalion, it had been knocked into shape, in great secrecy, from what its commanding officer once described as the 'most miserable, underfed, ragged and villainous' remnants of the FNLA. Its motto, *Proelio Procusi*, means Forged in Battle. What made the Buffalo soldiers unique, besides their ferocity on the battlefield, was that in the Defence Force, which mirrored the vicious racial segregation of apartheid South Africa, they were the first outfit in which white South African officers and black Angolans fought side by side.

The unit's founder, Colonel Jan Breytenbach, was a living legend. Despised by many SADF top brass and mistrusted as a maverick, Breytenbach fostered unstinting loyalty in the troops he commanded. He led them from the front, not from the safety of the backline. 'He was, and still is, highly unorthodox and eccentric,' Burman says. 'Whatever he put his mind to, he pulled off. He was an absolutely powerful man, legend-wise, and not to be crossed. Even today, if he puts out a call, the boys will be there, for whatever circumstances.'

In conservative Afrikaans society, Breytenbach was regarded as an oddity. He'd served with the *Engelse* in the British Royal Navy, participated in the Suez landings in 1959 and, shockingly, married an Englishwoman. His brother, Breyten – one of South Africa's great literary figures – was deemed a 'terrorist'. A committed opponent of apartheid, he left South Africa in the 1960s and settled in Paris, where he married a French–Vietnamese woman. Apartheid legislation classified her as 'non-white', and in terms of the Immorality Act – a law that criminalised interracial marriage – they could be arrested if they travelled to South Africa. In 1975, while Jan Breytenbach was leading the men of 32 Battalion into battle, Breyten, travelling on a false passport, was taken into custody at Jan Smuts Airport in Johannesburg and charged under the Terrorism Act. He was convicted of high treason and would spend seven hellish years in jail, later publishing a prison memoir, *The True Confessions of an Albino Terrorist*.

Jan Breytenbach was a ruthlessly efficient soldier. Conversely, he was also an avid conservationist who hand-reared three lions and a leopard while the war raged. Military Intelligence officers thought he had a 'screw loose' because he 'befriended big cats'. In the mid-1980s, while overseeing training camps for UNITA guerillas in the Caprivi Strip, Breytenbach was appointed as a conservator by the Department of Nature Conservation in Windhoek. The western Caprivi, where Breytenbach had a base on the banks of the Cuando River, is a declared nature reserve. He argued, somewhat quixotically, that military training in the area had to be 'conducted with minimum disturbance to wildlife'. The brass scoffed at him. There was no place for conservation in wartime.

Breytenbach has vivid memories of the time he spent in the southern Angolan province of Cuando Cubango, north of Rundu, in the 1970s, when South African troops invaded during Operation Savannah. This was where UNITA was based. But it was also an area of staggering beauty, teeming with game.

'It was breathtaking,' he would say years later. 'I'd never seen anything like it in my life before ... The number of animals and the diversity of wildlife species were such that it put the Kruger National Park completely in the shade. When we're talking about elephants, we're talking about tens of thousands of elephants roaming around all over the place, hundreds of rhino, huge herds of buffalo, especially along the Luiana River, sables, roan antelope, tsessebe, blue wildebeest, zebras. There were just vast numbers of game. I think the reason for that is that ... there's a lot of tsetse fly there, so people didn't go there much. At night, you could barely sleep because of the noise of the elephants and rhinos storming up and down.'

In the western Caprivi, Breytenbach set up a camp that became known as 'Rhino Base', named after the twenty black rhino that lived in the vicinity. There must have been several hundred more in the western Caprivi as a whole.

'On various occasions when we went into Angola and crossed the *kaplyn*, we came across black rhino bulls. The damn things would chase us,' Breytenbach laughs. 'We would be in a Land Rover in the sand trying to drive like madmen because the rhinos were catching up with us. There must have been dozens of them in that area.'

———

In the winter of 1986, Breytenbach returns to Cuando Cubango as a military advisor to Savimbi. Accompanied by some of his men, he drives north in a convoy of heavily armoured Casspirs. The landscape is still as beautiful as he remembers, but it is eerily quiet. 'The teeming herds of the past had completely disappeared,' he later writes. 'Now there was nothing at all, not even a duiker or a steenbuck ducking and diving to get away from the labouring Casspirs. The tall red syringas were as profuse as ever ... The extensive reed and papyrus swamps were still there. But over it all hung an atmosphere of utter desolation. There was no life.

'The further north we went ... the stronger the contrasts became. As the tree canopies got higher and the forests got thicker, the silence in them became deeper and more oppressive, like the deathly silence of the grave ... Where did they go? There was no doubt in my mind that they were shot, brutally exterminated in their thousands in ten to fifteen years.'

After his return to base, Breytenbach tallies up the score. On the 4 000-kilometre journey, he had seen the spoor of five elephants and one kudu, and noted sightings of an owl, a sitatunga, two reedbuck and a dozen pairs of wattled cranes.

Often wounded elephants cross south over the 'cut-line'. Many are riddled with bullets. In the sand one can see the drag marks left by a wounded animal. In 1986 or 1987, Breytenbach flies by chopper to a base in the western Caprivi. From the air, he counts twenty elephant carcasses – the tusks removed – scattered over ten square kilometres.

Journalists flown on propaganda junkets to meet Savimbi in Jamba are regularly shown pockets of elephant, giraffe, buffalo and zebra as proof of UNITA's commitment to conservation. But Breytenbach knows the conservation areas are also used as hunting grounds for Savimbi and his cronies, as well as visiting delegations of politicians, army generals and economists. He also knows that ivory and rhino horn is being stockpiled at Jamba. But how is it getting out?

One of Savimbi's admirers at the time is the British journalist Fred Bridgland. He gains unprecedented access to the man supporters called *O*

Mais Velho, The Eldest One, and will later be accused of being a Savimbi apologist. In 1986, Bridgland – who subsequently grows increasingly disenchanted with UNITA's inherent totalitarianism – publishes a biography, *Jonas Savimbi: A Key to Africa*. It includes a telling admission. 'We export ivory, rhino horn and leopard and antelope skins to help pay for our war,' Savimbi is quoted as saying. 'But we have declared some conservation zones where hunting elephant, giraffe and black sable is banned.' He also claims that South Africa has to be paid for its assistance in ivory and diamonds.

Breytenbach is astounded by Savimbi's claims. 'I know that the support budgeted by Military Intelligence in 1986/87 amounted to R400 million … [W]ith that money, the South Africans bought virtually all [of] Savimbi's military hardware, fuel and clothing.'

———

It is to Breytenbach that Burman eventually turns. He tells him the story about the CSI store, his confrontation with Oelschig, the threat from D'Oliviera and the poachers he was forced to release. Breytenbach is enraged. 'I was the fucking *bliksem* in,' he recalls in March 2012. 'I was the *moer* in.' The pieces of a disturbing puzzle are beginning to take shape.

One of Breytenbach's sergeants hears that Lobbs has bought a small shop and service station in Katima Mulilo, the commercial centre of the eastern Caprivi. Situated on the banks of the Zambezi River, the town provides easy access to Angola, Zambia, Zimbabwe and Botswana. In the centre of the town is a strategically important SADF base. Breytenbach regards it as the 'most corrupt place' he has ever come across.

'Virtually everyone in town was involved [in] some racket or another, be it the illegal export of wood, smuggling of ivory and rhino horn, selling unlicensed and unroadworthy second-hand vehicles to the local inhabitants, diamond smuggling, dealing dagga, smuggling Mandrax from Lusaka to Johannesburg, or providing the black market in Sesheke, in Zambia, with luxuries stolen from government stores and warehouses on the Namibian side of the Zambezi River.'

A man named Coimbra manages the shop for Lobbs. Coimbra's two sons are both in the SADF. Breytenbach's sergeant, who is friendly with one of the sons, tells him that they have a 'pipeline' to smuggle consignments of ivory, rhino horn, diamonds and Mandrax to Lobbs in Rundu.

A Namibian police (SWAPOL) inspector, Hennie Brink – head of the Diamond Branch – tells Breytenbach he knows about the 'pipeline' and has been investigating it for some time; all the evidence points to Frama, the MI front company. Brink claims that senior SADF officers are involved in the trade.

'It goes very, very high up in the hierarchy,' he tells Breytenbach, adding: 'As a matter of fact, I thought you were one of them, otherwise I would have approached you long ago.' A decade later, Brink is killed in Cape Town – blasted in the back with a shotgun.

Manie Grobler, a biologist and nature-conservation officer who is friendly with Breytenbach, approaches him one day and asks if he has any knowledge of a consignment of ivory, worth several million rand, which is apparently waiting to be picked up at an airstrip in the Caprivi. Breytenbach suspects it is a dirt strip in Buabuata, used by Military Intelligence, and that the consignment forms part of the UNITA stockpiles. He gives Grobler the name of a colonel to contact. Via a middleman, the colonel sends Grobler a message: Lay off or you will 'get sorted out'.

There are also questions about the death of a senior nature-conservation official. The man, Jan Muller, obtained 'incriminating tapes', which he tells Grobler implicates SADF officers in the smuggling of ivory and rhino horn. He's taking them to Grootfontein, a 250-kilometre journey from Rundu on the Golden Highway. The tapes are in his briefcase. Suddenly, a grader pulls into the road in front of him. His car slams into it head-on and he is killed instantly. The tapes are never found.

A friend of Breytenbach's, a commandant in 32 Battalion, tells him that some of the former FNLA troops who had served in the battalion started working for Lobbs after they were discharged from the Defence Force. They are being used as poachers, he says. One of them has been caught with eighty-two elephant tusks in his backyard. The case is quashed.

'This was the sort of thing that was going on the whole time,' Breytenbach says in an interview. 'Every time something crops up, you know somebody's caught with ivory or somebody's caught with this, that or the other, then it gets squashed, or they pay a fine and that's the end of the story.'

In 1987, the head of the roads department in Namibia approaches an army brigadier and requests permission to stop Frama trucks plying routes along the highway. He says he suspects that they are carrying contraband, but each time they are stopped, the drivers display military-issue cards, saying that they have the right of passage.

'Be my guest,' the brigadier says. A truck is stopped. Inside it is a cache of ivory and the driver is arrested. The brigadier is hauled over the coals by a general. 'Leave this alone,' he's told. 'It's got nothing to do with you.'

───────

Breytenbach had earlier scoffed at a series of 'incredible' investigative reports written and published in the *Windhoek Observer* by its eccentric editor, Hannes Smith, better known as '*Mal* Smittie' or 'Mad Smittie'. Week after week there were lurid revelations about the underworld activities of the 'Godfather' of Rundu. It was Lobbs. Matters came to a head when Smittie scaled the security fence surrounding a property belonging to Lobbs. The next day, the front page of the newspaper carried a photograph of a scowling Portuguese man in a cowboy hat waving a rifle at the editor.

But Smittie pressed on, revealing that seventy elephant tusks had been dug up in the home of one of Lobbs's employees. Another stash of ivory – 270 tusks in all – was nabbed in Namibia. The two smugglers, both Angolans, escaped with a 'ludicrously small fine'. Both men worked for Lobbs.

Breytenbach, who once 'laughed with the best of them over the editor's fertile imagination', is now coming to a grim conclusion: 'The picture that gradually began to emerge was an ugly one and, at first, I found it hard to believe. Not in my worst nightmare could I have imagined that officers in the SADF would get involved in something that would be worthy of the Mafia. This extremely effective and secret pipeline was operating under the protection of the Official Secrets Act for the illegal export of ivory and rhino horn.'

Breytenbach, who planned to retire from the army in 1987, accepted a post as park warden for the eastern Caprivi. One night, over beers and the glowing coals of a fire, he tells a senior intelligence official about his 'suspicions and misgivings, including the Mandrax that was being transported along the pipeline from Lusaka to Johannesburg'. He urges the man to crack down on the smugglers, get rid of the 'Portuguese mafia' and 'take urgent steps, since the elephant herds and few remaining rhinos were being slaughtered'.

The man says little. A few weeks later, Breytenbach is informed that his appointment as park warden has been withdrawn at 'the insistence of the SADF'. He appeals to the Chief of the Defence Force, General Jannie Gelden-huys, and is reinstated. But Military Intelligence officers have other ideas and lean on the man who offered Breytenbach the job. Somehow they succeed in having the appointment withdrawn again. There will be no reprieve this time.

———

For years, mutterings of SADF involvement in elephant and rhino poaching have been swirling in conservation circles in southern Africa. Animals are being decimated in southern Angola, it is said. But there is little hard evidence and Angola remains off-limits and largely 'opaque to the media except for military propaganda'.

In 1974, Garth Owen-Smith, a lanky, bearded conservationist, is hiking near the Otjihipa Mountains on the border between Angola and Namibia. The trek takes him along the Kunene River on the last 100 kilometres of its journey to the sea. The silence is shattered by the 'clatter of a helicopter flying upstream'. From a rocky ridge, Owen-Smith spies a tented camp, 'presumably belonging to the SADF, where the helicopter landed'. The hikers press on and soon forget about the intrusion. They camp overnight.

'[A]n hour before sunrise, we again heard the helicopter's aggravating racket as it flew downriver,' Owen-Smith writes in his book, An Arid Eden. 'This time we just stood beneath a large winter thorn tree and let it go over-head before continuing our walk. An hour later it came back, and in the course of the day flew over us another four times ... I assumed it was patrolling the river to make sure no SWAPO guerillas infiltrated the Kaokoveld from this part of Angola. But I was wrong.

'The next morning we discovered the real reason why the helicopter had flown over us so many times the previous day. On the bank of the Kunene was the fresh carcass of an elephant bull. A chainsaw had been used to cut through the skull to remove its tusks. All four feet had also been sawn off, and a piece of skin cut from its flank. On closer examination I found a number of bullet holes in the carcass, at least one of which was fired from directly overhead. There were also boot prints from the site to a rocky ledge where the helicopter had landed ...

'About six kilometres further west, we found the clear imprints of a heli-copter's wheels in the soft sand. Nearby, in the dense vegetation, were more boot prints, and close to the riverbank a pool of dried blood indicated where a large animal had been killed. Around the site was the fresh spoor of at least one lion. I also picked up four empty 7,62 cartridge cases of South African military origin. It was clear that one or more lions had been shot there, and a drag mark to the place where the helicopter had landed showed that at least one carcass had been loaded onto it.'

Years later Robbie Hawthorne, the principal nature conservator for the southern port of South West Africa, tells Owen-Smith that elephants are being 'killed on a massive scale in Angola, and that those involved [include] senior government officials'. One of Hawthorne's key informants is Muller. When he is killed in the collision with the grader, Hawthorne remarks bitterly to Owen-Smith: 'They got him.'

Hawthorne also tells him about a strange incident that occurred when security forces ambushed a group of men they believed to be SWAPO guerillas. One was killed and others were wounded in an exchange of fire. A large quantity of ivory and rhino horn was recovered. The men, it seemed, were 'just a gang of poachers'. But among their number was an odd grouping of 'white Angolan refugees'. The case was quashed before it could go to court. 'They couldn't be charged, because they knew too much,' Hawthorne says.

By the mid-1980s, Owen-Smith recalls, 'Strong rumours were surfacing of elephants and other wildlife being decimated in south-east Angola, where South African forces were operating in support of UNITA.'

In 1980, Clive Walker, then director of the Endangered Wildlife Trust (EWT), red-flags the 'large-scale destruction of wildlife and, in particular, of elephants and rhinoceros' throughout northern Namibia in a paper presented at a conference in Nairobi. He expresses concern about the status of the animal population in Angola, and notes that there are 'considerable rumours and allegations' about the perpetrators of the poaching. An aerial survey of the Kaokoland, an arid, mountainous region in northern Namibia known for its striking beauty, reveals that there are fewer than fifty elephants and fifteen rhinos left. The mummified carcasses of five elephants, their tusks removed, are discovered. Spent cartridge cases from automatic weapons litter the ground around them.

In 1982, Hawthorne ignores a standing instruction prohibiting Frama trucks from being searched. He pulls one over, breaks open the locks of the container and discovers it is filled with green army *trommels*. Before he can inspect the cargo, the driver makes a call to Pretoria. The SADF sends Hawthorne a message via Polla Swart, the head of nature conservation in Namibia: the truck must be allowed to proceed.

Swart is aware of the agreement between the SADF and his department that Frama trucks will not be subject to searches. Shortly after his appointment in 1981, he had been visited by an SADF colonel attached to Military Intelligence. The man reminded him that Frama trucks conveying wood and ivory were not to be stopped – on instruction from 'the highest authority' in South Africa.

Further evidence pointing to South African government complicity in the trafficking of rhino horn and ivory emerges in 1982, when another conservationist and a leading authority on the illicit trade, Dr Esmond Bradley Martin, publishes his book, *Run Rhino Run*. His investigations reveal that South Africa's officially reported exports of rhino horn don't tally with the corresponding import records in Hong Kong, Japan and Taiwan.

In 1978 – the year following the imposition of an international trade ban on rhino horn by CITES – South Africa reports exports of 149.5 kilograms of horn to Hong Kong. Records show that the horn originated from the Natal Parks Board. But careful scrutiny of trade data in key Asian countries shows there have been other undeclared exports. Between June 1978 and February 1979, 344.7 kilograms of horn were imported into Hong Kong from South Africa. Japanese records show imports of 350 kilograms of horn for 1978. In

Taiwan, there are records showing a further 166 kilograms originating from South Africa that year.

The Natal Parks Board – which until then had been the main seller of rhino horn in South Africa – stops trading after the 1978 sale to comply with the CITES ban. More than 100 horns are locked away in a safe in Pietermaritzburg. By late 1979, authorities in most South African provinces officially prohibit the export of rhino products. Despite this, Japan's statistics show 587 kilograms of horn imported from South Africa in 1980. Bradley Martin believes the horn is being routed from Angola, Namibia, Zambia and Tanzania through South Africa and on to Asia. But who is doing the killing?

Johannesburg ivory and rhino horn traders tell Bradley Martin that the nexus of trade lies in Rundu. One of them claims that between 1976 and 1979, he bought a ton of dried rhinoceros hide and 600 kilograms of horn there. He estimates that his purchases accounted for 40 per cent of the trade in Rundu at the time.

———

The shroud of secrecy surrounding the South African military and government's role in ivory and rhino horn smuggling is shattered in June 1988. Craig van Note's testimony to a US congressional oversight committee and his accusations that South Africa is 'one of the largest wildlife outlaws in the world' sends the SADF brass scurrying. In a clear reference to the 'Rundu mafia', Van Note says: 'The Angolan ivory trafficking is managed by two former Portuguese colonists from Angola who have close ties with the South African military ... Remarkably, nobody in Africa – or even in CITES – wants to talk about this scandal, which makes other, more publicised poaching in East Africa pale by comparison.'

Just over five months later, the SADF completes its cover-up. A sham military board of inquiry, chaired by Brigadier Ben de Wet Roos, completely exonerates them, saying there is 'no evidence to prove the Defence Force was responsible for or involved in' poaching. The only concession is that, over an eighteen-month period beginning in 1978, 'small quantities of ivory, captured by UNITA from poachers and others in Angola, were transported by the Defence Force on behalf of UNITA … This practice was stopped by the Defence Force and UNITA at the end of 1979.' As far as the SADF is concerned, the matter is closed.

But not for Breytenbach. Behind the scenes, he lobbies senior SADF generals, asking them to confront what they don't want to know – that the allegations and rumours are true. He writes a letter to the Minister of Defence, Magnus Malan, setting out his concerns. The letter is ignored.

Finally, on 28 October 1989, Breytenbach breaks ranks and does the unthinkable. He drafts a letter, attaches an emotional account of what he saw in northern Namibia and Angola, and sends it to *Sunday Times* editor Tertius Myburgh. Weeks later, the *Sunday Times* publishes Breytenbach's devastating revelations of the 'ivory and rhino horn smuggling racket' and an exposé of Frama Intertrading under the headline: 'Veteran links SADF to UNITA ivory slaughter'. But it will take the death of apartheid and another six years for the veil of secrecy to finally be lifted.

In October 1994, five months after South Africa's historic first democratic elections, the country's new president, Nelson Mandela, signs an order appointing a commission of inquiry into the allegations. It will be chaired by appeal court judge Mark Kumleben. At sixty-seven, Kumleben is one of South Africa's most highly regarded judges; a man of unimpeachable honesty, known for his razor-sharp intellect, fairness and gentle manner.

By then, Frama is no more. The SADF had discovered, somewhat belatedly, in 1986 that Lobbs and Maia had been ripping them off and owed the Defence Force R3.2 million. In February 1988, days before the SADF approached a court for an order liquidating the company, its name was abruptly changed to Elegant Food Distributors. The SADF did not want Frama to feature as a respondent in proceedings. On liquidation, the company's only asset was a cash amount of R2 599, hidden in a trust account.

The Kumleben commission's terms of reference are unusually broad, allowing it to investigate the smuggling of ivory and rhino horn, particularly of Angolan and Mozambican origin, through South Africa; the involvement of South African citizens in the illicit trade; and the illegal trade of ivory and rhino horn of South African origin. But while it can make recommendations, it is not empowered to bring the guilty to book. Witnesses are also able to rely on the legal privilege against self-incrimination.

Twenty-three people are called to give evidence at public hearings held in Durban in August and September 1995. Breytenbach, who is there every day, listens with growing anger to the 'lies' of some of the country's top generals. So is Burman, who is flown to Durban and booked into the Holiday Inn Garden Court at the commission's expense. Kumleben's quest for evidence is a mammoth task. Over the course of a year, the commission approaches nearly 140 potential witnesses, from government departments and organisations across southern Africa, the United States and Europe, for information.

At the heart of its inquiries are the allegations that South Africa, from the 1970s, had served as a 'clearing house' for the covert, illicit and large-scale handling and disposal of ivory and rhino horn originating from other African countries and sent overseas, principally to the Far East'; that the SADF was 'covertly involved in the receipt, transportation, sale and export of *inter alia* ivory and rhino horn'; that the SADF 'aided and abetted the slaughter and destruction of elephant herds and rhino ... in Angola and Mozambique'; and that these operations were 'sanctioned by highly placed personnel of the SADF, State officials and Ministers of State'.

In January 1996, Kumleben releases his report. Running to 226 pages, it reads, despite the dry legalese, like a thriller. It unsparingly strips apart the Defence Force's lies. The SADF, Kumleben finds, 'officially, though covertly, participated in the illicit possession and transportation of ivory and rhino horn from Angola and Namibia' to South Africa between 1978 and 1986. 'The evidence establishes that the SADF involvement in the handling and transport of ivory and probably rhino horn, directly and in conjunction with Frama, was illegal.'

The SADF was involved in Frama from 'the womb to the tomb', he finds, and the ham-handed Roos inquiry was a 'charade' that can accurately be described as 'slapdash and superficial'.

Breytenbach and Burman are vindicated. But no arrests or prosecutions ever flow from the commission's findings. Breytenbach will never forget the 'inherent deviousness' of the SADF and the 'calculating way in which those beautiful animals were appraised by the scheming eyes of South African Military Intelligence officers ... To them, an elephant was a huge piece of worthless, mobile meat, carrying towards its front end valuable tusks under its ludicrous, hosepipe nose.'

4

Operation Lock

The file was meant to have been destroyed twenty-two years ago. But the old man kept it, hoarding it among a stack of documents in a locked filing cabinet. 'I felt at the time that it was important,' he explains. The creased manila folder is marked in red, 'Private and confidential', and stamped: 'Investigations. Subject: Operation Lock'. There's a note pencilled on the cover: 'Illegal rhino horn smuggling'.

He opens the file, crooked fingers grasping at yellowed pages. 'You didn't get this from me,' he says softly, as if the ghosts of a forgotten scandal might hear us. He leafs through it. '*Secret: No unauthorised dissemination ... Warning. Compromise of contents or part thereof of this document could lead to the death of personnel involved in the operation.*'

The folder contains details of a disastrous covert operation aimed at targeting, and even killing, rhino and ivory-poaching kingpins in the late 1980s. The ensuing scandal reached into the highest echelons of the World Wide Fund for Nature (WWF), the Dutch royal family and a British mercenary firm staffed by some of the most decorated veterans of Britain's Special Air Service (SAS). It is the story of gamekeepers turned poachers and men who may well have become the willing pawns of apartheid's spies.

―――――――

The seeds for what became Operation Lock are planted in early 1987, when Prince Bernhard of the Netherlands, the WWF's founding president, embarks on a field trip to visit conservation projects in Nigeria. He is accompanied by the organisation's head of Africa programmes, Dr John Hanks, an internationally respected biologist and conservationist with a doctorate from Cambridge. Hanks had worked as a biologist in the Kafue and Luangwa Valley national parks in Zambia, had headed the biological sciences department at Natal University and been director of research at Natal Parks. Few could match his experience or credentials.

Bernhard is appalled by the plight of the continent's rhino population. Black rhinos, in particular, are under severe threat. At the start of the 1970s there had been an estimated 65 000 of them. Twenty-seven years later, only about 4 000 remain. Millions of dollars have been spent on security and rangers, but little is being done to gather intelligence on the middlemen and kingpins driving the illicit trade.

Bernhard asks Hanks if he knows of an organisation that can be tasked with tracking down and exposing the smugglers. It will be 'extremely dangerous and sensitive' work, he says. He is prepared to fund the project and, according to Hanks, 'he stressed that he wanted to do this in his personal capacity, using his own money, because he realised it was a sensitive topic and one that he felt should not be registered by the WWF as a project and the funds should not go through WWF books'.

———————

Dubbed the 'flying prince of conservation', Bernhard, the German-born consort of Queen Juliana of the Netherlands, was president of the WWF for fourteen years until his disgrace in a 1976 bribery scandal. He had accepted a $1.1-million kickback from the Lockheed aircraft company to promote the sales of its fighter jets to the Dutch Air Force. He later claimed he had donated the money to the WWF. A commission of inquiry found that the prince had 'shown himself open to dishonourable favours and offers' and had 'harmed the interests of the State'.

Bernhard was forced to resign from all public offices, including the WWF, and also as inspector-general of the armed forces. Humiliatingly, he was stripped of military honours and forbidden from wearing a uniform.

Bernhard had been dogged by controversy before. His insatiable appetite for money was matched only by his appetite for women. The prince kept a mistress in Paris and had numerous extramarital affairs that produced at least two children. As a young university student in Berlin, he had been a member of the Nazi SS. After his marriage to Queen Juliana, he resigned from the party, reportedly signing his resignation letter, 'Heil Hitler'. He later vocally denounced Hitler, renounced his German citizenship and, during the Second World War, served as a pilot with the British Royal Air Force before taking charge of the Dutch resistance to the Nazis.

Following the 1976 scandal, Bernhard remained an influential figure in the WWF and its secretive 1001 Club. The club – which never really existed as a physical entity – was the brainchild of Anton Rupert, one of South Africa's wealthiest businessmen. He had made his millions as owner of the Rembrandt Group and the Rothmans International tobacco company. Bernhard was a close friend of Rupert's and was seen as sympathetic to the apartheid government.

Rupert, who joined the WWF board of trustees in 1968, is credited with conceiving a plan to raise vast sums of money for the then struggling organisation. It would be called the 1001 Club. Bernhard would be the 'one'; the other thousand members would be a moneyed elite: billionaires, bankers, financiers, politicians and international wheeler-dealers. Many of them were drawn from Bernhard's extended network of business associates and friends.

'Bernhard had an extraordinary circle of friends,' says Stephen Ellis, a professor and researcher at the African Study Centre in Leiden, Holland. 'He knew everybody, from gang bosses to crowned heads of state. There were Nazis, crooks, fraudulent merchant bankers and Third World heads of state. He was even in with the CIA.'

Each member of the club would be persuaded to part with $10 000, ensuring them lifetime membership of an elite association whose membership list would be a tightly controlled secret. The fees would provide WWF with an endowment of $10 million.

Details of the membership list were first leaked to the British satirical magazine *Private Eye* in the 1980s. The generous patrons included men like Henry Ford II, the former president and chairman of the Ford Motor Company, former US defense secretary Robert S. McNamara, San Francisco businessman and political power broker Cyril Magnin, beer billionaire

August A. Busch Jnr, and former IBM president Thomas Watson Jnr. There were other, far less savoury members, among them Mobutu Sese Seko, Zaire's corrupt and murderous president, Agha Hasan Abedi, the former president of the Bank of Credit and Commerce International (BCCI) and the perpetrator of one of the largest frauds in financial history, Daniel K. Ludwig, a reclusive billionaire whose companies obliterated thousands of kilometres of rainforest in the Amazon, and Tibor Rosenbaum, a reputed Mossad agent whose Swiss bank laundered drug money for organised crime cartels.

The club also attracted an influential grouping of at least sixty South Africans. Many of them were members of the Broederbond, the secretive Afrikaner-nationalist society that exerted a powerful presence in South African politics and business. Among them were Johannes Hurter, the chairman of Volkskas bank, Pepler Scholtz, the former MD of insurance giant Sanlam, and Etienne Rousseau, an influential businessman who, at various times, had held directorships at Sanlam, Sasol, the Reserve Bank and Afrikaans mining finance and exploration company Federale Mynbou. Both Rousseau and Hurter had served on the Broederbond's executive council.

Hurter and another 1001 Club member, Dr Frans Cronjé, sat on an advisory body that counselled the government on the armament requirements of the SADF. Louis Luyt, Rupert's former business partner and a prominent figure in the Information Scandal, which ended the political career of South African prime minister John Vorster, was also a member of the club, as were seven of Rupert's relatives.

For the South Africans, the 1001 Club was about more than conservation. Veteran *New York Times* investigative journalist Raymond Bonner observed that, at the time, 'Not many international clubs welcomed South Africans, and membership in the 1001 provided them [with] an opportunity to mingle and do business with tycoons, as well as with Prince Philip [the head of the British chapter of the WWF] and Prince Bernhard.'

South African influence extended further. In 1971, Rupert suggested that Charles de Haes, an executive at Rothmans International, be seconded to work at WWF headquarters as Bernhard's personal assistant. De Haes, a Belgian national, had studied at the University of Cape Town and lived in South Africa for many years. Rothmans would pay his salary.

And it was De Haes – a skilled fundraiser – who set in motion Rupert's idea for the establishment of the 1001 Club, creating the endowment that ensured the WWF's international headquarters could be financially independent from its national sections. Six years later, De Haes would be rewarded with an appointment as WWF's director-general.

———————

On his return to WWF headquarters in Gland, Switzerland, John Hanks begins making a 'number of discreet inquiries about suitable candidates for the required undercover work'. In July 1987, he discovers the existence of a shadowy British private security and intelligence firm, KAS Enterprises. The company had been established by Sir David Stirling, the legendary founder of the SAS. Its name was derived from Kilo Alpha, the SAS call sign, and it formed part of a loose network of private security, risk-assessment and body-guarding entities run by retired SAS operatives, known collectively as 'The Circuit'.

One former SAS soldier later wrote: 'KAS was obviously the Rolls-Royce of security companies – the right address, the right contacts and the right people at the top. It was like the civilian wing of the Regiment. Another squadron, only better pay.'

In October 1987, Hanks flies to London for a meeting with Sir David and his men. KAS's offices are situated at 22 South Audley Street in London's chic Mayfair district. The address is an in-joke among KAS employees. Reduced to an acronym, it reads '22 SAS'.

Stirling, at seventy-one, is an imposing six-foot-six figure with an aristocratic bearing and the quiet authority of a man who is used to being obeyed. Hanks is impressed. He gives the men 'some background literature and information on the rhino poaching problem' and commissions KAS Enterprises to produce a feasibility study 'on ways of investigating the illegal trade'. Stirling's man for the job will be KAS's managing director, Colonel Ian Crooke.

In the annals of the SAS and the rah-rah hagiographies of the British tabloids, Crooke, known to friends as 'Crookie', is portrayed as a dashingly heroic figure. A rare photograph shows a man in an immaculate grey suit with a beakish nose, neatly parted hair and sun-wrinkled eyes. A British tabloid once quoted a former SAS officer, Colonel Clive Fairweather, as describing Crooke as a man who 'really didn't give a damn. He liked to brawl and raise hell ... but he always got the job done ... He was a drinker, a fighter, a womaniser and a genuine rogue to a certain degree. But he was born to be a soldier.'

Crooke had risen through the ranks of the SAS, eventually becoming the officer commanding 23 SAS. In May 1980, he is said to have played a pivotal role in the planning stages of the raid that ended the siege of the Iranian Embassy in London. Five hostage-takers were killed and nineteen hostages freed.

His most famous exploit came a year later, when 400 Marxist rebels seized control of The Gambia in West Africa. Five hundred people would be killed in the ensuing fighting. Crooke, who had been sent to the country's capital, Banjul, along with two other SAS officers with strict instructions to 'observe and advise', spectacularly exceeded his remit. Members of the president's family and other senior government officials were being held hostage at a hospital. Crooke and his men donned white coats and stethoscopes and caught a taxi. They took the rebels by surprise, disarmed them and freed the hostages.

Next, Crooke assumed command of a unit of French-trained Senegalese paratroopers who had been sent to the country to help crush the coup. He led a counter-attack that dislodged the rebels from key positions and drove them from Banjul. His military superiors in the UK were appalled and threatened him with a court martial. In the end, they gave him a Distinguished Service Order.

---

16 November 1987

Hanks writes a letter to Crooke. The letter – as with so many others that eventually leak out – is marked 'confidential'. Thanking Crooke for his proposals on the poaching investigation, Hanks arranges to meet him in London in December for 'detailed briefings on our requirements'.

'On receipt of the signed contract, I will authorise payment of fifteen thousand pounds to KAS Enterprises Ltd, the balance of five thousand pounds to follow on receipt by me of an acceptable report and one or more meetings with your operator. I would like to confirm that this whole operation should NOT be regarded as a WWF-funded activity. I can also confirm that none of the WWF staff knows of this project nor will they be informed of any of the activities until the project has been completed and the operators have left the field.'

But the following month, Hanks prepares a discussion paper for consideration by WWF's conservation committee. He calls for 'a major effort to halt the illegal trade by supporting intelligence gathering and the resulting follow-up operations. 'Anecdotal and unsubstantiated reports of involvement of government officials and foreign diplomats are no substitute for well-documented specific information incriminating the individuals concerned.'

Such an intelligence-gathering operation is 'not the domain of committed amateurs but that of the professional investigators who should be commissioned accordingly to undertake this work', Hanks says, adding that 'immediate action' is required. He states that within six to nine months, 'comprehensive dossiers should be assembled on the whole illegal trade network'.

Then, in a clear reference to KAS, he writes: 'Professional investigations as described, funded by external sources, were initiated in November 1987. The investigating team has been provided with the information and contacts presently available to the WWF. The first report from the team will be made available by 1 March 1988.'

Hanks believes that 'this is a major and significant new development, which should have far-reaching consequences for conservation activities in Africa'.

On 27 December, he pens a note to Crooke: 'P.B. [Prince Bernhard] phoned me on Christmas Eve to confirm that the balance of the initial £100 000 was on its way to you.'

————

Over the next year, plans are drafted and redrafted and strategies devised to infiltrate and gather intelligence on poaching syndicates. Crooke chooses the code name 'Lock' for the operation. It is his wife's maiden name. Stirling discusses the project with Sir Laurens van der Post, the South African author and conservationist best known for his books about the Kalahari and the San Bushmen. Van der Post, who served in the British Army during the Second World War, is also a close friend of Prince Charles, an unofficial advisor to British prime minister Margaret Thatcher, a supporter of the Zulu national-ist movement Inkatha, and a vocal critic of the African National Congress (ANC).

A dozen men, the majority of them retired SAS soldiers, are selected to participate in Crooke's little African adventure. Among them is Ken Edwards, a KAS director and a man later described in a newspaper report as 'a profes-sional arms dealer who also dabbles in pornography'.

Harry Taylor is a former British Royal Marine, SAS commando and veteran of Northern Ireland's 'Troubles'. In 1988 he had become the first person to conquer Mount Everest's 'unclimbed ridge'. In the years that follow, he will mount another five Everest expeditions.

Eddie Stone, a tough-as-nails staff sergeant, had served in Northern Ireland, the Falklands, the Middle East, and South and Central America. Thirteen years after Lock, he would make a name for himself as a presenter of a BBC reality television series called *SAS: Are You Tough Enough?*

Then there's Nish Bruce, a respected and 'glamorous, all-action hero', who had served in the British Paras, the SAS and been a member of the Red Devils parachute team. He's a secretly tortured man, haunted by horrors that 'most people would not believe'.

'In the Falklands I saw dead men so deformed that their own mothers wouldn't recognise them – boys of eighteen who had tried to slit their own throats because they had been so badly burned.'

Bruce will kill himself in January 2002, leaping 1500 metres to oblivion from a light aircraft piloted by his girlfriend.

Kauata 'Fred' Marafono, known as 'Big Fred' and 'Fearless Fred', is a likeable Fijian with a legendary reputation in the regiment. He always carries a Boeing hunting knife, tucked in at the back underneath his shirt. There are jokes that he'd never cut someone's throat without apologising first. Marafono had been awarded an MBE by the Queen, although he remained purposefully vague about the reasons. On the point of being demobbed from the SAS, he was snapped up by Stirling. He will go on to work with the South African mercenary outfit, Executive Outcomes, eventually settling in Sierra Leone, where he will play a role in ending the country's 'Blood Diamond' wars of the 1990s.

Finally, there is Evelyn le Chêne, a favourite of Stirling's. He affectionately calls her 'Blondie'. For a time, she seems to have been Lock's keeper of secrets and is said to have even conducted some of the early reconnaissance for the project. (She will later claim that she was 'never a member of KAS staff' and was 'only retained as a consultant to produce an initial report'.) Her ties to Britain's intelligence services date back more than four decades to her marriage to Pierre le Chêne, a British agent in Nazi-occupied France who had survived the Mauthausen death camp.

A historian who documented the horrors of Mauthausen in a 1971 book, she had testified against Klaus Barbie, the Nazi 'Butcher of Lyon' during his 1987 war-crimes trial. Le Chêne, a dedicated 'anti-communist campaigner', also belongs to the exclusive Special Forces Club. Membership of the club is limited to current and former members of military and intelligence services. She is reputed to be 'very good at running agents'. In 2003, Le Chêne will be exposed by Britain's *Sunday Times* as the 'mastermind of a vast private-intelligence-gathering network that collated the identities and confidential details of nearly 150 000 left-wing activists and offered them at a price to British industrial companies', including arms giant BAE Systems.

———

As Operation Lock develops, regular progress reports are supplied to Bernhard. KAS operatives, including Crooke, visit the prince at the Soestdijk Palace near Utrecht to brief him in person. Marafono remembers accompanying Crooke to meet the prince and spending the best part of a day talking about the project. The completed feasibility study finds – unsurprisingly – that Johannesburg is 'growing in importance as an entrepôt for rhino horn and ivory'. The KAS team feels the project should be based there.

Hanks asks Frans Stroebel, the executive director of WWF's South African affiliate, the SA Nature Foundation (SANF), to help pave the way and make introductions. A former private secretary to South Africa's foreign affairs minister, Pik Botha, Stroebel had also served as a diplomat at the South African mission to the United Nations in the 1970s. He is close to Anton Rupert, who is the SANF's president.

Stroebel agrees to allow the SANF to be used as a conduit for funds to the Lock team once it's in place. KAS also has its own, more questionable, connections in southern Africa. One senior KAS employee had assisted the Angolan rebel movement UNITA with a propaganda campaign and had close ties with the South African military attaché in London. Stirling had also published and disseminated pro-UNITA propaganda material through an organisation known as the Better Britain Society.

These ties are significant, given Craig van Note's July 1988 accusations that South Africa and UNITA were complicit in a 'massive smuggling ring' and that UNITA had virtually exterminated Angola's elephant and rhino populations. Despite this, Hanks and Bernhard press ahead with KAS.

In December 1988, Sotheby's auctions off two oil paintings on behalf of Bernhard – 'The Holy Family' by the seventeenth-century Spanish Baroque painter Bartolomé Esteban Murillo, and 'The Rape of Europa', by Murillo's Italian contemporary Elisabetta Sirani. Both belonged to Queen Juliana. Together, they fetch £610 000 from an anonymous buyer. On Bernhard's instructions, the proceeds are donated to WWF International. Weeks later, Bernhard calls the administrator of the 1001 Club and asks her to transfer an amount of £500 000 from the WWF to his wife's account in the Netherlands. The money is routed to Lock.

———————

18 January 1989

Two former SAS 'hard men' cross the tarmac at Jan Smuts Airport in Johannesburg, wending their way through a crowd of weary passengers disembarking from the London flight. Ray Harris and Jim Hughes are Crooke's advance party. They have reservations at the Mariston Hotel in the Johannesburg central business district, and a shopping list. The team will need vehicles, safe houses and, most importantly, information. Stroebel is their fixer, introducing the Lock men to key conservationists and police officials, among them Captain Piet Lategan, head of the police's Endangered Species Protection Unit (ESPU).

The ESPU is only a few months old. Lategan, the desk officer at the police's Stock Theft Unit, had been approached in 1988 by the then Minister of Law and Order, Adriaan Vlok, and asked to establish a specialised wildlife crimes unit. There were growing concerns about the levels of poaching in South Africa and in the Kruger National Park, Vlok said. He asked Lategan to come up with a name for a new unit. 'All I could think of was the Endangered Species Protection Unit. I gave the name to Vlok, he made an announcement at a wildlife conference and that was it. But for a year or two all the unit consisted of was me and the stock-theft guys,' Lategan recalls in an interview in 2012.

Van Note's accusations and the revelations of the Lukman case in late 1988 increase the pressure. Vlok and the South African government need to save face and they want results. And Lategan – with his limited resources – will take any help he can get. The arrival of the SAS team seems like manna from heaven.

'Stroebel got hold of me one day and told me there are some guys coming to South Africa who are going to be working with us, and that the minister is aware of it.' The Lock team provides Lategan with an equipment 'wish list'.

'It was stuff I didn't even know about or how to get, like earpieces and night-vision equipment.'

The list is daunting. Lock's surveillance team will require half a dozen vehicles, a motorbike, micro-cassette recorders, 35-mm cameras, long lenses, video equipment, night-vision gear and false passports. A computer will have to be purchased so that intelligence can be collated and sifted into a usable database. The more sophisticated military-grade surveillance equipment will also have to be imported into South Africa in violation of international sanctions. Lategan helps where he can.

He introduces the men to a journalist at South Africa's *Sunday Times* newspaper, De Wet Potgieter. Lategan and Potgieter had bonded over a campfire and beers during an operation in Swaziland the year before and had become firm friends.

'In those days, I was basically alone, so old De Wet was my back-up,'

Lategan says. The journalist latches onto the Lock team in the hope of a scoop. It is a relationship that quickly turns incestuous. He slips them names and details about smuggling networks he has been investigating and makes arrangements with an estate agent to find them a property in Pretoria they can use as a safe house.

Harris and Hughes become regular visitors at the *Sunday Times* offices in Pretoria, and Potgieter a frequent fixture at the house in Arcadia in Pretoria and, later, at another Lock safe house in Johannesburg.

The rest of the Lock team, led by Crooke, arrive in South Africa in late January and early February 1989. Stroebel introduces Crooke to executives at the Rhino and Elephant Foundation (REF) and asks that he be given support. The operation has the blessing of the WWF, Stroebel says. The Foundation's president is Mangosuthu Buthelezi, the controversial KwaZulu homeland chief minister and leader of the Inkatha movement.

Two years later, Buthelezi will be mired in scandal when the *Weekly Mail* newspaper reveals that Inkatha received covert funding from the South African police to oppose the ANC. There will be other revelations of Inkatha 'hit squads' trained at secret bases by South African Military Intelligence agents. A senior officer in the REF is also reputed to have been in the pay of Military Intelligence.

Crooke's point of contact at the Foundation is Dr Jeremy Anderson, who also serves as director of the Parks Board in the KaNgwane homeland on the border between South Africa and Mozambique. Anderson, a highly regarded conservationist, is instrumental in introducing the KAS men to a range of contacts. He believes they have a key role to play in training anti-poaching teams.

Anderson notes in a report: 'There is tremendous scope for KAS to carry out training tasks on behalf of the National Parks of Mozambique, Central African Republic and Togo ... this training cannot be carried out by South African personnel for obvious political reasons. The South African Foreign Affairs department is prepared to fund the bulk of this training.'

As the months progress, Lategan's unit becomes increasingly reliant on the Lock operatives. According to a secret KAS report from June 1989: 'It is evident that the Stock Theft Unit rely completely on the KAS surveillance team to develop their information and the intelligence acquired by both KAS and the SAP.'

The Lock team is given unfettered access to police 'intelligence on all matters relating to the illegal horn and ivory trade'. This includes 'routine research checks', including criminal records, vehicle registration numbers, addresses, company registration details, export licences, identity documents, and passport and visa details of targets. It is a 'two-way affair and of immense mutual benefit to both parties', the Lock report notes diplomatically. The police supply KAS with 'false passports for infiltration of the smuggling network as well as sensitive information which could affect KAS activities in foreign countries'.

With the aid of the police, the SAS men set about compiling dossiers on suspected smugglers and rhino horn dealers. A target list is drawn up and code names assigned to key figures in the wildlife trade. A copy of the list contains thirty-two names, including some of the largest ivory and curio dealers in Africa. Among them is Hans Beck (code-named Hotel 2), a German-born ivory trader and curio-shop owner based in Botswana; John Ilsley (Delta 1), an ivory dealer and owner of a Johannesburg company called Bushcraft Trading; Ian Parker (Charlie 1), a former Kenyan game warden turned ivory consultant; Chris Huxley (Lima 1), a zoologist and CITES ivory-trade expert; George Poon (Charlie 2), a notorious Hong Kong trader who made a fortune from poached ivory; Marius Meiring (Echo 2), the South African army major caught up in the Lukman scandal; and Chong Pong (Bravo 2), a Pretoria-based ivory dealer the police have tried unsuccessfully to entrap.

Also named is Tony Viera (Papa 2), a smuggler who was charged and convicted in 1988 after Botswana customs officials seized a truck registered in his name. Inside they found 382 raw ivory tusks, 34 carved tusks, 94 black rhino horns, 50 ivory bangles, 73 ivory necklaces, 10 pairs of earrings, 20 elephant sculptures, malachite and copper ingots. Part of the shipment was later linked to Pong.

But the list suggests that Crooke has a vindictive streak. Anyone who crosses him can be considered a legitimate target. This is true of Rowan Martin (Juliet 1), a respected conservationist and then director of research in the Zimbabwe Wildlife Department. Martin had rebuffed Crooke's approaches for information on the illegal trade in ivory and rhino horn, later telling a Reuters reporter that Crooke had been vague about his sponsors and objectives 'and seemed more interested in military technology than wildlife'. Crooke also hinted at 'some irregular methods', he said.

Another 'target' is Dr Richard Bell (Bravo 1), who runs anti-poaching operations in Zambia's Luangwa Valley and who had been a senior researcher in Malawi's wildlife department. Crooke had visited Bell in February 1989 and asked him for advice on investigating the trade in Zambia.

'I responded by asking whether their activities were known to the Zambian government and its security agencies,' Bell told Reuters. 'On being informed that such contacts had not been made, I informed them I could not be of any assistance to them until I was assured they had government approval.'

A secret situation report covering Lock's first four months of operation states: 'Unfortunately the presence of the KAS team on the ground was leaked to their [Zambia's] National Intelligence Service – probably by Dr Richard Bell – before the KAS team could laydown [sic] their basic infrastructure on the ground.'

The report also reveals that, in a bid to gain a foothold in Zambia, Stirling personally intervenes and enters into negotiations with President Kenneth Kaunda to secure a KAS contract to train a presidential guard. 'The scope in Zambia to combat poaching could be enormous, providing KAS secures the presidential contract and becomes indispensable to Kenneth Kaunda ... Once a foot has been well and truly secured in the office of the president, then it is time to diversify into anti-poaching areas.'

In Zimbabwe, Crooke enlists the aid of Glenn Tatham, the chief warden of Zimbabwe's national parks and the progenitor of Operation Stronghold, the country's controversial shoot-to-kill war against poachers. Tatham feeds Lock with 'a lot of information' about poaching syndicates operating in the Zambezi Valley and across the border in Zambia. Crooke – who appears to have no qualms about whom he'll do business with – begins developing 'unofficial' ties to spies in Zimbabwe's notorious Central Intelligence Organisation. Lock, operating on a 'need-to-know' basis with a 'small group' of CIO officers, has grandiose plans to entrap North Korean embassy officials in a rhino horn deal. The Lock team plans to smuggle the horn into the country from South Africa. The CIO will 'provide the right black man specially selected by it to carry out this deal'.

Crooke also turns his attention to Swaziland, the tiny landlocked kingdom bordered by South Africa and Mozambique. 'All intelligence indicates that Swaziland has become a major smuggling route into the RSA – not only for horn and ivory, but also for all types of illicit trophies and goods.' A key target is the Taiwanese embassy in the kingdom's capital, Mbabane. The previous Taiwanese ambassador 'was known to be involved in [the] smuggling of horn and ivory through diplomatic bags [and] intelligence indicates that members of his staff are still involved in this illicit trade'.

The June 1989 Lock report reveals that 'KAS has at last developed a small team with the necessary credibility to infiltrate the smuggling network. It has taken a lot of time, patience and hard work to develop this credibility that is so essential to anyone operating within the smuggling ability.'

Crooke's plan appears simple, but it transgresses the bounds of legality. In order to catch the smugglers, Lock's 'infiltration team' will have to become smugglers and dealers themselves. To do this, they obtain 178 rhino horns. The bulk is sourced from stockpiles in Namibia. The Lock report states that, of that number, '78 [horns] are immediately available to KAS and is [sic] being held in a secure place within [the] RSA'.

According to Ellis, who, as a journalist, dug deeply into Lock's activities: 'Internal KAS documents show that KAS hoped to eventually become self-financing by the purchase and sale of rhino horn, which would have made it itself one of the region's biggest traders ... According to one South African who worked with KAS, shortly before Namibia's independence elections in 1989, the company acquired some seventy-five rhino horns, which were in official hands in Namibia. Some of these are believed to have been horns cut from live animals as part of a programme to de-horn rhinos so as to discourage poaching.'

Lategan says he recalls helping them to obtain 'no more than twenty horns' from the Natal Parks Board (NPB). The figure is closer to fifty. Dr George Hughes, the NPB's director, supplied the horn only after receiving approval from the head of the police's criminal investigation division and

Vlok. But he didn't part with it for nothing. A price of R250 000, in the form of a donation to the Natal Parks Board Trust, was agreed on. The money was paid by the SA Nature Foundation.

'The KAS infiltration team is now ready to commence smuggling operations in both Swaziland and Mozambique where the required contacts have now been set up and business deals agreed in principle,' Crooke's report reads. 'In [the] RSA there is an on-going deal concerning 2 tons of ivory smuggled into the Northern Transvaal from Mozambique.'

He adds that the police 'will only allow KAS to carry out illegal dealings in horn and ivory within the RSA providing the operations are monitored by a surveillance team, which covers them legally in this type of covert operation'.

But the South African police have limited control over KAS's other planned smuggling operations in Swaziland and Mozambique. In Swaziland they make approaches to dealers, and establish 'good links into the Taiwan embassy'.

The team's 'main aim will be initially to infiltrate the Swazi and Mozambique smuggling network to enhance their reputation for future operations'. Secondly, they will 'commence dealing with the Taiwan embassy in order to get irrefutable proof of their involvement through photographic evidence gained by the KAS surveillance team'.

In his autobiography, Marafono describes their work as 'very, very enjoyable'.

'We were attacking at two levels: one group was to do the training with game wardens ... And then the other group were [sic] stationed in a base and had to try and get to the people who were actually dealing in those endangered animals.'

But it was by trying to get to the dealers that Crooke and his men would lose their way.

5

The Superspy

Of all the bad decisions that dogged Operation Lock, one stands out.

It is early 1989. Crooke is in a meeting with the head of a private security company in Johannesburg. The man seated across from him is bearded and grossly overweight. He has an easy charm and a keen intelligence. His gaze is direct, inquisitive. Marafono will later describe him as 'very nice' and 'very helpful'. The businessman 'used to work for the South African intelligence service … [Y]ou cannot operate in South Africa without the approval of the South African government. Whether you like it or not, that is the reality.'

The man's name is Craig Williamson. In South Africa, he is known as 'apartheid's superspy'. How Crooke and the KAS team made their initial contact with Williamson remains unclear. There are suggestions that Le Chêne provided the introductions. It is a claim she has never denied, although she is on record as stating that it would be 'unprofessional to respond to unsubstantiated claims'.

It was an unlikely alliance. A former police spook who ran covert operations for Military Intelligence, Williamson had been at the heart of the National Party government's bloody covert war against the ANC. In a security establishment dominated by Afrikaner nationalists, Williamson cut an incongruous figure. The product of privilege, he was an English South African from an upper-middle class Johannesburg family who had been privately schooled at St John's College in the city. An exceedingly bright student, he was accepted to study law and politics at the University of the Witwatersrand. By then, he was already on the payroll of the South African police's Security Branch.

In 1975 Williamson was elected vice-president of the anti-apartheid National Union of South African Students (NUSAS), all the while feeding reports back to his security-police handlers. He wormed his way into the

International University Exchange Fund (IUEF) in Geneva and used it to establish contact with the ANC. One of the fund's primary objectives was to assist students who were political refugees from southern Africa. Williamson, who became the IUEF's deputy director, went on to represent it at a number of anti-apartheid conferences and meetings with Geneva-based United Nation's organisations.

Ironically, it was Williamson's lobbying that led the IUEF to recognise the ANC as South Africa's primary liberation movement. It was all in aid of 'Operation Daisy', a plan hatched by Williamson and his handlers to disrupt the ANC and gain high-level intelligence on the organisation.

And Williamson, abusing his trusted position, seized the opportunity to loot the fund, diverting vast sums of money away from humanitarian causes to the Security Branch, political entities with links to the South African government and South African projects of questionable veracity. Some of the money was used by the Security Branch to buy a farm near Pretoria. They named it Daisy.

Williamson's cover was blown in 1980. On his return to South Africa, apartheid's propagandists lauded him as a hero who had achieved the impossible and infiltrated the ANC. His new-found status precipitated him even deeper into the dark nexus of the secret war. In 1982, Williamson – now head of Section C2, the Security Branch's foreign division – 'commissioned' the letter bomb that killed Ruth First, the wife of Joe Slovo, a leader of the South African Communist Party, in Mozambique.

Two years later, Williamson was instrumental in another parcel-bomb attack in Angola. It killed Jeanette Schoon, an exiled South African whose husband, Marius, was an ANC activist, and their six-year-old daughter, Katryn. Williamson knew his victim. Jeanette had served alongside him on the NUSAS executive in the 1970s, unaware that he was a spy.

Williamson would later tell South Africa's Truth and Reconciliation Commission that '[I]t made very little difference to me whether Joe Slovo was killed or Ruth First was killed or Jeanette Schoon was killed or Marius Schoon was killed, but I never in my life targeted an innocent child.'

In 1985, Williamson left the police, ostensibly to pursue business interests. But that, too, was a ploy. He established Longreach (Pty) Ltd, a Military

Intelligence front company that was used to carry out foreign intelligence and sanctions-busting operations. Williamson would later be implicated by his close friend, Eugene de Kock – the commander of the Vlakplaas police death squad – in the assassination of Swedish prime minister Olaf Palme in February 1986. It is a claim Williamson has dismissed as 'pure fantasy'.

By 1987, Williamson had become a National Party member of the State President's Council, an influential advisory body reporting directly to South Africa's finger-wagging head of state, P.W. Botha. Williamson would later stand as a National Party candidate for the wealthy constituency of Bryanston in northern Johannesburg.

———

Aside from Williamson's close proximity to the apartheid regime's intelligence agencies, there is another reason for Crooke to be circumspect. One of Lock's targets, designated 'Alpha 2', is James Anthony White, known as 'Ant'. White is one of the founding members of Longreach and a close friend of Williamson's. A notorious former Rhodesian Selous Scout and assassin, he is implicated in at least two failed attempts to kill Joshua Nkomo, the Zimbabwean liberation leader.

He is also accused of being a major ivory smuggler. There are allegations that White ran ivory-smuggling operations while still in the Selous Scouts in what was then Rhodesia. According to Ellis, 'during the late 1970s, Selous Scouts fighting in the bush had often acquired poached ivory, often from elephants which had trod on land mines ... White was widely known as one who had smuggled ivory from Mozambique and Rhodesia and sold it to his contacts in the security forces in South Africa.'

In the late 1980s, White is accused of smuggling tons of Burundian ivory to Mozambique, where he would later buy a sawmill near Beira. In April 1988, both Williamson and White are alleged to have made a failed bid to buy Burundi's eighty-four-ton ivory stockpile. The London-based sector of the Environmental Investigation Agency describes White as a major ivory dealer.

White will also become one of Lategan's informants: 'He's the smartest guy thinkable,' Lategan says. 'He knew what was going on in Africa with ivory, and he himself had taken ivory out. With permits and everything. Ant is a very agreeable guy and we worked well with him. He gave us a lot of information.'

In the mid-1990s, De Kock's predecessor at the Vlakplaas hit squad, Dirk Coetzee, will claim that White was the triggerman who killed Palme. In interviews, White will vehemently deny any involvement, and little evidence will emerge to substantiate the claim.

———————

Soon after Crooke leaves his office, Williamson picks up the phone. He calls Mike Richards, a man later described by Judge Mark Kumleben as having had a 'chequered and umbrageous career in the underworld of intelligence and security operations'. Richards had previously served under Williamson. Until 1987 he had worked for the Security Branch in the South African Police, where he had been involved in 'all aspects of surveillance, the gathering of intelligence through informers, sources and technical means'. After his resignation, Richards joined the counter-intelligence directorate of Military Intelligence and, in July 1987, helped establish a front company, Richards & Tyrrel-Glynne, also known as R&TG Consultants International CC.

'We operate in the private sector. We penetrate undercover agents into commercial areas who [sic] are suffering losses due to criminal activities,' Richards declares in a 1991 affidavit.

R&TG falls under the auspices of another Military Intelligence front company, Pan African Industrial Investment Corporation CC (PAIIC). Central to the close corporation's activities is the acquisition of 'specialised technical equipment for the Security Branch and Military Intelligence'. Much of it has to be obtained in contravention of international sanctions on apartheid South Africa. R&TG also assists with the development of 'technical surveillance systems' for field operations, the installation of 'technical equipment during covert operations' and, as mentioned, the infiltration of spies into businesses that experience losses due to 'internal criminal activity'.

Williamson tells Richards that he has 'been approached by an ex-colonel who had commanded the British Special Air services regarding helping them with an investigation concerning the World Wildlife Trust'. He says he told Crooke he would be unable to assist, but could strongly recommend someone who would be capable of 'handling all their needs'. He is 'worried about a possible British intelligence link with Mr Crooke and his fellow operatives', and suggests that Richards pass the information on to his Military Intelligence handler.

The handler is dismissive, but leaves the decision of whether or not to infiltrate the group up to Richards, provided it doesn't affect other operations. Richards places another call, this time to Lieutenant Colonel André Beukes at the security police. He's more receptive and has some knowledge of Crooke and his men.

There is 'reasonable cause for concern', he says, adding that another intelligence agency has 'already expressed their dissatisfaction at the presence of Crooke's team'. Left unspoken is the very real concern that Lock could stumble on evidence of the SADF's involvement in ivory and rhino horn smuggling. A decision is taken: Richards and his partner, Leon Falck, will 'penetrate the British group' and dig up any information they can get on their finances, structure, countries of operation and the names of their 'principal controllers in London'.

To do this, they need false papers and new identities. Richards adopts the name Harold Michael Stephens. Falck assumes that of John Leonard Bailey. Richards sets about establishing a 'legend or background history' for Stephens. He opens bank accounts in the name of an entity called HMS Trading and obtains a variety of credit cards in Stephens's name.

According to a statement given by Richards, which was submitted to the Kumleben Commission, 'Various other financial transactions [are] later concluded by HMS for the purpose of having a credit history, such as a vehicle lease with Wesbank, home loan account with First National Bank [and] a hire purchase agreement with Union Bank.'

Richards quickly gains the Lock team's trust. He arranges false passports and driver's licences for Marafono and Nish Bruce. According to Marafono, a decision is taken that 'since I look like a Malay, and I could speak Malay … my background was that I was to be a Malay from Woodstock … in Cape Town. That was my cover.'

In the weeks and months that follow, Richards amasses a wealth of data about their plans and strategies. The Brits, he finds, are setting up 'their own black market system' and have established links with military, intelligence and government officials in a host of southern African countries. In the course of their investigations, they have also obtained information about arms smuggling, drug dealing and the 'movement of fugitives plus criminals, not excluding terrorists'. This intelligence will be 'traded with the South African authorities'. The South African's intentions for Lock are spelt out in a document dated 21 August 1989, marked confidential and headed: 'World Wild-Life Project'. Later dubbed 'Document Q', it appears to be written by someone with an intimate knowledge of Lock's activities; in all likelihood, by Richards. It offers an appraisal of Lock's capabilities and command structure, and identifies key problems and advantages of the operation which could be manipulated to the benefit of apartheid's security structures.

It notes that Lock's operations are similar to those 'needed for the collection and collation of intelligence directly related to the activities of anti–South African countries, forces and people'. Crooke's men – 'with their foreign backgrounds, passports and, so to speak, legitimate activities' – have a level of credibility to operate in African countries.

'If tasked correctly, [they] could bring back valuable information which could be put to good use by the necessary South African information-collecting departments.' Crooke, it adds, has offered to co-operate in the 'monitoring of anti-South African bodies which are situated overseas'.

The Lock team also apparently agrees to turn a blind eye to SADF involvement in smuggling. 'It is known that various SADF operations make use of smugglers and smugglers' routes to channel information from neighbouring states back to the RSA,' the report reads. It continues:

This point is recognised by the investigation team and at the beginning of the operation in February 1989 a decision was taken to avoid any possible contact with SADF personnel … A … problem exists whereby information may be received of dealers within the rhino horn and ivory trade and upon investigation it is found that these dealers are actually permanent force SADF members …

Another problem which was recognised at the beginning was the activities of South African-backed RENAMO and UNITA, which have large-scale rhino horn, ivory and other endangered species smuggling routes in operation. Once again, a decision was taken to avoid possible confrontation in this area as far as possible.

The last and most spoken-about problem was the possibility of giving South Africa bad international publicity if the media were to take the information and put it across to the world that the South African government is tolerating the smuggling of endangered species and wild-life products as part of the destabilisation process of its neighbouring states. This point has received much attention at the liaison and command level and an early decision was taken to closely co-ordinate all investigation actions with the South African authorities to, as far as possible, avoid such a repercussion, which would have a serious detrimental effect, not only on the host country, being South Africa, but also on the British subjects involved in this operation.

———————

By mid-1989, Lategan is growing increasingly agitated. Crooke has kept him in the dark about the rhino horn sourced from Namibia and has failed to account for the horn that Lategan arranged for them. 'As far as I was concerned, the money they obtained [from rhino horn deals] was never declared to me … [M]y concern was mostly what was happening to the rhino horn, and there was no positive follow-up after illegal or undercover operations. It simply disappeared somewhere.'

Crooke and his men, he later tells the Kumleben Commission, 'had all sorts of weird ideas of how to deal with people. They just thought that a "shoot-to-kill" policy would also work and they came [up] with various ideas … which I had to veto and say, "We won't take part in that operation. It can't work like that," because as ex-soldiers they wanted to go with the maximum force policy and we differed on that one'.

Those 'weird ideas' include murder. Assassination is a relatively simple alternative to the arduous task of gathering hard evidence and entrapping and arresting a suspect. And killing is something that Crooke and his men do well. In his statement, Richards says Lock identified 'certain key players for determination of possible assassination'. Interviewed at his home in Centurion in February 2012, Lategan says, 'They wanted to take people out. As police, we can't go around behaving like Rambo. We investigate a crime, make arrests and take it to court. Just because someone is said to be part of a syndicate, we can't go and kill them and say the syndicate is now finished.'

Lock's primary target for 'elimination' is Hans Beck, the German-born ivory trader code-named 'Hotel 2'. Beck is based in Francistown in Botswana. He had been the subject of a 1988 investigation by Potgieter and the *Sunday Times* after his live-in lover, a supposedly 'striking platinum blonde', had chosen to 'reveal everything she knew about the multimillion-dollar smuggling racket' to the newspaper. On a copy of the Operation Lock target list that I obtained, someone has written the word "Assassinate' next to Beck's name.

In his 1995 book *Contraband: South Africa and the International Trade in Ivory and Rhino Horn*, Potgieter claims he was present, along with Lategan, at Lock strategy meetings where Beck's 'murder' was discussed on 'numerous occasions'. Initial plans to kill Beck in his Francistown home are scotched after months of planning because of concerns that the South African government could be politically embarrassed. Another plan is to lure Beck to a farm near Rustenburg in the north-western Transvaal with an ivory deal as the bait. He will then be murdered and his corpse dumped across the border in Swaziland. A dry run is carried out but, at the last moment, the hit is called off.

––––––

Operation Lock is in trouble. Towards the latter half of 1989, its funds begin to dry up. According to Richards, there is talk of severe 'internal' problems and suggestions that finances for the project, amounting to £250 000, have been misappropriated by Crooke's London partners. To sustain Lock and generate an income, the focus of some of the operations is diverted to training programmes. In Namibia, the Lock team assists in retraining former members of the notorious police counter-insurgency unit Koevoet as game wardens.

Eddie Stone is dispatched to help the KaNgwane Parks Board train a group of fifty Mozambican men as game scouts for parks in the south of their country. There are rumours that the men will be used by South African Military Intelligence in 'third-force' operations to destabilise the Mozambican government, a claim Anderson, the KaNgwane Parks Board director, dismisses as 'the biggest load of crap out there'. Lock also trains bodyguards for Enos Mabuza, the KaNgwane homeland's chief minister.

Lock's training programmes are the subject of some controversy. Were they legitimate exercises or part of something more sinister?

Since 1987, a bloody civil war had raged in townships and rural communities across the Natal Midlands. Thousands had died in a struggle for territorial sovereignty between Inkatha and the ANC-affiliated United Democratic Front. By 1990, following the unbanning of the ANC and the release of Nelson Mandela, the violence – much of it fomented by the National Party government's security forces – would sweep north into townships, squatter camps and mining hostels around Johannesburg. In a desperate last-ditch bid to prevent the inevitability of an ANC government, apartheid's covert warriors and counter-insurgency specialists had thrown their weight behind Inkatha.

In October 1990, *City Press* newspaper revealed that unemployed young men seeking work as game scouts in the Gazankulu homeland had received military training from white army officers at a secret camp. More than 800 Zulus linked to Inkatha were also being trained there. In subsequent years there would be more revelations of covert funding to Inkatha by the police's Security Branch, and disclosures that the movement's so-called 'self-protection units' received vast quantities of materiel from Eugene de Kock and the Vlakplaas death squad. The weapons included AK-47 and SKS assault rifles, pistols, thousands of grenades, AK-47 rounds, hundreds of kilograms of explosives, mortars and even anti-tank mines. There will be evidence, too, that the SADF secretly trained a 200-strong Inkatha 'impi' in the Caprivi in northern Namibia – a paramilitary unit that would later be at the heart of the bitter conflict between Inkatha and the ANC.

Although there is little evidence that Lock participated in training similar 'third-force' elements, Ellis believes they may have served another purpose.

'Operation Lock was known in conservation circles to have WWF backing, and the South African press gave some publicity to its work, training game wardens in KaNgwane. The presence of such a high-profile training programme, run by foreigners and having the blessing of the Mozambican government ... provided a perfect cover for SADF Military Intelligence officers or others concerned with supporting Inkatha and RENAMO in paramilitary operations to train personnel ... in the pretence that they are training game wardens for use against poachers in a legitimate environmentalist operation.'

On 5 July 1989, Lock's cover is blown by Robert Powell, a Reuters news-agency correspondent in Nairobi, Kenya. The story carried by the agency's wire service to its clients around the world reads: 'Former British commandos based in South Africa say they are conducting a secret drive against elephant and rhino poachers in several neighbouring black states. But wildlife officials in Kenya, Tanzania, Zimbabwe and Zambia have declined to cooperate with them, suspecting their motives.'

The report quotes Zimbabwean security minister Sydney Bekeramayi expressing his concern that Lock could be used by South Africa 'in an intelligence-gathering role as part of destabilisation activities against Zimbabwe ... Security authorities in Zimbabwe have been aware for some time of the activities of these former SAS men ... Zimbabwe has no use for the purported anti-poaching unit.'

Contacted prior to publication, Stirling had attempted to dissuade Powell from running the report. Crooke was hastily dispatched to Nairobi to talk to Powell. During their meeting, Crooke refused to identify the operation's sponsors, saying only that they were based in Britain, Europe and the United States. 'What the sponsors said was we do not want any more bloody papers written. We want some effective action on the ground,' the article quotes Crooke as saying.

Powell is unable to link the WWF to the operation. Hanks tells him that the WWF is 'not funding any intelligence-gathering operation on the trade in rhino horn or ivory'.

Ellis, then the editor of *Africa Confidential*, a fortnightly newsletter devoted to the continent's politics, picks up where Powell's article leaves off. On 28 July, he publishes further details about the operation, linking KAS and Longreach, the South African Military Intelligence front company run by Craig Williamson. Stirling goes ballistic.

'The owners of *Africa Confidential*,' Ellis says, 'were old friends of David Stirling's and they basically said to me: "You foolish boy. What have you done now? Just print a damn apology." I was humiliated, but that's what happens to journalists.'

Crooke heads to London for a crisis meeting with Stirling and KAS executives. Growing increasingly senile, Stirling is wasting away from a lung disease and spends most days bedridden in his Chelsea flat, the Lock files close at hand. KAS sues Reuters and *Africa Confidential* for libel. Both defendants settle, in large part because Britain's notoriously stringent defamation laws are heavily skewed in favour of the plaintiff. Should the case go to court, there will be no legal onus on KAS to prove that the contents of the articles are false. The company merely has to show that its reputation has been harmed.

In a note to subscribers, Reuters says it 'regrets any implication in its story that KAS was set up to destabilise black African countries under cover of wildlife conservation'. Ellis also publishes an apology to KAS, Stirling and Crooke, saying that *Africa Confidential* is 'happy to emphasise their commitment to wildlife preservation'.

But Ellis isn't finished with them yet. Commissioned by Britain's *Independent* newspaper to investigate Lock, he digs ever deeper.

———

Despite the fallout from Powell's article, Lock's operatives press ahead. Between February and July 1990, according to a report compiled by Richards, Lock's 'penetration team' sells ninety-eight rhino horns to smugglers, netting about R210 000. In the same period the team purchases two horns, paying just over R19 000 for them. None of the transactions leads to arrests and the money is never properly accounted for.

By now, Lategan is at his wits' end. 'I'd never really felt that comfortable with the whole thing. Some of the transactions just didn't look right to me,' he says. Late one night in mid-1990, with Potgieter in tow, he raids the Lock safe house in Johannesburg and seizes the sixteen remaining horns from the operation's stockpile.

Gradually Lock's activities sputter to a halt. Stone continues training programmes in KaNgwane. Marafono is headhunted by the mercenary firm Executive Outcomes. In November 1990, not long after being knighted, Stirling dies. Crooke settles in Johannesburg with his wife. They buy a modest house in the Johannesburg suburb of Rivonia. It is not far from Liliesleaf, a farm the ANC used as a safe house in the 1960s and where many prominent ANC figures were arrested, leading to the 1963 Rivonia Treason Trial.

In March 1993, during a Special Forces get-together in the city, Crooke participates in a free-fall parachute jump. He suffers a stroke mid-air, loses consciousness and falls hard, landing on the canopy of his parachute.

'He was a vegetable for nearly two years,' his wife Lesley says in May 2012. 'He's still far from right, but at least he's alive.'

———

On 8 January 1991, the *Independent* publishes Ellis's article, revealing the extent of Prince Bernhard and the WWF's links to Lock for the first time. The article, a much lengthier version of which is published later that year in the Dutch newspaper *De Volkskrant*, is damning.

> The World-Wide Fund for Nature (WWF) approved and participated in a covert operation which employed former members of an elite unit of the British Army and collaborated with members of the South African security services, some of whom were major traders in ivory and rhino horn …
> The WWF has consistently denied any responsibility for it.
> However, according to documents seen by the newspaper, the

Conservation Committee at the headquarters of WWF International in Switzerland was told in December 1987 that the project was being set up to investigate the trade in poached rhino horn in southern Africa.

In fact, the British soldiers who worked on Operation Lock, and who received at least £800,000 from Prince Bernhard, one of the initiators of the project, went far beyond investigating the rhino horn trade. They bought and sold rhino horn themselves. They made plans to assassinate suspected traders. They imported sophisticated military equipment to South Africa in defiance of international sanctions. Using millions of rands' worth of military equipment, which they had purchased from the South African Defence Force (SADF), and working closely with the South African authorities, they set up camps for giving paramilitary training to game warders in Namibia – while it was still under South African colonial rule – and in South Africa.

Ellis reveals that, in January 1988, Hanks wrote a note, on paper bearing a WWF letterhead, to someone with whom he had discussed the plan that 'the operation has started ... Our involvement in this project was conveyed to you by CITES.'

In the days leading up to the publication of Ellis's article, the WWF attempts, unsuccessfully, to convince him to 'refrain from publishing his story'. In a statement faxed to Ellis on 5 January 1991, WWF spokesman Robert SanGeorge claims: 'It is, and always has been, the policy of the WWF not to engage in clandestine or covert operations which might be considered unethical by governments, the public, or supporters of WWF.'

John Hanks, he claims, initiated the project and 'involved himself in the operation without the knowledge or approval of WWF International's management or executive committee ... WWF wishes to make it clear that, while it accepts that Dr Hanks behaved with the best intentions, WWF nevertheless does not accept that any member of its staff should in matters of this sort act on his or her own initiative.'

Attached to the fax is a statement from Hanks and a terse note from Bernhard confirming its contents and stating that he had 'ceased to fund or be involved with Operation Lock since 1989'. Hanks claims, unconvincingly, that Lock was conducted 'without the knowledge of any of the WWF staff or board members in Switzerland or anywhere else in the world'.

The Nature Foundation's involvement also took place 'without the knowledge or approval of WWF International', he claims, and he pleads with Ellis not to publish because 'he could jeopardise a process that was carefully built up over a three-year period, and by so doing hasten the decline of the remaining populations of elephants and rhino'. He offers to provide Ellis with 'exclusive information and interviews when details can be divulged without threatening ongoing undercover operations and the lives of those involved in trying to stop the illegal trade'.

Ellis doesn't fall for it.

Behind the scenes, other letters and statements are hastily being drafted. On 6 January 1991, two days before Ellis's story breaks, Stroebel writes to Prince Philip. De Haes, WWF's director-general, received 'a number of comprehensive briefings on the project since I first became involved', Stroebel writes. 'In May 1989, I gave him full details. He then went to HRH Prince Bernhard to confirm that Prince Bernhard was indeed the sponsor. Mr de Haes satisfied himself with the developments, and in subsequent discussions with me he never expressed any concern about my involvement, or, for that matter, the covert programme itself.'

In a separate letter, Stroebel writes: 'The funds for Operation Lock were actually WWF funds.'

The ghosts of Lock are resurrected in 1995 during the Kumleben Commission of Inquiry into the smuggling of ivory and rhino horn. Hanks testifies and is adamant that WWF officials were not party to it. Judge Mark Kumleben is unconvinced. He writes:

That WWF had knowledge of, and an association with Lock for an undetermined period of time can hardly be gainsaid. On the evidence available to this commission, one must conclude that Lock was not a WWF venture but that the latter cannot contend that it had no knowledge of Lock or was totally divorced from it.

Although Lock was initiated with a worthy aim, its fatal flaw was that it was a covert operation involving persons with a reputation for carrying out unorthodox exploits to achieve their goals. They were accountable to no one. Thus suspicion regarding them was inevitable, particularly since there has been no disclosure of the fate of rhino horn delivered and not recovered. With the benefit of hindsight, Hanks candidly conceded that this operation was not a propitious one.

Two unrelated projects in which the WWF became involved demonstrate that the organisation was not averse to controversial and questionable operations. In the late 1980s, the organisation gave funds to Zimbabwe's national parks, enabling them to buy a helicopter, which was used with deadly effect against poachers in the Zambezi Valley. Dozens of poachers were reported to have been killed in 'contacts' with anti-poaching units dropped into combat, sparking an outcry from human rights groups.

In the early 1990s, the WWF and other conservation organisations actively encouraged the hunting of saiga – an antelope that thrived on the steppes of Central Asia – and promoted the animal's horns as an alternative to rhino horn. In the course of a decade, the saiga population was virtually exterminated, falling from a population estimated at over a million in 1993 to just 30 000 in 2003. The journal *New Scientist* reported that '[s]ince the collapse of the Soviet Union, a lucrative market in [saiga] horns has opened up, with hunters using motorcycles and high-powered weapons to chase and kill their quarry'.

'In China … horns fetch around $100 a kilogram. Organised gangs illegally export the horn by train from Moscow to Beijing, or across the border from Kazakhstan.'

The strategy to promote saiga horn as an alternative to rhino horn had been spearheaded by rhino trade expert, conservationist and WWF consultant Esmond Bradley Martin. Later, after the devastation of saiga herds became apparent, he publicly recanted the idea. The WWF has since tried to distance itself from the fiasco.

Today, the WWF lists the saiga as a 'priority species' and says it is facing extinction.

———

Two decades after Operation Lock came to its ignominious end, an embarrassed code of silence still binds the few surviving participants. John Hanks, who at the time of writing was contracted to the WWF, says that the 'true story has never been properly told'. He claims that he is planning to write a book about the operation 'when I find the time', and says he would rather not speak about it.

Craig Williamson is equally reticent to discuss either his past or Lock. 'I'm out of that now,' he says. Pressed for more, he answers reluctantly. 'I was on the President's Council at the time and was involved with liaison when the idea came up. I was involved in discussions between them [Lock] and the security and political establishment. Everybody was suspicious of everybody at the time, so obviously one would keep an eye on them.'

He won't be drawn on whether Lock was exploited by apartheid's spies, saying only: 'The thing fell to pieces mainly because everyone thought these people, operating in Africa against poaching, would be gathering intelligence for the dreaded apartheid regime.'

Marafono also declines to be interviewed. In a message he sends via the ghostwriter of his autobiography, Hamish Ross, he says bluntly that he 'does not want to be in contact about Project Lock'. Richards is dead, killed in a car crash.

Crooke, now seventy, has never recovered from the parachute accident that stripped him of his faculties and his memory. 'He can hear what you are saying, watch television and laugh at the funny bits, watch rugby and so on, but he can't talk very well,' one former associate says of him. Says Anderson: 'He's not in a position to talk, really. It was a nasty accident. Very, very sad.'

'My husband's recall is pretty much zero,' his wife, Lesley, tells me. 'The fact that he's made any sort of recovery is remarkable, considering that he landed on top of his parachute from God knows how many feet. Not many people survive that.'

As for the others who were involved, 'most have died', she says.

'It's pretty much just a row of dots now.'

Ellis says he can understand why 'certain people remain embarrassed about it, especially John Hanks'.

'Hanks really got hung out to dry. He was made the fall guy. I think he never really understood what it was all about. He's not a military man. Despite this, he remains on very good terms with the WWF. If Hanks had been a really bad boy and done this without their knowledge, I think the WWF director would have said: "Hanks, you're fired and I never want to see you again."

'I say this with some reluctance, but Lock had all the hallmarks of a conspiracy – a small group of people running an operation and trying to keep it quiet. But in the end, they achieved almost nothing,' Ellis says. He believes their silence now is an indication that they 'don't want to be associated with something quite so incompetent or something that was such a total and utter fiasco'. There may be another reason, he speculates. 'Perhaps there was also something we don't know that was deeply unpleasant about Lock.'

Piet Lategan, who oversaw the ESPU until 2000, is one of the few prepared to discuss Operation Lock and its failings.

'We got a lot of information out of Lock,' he says. 'A lot of surveillance photos were taken and a lot of information was obtained. But did it lead to any arrests? Not really. Was any of the information usable? I can't remember that it really was.' Despite this, Lock's influence seems to have continued long after its demise, and permeated many of the ESPU's subsequent undercover operations.

The ESPU demonstrated remarkable successes in its early years. Between 1991 and June 1995, for example, it investigated 792 reports of ivory and rhino horn smuggling, confiscated 403 rhino horns, 34 000 cubes of ivory and more than 1 000 tusks. Its investigations resulted in 529 prosecutions and a reported 90 per cent conviction rate. There were spectacular arrests: a Taiwanese national found with 115 rhino horns; two men caught trying to flog fifty-five rhino horns; the arrest of an American businessman in Cape Town who illegally exported twenty-nine tusks to Kobe in Japan in 1992; the seizure of nearly 10 000 cubes of ivory packed into a shipping container in Durban harbour; and the arrest of thirteen suspects linked to rhino poaching in KwaZulu-Natal. South Africa lost only seventy-eight rhinos and eighty elephants between 1990 and 1995; most of the horns and tusks seized by the ESPU originated north of its borders.

'We had to think creatively,' Lategan tells me. 'That's what we tried to do with undercover operations. For the first time, the Chinese buyers didn't know who they were buying from: was it a genuine seller or a police trap?' In executing its plans, the ESPU emulated Operation Lock's attempts to infiltrate smuggling networks. Between 1989 and 1993, the unit set up 'front shops', using existing curio dealerships, to entrap ivory and rhino horn smugglers. The primary front was a company called Around the Clock Import-Export, which had offices on the fifth floor of Pan African House in central Johannesburg. Lategan adopted the cover name 'Piet Pieterse'. In hindsight, Lategan says, it was an 'amateurish' scheme, but it nevertheless worked well.

The front operations proved 'remarkably successful', Judge Mark Kumleben noted in his 1996 report, and led to the exposure of various smuggling syndicates, 300 arrests and the recovery of at least 500 tusks and large quantities of rhino horn. But critics denounced the operations on the grounds that they encouraged poaching by, in effect, creating a market for ivory and rhino horn. Kumleben wrote that it 'seems a fair inference that these "front shops" may well have contributed to the perception that trading in tusks and rhino horn was a flourishing business in [South Africa] which was not receiving sufficient police attention'.

By the late 1990s, the ESPU was struggling financially. In the years following the collapse of apartheid in 1994, South Africa's government had steadily slashed funding for environmental programmes in favour of a strong socio-economic agenda. A trust was established by a group of businesspeople in response to the unit's appeals for funding. Then, in 1999, a scandal erupted after the ESPU was secretly thrown a R2-million 'lifeline' by the International Fund for Animal Welfare (IFAW), a controversial US-based NGO. In exchange, Lategan effectively allowed the unit to be privately contracted by IFAW to carry out a year-long investigation into the illegal ivory trade in ten African countries. It was code-named 'Operation Jumbo'.

'The fact that the investigating activities of the ESPU, a branch of the SA Police Service, were dictated by a foreign organisation is of grave concern,' the Rhino and Elephant Foundation said in a January 1999 statement that revealed details of the operation for the first time. A report produced by the ESPU following its investigations was 'largely anecdotal' and an 'absolute waste of donors' money'. South Africa's EWT also weighed in on the controversy, raising concerns about the secrecy that had accompanied the funding (the ESPU Trust was not made aware of it, despite the fact that an IFAW representative was a trustee), the fact that photographic and video evidence obtained by the ESPU had been handed over to IFAW and, perhaps most significantly, that the ESPU had joined forces with an organisation whose views were 'diametrically opposed to official South African policy on sustainable wildlife utilisation'.

Lategan defended the operation, saying that the funding had been officially declared to the Minister of Safety and Security, that the ESPU's trips to ten African countries had been sanctioned by their governments, and that IFAW had 'never attempted to influence' the ESPU or its report. But the damage was done.

Nine months later, another scandal erupted when *Rapport* newspaper published shocking stills of a 'hunting orgy' on a private game reserve in Northern Province. These included images of a lion being shot six times in an illegal 'canned hunt'. The owner of the Kapama Game Reserve, where the hunt took place, was a businessman named Johann Roode. He was also a founder of the ESPU trust and a prominent member of South Africa's National Parks Board.

It wasn't the first time Kapama had been linked to 'canned' lion hunts. In 1997, Britain's ITV had broadcast an investigative documentary in which the reserve's resident professional hunter, Keith Boehme, told an undercover reporter that lions were 'drawn in' using bait and could be shot from a hide, if necessary.

Not long afterwards, Lategan left the ESPU. 'I realised it was a dead-end street,' he tells me. 'I just saw all these promotions passing me by.' He later took early retirement and left the police. Today he works as an investigator for South Africa's Road Accident Fund.

In 2002, the ESPU fell victim to police commissioner Jackie Selebi's controversial strategy to disband specialist police units and deploy their staff to police stations. According to research conducted by the Institute for Security Studies, the demise of the Endangered Species, Anti-corruption, Child Protection, Sexual Offences, Crime Combatting and suchlike units contributed to large increases in crime. This was also true of wildlife crime.

———————

Twenty years after the operation's demise, questions persist. Most will probably never be answered. Did the Lock team become pawns in a much bigger scheme? Were they co-opted by apartheid's securocrats into some sinister 'third-force' operation? Although it seems unlikely, a secret 1992 military report offers some tantalising, if inconclusive, clues. It was drawn up by the South African Defence Force chief of staff at the time, General Pierre Steyn, following a probe into revelations about a shadowy Military Intelligence unit and its links to death-squad operatives and political violence. Steyn reported his findings directly to the then state president, F.W. de Klerk. It led to a military purge dubbed the 'Night of the Generals' in which twenty-three senior officers were sacked.

De Klerk told Parliament that Steyn had reported verbally to him, and for years South Africans were led to believe that nothing existed on paper. Two years later, in 1994, the ANC swept to power in South Africa's first democratic elections, and in 1997 the existence of a written report was finally confirmed by the Truth and Reconciliation Commission. But it would be another decade before it was declassified, and only due to the persistence of the South African History Archive (SAHA), an independent research institution.

The report provides details of a clandestine operation run by the Special Forces reconnaissance directorate. Project Pastoor, as it was known, is described as a 'peg for nearly all official operations/activities of Directorate Reconnaissance'. And many of those activities were illegal.

According to the report, Pastoor was linked to 'alleged weapons caches in Portugal for utilisation during an internal uprising, weapons caches in the RSA and southern Africa, and clandestine transport of weapons by means of a modified aeroplane; alleged instruction to murder two Portuguese operators in detention; alleged training provided to resistance movements of other countries; alleged involvement in [political] violence on the East Rand and alleged involvement in train murders ...'

Buried in an annexure is this reference: 'Fronts of Operation Pastoor are in Kenya, Zambia and Mauritius, mainly in nature reserves. Strong contact with the British SAS exists.' It notes that there is documentary evidence of this and that the allegations are 'probably true'.

'Could it be,' asks Ellis, 'that Operation Lock really did get hijacked by the South African Special Forces?'

6

The Hunters

A diminutive Vietnamese woman peers uncertainly down the sights of a rifle balanced on a tripod. Her stance is unnatural. Her clothes betray her inexperience: white sneakers, fake Levi's and a bright-red pullover worn underneath an oversized two-tone bush shirt.

Three burly South African professional hunters – or PHs, as they're commonly known – crowd around her, guiding her aim. She squeezes off two shots in quick succession. Forty metres away, a white rhino lets out a high-pitched squeal, falls – legs thrashing – and bleeds out into the dust. The young woman poses for photographs with her kill, arms held rigidly at her sides, her head bowed. She doesn't smile.

In other snapshots she can be seen standing behind the carcass, its head propped up on a rock. A Vietnamese man – also dressed incongruously in jeans, white tennis shoes and a pink shirt – poses beside her.

'She didn't have a clue,' a witness to the hunt tells me later. 'She had clearly never fired a rifle before and seemed almost embarrassed to be there.'

———

South Africa and the tiny kingdom of Swaziland are the only countries in the world where rhinos can be hunted for sport. Over the past decade, the demand for rhino trophies has grown dramatically. But the vast majority of recent trophy hunters have not been wealthy Europeans or Americans thirsting for a 'big African adventure' or living out fantasies of the 'Great White Hunters' who once cut a bloody swathe across the continent. The trophies that recent hunters have bagged would not be mounted over a bar or in a living room as a stimulus for tall tales of escapades in the rugged African bush.

Like the young woman, they hunted in jeans, tennis shoes and brightly coloured T-shirts, not the neatly pressed designer safari gear that the Americans and Europeans pick off the shelves before flying to 'Africa'.

Most of these hunters came from Vietnam, a country with no tradition of big-game sport hunting and no recognised professional hunting associations. They didn't go on luxury safaris. They would arrive and leave in a hurry. In most cases, their trips were sponsored by unnamed benefactors and they had just enough money to get by for a few days. Many of them were poor, drawn from crowded tenements and crumbling slums, or ramshackle rural hamlets and villages.

If you dig through the jumbled reams of spreadsheets listing details of rhino hunting permits issued by South Africa's Department of Environmental Affairs, you'll find discernible patterns: clusters of hunters' addresses situated in the same cramped areas of Vinh City, Hanoi, Ho Chi Minh City and Lang Son. Some are congregated in cross-streets near the same anonymous office blocks. The names of the same rural communes recur. And sometimes you'll find the same names and passport numbers; people who obtain a permit to hunt a rhino one year and return the next for another.

The numbers of permits and dates on which they were issued also show a definite pattern. For example, take the Ngaka Modiri Molema District in South Africa's North West province, near the Botswana border. The provincial capital, Mafikeng, lies at its heart. On 9 June 2010, eight consecutively numbered permits to shoot white rhinos were issued to a party of Vietnamese nationals. The following month, four permits were issued in a single day to Vietnamese hunters.

Move across to the neighbouring Dr Ruth Segomotsi Mompati District, which accounts for the vast majority of these rhino 'hunts', and you'll find batches of permits issued over the same period in twos and fives to groups of Vietnamese hunters. For instance, on 23 July 2010, records show that permits numbered O 21436 through O 21440 were issued to Le Viet Tuan, Dang Cong Tuan, Vo Hien Nha, Nguyen Dinh Hoang and Phan van Tanh. Two of the permit-holders came from the hamlet of Nghi Khanh, a rural community surrounded by rice fields and farmland just north of Vinh City in northern Vietnam. The other three all came from Vinh City itself.

A similar pattern is evident in North West's Dr Kenneth Kaunda District. On 28 July 2009, three permits were issued to Vietnamese hunters; 20 November 2009 – four permits; 14 December 2009 – three permits; 15 December 2009 – six permits; 25 March 2010 – three permits; 15 April 2010 – five permits.

———————

'None of the Vietnamese can hunt,' says Dawie Groenewald, the notorious safari operator who faces hundreds of criminal charges related to allegations of illicit rhino horn deals and illegal hunts. 'I'll be straight with you. They are not here to hunt. They are here to get the horn. That's it. These guys are making so much fucking money out of rhino horn. They've been trading in it for thousands of years and we'll never stop it.

'I make very good money out of the hunts. When the Vietnamese came in, all of a sudden they started paying R50 000, R60 000 and R70 000 a kilogram. Rhino prices shot through the roof. American hunters won't pay that. A guy who sells a rhino hunt to an American is fucked up, because he's not going to make any money. What does it matter who shoots a rhino, an American or a Vietnamese? You go with whoever can pay the most money. That's the way it works. It's not my problem what they do with the horn over there.'

It's called 'pseudo-hunting'. It isn't hunting, it's shooting. And the 'hunters' are little more than pawns recruited by criminal syndicates to acquire horn for the medicinal black markets of Southeast Asia and China. Everyone knows it, from the outfitters and professional hunters who arrange the hunts to the permitting officials and bureaucrats who are meant to enforce the regulations.

In July 2009, the Professional Hunters' Association of South Africa (PHASA) took the unprecedented step of advising members 'not to book and conduct hunts with nationals from Vietnam or other Far Eastern countries' until the government had 'removed this abuse from our legal system'.

In a statement, PHASA's then president, Peter Butland, said that 'expert evidence from enforcement and trade monitoring agencies [has] indicated a direct link between the export of rhino horn from recent legal rhino hunting by Vietnamese, from rhino poaching on private and state land, from cross-border smuggling, from the theft of rhino horn … and Far Eastern syndicates'.

It was a warning that went largely unheeded.

———————

The first Vietnamese 'sports hunter' to be issued a permit to shoot a rhino in South Africa arrived in the country in 2003. Others soon followed. Records show that nine rhino 'trophies' and two rhino 'horns' were exported from South Africa to Vietnam that year. This implies – if you take into account that a trophy comprises both front and back horns – that at least ten white rhinos were shot and twenty horns obtained in pseudo-hunts.

The following year, three trophies were taken and then, according to the CITES trade database, the market escalated dramatically. Twelve trophies – twenty-four horns – left South African shores in 2005, bound for Vietnam. In 2006, at least ninety-eight horns were shipped. By 2007, that number had jumped to 146 horns. In 2008, it dipped to ninety-eight horns, then rose again sharply to 136 horns in 2009 and 131 in 2010.

In total, over a seven-year period, at least 329 rhinos were 'hunted' by Vietnamese nationals, netting about 659 horns. Assuming that the average rhino horn weighed between three kilograms and five kilograms, this means that between two and three tons of horn were 'legally' exported to Vietnam over that period. In black-market terms, that's worth anywhere been $200 million and $300 million. A bargain for the syndicates, considering that the hunts set them back only about $20 million in trophy fees.

The figures for the number of rhino hunts are problematic and could potentially be higher. A report issued by the international wildlife-trade-monitoring network TRAFFIC in August 2012, suggests that as many as 400 rhino were shot in pseudo-hunts. The South African Department of Environmental Affairs' records on rhino hunting permits and trophy exports are notoriously chaotic. In 2010, for instance, CITES data shows that South Africa reported exporting twenty 'trophies' and ninety-one 'horns' to Vietnam. The previous year it reportedly exported thirty-seven 'trophies' and sixty-two 'horns'. But both CITES and South Africa's Threatened or Protected Species (TOPS) regulations prohibit the trade of individual rhino horns and allow only for sports-hunted trophies to be legally exported.

The department readily admits that there are severe inconsistencies. These, they say, are due to a variety of factors but, most significantly, the complexity of the reporting requirements – which many provincial officials fail to grasp – and the lack of a centralised computer system linking all nine provinces and their data to the national department.

'The big problem,' says Sonja Meintjes, the department's deputy director for biodiversity compliance, 'is that we do not have an integrated electronic permitting system … To find out how many permits have been issued, we have to write to each of the nine provincial permitting offices to ask for the data. After a week, we might get four or five provinces responding to us. It is a nightmare. We see the strangest things in provincial reports: species that are not species; or numbers that are incorrect. Three thousand when it should be three hundred, or even thirty. You get things listed like lion horns. Have you ever seen a lion horn? Or even things like ivory from a lion. That is why it is so dangerous to work with that information.'

TRAFFIC says South Africa's initial response to the crisis was 'flat-footed and slow'. In November 2009 a TRAFFIC investigation red-flagged massive discrepancies between South Africa's recorded exports and Vietnam's recorded imports of rhino horn trophies. According to TRAFFIC's report: 'Vietnamese nationals reportedly conducted 203 white rhino hunts in South Africa in 2005–2007, which would have yielded 406 rhino horns. South African exports, however, only account for 268 horns to Vietnam during this same period, suggesting that one-third of these hunts took place without the subsequent acquisition of CITES documents. In effect, the trophies from sixty-nine hunts could not be accounted for.'

Official import figures for Vietnam for that period show that only thirty-eight rhino horns were declared at the time of their importation into the country. This means that a staggering 87 per cent of trophies simply vanished after leaving South Africa. Similar discrepancies exist for 2010, when roughly 130 horns were exported to Vietnam. Fewer than thirty imports were declared.

TRAFFIC's investigations also indicated that 'unsurrendered permits were allegedly reused (until their eventual expiration) to accompany additional shipments of rhino horns acquired through illegal means'.

According to the report:

Investigations in South Africa have revealed disturbing evidence of organised crime, including: the frequent involvement of a small number of Vietnamese nationals in rhino hunting, often on the same game ranches repeatedly; numerous cases whereby Vietnamese 'trophy hunters' paid above market price for rhino hunts, but then had to be instructed how to shoot and would completely forego any proper trophy preparation; the issuance of export permits for rhino trophies to Vietnamese nationals who had previously been identified in ongoing rhino crime investigations; the repeated involvement of Vietnam Embassy personnel or vehicles in the illegal procurement and movement of rhino horns within and out of South Africa, one of whom invoked 'diplomatic immunity' to avoid arrest; the belief in law enforcement circles that various rhino poaching incidents have directly involved Vietnamese buyers; and arrests of Vietnamese men and women in possession of illegal rhino horns.

————————

It is late January 2011. Two men are locked in conversation in the drab face-brick quadrangle of the Mokopane Magistrate's Court, about 250 kilometres north of Johannesburg in Limpopo province. One of them – the lawyer – is a greying ambulance-chaser with the lined, papery skin of a chain-smoker. His shirt is rumpled, his tie askew. The other – the client – has a dark tan, the colour of coffee. He's in his forties, balding, fit and a little unshaven. It is him I've come to see. Chris van Wyk, I've been told, is the man 'who started it all'.

The court convenes. A handful of spectators files into the lines of hard, wooden benches. Van Wyk takes his place in the dock. He stands upright, shoulders back, face expressionless. 'All rise!' an officious court orderly commands as Magistrate Gerhard Pretorius, robed in red and black, enters the room. Van Wyk knows the drill. Twice before, he's been found guilty and convicted of illegally trading and transporting rhino horn and elephant ivory. In one instance he was out on bail, awaiting trial, when he committed the offence. In another he was caught in a police sting operation trying to buy rhino horn. Both cases resulted in fines.

Sentencing is quick. Pretorius sums up the case: It was 27 April 2006. Freedom Day. Van Wyk, a PH and taxidermist from Mossel Bay, and his Vietnamese client, Nguyen Tien Hoang, were at the Leshoka Thabang Game Lodge in Roedtan, Limpopo, to hunt a rhino. They had gone out with another group of South Africans, including the father and wife of the safari owner who had arranged the hunt.

The hunters found their prey easily enough. The hunting permit was in Nguyen's name. Consequently, he was required to fire the first shot. Instead, he turned his back on the scene and walked away, stopping after a short distance. Three of the others, including Van Wyk, then took aim and fired. The rhino was hit four times at a distance of between fifty and 100 metres. None of the shooters had hunting permits. After they were arrested, two of them turned State witness against Van Wyk. In exchange, the charges against them were dropped.

Magistrate Pretorius is cutting. The hunt, and others like it, is 'a circus in which twenty-three people get in a vehicle and watch as animals are shot dead', he says.

'The prison doors are coming closer and opening wider for you,' he warns Van Wyk. But not today ... Van Wyk is fined R30 000 or, if he can't pay it, 1 000 days in prison. The rhino trophy from the hunt and a Musgrave .375 rifle are to be forfeited to the State. Van Wyk is also disqualified from obtaining any hunting permits to hunt in Limpopo for the next three years. But there is nothing preventing him from hunting elsewhere. Significantly, the court does not declare him unfit to possess a firearm.

The fine is quickly paid. It is what Van Wyk and his lawyer had been expecting. Twenty minutes later, we're in a noisy coffee and internet cafe across the road. Van Wyk is smiling, relieved. He speaks softly, his voice barely rising above the din. He trots out the usual platitudes. The sentence is fair, he says. Anyway, it was all a 'technical mistake'.

I tell Van Wyk what I've heard about him: that he's the man who opened the floodgates to Vietnamese pseudo-hunters and, in effect, 'created' the Asian demand for trophies as a 'legal' source for black-market medicine.

'I wouldn't say I created it,' he says. 'There was always a market. I just filled it.'

He says he was approached by an exporter in 2003. He won't name him. The man asked him if it was legal for Vietnamese nationals to hunt rhino in South Africa. Van Wyk said that it was. The man then asked him to make the arrangements. The hunt took place in KwaZulu-Natal. 'It was a legal hunt,' Van Wyk hastens to add.

Seven years later, 'the rhino market is Vietnamese'.

'There are three or four agents who contact me about clients. There are probably about fifteen to eighteen hunters who regularly deal with the Vietnamese … I'm one of the smallest. I deal with it like I would deal with any hunting inquiry I get. I assess whether it is viable, whether it is possible and whether it is legal. If those three criteria are met, then I send them a quotation and, if the hunter accepts it, then that's that.'

And the clients are prepared to pay *big* money, he says; anything from R300 000 up, depending on the weight of the horn. Van Wyk has no interest in knowing what happens to the trophy after it is shipped. 'I've never been overseas. I don't know what goes on there. All I do is when the hunter comes out, I apply for the permit, arrange the hunt, prepare the trophy and crate it.'

It is the same wilful ignorance I frequently encounter in discussions with other professional hunters about the Vietnamese hunts.

Van Wyk blames the dramatic increase in poaching since 2003 on progressively tighter government regulations. Legal hunting, he argues, offers a pressure release of sorts. 'Poaching grew as the regulations were tightened. I think that when the Vietnamese could hunt legally, it limited the demand [for poached horn] to some degree. There are now major impediments being put in the way of the guys who really want to hunt legally. And because it is getting increasingly difficult for the Vietnamese to get their hands on rhino horn through legal hunting, a much bigger illegal market is being created.

'At one stage there were about 100 rhinos being hunted by Vietnamese. Now suddenly it has dropped to twenty. But the demand remains 100. That won't change over the next five or ten years. There will always be a demand. Poaching continues because the market still exists.'

Van Wyk argues that legal trade should be allowed, although under strict conditions.

'Private farmers and entrepreneurs ploughed millions into conservation and have done more for wildlife than the state or any province. Despite this, those guys have got no say over what they can do with their rhinos. To dehorn rhinos and lock the horns in a safe doesn't work. All you're doing is creating a market for yourself in the hope that the laws will change and trade will be allowed.'

Van Wyk claims, without any apparent irony, that he and other hunters are being unfairly tarred. 'Not all BMW drivers are road hogs. So if one guy goes and does things in a manner which is not ethical, he gives everyone a bad name.'

Not long after our meeting, according to hunting records, Van Wyk accompanied two more Vietnamese clients, Tran Khanh Toan and Trinh Tich Nam, to hunt rhinos on Leeuwbosch farm in Stella, North West province.

And it would seem that Nguyen Tien Hoang, the Vietnamese client who caused all the trouble, wasn't scared off either. He returned to South Africa and was issued a permit to hunt a rhino in April 2010.

———————

'If it pays, it stays' is the refrain commonly heard in hunting and game-farming circles. To survive, animals must have a commercial value that can be exploited. The rarer the species, the greater the value, the more the demand ... They call it 'sustainable use', a nebulous term that can mean vastly different things to different people. The term gained currency in conservation circles in the late 1980s. Today it has become a hackneyed buzz-word, used frequently and unthinkingly.

Steve Irwin, the late Australian environmentalist and television presenter, dubbed the 'Crocodile Hunter', dismissed 'sustainable use' as the 'greatest propaganda in wildlife conservation at the moment'. Elsewhere, it has been called the 'most volatile and divisive conservation issue of the decade'.

Dr Rosalind Reeve, an environmental lawyer and associate fellow at the Royal Institute for International Affairs in London, who has conducted extensive research on the CITES treaty, argues that while some promote the idea of sustainable use 'in the genuine belief that it provides the only means to save endangered species in the wild, others undoubtedly misuse it for their own ends ... Unscrupulous traders often find it a convenient peg on which to hang their activities and justify what sometimes amounts to little more than habitat-stripping'.

Michele Pickover, a leading animal-rights campaigner in South Africa, says South Africa's 'current policy of "resource use" has the effect of reducing biodiversity significantly and increasing the number of threatened species, because it alters the way ecosystems function'. South Africa, she writes, has 'the highest estimated rate of extinctions for any area in the world, with 37 per cent of its mammal species threatened'. And environmentalist Gareth Patterson describes the 'lethal use of wildlife in South Africa [a]s a blood-thirsty, money-hungry blot on the national landscape'.

Dr Hector Magome, head of conservation at SANParks, the national parks authority, speaks bluntly about 'business-orientated conservation'.

'Wildlife must be used to reduce poverty, otherwise we will lose our parks,' he has often argued. For both SANParks and the private game industry, rhinos are a money spinner. Between 2008 and 2011, for example, sales of white rhinos generated R236 million (about $35 million). SANParks alone made over R100 million in those three years.

John Hume, the largest private rhino owner in the world, contends that 'just as we would accept sacrificing a number of animals to their natural predators, we should be prepared to sacrifice a number of them to humans to eat or use as trophies or for any reason that makes them more commercially viable and therefore more desirable for farmers to want to farm with them'.

Game farmers I interviewed routinely had the same thing to say: 'This is not a charity; it's a business. We spend millions on keeping and feeding our animals and we expect a return on our investment.'

Ian Player, the doyen of South African conservation and the man credited with saving South Africa's rhinos from extinction in the 1960s, argues that there is no place for sentimentality, or 'eco-emotion', as he calls it, when it comes to conservation.

'Through death there is life,' he says. 'The great irony is that rhino were nearly wiped out in the nineteenth century by hunters. But it is through hunting in the twentieth century that rhino populations have exploded. When South Africa put the rhino back on the hunting list in the late 1960s and early 1970s, [it] was the beginning of the game-ranching industry. The game farmers were buying rhino for a couple of hundred rand, selling them to European and American hunters for $25 000; then taking that money and putting it back into conservation and buying more land and buying more rhino.'

Legal sport hunting of white rhino resumed in 1968. At the time there were only 1 800 of the animals in the entire country. Forty-five years later, that number has increased tenfold. TRAFFIC's August 2012 report – a wide-ranging study of the 'rhino horn trade nexus' between South Africa and Vietnam – states that: 'Rather than hindering population growth, trophy hunting is widely regarded as having been a positive force by contributing to biological management, range expansion, the generation of revenue for conservation authorities and incentives for wildlife conservation …'

The 1970s saw poaching in Africa and Asia reach terrifying new levels. A severe drought in much of Tanzania and Kenya had a devastating effect on elephant and rhino populations. Rhinos, competing with elephants for what little bush there was to eat, starved by the hundreds. In 1969, Kenya had as many as 20 000 rhinos. By the early 1980s, as a result of drought and poaching, that figure had plummeted to 1 500.

In Uganda, the murderous dictatorship of Idi Amin – in which half a million people were killed between 1971 and 1979 – also saw wildlife, including rhino, being slaughtered on an unimaginable scale. The Tanzanian soldiers who ended Amin's bloody rule continued the killing.

Tanzania itself lost half its rhino population. In the north of the country, where poaching was rife, 80 per cent of the rhino population was wiped out. In 1973, there were between 4 000 and 8 000 rhinos in Zambia's Luangwa Valley. By the early 1980s, only 1 500 were left. Elsewhere, the picture was equally bleak. In Angola, there were said to be only 200 rhinos left; Mozambique, 300; Zimbabwe, 1400; Chad, twenty; Uganda, possibly twelve; and Rwanda, between twenty and forty.

At the beginning of the 1970s, there were an estimated 65 000 black rhino in Africa. A quarter of a century later, only 2 400 remained. In 1982, the conservationist, Esmond Bradley Martin, wrote grimly: 'Over the last 160 years 95 per cent of the entire African rhino population has been lost. Even more alarming is the fact that there were twice as many African rhinos in 1970 as in 1980.'

In July 1975, the CITES treaty formally took effect. South Africa was the fifteenth country to ratify it. (It is worth noting that China became a member in 1981, Thailand in 1983, Vietnam in 1994 and Laos only in 2004.) CITES is an environmental trade agreement, nothing more.

Today the convention has 175 signatories. Intended to ensure that transactions involving wild animals and plants do not threaten their survival, it is heavily dependent on self-regulation by the signatories. In many ways, CITES is only as good as the information it receives from member states, which enables it to track and evaluate trade. CITES officially meets every three years to debate proposals put forward by the various states. The next 'conference of parties' is scheduled for March 2013.

CITES requires that each member-country enacts national legislation that gives effect to the convention and ensures that trade is monitored and policed. Any exports of endangered or threatened wildlife products must travel with CITES-compliant export paperwork issued by the originating country. Corresponding paperwork is required from the importing country.

Animal rights activists, like Pickover, claim it is a 'weak treaty, promoting trade rather than preventing it'. The Green Movement often refers to CITES as the 'animal dealer's charter'.

'Unscrupulous traders take advantage of its many loopholes and its lack of power to enforce minimum standards of compliance,' Pickover writes. These include 'inadequate national laws and feeble implementation, and the general lack of political will … Fraud, corruption and abuse are rife, including the forging of documents and the issuing of re-export certificates for smuggled specimens.'

Michael 't Sas-Rolfes, an economist best known for his arguments in favour of legalising trade in rhino horn, has a contrary view on why CITES is 'very limited in its potential effectiveness as a conservation tool'.

'As it is currently structured, CITES primarily operates as a restrictive mechanism, rather than an enabling one. Implicit in its existing structure is an assumption that all trade is somehow bad for conservation unless proven otherwise.'

By 1977, in response to the poaching crisis in Africa and Asia and a massive decline in rhino populations, trade in rhino horn was banned. All species of rhino were classified under CITES Appendix I: Animals and plants that are threatened with extinction and are prohibited from being traded except in rare instances. Exports to zoos and museums for non-commercial educational or scientific purposes were still permitted.

In South Africa, trophy hunting remained an exception to the rule. The import and export of personal 'sport-hunted' trophies was classed as 'non-commercial' trade. Trophy hunting was seen as a necessary means of controlling rhino populations. And it brought in money that, in theory, would benefit conservation. At least 820 white rhino are believed to have been hunted between 1968, when trophy hunting of white rhino resumed, and 1994 – an average of about thirty a year. From 1995 to 2011, a further 1 300 were shot in trophy hunts.

The 1977 CITES trade ban assumed that demand for rhino horn products would gradually fade and, with it, poaching would cease. Instead, the black-market price for rhino horn skyrocketed. In Taiwan, for instance, a kilogram of rhino horn could be bought for US$17 in 1977. By 1980 – just three years later – it cost US$477. In Yemen, where rhino horn was used to make the ornate hilts of ceremonial jambiya daggers, the price nearly doubled between 1980 and 1985, from US$764 a kilogram to US$1159. And poaching continued unabated.

Over the next seventeen years, various increasingly stringent resolutions were adopted to try to halt the illegal trade, but with little effect. In 1994, South Africa pushed CITES to 'down-list' the southern white rhino population and legalise trade.

'The strategy of banning all trade in rhinoceros products has ... failed to provide any significant protection to rhinoceros populations in the wild and should be discarded as a viable conservation measure,' it said in its proposal.

South Africa argued that while large-scale poaching continued elsewhere in Africa and Asia, its own rhino populations were stable and flourishing. (At the time, the country had about 6 000 white rhino, up from only 3 800 in 1984. By 2011, the population had grown to an estimated 18 800.)

CITES should allow 'controlled utilisation' of rhinos, it said. This would include regulated trade in horn, skin and toenails from natural mortalities, the slaughter of seriously sick and post-reproductive animals for a 'wide range of rhino products', and the commercial ranching of rhinos for their horn.

'Revenue accrued from the sale of rhinoceros products will be available to maintain and improve the conservation management programmes on which the various rhinoceros species depend.'

The submission was sharply criticised by environmentalists. Newspapers ridiculed it. 'End tables made from elephant ears. Designer boots fashioned from rhino skin. If officials here [in South Africa] have their way, such goods, now illegal, could soon be coming to a mall near you,' read one unbelieving report from the Knight News Service.

South Africa's call for the unbanning of trade failed to garner the necessary support. But CITES members were prepared to allow for the 'down-listing' of white rhinos from Appendix I to Appendix II: species that are not currently threatened with extinction but may become so unless trade is strictly regulated. This would enable limited commercial trade in live specimens to 'appropriate and acceptable destinations'. In 2004, the down-listing was extended to Swaziland, and both countries were allowed limited quotas of black rhinos to hunt.

South Africa made another bid to push for the legalisation of trade at the 1997 CITES conference in Harare. According to Sonja Meintjes, who attended the meeting, 'The conference was overshadowed by issues around elephants and ivory. The voting was by a show of hands. In order for their votes to be counted, the parties had to be present in the room. There was a mishap and some of the people we counted on were not there. We lost by one vote.'

South Africa's relationship with CITES has been prickly. The country's past track record of compliance with CITES requirements has been described as 'abysmal'. In 1992, the CITES secretariat announced a far-reaching national legislation project that was designed to ensure that all participating countries enacted national laws that met the basic requirements of the convention. Five years later, South Africa was warned that it faced a blanket trade suspension if it did not comply. But the country continued to miss deadline after deadline. It would be another seven years before South Africa finally enacted national legislation and a further six years before adequate regulations were put in place.

A 1996 report by TRAFFIC found that while South Africa had 'earned a positive reputation for conserving native wildlife', this was 'being undermined by the government's inability to adequately control trade in wild animal and plant species'.

Significantly, TRAFFIC criticised the 'poor quality control' around the issuance of CITES permits and South Africa's annual reports to CITES, which 'showed numerous cases where permit information was inaccurately or incompletely reflected'. It also highlighted 'poor co-ordination and information sharing', and investigations 'characterised by informal communications rather than formalised co-operation ... [which] often owe more to good will and individual personalities than necessity'.

And it found fault with the 'compartmentalised nature of provincial wildlife trade controls', which were 'neither efficient nor effective'. Sixteen years later, many of the complaints persist.

'For many years, South Africa's CITES compliance was extremely poor,' says David Newton, regional director for TRAFFIC East and southern Africa. 'But there has been quite a dramatic improvement in recent years. There has been a sharp improvement in the skills available and there is a lot of interest from government to make sure their bases are covered, and they seem very willing to entertain ideas and adopt measures.'

As recently as 2010, the country came 'within a cat's whisker' of trade sanctions being imposed for its failure to publish national CITES regulations.

'The government really dragged its feet over that legislation,' says Newton. 'It moved dreadfully slowly and took years to enact.'

The threat of a blanket trade ban saw the regulations hastily gazetted on 5 March 2010, just eight days before the fifteenth CITES conference of parties, which was held in Qatar.

'There were mistakes. It wasn't perfect,' Newton says. Even now, in 2012,

South Africa remains on a short leash and CITES has flagged the country for attention because of the high levels of poaching, inadequate reporting of numbers of rhinos and horn stockpiles on private land, and pseudo-hunting. South Africa still has some way to go before it will be regarded as a 'Category 1' or 'fully compliant member state'.

Newton says the lack of a centralised computer database to manage permits is a matter of grave concern. 'For years there has been talk about a system linking all nine provinces. The software was specially developed for the country twelve years ago and never implemented. It is probably out of date by now, and apparently the software developer left the country and the department forgot to buy the code.'

Says Meintjes, 'At the end of the 1990s, there was a Danish project to develop an integrated electronic permitting system. Our IT people were not involved at the beginning and only came in during the last phases. They discovered they couldn't marry it with our existing system. And by then the consultant who [had] developed it had left for the United States and we didn't have the intellectual property rights to make changes to it.

'We have been working on it forever. We tried one company, but they couldn't deliver. We had a working group that also looked at three existing systems, but none of them can be integrated into our system. Limpopo, for instance, has paid a lot of money to a company from India to develop a system for them. But it's not even up and running yet and it's already full of glitches.'

Properly implemented, the technology would enable the department to monitor the issuing of permits in real time, and extract data that could identify anomalies, detect new trends, and prevent the type of permit abuses that accompanied the Vietnamese and Thai pseudo-hunts.

'We need a business-analysis system where we can gather information and analyse it,' says Meintjes. 'We need to be able to flag instances where, for instance, someone like Dawie Groenewald applies for a permit.'

In June 2012, the department was still trying to find funding for the project and proposals were 'with senior management to be signed'.

Another key challenge remains the ungainly provincial nature conservation ordinances that have for so long formed the backbone of CITES implementation in the country. They differ, sometimes markedly, from province to province. As inconsistent, patchwork laws, they often serve to undermine any efforts at cohesive hunting and wildlife trade policies.

'It would have been much easier if nature conservation was a national-government competency,' says Meintjes. 'But it isn't and it will most likely not be changed in the near future. That makes things difficult, because we now have to co-ordinate with all nine provinces. We're trying our utmost best, but it isn't easy.'

The national department's ability to intervene, even in provinces like North West, where abuses appear to have been rife, is limited, says Meintjes. 'It is not our job … It is the provincial department that must take disciplinary steps or conduct audits … If [officials] tamper with the permits they issue to the public, we can't investigate that. The South African police must investigate that. If a province can't fulfil its function, then the national minister can step in and take over that function. But then there's a whole process that has to be followed.'

Adri Kitshoff, the CEO of PHASA, says provincial ordinances are 'unmanageable'. 'National government issues norms and standards to the nine provinces, but each province legislates itself. Some provinces are stricter than others. It is unmanageable.'

Professional hunters are required to be registered in accordance with the regulation of the province in which they hunt. To hunt in all nine provinces, a PH has to apply for registration nine times.

'To operate, he has to do his training and then write a practical exam and apply for a hunting licence.'

Kitshoff attributes some of the legal infractions by hunters to the unwieldy nature of the hunting regulations. 'We would like to see one national system. If the government makes it difficult for you to do things correctly, then it becomes a case of impossibility. Say I go and hunt in Kwa-Zulu-Natal and I don't realise that I need a hunting licence – I would actually be hunting illegally.'

Provincial nature conservation offices that issue hunting permits are also open to abuse. Corruption is said to be rife, particularly in North West and Limpopo provinces. Personal relationships quickly develop between professional hunters, game farmers and provincial conservation officers. Often, they move in the same small circles. In one province, for instance, officials had been stranded without working vehicles. Because regulations require that a conservation official be present during a rhino hunt, the game farmers would arrange to pick them up the evening before a hunt and accommodate them overnight so that they could go out with the hunting party at first light.

Chris Mercer, a retired advocate who has championed efforts to outlaw the canned hunting of lions, says that 'the hunting industry and provincial conservation officials are often one and the same', and compares their oversight role to 'asking Al Capone's henchmen to monitor his activities'.

————————

It takes a particular sort of hunter to shoot a rhino. You have to be rich – unless, of course, you are on an all-expenses paid holiday courtesy of a crime syndicate. Killing a rhino doesn't pose much of a challenge, so you have to be in it for the trophy. Trophy hunters are collectors. Each head is a notch on an unwritten list. A hunter who hunts the Big Five wants all their heads on a wall. For some, it becomes an obsession. In the case of a rhino, whether you're a trophy hunter or pseudo-hunter, it is all about the horn. For many hunters, though, a rhino hunt remains an unchallenging and unpalatable exercise.

Shooting a rhino is 'about as sporting as shooting a horse', Bradley Martin once wrote. The late professor Charles Guggisberg, a naturalist who lived for years in Kenya studying its rhinos, regarded hunting as 'a good sport', but felt 'its participants should never become accomplices in the extermination of a rapidly diminishing species … To go out in a Land Rover, accompanied by a highly efficient professional hunter, in order to shoot an animal which is under heavy pressure from poachers … can hardly be rated as a sporting achievement'. Even Dawie Groenewald – who claims he has never hunted a rhino himself – says he fails to see the challenge in taking one of them down.

Former US president Theodore Roosevelt, who hunted rhinos on a bloody safari with his son Kermit in what was then British East Africa in the early 1900s, said that he considered the 'rhinoceros the least dangerous of all real dangerous game, although many good hunters hold the contrary view'. Frederick Selous, the nineteenth- and twentieth-century British explorer and hunter, described white rhino as the 'most harmless and inoffensive of beasts' and black rhinos as 'by no means the surly, morose and dangerous beast that some travellers would have one believe. They are, as a rule, very easy to shoot on horseback ... They die very quickly when shot through the lungs or the upper part of the heart; but if shot from in front, and a bullet perforates one lung, they will go on to all eternity, though throwing blood out of their mouth and nostrils by the gallon.'

Peter Hathaway Capstick, the American hunter and author whose books influenced a generation of hunters in the 1970s and 1980s, wrote that rhinos are 'the only critters that really give me a sense of sadness to hunt. Except in a charge, they are relatively easy to flatten with a bullet of proper size, and with the passing of each one, I have a terrible, hollow feeling of having smashed a priceless artefact ... Today he's like an arthritic, old soldier, a one-too-many-fight boxer who is losing his battle for survival. He's dimwitted right off the bottom of the scale, a non-achiever in the changing struggle for existence.'

Aside from Asian syndicates, South Africa has attracted its share of unscrupulous rhino hunters, from Eastern European gangsters and business-men with suspected ties to *Vory v Zakone*, or Thieves in Law – the Russian mob – to the playboy son of slain Libyan dictator Muammar Gaddafi, and the son of a former American presidential candidate.

Hunting records show that Saadi Gaddafi – footballer, businessman and all-round 'black sheep of the Gaddafi family' – hunted and killed two rhinos in 2009 and 2010. The first hunt took place in the Bojanelo District of North West province some time between 16 and 22 May 2009, three months after Saadi's father was elected chairman of the African Union. In the same year, Saadi visited the Masai Mara National Reserve in Kenya and reportedly 'threw a tantrum' when he was refused permission to hunt there.

His second hunt was conducted at the luxury Lalibela Game Reserve near Grahamstown in the Eastern Cape in June 2010, seven months before the uprisings that saw the eventual overthrow of his father's regime.

A colourful diplomatic cable sent by the US embassy in Tripoli to the State Department in 2009 provides a rare profile of Saadi Gaddafi. Its subject heading: 'Black sheep made good?' A former professional footballer who enjoyed a season with Perugia, Saadi owned a significant share in one of

Libya's two main soccer teams and had briefly served as an officer in a Special Forces unit. His focus later 'drifted' to movies, and he set up a film production company. According to the cable, he had a 'troubled past, including scuffles with police in Europe, abuse of drugs and alcohol, excessive partying and … profligate affairs with men and women. His bisexuality was reportedly a point of extreme contention with his father and partly prompted the decision to arrange his marriage.'

Following the fall of the Libyan capital Tripoli to opposition fighters in August 2011, Saadi Gaddafi fled to Niger, where he remains. An Interpol red notice in September 2011 calls for his arrest on charges of 'misappropriating properties through force and armed intimidation when he headed the Libyan football federation'.

Another controversial hunt took place in July 2009 at the Mkuze Falls Private Game Reserve in KwaZulu-Natal and involved Henry Ross Perot Jnr, the son of the Texan billionaire and former US presidential candidate Ross Perot. Accompanying Perot Jnr on his African safari was his twenty-seven-year-old son, Hill. Hunting permits had been issued to both of them. Records indicate that Hill Perot shot and killed one rhino. His father, however, either missed or wounded a rhino, which escaped into the bush. For two days trackers followed the animal's spoor and then lost it.

Ezemvelo KZN Wildlife's position is that if a trophy animal is wounded and not found during the hunt, the trophy is forfeited. An ugly legal battle ensued. Perot Jnr – who was featured on the 2010 Forbes list of the world's billionaires at No. 721, with an estimated net worth of US$1.4 billion – got his lawyers to fire off a letter of demand. If the animal was found, they insisted, it had to be killed and the trophy shipped to their client.

'I've paid for it and I want it,' was Perot's blunt demand. Ezemvelo dug in its heels. Jeff Gaisford, a spokesman for Ezemvelo, said that never before had a hunter demanded a trophy despite failing to make a kill. 'This is a bit of a first,' he later told the Telegraph newspaper. 'We will argue that one in court if needs be.'

Gaisford was disparaging of Perot Jnr's hunting abilities. 'It would be a bloody awful shot, like missing the barn wall at two paces. These animals are not difficult to hunt; they are very placid. It's a bit like shooting a cow in a field. But anyone can duff a shot. Maybe he was nipped by a bee as he pulled the trigger or wet his pants, who knows?'

Gary Kelly, the professional hunter who accompanied Perot Jnr, defended his client, saying the animal had moved as the shot was fired. 'That could happen to anybody. He's a very good shot, a great guy and a wonderful hunter.' The rhino, meanwhile, appeared to have survived with a minor flesh wound and rangers were unable to find any trace of a carcass or wounded animal.

In November 2009, after months of legal wrangling, conservation authorities agreed to allow a 'follow-up' hunt. If it succeeded, Perot Jnr could have the animal's head. But at the last minute, the hunt was called off. Writing in the *Mercury* newspaper, environmental journalist Tony Carnie said that the 'initial decision to allow Perot's agents to have a "second bite at the cherry" drew strong opposition after it emerged the animal would be shot by Ezemvelo KZN Wildlife if there was a visible bullet wound from Perot's large-calibre hunting rifle'. Perot later relinquished his claim after it emerged that the animal he had shot at was alive and appeared to be uninjured.

———————

Whenever a hunter or safari operator is arrested in connection with illicit trade in rhino horn, Adri Kitshoff hastily checks her membership lists to see if there is a match. 'Every time a name gets mentioned, I rush off to check the lists, because in all likelihood it is going to happen that one of our members is arrested,' she says. Since her appointment as PHASA CEO in November 2009 – the first woman to hold this position – she has become the public face and voice of the hunting industry. It is her job to put a positive spin on an industry that is drawing increasing criticism. These days, she has her work cut out for her.

'It is heartbreaking what some people are doing,' she says of the Vietnamese pseudo-hunts. 'The man in the street, the man who reads a newspaper, doesn't differentiate between those hunters and others who operate properly. All he sees is that the professional hunting industry is rotten. And your local hunter, who has never in his life shot a rhino, is going to look at the situation and say: "*Ja nee*, it's these damn PHs. Look at them carrying on like cowboys and crooks." This is our industry. And for me, it is really heartbreaking that there are people out there dragging it down.'

Ian Player says the hunting industry should have 'moved quickly and taken these guys to task. There are those in the game-ranching fraternity who've done tremendous harm, not only to conservation, but to South Africa ... The pictures of the savagery and barbarism with which these rhinos have been treated ... it's not doing our country any good'.

PHASA's problem lies in the fact that it is not a regulatory authority; it can do little more than suspend, expel or blacklist members found guilty of rhino crimes. Membership is voluntary and at least half the estimated number of professional hunters in South Africa do not belong to it. In an attempt to mollify critics of the hunting industry, the association has taken to aggressively promoting the 'positive role that hunting plays'. In radio and newspaper interviews, Kitshoff repeats the association's catchphrases over and over. 'No other industry can create the value for wildlife that hunting does ... Without the value, we wouldn't have the wildlife in South Africa that we have today.'

There are the untested claims: 'Since we introduced controlled hunting in the middle of the last century, our wildlife has increased from half a million heads of wildlife to more than 18.5 million.' And there's the economic message: foreign hunters bring in 'about R2 billion a year'. But critics argue that eco-tourism generates a much greater income, with one study suggesting that it brings in 'more than fifteen times the income of livestock or game rearing or overseas hunting'.

PHASA, which was formed thirty-five years ago, today has just over 1000 members. The vast majority are uncomfortably white and male. At PHASA's annual gala dinner, which I attended, the contrast between the sea of white faces at the tables and the images of black children and game rangers being projected on a giant screen – the beneficiaries of PHASA's largesse – was stark. It seemed both patronising and an obsequious attempt to curry favour with the current government. There was something of an old boys' club about it all. This preponderance of 'pale males' is something of which the association has been made acutely aware.

'Professional hunting remains by and large white and male-dominated –

visibly separate from most South African communities,' the former Minister of Environmental Affairs, Marthinus van Schalkwyk, is on record as saying. Kitshoff is at pains to emphasise that perceptions of hunting as 'by and large an Afrikaans-speaking sport' are largely wrong.

In recent media statements on the growing number of pseudo-hunts channelling rhino to medicinal black markets, PHASA has walked a legal tightrope, condemning 'any illegal activities', but stopping short of pointing fingers or, as its former president did, calling on members to avoid conducting hunts with Vietnamese or Thai nationals.

This approach was based on legal advice, Kitshoff says. She doesn't recall Butland's statement. 'We have specifically stayed away from singling out specific countries. You have got to be careful about generalising about a country. We all know that it appears the Vietnamese are sitting behind all of this and are involved in it. But the outfitter's responsibility lies with the permit. He must be responsible. At the end of the day, it is his choice about whom he hunts with or not. There are many who would quite simply not conduct hunts like that and others who would.'

I tell her that many of the professional hunters and outfitters I've spoken to have said that they are fully aware of the fact that the Vietnamese hunters are here for the horn and not the trophy. Kitshoff seems surprised. 'The general feedback I've received is definitely not that,' she says. Later, I send her an email with Butland's 2009 comments on Vietnamese hunters. She writes back: 'I would appreciate it if we could just keep to our latest press releases.'

PHASA's balancing act seems designed to ensure that it doesn't alienate its members. 'You must remember [that] we are not just there to grind our members. We are also there to stand up for them,' Kitshoff says.

Dawie Groenewald is the only PHASA member to have been expelled from the association in recent years. His expulsion in 2006 was in relation to unrelated 'breaches of PHASA's constitution', including 'violations of laws' and hunting activities in Zimbabwe that 'had nothing to do with the rhino thing'.

Following the arrest of Groenewald and several others in 2010, Kitshoff told a newspaper: 'We are looking at blacklisting any professional hunters implicated in this scandal. If any of the other people arrested are PHASA members, they will be immediately suspended. If they are convicted of poaching, or anything related to the case, they will also be expelled.' But she cautioned that 'in South Africa, you can still be a professional hunter after losing your PHASA membership'.

At least one PHASA member, Randy Westraadt – a professional hunter based in Bloemfontein in the Free State – played a pivotal role in the growth of the Vietnamese trophy industry. I first heard his name from Groenewald. 'There are about ten guys who shoot an awful lot of rhino. I don't have a patch on them,' he complained. 'Randy Westraadt and people like that are shooting ten times more rhinos than we do.'

Westraadt has previously attracted controversy over his involvement in lion hunting. In 2012, he represented the professional hunting industry on the executive committee of the South African Predator Breeders Association, an organisation accused of championing captive or 'canned' lion hunting.

Hunting records show that between September 2009 and November 2010, Westraadt was involved in at least thirty-four rhino hunts with Viet-namese clients. In at least four cases, the agent acting for the clients was Chris van Wyk. Westraadt's website, choiceafricasafaris.co.za, quotes the prices of rhino hunts by the trophy inch. A white rhino-bull trophy would cost US$4 000 an inch for a horn of up to twenty-four inches in length. Above twenty-five inches, the price rises to US$4 500 an inch. A twenty-four-inch horn would therefore cost US$96 000.

Westraadt's closest competitors at the time appear to have been hunter Frikkie Jacobs and his father, Kobus. Between them, according to the records of hunting permits issued, they took part in at least forty-two rhino hunts with Vietnamese hunters between August 2009 and July 2010. Many of the hunts took place at the Jacobs family's Shingalana Lion & Rhino Game Reserve in North West province. Another PH, Brad Rolston, conducted at least twenty-four hunts over a fifteen-month period between 2009 and 2010. A key link is safari operator Alexander Steyn, who was the outfitter for several of the Vietnamese hunts conducted by Westraadt and Van Wyk.

In 2010, Steyn was also a major rhino buyer, purchasing about seventeen rhinos from SANParks for just over R4 million. Steyn is a controversial fig-ure who has been implicated in the 'canned' hunting of cheetahs. In 2005, an undercover journalist from the *Mail & Guardian* newspaper reportedly negotiated with Steyn for the purchase of two captive-bred cheetahs for a hunt. When Steyn was eventually confronted and asked if he was involved in canned hunting, he replied: 'What is canned hunting? Canned hunting takes place in a fenced-off area. Yet the whole of South Africa, the whole of Africa, is fenced. The whole of Africa is canned.'

What is apparent from the records and hunting registers – which one investigator laughingly describes as a 'great suspect list' – is that a relatively small group of a dozen or so hunters are the key protagonists in trophy hunts involving Southeast Asian hunters.

In March 2012, South Africa's environment minister, Edna Molewa, announced, somewhat belatedly, that her department had asked Vietnam's Ministry of Agriculture and Rural Development to conduct inspections to determine whether trophies shot in South Africa by Vietnamese citizens were still in the hunters' possession. A list of names and addresses taken from hunting-permit applications was provided to the Vietnamese authorities. Until the verification process had been completed, South Africa would refuse all hunting permits to Vietnamese hunters, she said.

In the same month, Walter Slippers, a safari operator who had been involved in a number of rhino hunts, brought an urgent application in the North Gauteng High Court to force the Limpopo provincial wildlife author-ities to issue hunting permits to five Vietnamese hunters. The permits had initially been authorised, but, following an advisory from the national department calling on provinces 'not to issue hunting permits to Vietnamese citizens due to various concerns regarding illegal hunting practices', the per-mits were withheld.

The court ordered that the permits be issued, subject to the Vietnamese hunters being interviewed by wildlife officials. Should the interviews call into question the legitimacy of the hunt, the department could return to court, the judge said.

The arrangements for the interviews were made, but on the appointed day, Slippers conceded that his clients were not even in the country. The interviews were scrapped, the department went back to court and, based on their 'legitimate concerns', the court ordered that the hunting permits need not be issued.

In April 2012, Molewa gazetted a revised set of norms and standards governing trophy hunting, the microchipping of horns, the marking of live rhinos and the manner in which samples should be collected for DNA profiling.

Rhino hunts now have to comply with seventeen specific requirements as opposed to eleven under earlier 2009 guidelines.

All hunting permit applications have to be accompanied by a raft of supporting documentation. Foreign hunters have to prove that they belong to a hunting association recognised by their government, and provide a CV detailing previous hunting experience or 'proof of previous experience in hunting any African species'. Permitting officials are now also required to consider 'whether the country of usual residence of the hunting client, where the rhinoceros horns and the rest of the hunting trophy will be imported to, has adequate legislation to ensure that rhinoceros horns and the rest of the hunting trophy will be used for the purpose as indicated on the CITES export permit'.

Magdel Boshoff, a deputy director of policy development in the Department of Environmental Affairs, says nature conservation officials can now refuse hunting permits where previously they had no grounds on which to do so.

'Before, if the hunter complied with all the provisions, we didn't have any measures in place to refuse a permit. It was the exception to the rule for a permit to be refused. Now we need all that supporting information and, if it isn't there, we can refuse to issue a permit. We're in a position to refuse a permit on the basis that someone isn't a bona fide hunter.'

By early 2012, the Vietnamese pseudo-hunts had ground to a halt. But already there were worrying signs that the syndicates were adapting and were looking for other fronts for their operations. New patterns had begun to emerge in the hunting registers, including a curious spike in rhino hunts conducted by hunters from the Czech Republic and Poland. Since July 2009, they had shot thirty-four rhinos.

'The Czech hunters are being specifically recruited by the Vietnamese to hunt rhinos,' a senior South African investigator told me. 'When the Czech police went and interviewed the hunters, the guys confessed and said, "Yes, we were recruited by the Vietnamese to go and shoot, this is what we were paid and here are the permits." That is how big this thing is. It is a worldwide phenomenon, and the syndicates are always one step ahead.'

7

The 'Boeremafia'

18 June 2011

Dawie Groenewald would shoot a hundred rhinos a year, given half a chance. 'It's a good business,' he says. In fact, right now he'd probably kill every rhino he could lay his hands on. 'I feel so fucking angry about the system that I want to shoot as many rhinos as I can get,' he tells me. 'And that's not right.'

It is almost a year since Groenewald, his wife Sariette and nine others, including professional hunters, veterinarians, a pilot and farm labourers, were arrested by the police's organised crime unit. The fifteen-month investigation – called 'Project Cruiser' – was described by police as 'a huge stride in our undying effort to thwart rhino poaching'. An SAPS spokesman, Colonel Vish Naidoo, claimed that the Groenewald syndicate had been linked to literally 'hundreds of rhino poaching incidents'. Newspapers were filled with grisly accounts of the 'Rhino Slaughter Farm' and the rotting carcasses exhumed from mass graves. Outside the Musina Regional Court, where the suspects appeared, demonstrators held up placards exhorting: '*Sny Dawie se horing af*' (Cut off Dawie's horn). There were cries of 'Rhino killer!' as Groenewald arrived at court with his wife.

Prosecutors threw the book at him. The indictment in the matter of the *State v Dawid Jacobus Groenewald* and ten others runs to 637 pages, and there are 185 witnesses lined up to testify. Groenewald himself faces 1736 counts of racketeering, money-laundering, fraud, intimidation, illegal hunting and dealing in rhino horns. He is accused of killing fifty-nine of his own rhinos for their horns, then getting rid of the carcasses by burying them, burning them or selling them to a local butchery. In addition he's charged with illegally dehorning dozens of the animals and selling at least 384 rhino horns over a four-year period. The case – which at the time of writing in late 2012 had yet to go to trial – could drag on for years.

But Groenewald is adamant. 'I am not a poacher,' he tells me as we sit on the deck of the hunting lodge at his farm Prachtig, sixty kilometres south of Musina. 'That word makes me sick. It is not necessary for me to poach a rhino.'

I first heard Groenewald's name in Zimbabwe a few months before his arrest during my initial inquiries into Johan Roos, the Musina poacher accused of supplying silenced rifles to poaching gangs.

I had gone to meet Charles Davy, the founder and driving force behind the Bubye Valley Conservancy in Zimbabwe's south-eastern Lowveld. It was there that two silenced rifles – including one stolen during a farm attack in South Africa – had been recovered and linked to Roos.

Davy is a controversial figure. He has made millions through property development, game farming and hunting. Until 2006, he had been a director and shareholder of HHK Safaris, one of Zimbabwe's largest hunting operators.

Dubbed the 'great white survivor' by a British press fixated on his daughter Chelsy's long on-again, off-again relationship with Prince Harry, Davy was one of the few white farmers to weather the storm of Robert Mugabe's land grabs. Davy said it had come at a price: 'I have given up rather a large part of my life to end up with the bit that I have left.' Four of his farms, covering an area of about 56 000 hectares, were ceded to the government for resettlement. Despite this, rumours persist that he is somehow protected because of his ties to leading figures in Mugabe's government. The opposition Movement for Democratic Change (MDC) has accused Davy of 'sustaining' the Mugabe regime, a claim he denies.

But they point to his friendship with Webster Shamu, Zimbabwe's information minister and one of the old guard close to Mugabe. Davy claims he has known Shamu since the mid-1990s and that they have a 'legitimate, long-standing business partnership' in a safari business. 'He's a person I like and get along with,' he told me.

Once Chelsy met Harry, Davy's business interests and his links to Mugabe's government became grist for the tabloid mill. In 2009, Britain's *Daily Mail*, a newspaper with a reputation for allegedly fabricating stories, published an article linking Davy to a rhino-poaching cartel called the 'Crocodile Gang'. It was a name unimaginatively plucked from the annals of Zimbabwe's independence war. The report, littered – by the writer's own admission – with a 'cast list lifted straight from the pages of a Wilbur Smith novel', suggested that Davy was somehow linked to a syndicate led by Emmerson Mnangagwa, a Mugabe confidant known as the 'butcher of Matabeleland'. It was a story calculated to cause damage. Harry's brother, Prince William, is an ardent conservationist and has spoken out repeatedly against the illegal trade in rhino horns, describing it on one occasion as 'ignorant, selfish and utterly wrong'.

Davy was outraged by the *Daily Mail*'s allegations. In a rare interview, he told the *Telegraph* that he had had 'enough of this nonsense'.

'I have spent a good part of my life building up game sanctuaries and protecting wildlife ... I doubt that you will find anyone who has done as much for the conservation of wildlife with his own money as I have.'

Raoul du Toit, the director of the Lowveld Rhino Trust and the man credited with saving Zimbabwe's rhinos from extinction, came to Davy's defence, saying that he was a vital cog in protecting Zimbabwe's dwindling black rhino population.

The *Daily Mail* article was later quietly removed from the website.

———

The sprawling, thatched-roof Davy family homestead sits on a hilltop overlooking the Bubye Conservancy and a vast expanse of acacia trees, granite *koppies*, veld and mopane woodlands that stretch as far as I can see. There is a pool and a tennis court. Below it lies Towla, the conservancy's headquarters. Over coffee in his office, Davy is emphatic. Dawie Groenewald, he tells me, is a 'bad bastard'. He leans forward. 'Groenewald has bought $4 million worth of rhino at auctions. He bought them because he's chopping off all the horns.' It was the first I'd heard of it.

The two men have never met. But they despise one another. At the root of their enmity lies a long-running feud over a prime government hunting concession in the Matetsi Safari Area, near the Hwange National Park in north-western Zimbabwe. Davy alleges that in about 2003, Groenewald conspired with his former business partner, Ed Kadzombe, and 'other political elements' to strip him of the concession.

'After we lost the concession, one of our skinners stayed behind. He told me later that hunters had shot sixty lions. It was absolutely terrible.' Davy also alleges that Groenewald has been involved in large-scale hunting on farms in the Gwaai Valley Conservancy near Hwange, which had been occupied by squatters as part of Mugabe's 'fast-track land-reform programme'. According to conservationists, 'whole herds of animals' were shot there.

Later, when I ask Groenewald about the accusations, he admits to hunting on occupied farms, but says that accusations of illegal hunting are prompted by jealousy and racism. 'You know what the white Zimbabweans are like to the white South Africans,' he says. 'They don't want us to hunt there in their kingdom. In 2000, when the farms were being taken back from the whites, there were ex-parks guys who each got a piece of land. And I started hunting there. I wasn't the only South African in Zimbabwe doing that. But then I began hunting with the boys. And people said that was wrong. How could a white guy go hunting with a boy? It just doesn't work like that.' (In this context, the word 'boy' is used as a demeaning term for a black African man.)

Groenewald continues: 'So when I began hunting with the boys, that is when the stories started coming out that I was hunting illegally, that I was slaughtering Zimbabwe's wildlife, that I was sending planes in to smuggle stuff out.'

Groenewald says that the Matetsi concession was the cause of his 'biggest shit' in Zimbabwe. 'It is the best hunting in Zim but, *jirre*, I lost a lot of money there.' He claims he was harassed in a concerted campaign to get him off the concession. 'It was police every second day, accusations that we were hunting illegally, all that bullshit, all the time. It was a nightmare. It was all just because we had the most clients.'

For years Groenewald's hunting business, Out of Africa Adventurous Safaris, had been dogged by allegations of illegal hunting in Zimbabwe. 'This is an unscrupulous organisation that doesn't respect the environment and pursues unsustainable quotas,' David Coltart, an opposition politician in Zimbabwe, told a *Newsweek* reporter in 2005. According to the article, 'critics, including the Zimbabwean Association of Tourism and Safari Operators, say the group ... overhunt species in violation of the Zimbabwean government's hunting rules'. That same year, the influential US-based *Hunting Report* newsletter stated that Out of Africa was 'widely known to take people onto seized properties in Zimbabwe' and was 'deeply resented by the professional hunting establishment'.

In 2005, the Zimbabwe Parks and Wildlife Management Authority also issued a letter 'banning' Out of Africa's operations in Zimbabwe. Dated 20 January and signed by Dr Morris Mtsambiwa, the then director-general of Zimparks, the letter stated that Out of Africa is 'not allowed any hunting nor any safari operation in the whole country of Zimbabwe'.

When I asked Groenewald about the banning letter in June 2011, he said it was 'bullshit'. He showed me another letter, also on a Zimparks letterhead and signed by Felix Matenda, a senior investigations and security officer in the Bulawayo office. Dated 17 August 2010, it stated that there were no allegations being investigated against Out of Africa.

'How can you ban someone in Zimbabwe? I'm still hunting in Zimbabwe,' Groenewald said. 'We're hunting in [Hwange] National Park now, with permits. Elephant and buffalo. We shot five or six elephant there last year. That is how bad it is over there.'

Strictly speaking, Zimbabwe's National Parks Act prohibits hunting in national parks. But in recent years the regulations have been waived to allow the country's cash-strapped parks authorities to earn an income through 'non-trophy' elephant hunts. Under normal circumstances, the animals would be culled and the meat given to parks officials and local villagers. Now a hunter, paying as little as $10 000 for a seven-day hunt, can shoot an elephant, pose for a photograph with the kill and get a cast of the tusks as a keepsake.

'There is a total overpopulation of elephants there,' Tielman Erasmus, a professional hunter and one of Groenewald's co-accused, said. 'So what a way to get rid of them and make money.'

The Zimbabwe Professional Hunters and Guides Association has described the practice as 'unethical'. 'If we start hunting within a national park, it destroys the entire purpose of having national parks,' it said in a 2011 statement. According to the Safari Operators' Association of Zimbabwe, the practice is 'not ideal or desirable, but it is legal'. One Zimbabwean professional hunter I spoke to, Blondie Leathem, remarked: 'Only guys like Groenewald would have such low ethics that they are prepared to hunt in a national park – the typical lowlife who believes that money comes before everything else in life.'

The Zimbabwe allegations seem to have had repercussions in South Africa. In 2006, Groenewald was expelled from PHASA. While the exact nature of the complaints filed against him was never made public, some were said to relate to his activities in Zimbabwe. Adri Kitshoff, PHASA's CEO, told me in 2012 that most of the charges related to 'transgressions of laws' and permit violations. She wouldn't be drawn on the details.

Groenewald maintains that he did nothing illegal in Zimbabwe. 'We are not angels,' he told me. 'You can never do anything 100 per cent right. You might pay a bribe in Zimbabwe to go through the border or give a guy a $100 and say, "I don't want to wait a week for a permit. Give it to me in a day." But we never stole [anything] from [anybody].'

———

As Groenewald tells it, his is a classic rags-to-riches tale – the story of a local boy who defied the odds to become a multimillionaire.

He was born into a working-class Afrikaans family in Pietersburg – now Polokwane – in 1968. Groenewald's mother was a hairdresser. His father worked in construction. He doesn't talk about him much. 'I see very little of him. We don't have a relationship. It is difficult. My mother and father separated early. My mother raised us and then we went to boarding school.'

When he finished school, his mother didn't have the money to send him or his brother Janneman to university. They were left with a simple choice – the army or the police. In 1987, all young white men were subject to compulsory military service in the armed forces of the apartheid state. There were few exceptions to the rule. One of them was joining the police. Groenewald weighed up his options. The army was a two-year stint. If you opted for the cops, it was four years. The army paid R120 a month, the police force, R600. Groenewald joined the police, as did Janneman.

The two were eventually assigned to the narcotics bureau, and spent much of their time chasing down dagga dealers. 'We didn't even know what stuff like cocaine looked like back then,' Groenewald says. He also found time to make a name for himself playing rugby for the police and then for the Far North rugby union. He was a fullback. 'That was a great time,' he says wistfully.

But in 1993, the brothers left the force under a cloud. There were whispers that they were somehow linked to a syndicate that smuggled stolen cars across the border into Zimbabwe.

'The whole thing was blown completely out of proportion,' Groenewald says, taking a sip of Coke. 'We had left narcotics and were working at the vehicle theft unit. You get a lot of stolen cars coming in and you don't know who the owner is. Engine numbers are filed off, but you can etch them out and then trace the car. At that stage we didn't have a private vehicle, so one day in came a fucked-up old Toyota bakkie. We got the number, found out who the owner was, called him up and asked him if we could buy it. He said sure, and we paid R7 000 for it.

'We drove it to work at the police station every day. It's not like we were hiding it. Then the bomb burst and we were accused of fraud. Afterwards we found out that the guy who had sold us the bakkie wasn't the real owner. My brother was fined R3 000 for fraud. I wasn't found guilty. It was a ridiculous case. If we wanted to steal a car, we wouldn't drive it to work at the fucking police station.'

'It was about jealousy,' Groenewald says, touching on what is to become a recurring theme in our discussions. 'We always did nicer things than the others in the unit. The other guys always had a knife out for us.'

Not long afterwards, Janneman left South Africa and went to the United States. He has never been back, his brother says.

Out of the police and out of work, Groenewald turned to selling fresh produce. 'I was selling bananas, peaches and watermelons on the street corners and in the taxi ranks. At 5 a.m., I'd be sitting in a taxi rank selling bananas, just to make money. I'd go to the farmers, buy some Impala, cut it up into small packets and sell it on the street.'

Everything changed in 1997. That was the year Groenewald and three friends started a hunting business that would become Out of Africa Adventurous Safaris. It was the year that he attended his first Safari Club International (SCI) convention in the United States. Billed as the 'largest hunting shows on earth', the annual SCI conventions draw thousands of hunters from across the United States and around the world. Every safari outfitter worth his salt is there looking for clients. It is a cut-throat business. 'This is the dirtiest business out there,' Groenewald's wife, Sariette, says. 'One day everyone is nice to you at the show, and the next you are their biggest enemy and you mustn't come within ten metres of their little stall because you're then stealing their clients.'

Groenewald quickly found his first clients at the SCI convention. 'We hired a camp from someone for them to stay at and arranged the hunts.' Three years later, Out of Africa expanded its operations into Zimbabwe as the first farms were seized and bread riots erupted in Harare.

In 2002, Groenewald bought Prachtig. 'It cost R4 million for only 2 500 hectares. That was expensive back then.' Two of his partners in the hunting business pulled out in 2004 to pursue other interests. That year Groenewald bought his first sables and, a few years later, his first rhinos. Later, he partnered with a Spaniard and bought the neighbouring farm, Krige. He was doing well. An Out of Africa safari brochure for the 2008 to 2009 hunting season shows hunters posing with a variety of kills – eleven lions, ten leopards, twenty elephant, thirty-five buffalo, four rhinos, three hippo and three crocodiles. At the time, Groenewald was charging between $10 000 and $12 500 for an elephant trophy, $5 000 for a lion, $4 500 for a crocodile and a hippo, and $3 000 for a buffalo.

The first rhino hunts took place on Groenewald's farm in about 2008. 'A guy called Alexander Steyn came and hunted here. I bought the rhinos for him to hunt. And it was through him that I met the Vietnamese agent,' Groenewald says.

Steyn had previously been implicated in the 'canned' hunting of cheetahs. According to records held by the Department of Environmental Affairs, he was also the outfitter in a number of rhino hunts conducted by Vietnamese nationals. Groenewald won't be drawn on the identity of the mysterious Vietnamese agent – a man who is apparently based in Pretoria.

Groenewald bought dozens of rhinos on auction from SANParks. 'Through the years, they have been the biggest supplier of rhinos in South Africa,' he tells me. 'I don't believe they can make a profit without selling rhinos.' In 2008, SANParks made R22 million from rhino sales to private entities. The following year, the amount increased to R52 million. Many of the biggest buyers were also the biggest organisers of rhino hunts for Vietnamese clients.

Groenewald says he bought forty-four rhinos from SANParks between 2008 and 2009. 'Ten were bulls and thirty-four were cows and calves,' he tells me. Prosecutors contend that a total of at least forty-eight rhinos were bought and moved to Prachtig between June and December 2008.

Feeding them costs money. 'It costs me R3 million a year just to feed the animals on this farm,' Groenewald says. 'People don't understand that. Now and then you have to hunt a rhino to make some money to run the farm.

'Back then I was selling a rhino hunt for $35 000. At that time you could buy a rhino for R150 000 (about $18 000). When the Vietnamese came in, all of a sudden they started paying R50 000, R60 000 and R70 000 (about $8 000) a kilogram. Rhino prices shot through the roof. Now that rhino would [cost] R450 000 (about $55 000).'

The Vietnamese are 'making a lot of money out of rhino horns'.

'I must be honest with you – for me, to do these hunts is very good money. It is *really* good money. And for those guys [the Vietnamese] it is good money.' As the South African government has slowly closed the tap on hunters from Southeast Asia, Groenewald has been lobbying behind the scenes to keep them going. His lawyer has visited Vietnam at least twice to hold discussions with CITES authorities there, and Groenewald has threatened to launch a legal challenge to increasingly stringent rhino hunting regulations.

But the Vietnamese are not hunters, he says frankly. 'The Vietnamese want the horn, that's it. That's what makes it worse. You're killing a rhino with a guy who is actually not a hunter, just for the horn. But we make them fucking shoot, so they're doing it all legally.'

Groenewald blames the 'system' for the killing. 'I don't enjoy killing rhinos ... but I'm killing them because of the system. We are forced to shoot them because that is the only way the trophies can be sold and exported. You have to kill the animal to sell its horns.'

And, he says, 'Everyone who has rhinos has done hunts with Vietnamese clients. Everyone, except John Hume. That guy has lots of horns.'

———————

19 January 2012

John Hume likes to say that he would buy rhinos from the devil himself. Today, the devil – at least as far as the demonstrators outside the Musina Regional Court are concerned – is seated opposite him with a Knysna loerie on his shoulder and a klipspringer nuzzling his hand.

Dawie Groenewald had flown in earlier to see '*Oom* John' (Uncle John), as he calls him, about a sale of buffalo. Hume's office, on his farm Mauricedale in Mpumalanga near the southern boundary of the Kruger National Park, opens onto a magnificent aviary. A stained white towel covers his computer keyboard to protect it from the droppings of birds that constantly fly in and out. There are thirty or forty buck inside the aviary, including tiny suni antelope, red duiker, blue duiker and klipspringer, along with dozens, if not hundreds, of exotic birds.

The klipspringer licking Groenewald's hand with a wet, black tongue is a particular favourite of Hume's. 'She's always been like this,' he says. 'That is, until about three months ago, when she started to take umbrage to every second man and she'd go fucking moggy and try and bite them. Now she's calming down again. She's pregnant with her fourth kid.' The klipspringer makes no attempt to bite Groenewald and eventually hops up onto a chair before wandering out the door.

Hume – the largest private rhino owner in the world – is trying to persuade Groenewald to do an interview with a television crew. 'You people need to go on camera and talk about this,' Hume says. 'Somebody will ask you, "Do you shoot rhino?" and you'll answer, "Yes, we do. We hunt rhino with permits."'

'Some without,' Groenewald laughs, and winks at me. He decides against doing the interview. Later, as Hume takes me to see the rhinos on his farm,

Groenewald calls him on a cellphone from his helicopter. His voice is barely audible over the clatter of rotor blades. 'Typical fucking Dawie,' Hume says, shaking his head. Theirs is an odd relationship. 'John lets me do all these things for him,' Groenewald says. 'He trusts me with a lot of money and the things we do together.' Much of Groenewald's time has been spent sourcing rhinos for Hume's farms.

'I like John's operation,' he tells me. 'That man has so much horn. If they legalise rhino horn tomorrow, he is going to be one of the richest men in the fucking world because he's got tons of horn ... But if I had his money, I would do it in a much better way than he's doing it.'

When I ask Hume about the rhino deals he's transacted with Groenewald, he answers bluntly: 'I will buy rhinos from the devil himself, especially if I think I may be saving the rhino's life. Bring me any fucking crook, murderer – doesn't matter what [they are]. If he's offering to sell me a rhino and it suits me, I'll buy it anyway.'

He seems to have a gruff fondness for Groenewald, although he is quick to point out that 'Dawie is always bloody wheeling and dealing.'

'He's what we in Rhodesia would have called a "wide boy". In other words, he's a wheeler and dealer, a ducker and diver. You'll never change Dawie. Where he sees a gap to make money, he'll take it; if it [means] bending the law, he'll do it. I think he does have some morals, though. He certainly doesn't mind killing animals but, as far as robbing a bank or poaching – I don't think so. Dawie's opinion is definitely that "I own the rhino, I bought it and if I want to kill it, I'll kill it. But give me the incentive to keep it alive, then I'll keep it alive." And in that way, he's no different from ninety-nine out of a hundred farmers.'

'There is no money to be made out of rhinos without the legalisation of horn,' John Hume tells me as we bounce along a dirt road in his bakkie towards a cluster of about forty cement troughs, where herds of rhinos are gathered like cattle to be fed. 'If there is no money to be made, how are we going to get farmers to farm with them?'

Hume bought his first black rhinos, six of them, on auction from the Natal Parks Board in 1996. 'It was to be a retirement project,' he says. 'I wanted a place where I could retire and farm like a gentleman. That is when I struck on this idea of being a big-game rancher.'

He had spent his boyhood growing up on a farm in what was then Rhodesia. A precocious child, he displayed an early aptitude for business, roaming his father's farm collecting bones, wool from dead sheep, bits of copper, the lead from spent batteries, empty bottles – in fact, any scrap that he could find to sell at a profit.

He dropped out of school at fourteen, despite the valiant efforts of an English teacher who tried to persuade him to stay on another year so he could get into Cambridge University. Hume told him, 'Cambridge? What the hell do I want to go to Cambridge for?'

He bought his first farm at eighteen. 'I was some sort of natural trader, I suppose.' By the time he was twenty-five, he had three. But he quickly came to the conclusion that farming was a 'mug's game' and that 'there must be easier ways to make money'. He bought the Zimbabwe Ruins Hotel and later the Baobab Hotel in Wankie. Then a taxi company. By 1979, as white minority rule crumbled, Hume, like many other white Rhodesians, began to spirit his money out of the country to South Africa. 'I moved my money illegally from Rhodesia. There were so many bloody adventures, I tell you. I bought fucking gold mines. I took emeralds from one guy in exchange for a supermarket in Salisbury.'

In the late seventies and early eighties, Hume says he 'lost the plot' and made the mistake of investing heavily in Hollywood films. 'I had a hell of an adventure in movies and, for my trouble, I lost $1 million.'

One film – *Zulu Dawn* – starred Peter O'Toole, Burt Lancaster and Bob Hoskins. 'All of them were a bunch of arseholes,' Hume says. The only one Hume seemed to like was the South African actor Ken Gampu.

Hume recovered from his losses, and in the mid-eighties turned his attention to timeshare, building some of the first resorts in South Africa. He made millions. Today, he has a 'lot of fucking rhinos'.

'I don't like to talk numbers, but it is a lot of hassle, a lot of responsibility, a lot of worry … a lot of rhinos.' By some accounts he owns more than 800 and, according to the *Financial Mail*, boasts revenue of R25 million a year, of which about 80 per cent comes from selling live animals to farmers and exporters, and 20 per cent from trophy hunting.

In recent years, Hume has become perhaps the most vocal public proponent of legalising the trade in rhino horn. With the help of his assistant, Tanya Jacobsen, he writes a steady stream of letters to newspapers and does interview after interview arguing his case.

'My frustration and depression for the rhinos is that not one of the Dawie [Groenewalds] or Marnus Steyls would be killing a rhino if the trade was legal,' he says, referring to the lion breeder and rhino hunt outfitter Marnus Steyl. 'To me it is absolutely nonsensical that the only way you can legally change the ownership of a rhino's horn in this country is to kill the [animal]. I cannot for the life of me understand why we are killing the very goose that lays the golden egg; the very rhinos that are capable of saving their species from extinction.'

Hume argues that if the horns are harvested, 'every rhino could go on growing a kilo of horn a year for the next thirty years', which could be sold to meet the Asian demand for rhino horn.

'Legalisation is their only hope. Our problem is that we are losing the war. Poaching is rocketing. If we try legalising the trade and it doesn't work, what have we lost? We are losing anyway.' The possibility that legal trade might involve the same criminal syndicates that currently control the market, and serve to fund the trafficking of other wildlife and contraband, doesn't seem to perturb him.

'Quite possibly,' he says, 'but surely if you stand a chance of saving rhinos' lives, that should be paramount?'

Hume has stockpiled a vast quantity of rhino horn, which he claims is stashed away in trunks in the safety deposit rooms of banks across North West province and Limpopo. 'It is a pain in the arse,' he tells me, 'but the banks don't seem to mind.' He chuckles. 'Officially I'm an old-book collector … The trunks are obviously heavy.' His detractors say he is simply promoting legal trade to serve his own interests. In response, Hume – who turned seventy a few days after the interview – says: 'If I sold my rhino horn stockpiles – and it would be a huge shithouse full of money I'd get – I don't know what I'd do with that money. Put it in shares and lose it? Or put it in gold, maybe. But what [if] the broker [is] crooked or the fucking bullion house [goes] belly-up? [Rhino horn] is an asset that has [increased in value] more than anything else. I don't think my heirs will bitch if I don't sell it.'

His voice rises in anger. 'I don't want legalisation in a selfish way. The *rhino* needs legalisation ... There is only one victim in this whole fuck-up: the rhino. I don't mind being called names, but it doesn't help the bloody rhino.'

The legalisation debate is one of the most divisive and incendiary issues in conservation today. Ian Player has faced a 'torrent of abuse' for his tentative support of the idea. 'In conservation, you have to develop a skin as thick as the pachyderms' for which you are responsible,' he once told me during an interview. He believes that consideration should be given to opening trade for horns obtained 'from natural mortalities and shavings'.

Many private rhino owners and a fair number of conservationists have thrown their weight behind public calls for the 1977 CITES trade ban to be lifted. Within SANParks and South Africa's Department of Environmental Affairs there are a number of officials who privately express a belief that legal commercial trade may be the answer. Wildlife authorities in KwaZulu-Natal have also made a strong case for legalisation. '[A] rhino is worth more dead than alive,' says Ezemvelo KZN Wildlife rhino security co-ordinator Jabulani Ngubane. 'Today you can buy a rhino on auction for about R300 000. Tomorrow you can sell the horn of that animal for R1.5 million.'

The price of live rhinos is decreasing as poaching incidents increase and the animals become 'a liability rather than an asset'.

For the past twenty years, conservation economist Michael 't Sas-Rolfes has argued in favour of reopening legal trade in rhino horn. The CITES ban, he says, has succeeded only in driving the trade underground and making it nearly impossible to monitor. The spike in poaching in South Africa from 2008 and 2009 onwards coincided with increasing restrictions on hunting and a moratorium on internal domestic trade in rhino horns. He believes that farmers like Groenewald 'played a role in delaying an inevitable resurgence of poaching activity' rather than creating a market or 'fuelling a demand' for rhino horn.

'The fact that poaching levels started to rise dramatically after the imposition of restrictions on domestic trade and Vietnamese hunts suggests that the South African suppliers were not only not "fuelling demand", but had probably been acting as a buffer against potential poaching activity.'

Were it not for them, 't Sas-Rolfes believes the sudden increase in poaching would have 'started far sooner than it did'.

'The rhino horn trade ban no longer makes either economic or conservation sense,' he writes. 'The natural mortality rate of rhinos in Africa alone yields as much horn as has been poached to supply the market in recent years. Furthermore, rhino horn is a renewable resource that can be easily harvested without killing rhinos. And African conservation agencies and landowners already hold between fifteen to thirty years' supply of rhino horn [at the current rate of black market supply]. These stockpiles are worth millions of dollars, money that could be usefully spent on rhino conservation, but the ban will not allow them to be sold to raise this money.'

Tom Milliken, the regional director for TRAFFIC in East and southern Africa, disagrees. 'The notion of legalising the rhino horn trade is hugely problematic for the simple fact that all of the Asian consuming countries, including Vietnam, have banned its usage. So, if you legalise this commodity, and you start to trade it, who are you dealing with? You do not have the support, at least yet, of any Asian government who's willing to change their legislation. So, if you're going to market horn as a legal commodity, you're basically marketing it to criminals. Rhino horn presents a real challenge for a legalised trade at this time. As a commodity – you can't see it. It ceases to appear as a horn. It's ground up. Regulating a trade like this to try and keep the legal stream unpolluted by illegal horn laundered into it presents a challenge that, at this point in time, can't be effectively met. So I think, for the moment, it's completely off the table.'

In a 2012 newspaper article, Richard Vigne, the CEO of the Ol Pejeta Conservancy in Kenya, said there was a danger that legalisation would give legitimacy to claims that rhino horn had medical benefits. 'That, in turn, could stimulate increasing demand amongst two billion Far Easterners, far beyond the capacity of Africa's remaining rhinos to supply. Prices for horn would therefore be driven upwards rather than downwards. In the absence of absolutely watertight controls over the legal trade, the same criminals who currently specialise in killing rhinos would thus be incentivised to remain involved for short-term gain, and poaching pressure would increase rather than decrease.'

———————

It started with a leopard. In January 2010, Dawie Groenewald was arrested by the US Fish and Wildlife Service in Montgomery, Alabama. He was at the airport, about to board an aircraft back to South Africa after visiting his brother Janneman. A month later, a federal grand jury indicted him on charges of smuggling and infringements of the Lacey Act, the US wildlife statute.

Groenewald was accused of selling an illegal leopard hunt to a US sports hunter, Glen Davey, in 2006, but no permit was issued to the hunter that year. Two years later, when the trophy was finally exported, Groenewald attempted to cover his tracks by 'fraudulently' applying for a leopard hunting permit in the hunter's name. CITES export paperwork stated 'falsely' that the animal had been killed in 2008, not 2006.

Groenewald spent eight days in jail and two-and-half months under house arrest at his brother's home as the case dragged on. He eventually pleaded guilty, was sentenced to 'time served' and fined $30 000.

'The United States is not a good place to sit in jail,' Groenewald says. 'They treat you like a serial killer, my friend. I had flu. I was so fucking sick, I almost died. The guys were nuts in that place. They would block the toilets with toilet paper and flush the thing so the whole jail cell is under water. It was the worst time in my life. For a fucking leopard?'

He maintains that the hunt was legal, that he had a permit for the leopard, but that the paperwork got lost by nature conservation officials. Groenewald says while he was under house arrest in the US, his business in South Africa was losing money and he couldn't afford to remain in the US any longer. So, against his lawyer's advice, he pleaded guilty. 'Now I've got a felony conviction against me, so I'm kicked out of Safari Club International for five years and I can't go to their shows.

'It is not like we wanted to smuggle a leopard into the States. The stories doing the rounds are unbelievable – that we were smuggling rhino horn inside the trophy and that sort of shit. I can tell you, a lot of it is jealousy. Jealousy plays a big role in this.'

The Limpopo police Organised Crime Unit had begun 'Project Cruiser', their investigation into Groenewald's activities, in June 2009. The investigation was registered after two of Groenewald's farm labourers, Paul Mathoromela and Joseph Maluleke, were stopped by police near Pretoria. Four rhino horns were found in their vehicle and they were arrested. (The horns subsequently disappeared from a locked police safe in a forensics laboratory and were replaced with plaster copies. Three years later, a senior police administration clerk, Azarial Matjila, was arrested and appeared in court on charges of stealing the horns and defeating the course of justice. He denied any wrongdoing.)

It was while Groenewald languished in his Alabama jail cell, and then later at his brother's home in the US, that another incident occurred that piqued the police's interest. In February 2010, one of the professional hunters (PHs) working for Groenewald, Gys du Preez, filed a police report about a break-in at the farm. Thieves had stolen dozens of rhino horns, he said.

'I was on my "long vacation" in the States,' Groenewald tells me. 'About eighty horns were stolen. [They were hidden] under my couches and the beds in my room. Somebody just broke in and cleaned out [the place]. An inside job.'

Tielman Erasmus, another PH, who was present at the farm at the time, claimed that the horns had not been locked up in the lodge's walk-in safe because 'all our waiters and staff have got safe keys'.

'That is why we didn't keep it in there. They all go in and out of the safe all the time to get booze, etcetera.' What about the bank? I asked, thinking of Hume's stockpiles.

'The bank doesn't want to take it,' Groenewald says, 'and it takes six months or seven months to get Reserve Bank clearance.'

All the horns had been microchipped, he says, but it is 'so easy to take a chip out. You can just drill it out or break it.'

The police took another view. According to a statement by Colonel Johan Jooste, the head of the endangered species unit at South Africa's Directorate for Priority Crimes Investigations, the Hawks, 'police suspected something untoward', and investigations later 'determined that the house break-in was staged'.

According to Jooste, Groenewald had discovered a way he could 'score twice': dehorning rhinos and then selling the horns and the dehorned animals separately. 'During 2009, at least fifty-nine rhinoceroses were moved from the farm, of which nineteen were dehorned. This trend continued in 2010, when 100 rhinoceroses were moved from the farm, of which sixty-four were dehorned.'

Prosecutors will argue during Groenewald's trial that, while he was in custody in the US, he became increasingly worried that environmental inspectors might visit his farm and discover dozens of newly dehorned rhinos, but no horns. The 'break-in' solved that problem.

———————

Colonel Johan Jooste is almost always in a hurry. 'If I don't answer my cellphone, it is because I'm busy, not because I'm ignoring you,' he tells everyone he gives his number to. His phone never stops ringing. There are five detectives in his unit tasked with investigating wildlife crime – specifically rhino horn cases – across South Africa. Jooste's men don't investigate all the cases themselves, but they play a major support role in collating and distributing information, guiding local investigations and ensuring that big cases are pulled together properly.

In contrast, twenty years ago, when Jooste joined what was then the Endangered Species Protection Unit, it had thirty members.

Jackie Selebi, South Africa's disgraced former national police commissioner, saw to it in 2002 that the ESPU and other specialist units like it were shut down and their officers scattered to police stations. The long-term consequences were devastating. With the demise of the ESPU, Jooste joined South Africa's elite FBI-style crime-fighting unit, the Scorpions.

But the Scorpions fell victim to the political intrigues surrounding the abortive corruption trial of South Africa's president Jacob Zuma, and Jooste found himself back in the police at the helm of an endangered species 'desk' in 2009.

Months later, in response to the worsening rhino crisis, the desk was expanded into a unit. In January 2010, the National Prosecuting Authority also established a specialised organised crime component to work closely with Jooste's unit to bring rhino horn cases to book. It is headed by Advocate Joanie Spies, a seasoned prosecutor. Rhino poaching was declared a 'priority crime'.

Jooste believes that the hunting and game-farming industries need to be 'cleaned up'.

'I get the *moer* in with some of the farmers,' he says. 'When they all made money out of rhinos, everything was fine. But now that the shit has hit the fan, it is the police's fault. Some of them helped create the market [for rhino horn]. Some of them dealt illegally, and now that this thing has come back to bite them, it is the police's fault.'

The Groenewald case was the first major case investigated by the newly formed rhino task team. Political and public pressure for arrests had been steadily mounting. In May 2010, Jooste took over the faltering Limpopo Organised Crime Unit investigation. Five months later, Groenewald and his co-accused were arrested.

Jooste's investigations turned up evidence that rhinos were 'regularly being killed and dehorned on the farm'. Between June and August 2008, Groenewald sold twenty rhino carcasses to Daniel Karl Johnson, the owner of the Taste of Africa butchery a few kilometres from his farm.

In August 2010, he sold him a further nineteen carcasses. In all, it came to eleven tons of meat. But no permits had been issued in 2008 for rhinos to be hunted on Prachtig. When Johnson began refusing to buy more carcasses, Groenewald allegedly had them buried or burnt.

After Groenewald's arrest, a Kruger National Park veterinarian, Dr Markus Hofmeyr, who helped dart twenty-nine rhino on the farm, assisted police in collecting blood and tissue samples for DNA analysis.

'All the rhino we darted,' he wrote in a statement, 'had had their horns removed previously and some right down to the growing point. The horns on some rhino were clearly cut off with a chainsaw or the like, and other[s] had the horns removed at the growing point. The method of removal is not clear, but [I] suspect it was done by inserting a knife and separating the attachment area of the horn from the base of the skull or applying a large force and tearing the horn from the base.

'We also observed burnt rhino carcasses [and] ... other skulls at the pit where the burnt rhino carcasses were seen, highlighting the extent of the rhino killing that took place there.'

———

The last time I interviewed Groenewald – several months before police and prosecutors obtained an asset-forfeiture order seizing control of R55 million in assets belonging to him and his co-accused – he seemed confident about the case.

'The two main witnesses are people who worked here. The one is a drunkard, the other a liar. They won't last five minutes in the box. Let me tell you, they [the prosecutors] will eventually come and say there has been a mistake on a permit here, or something wrong there, let's sort it all out. Let's make arrangements for a fine.'

Tielman Erasmus – always the joker – cut in. '[One of our lawyers] says that if someone is lying, it takes him five minutes on the stand to show that he's a liar. If he isn't lying, it takes him fifteen minutes to show that he is lying.'

That afternoon, I joined Groenewald, Tielman, Sariette, two American hunters and their wives for lunch at the lodge. The Americans had spent the morning poring over a price list, trying to decide what to kill.

'John has to decide what he wants to hunt,' one of the wives said to me, referring to her husband. 'I'm still trying to talk him into a zebra. A zebra rug is really nice. But I don't want to watch [the hunt]. I don't want to see it.'

That next day, John gets his zebra. It moved when he fired the shot and the bullet hit it a little further back than he had planned. The animal ran a short distance along a dirt road that leads through the farm before collapsing. 'Tomorrow, wildebeest or sable,' one of the women said over dinner as John showed off his trophy pictures of the zebra.

Tielman chimed in: 'If it's brown, it's down; if it flies, it dies; if it's red, it's dead.'

'Did you know,' he asked the Americans, 'that a rhino's sexual organs are under his right foot?'

'No,' was the chorused reply.

'*Ja*, because if he puts his foot on you, you're fucked.'

––––––––––

The Groenewald case focused international attention on what animal activists would eventually dub the South African 'game-industry white guys' – a group of 'unscrupulous individuals hiding behind the cloak of conservation [who] are ferociously plundering South Africa's rhinos'.

They included vets, game farmers, helicopter pilots, game-capture specialists and professional hunters. In 2012, a US-based activist and writer, Sarah Pappin, raised concerns that of the twenty-nine 'white guys' arrested for rhino crimes since 2006, only two had been given prison sentences.

One was Jacques Els, a game-capture expert and farmer from Limpopo, who was sentenced to eight years' imprisonment and fined R1 million in March 2012. He had been arrested in October 2010 after buying thirty rhino horns from Tommy Fourie, the manager of the Maremani game farm near Musina. Both he and Fourie were arrested. A month later, Fourie climbed a hill behind his house, carrying a hunting rifle, and shot himself in the head.

That same year, Els's business partner in the game-capture business, Mark Tout, was accused of being linked to rhino poaching. The investigative television programme, *Carte Blanche*, broadcast a documentary identifying Tout as the pilot of a helicopter that had flown low over a game farm with its registration numbers taped over. At the time there were frequent reports in South African newspapers of helicopters being used to poach rhinos. Tout denied the allegations and was never charged, although it later emerged that he had been indemnified as a State witness. The helicopter raids largely ceased.

The other jailbird was a father of six named Deon van Deventer. In prison, they called him 'Rhino'.

––––––––––

I met Van Deventer in May 2012 in the town of Lephalale – previously known as Ellisras – near the South African border with Botswana. He was accompanied by his new girlfriend, a haggard, money-grubbing woman in her late forties, who did most of the talking. I was hoping to interview Van Deventer for this book and he had agreed to a meeting to discuss the possibility. She wanted to discuss the terms.

Van Deventer had done a number of jailhouse interviews in recent years, despite claiming that he feared for his life if he spoke out against the men he had implicated in a rhino horn syndicate. By his own admission, he had killed twenty-two rhinos between 2005 and 2006.

In 2011, shortly before his release from prison, he boasted to a *National Geographic* journalist that he had used a penknife to remove the horns of the rhinos he'd shot. 'You don't need a saw. It's quick, and the entire horn comes off clean, just like a bottle cap,' he told the writer, Peter Gwin.

He also claimed to have built a home-made silencer – using a metal pipe with washers soldered inside it – which he fitted to the barrel of a .30-06 hunting rifle. 'I shot a male [rhino], and a female standing two metres away didn't flinch before I shot her too.'

Van Deventer and his girlfriend had arranged to meet me at the Spur steakhouse in town. The place was busy and they decided against going there, and directed me to follow them to a coffee shop across town. At a corner table, Van Deventer spoke of remorse.

'What I did was a *moerse* ugly thing, and I don't know how I could have involved myself in something like that. I'm a good hunter. I hunted for many years professionally. The rhinos that I shot were shot clean. It was a shot to the brain every time and they fell to their knees and not on their sides. They didn't suffer. I took off the horns in the right way with a knife. *Woep-wap*, and the horn is off. That is how I operate.'

He says he is sorry, a claim he repeats in statements given to police after his arrest. But it is a lie. Van Deventer revelled in the killing. In letters he apparently wrote to his family, which I found while perusing court papers about the case, he boasted about stalking a rhino.

In one he described looking out of the bars of his prison cell. '[T]here was this cat that was stalking a dove ... It was very enjoyable for me. It took

A wounded poacher, Hardlife Nkomo, is questioned by game scouts. A hundred metres away lies a bloodied .303 rifle fitted with a silencer

Blondie Leathem and Magotshe Siziba – his former Zimparks sergeant – discuss a possible incursion by poachers into the Bubye Valley Conservancy. The two men have been at the forefront of Zimbabwe's 'rhino wars' for the past twenty-five years

Julian Rademeyer

A .375 hunting rifle, fitted with a custom-made silencer, which was stolen during a violent farm attack near Musina in South Africa, and later used to poach rhinos in Zimbabwe

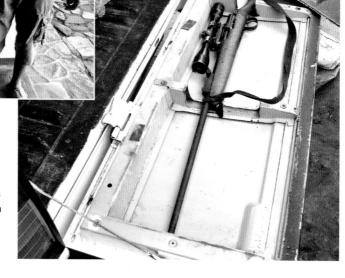

Another silenced rifle was found by Zimbabwean police in a hidden compartment in the tailgate of a South African–registered bakkie

Zimbabwean poacher Rodgers 'Teacher' Mukwena

Two game scouts, Godknows Zulu (left) and Sylvester Ncube (right) tracking poachers in the Bubye Valley Conservancy

Julian Rademeyer

Musina poacher Johan Roos photographed after his 2009 arrest in Zimbabwe

Julian Rademeyer

The Lemmer family, from left to right: Faan Snr, Faan Jnr and Christi in their Musina home in 2010. A .375 rifle, stolen during a robbery on their farm, was found in Zimbabwe, where it was used to poach rhinos

Julian Rademeyer

An orphaned rhino calf, one of several rehabilitated by Blondie Leathem and his wife Katrina, suckles on a milk bottle in a protected *boma*

Alleged rhino-horn-syndicate 'mastermind' Dawie Groenewald on his farm near Musina

Julian Rademeyer

A Vietnamese 'hunter' poses with her kill

The many faces of a wildlife trafficker. Chumlong Lemtongthai, aka 'Chai', poses for his webcam at his home in Thailand

Chumlong Lemtongthai (left) is ordained as a Buddhist monk, a nominal ordination that many Thai men undergo during their lives

Chumlong with the Hummer he paid for in cash

Chumlong (centre) and Punpitak Chunchom pose with labourers on a lion-breeding farm near the Cradle of Humankind World Heritage Site in Gauteng

Farm labourers with the skinned carcass of a lioness

Lion carcasses are stripped of flesh and the bones are cleaned

Chumlong Lemtongthai poses with a number of lionesses on another farm. It is unclear whether the animals are dead or sedated

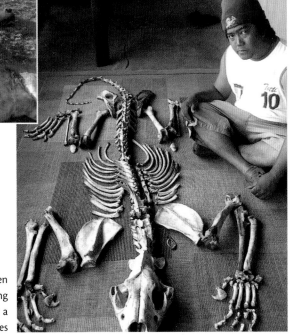

One of the Thai men working with Chumlong Lemtongthai poses with a complete 'set' of lion bones

Members of the Xaysavang syndicate photographed in Bangkok with an illegal consignment of ivory

Punpitak Chunchom and hunting outfitter Juan Pace with a pile of money that is believed to have been payment for the first rhinos that the Xaysavang syndicate shot

Chumlong Lemtongthai

Marnus Steyl

Punpitak Chunchom

According to Johnny Olivier, Chumlong Lemtongthai described his business with these words: 'We shoot, we cut, we weigh, then pay.' Chumlong watches farm workers with knives removing a dead rhino's horns

Punpitak Chunchom weighs a set of horns

A pile of cash drawn from ATMs at Emperors Palace Casino

A young Thai woman – one of the many allegedly recruited by the Xaysavang syndicate – poses with a rhino carcass

Julian Rademeyer

Game farmer Marnus Steyl poses with one of the Thai 'recruits'. When I later tracked her down (INSET), the woman – who only wanted to be identified as 'Wi' – denied shooting any rhinos

Chumlong Lemtongthai and a North West environmental services department official

Three of the young women allegedly recruited to pose as 'hunters' by the Xaysavang syndicate

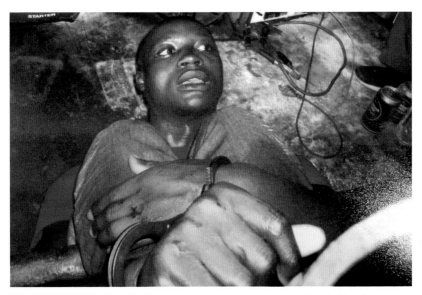

A photograph discovered on a camera belonging to ex-cop and alleged rhino horn smuggler 'Big Joe' Nyalunga. It was submitted to court during his bail hearing and appears to show an unidentified man in handcuffs being tortured. In the background is a car battery, jumper cables and cans of beer

Julian Rademeyer

Albert Zitha holds a photo of his dead brother Dario, who was shot dead in the Kruger National Park while trying to poach rhinos

Julian Rademeyer

Thando, the Musina con man, making one of his fake rhino horns

Left: Tommy Tuan's passport; below left: R1.2 million in cash spread out on the bed of his hotel room; below right: the embassy car he was driving when he was arrested in Kimberley

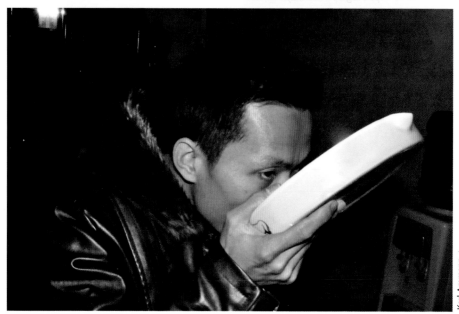

A Vietnamese man consumes rhino horn from a grinding dish in which it was ground and mixed with water

Karl Ammann

A rare photograph of Xaysavang boss Vixay Keosavang (left) and Chumlong Lemtongthai (right). Apparently taken in Thailand, it was obtained from a source with close links to Thai investigators

Company registration documents for Xaysavang Trading bearing a photograph of Vixay

ຕົ້ນສະບັບ

Lao People Democratic Republic
Peace Independence Democracy Unity Prosperity
****
Enterprise Registration Certificate
No : 0013 / ERO
(Translated from Lao Version)

Base upon the Enterprise Law No: 11/NA,Dated:09/11/2005, in accordance with the Application for Enterprise Registration Dated 8/8/2008.
The Enterprise Registry Office (Domestic Trade Department , Ministry of Industry and Commerce) has registered as enterprise for:
Mr. Vixay KEOSAVANG : Nationality : Lao , Acting as Director of:
- Name of Enterprise : Xaysavang Trading Import – Export CO.,LTD
- Name of Enterprise in English: Xaysavang Trading Import – Export CO.,LTD
- Form and Kind of Enterprise : Company Sole Limited
- Registered Capital : 13.050.000.000. kip.
- Location of Enterprise: Anusonxay Village , Pakxan District , Bolikhamxay Province
- Categories of Business (Stated on another side)

| 01-00000005 | 442 5 | (A,G,S,H,G/6) |

Instruction

Modified E/R No 0004 /MOC,ERO
Dated 10/01/2007

Vientiane Capital, Dated
Enterprise Registrar

Noyane NHOYSAVKNAM

XAYSAVANG TRADING EXPORT - IMPORT Co.,LTD

Mr. Vixay KEOSAVANG
Director
- Vice President of the chamber of commerce and industry of Bolikhamxay Province
- Vice President of Lao National Boxing
- Vice President of Lao National Swimming committee
Office : No.174 Ban Anousonxay Rd.
Paksan District, Bolikhamxay Province, Lao PDR
Tel/Fax : (856-54) 280102, 280101, (856-21) 710937
Mobile : (856-20) 5552219, (856-20) 2333366.
Email   : xaysavang@gmail.com
www.xaysavang.somee.com

Vixay's business card

Julian Rademeyer

Vixay's home and offices in Paksan in central Laos

Julian Rademeyer

Chumlong Lemtongthai in the dock of the Kempton Park Regional Court in South Africa. Investigator Paul O'Sullivan is standing in the background to the right

From left to right: Chumlong Lemtongthai, Punpitak Chunchom and Marnus Steyl in the Kempton Park Regional Court

my thoughts back to the rhinos that I stalked. Damn, I really enjoyed it. Although I'm now sitting here because of that, nobody can take that experience away from me.' The letter was signed 'Rhino'.

Deon and his brother Nicolaas killed rhinos in game reserves and game farms across South Africa, including the Hluhluwe-iMfolozi Game Reserve and a number in the Kruger National Park. In several instances, cows and calves were killed with hunting bows and rifles.

In statements given to investigators as part of a plea agreement, Van Deventer claimed he was paid R12 000 a kilo by the syndicate bosses. He also claimed that the syndicate was led by Clayton Fletcher, a Free State game farmer, hunting outfitter and businessman, and alleged that Gert Saaiman, a Pretoria-based pilot and owner of Saaiman Hunting Safaris and the Saaiman Game Ranch, was the 'middleman' in the syndicate.

The case of the 'Fletcher gang' was hailed as a major breakthrough in rhino poaching when it went to trial in October 2010. A day later, the case collapsed spectacularly when Van Deventer refused to testify, claiming that he had been intimidated in prison by private investigators who had threatened his children. He also claimed that his wife had been attacked in their home.

The truth of his claims remains murky, and there are suggestions that Van Deventer concocted details about the syndicate to get a reduced sentence. If so, he succeeded.

Once Van Deventer pulled out, the charges against all the accused were dropped, although, at the time of writing, there were suggestions that charges might be reinstated against Fletcher. The National Prosecuting Authority notified Saaiman in a letter that they would not be proceeding against him, as Van Deventer was their only witness.

In a statement given to me by his lawyer, Saaiman said that Van Deventer had worked for him in his hunting operation for a short while. 'Because he knew my business, daily routine, friends and family, it was easy for him to concoct a story implicating me in unlawful follies. It took me five years to prove my innocence.'

A few days after my meeting with Van Deventer, I received an email from a fly-by-night lawyer in Gaborone, Botswana, where Van Deventer and his girlfriend now live. Van Deventer – and probably more specifically, his girlfriend – wanted R250 000 for his story.

Clearly he was still after the money. I turned him down.

8

Johnny the Rat

23 July 2011

The man in the pink golf shirt and cheap, knock-off jeans is on edge, itching for a cigarette he doesn't have. He studies the faces in the crowd of Saturday shoppers thronging around him in the mall at Sandton's Nelson Mandela Square, eyes flicking uncertainly from one person to the next.

Johnny Olivier has reason to be afraid. The phone calls started a few days ago. Late at night. Sometimes, he thinks, he can hear someone breathing. Then silence. The caller ID always shows up as 'private number'. In the months that follow, there are more threats; messages sent to his Facebook account containing images of a cat, teeth bared in pain, being trampled to death by a woman in high heels, and a young girl lying dead in a bath with her head cut off.

They all know he's the *impimpi* – the rat who pimped them out to save his own skin. He's heard that they want him dead. Rats are vermin and should be exterminated. 'Johnny is scum,' a man who once had dealings with him tells me. 'He'll do anything for a quick buck. He's just like the rest, but he's fucking great at pretending he's an innocent.'

I had seen Johnny Olivier before, but only in photographs. In the dry scrub of a North West farm, under the shade of a tree, two men wearing Steyl Game Safaris T-shirts are cutting the horns off a dead rhinoceros. Olivier is in the background, next to a North West Parks official. His face is impassive. In another image he holds a rifle in his right hand and poses next to the hulking carcass. He doesn't smile.

I cross the square. A busload of Korean tourists grin manically as they pose for pictures in front of a bronze statue of Nelson Mandela. 'I want to make things right,' Olivier says to me in Afrikaans after we shake hands. I'd angered him by describing him in an article as a 'rhino horn dealer'. He wants to 'put the record straight', he says. He's not alone today. A government minder watches our every move. There is talk of him entering a witness-protection programme.

We wend our way through the crowds, all tarted up and gorging themselves on designer decadence. 'This isn't the kind of place I normally go to,' Olivier says as we walk. '*Jissus*, there's nothing here I can afford.' We pass a shop window displaying R250 000 Breitling watches, the kind favoured by disgraced ANC Youth League (ANCYL) leader Julius Malema. 'I love watches,' Olivier confides. 'I try and collect them. But not these, they're way out of my price range. All I've got is a Seiko and a Rolex I bought in Thailand.'

A meeting place has been arranged in one of the open business lounges that overlooks the Michelangelo Hotel foyer. This isn't Johnny's world. He's blue collar, as *plat* as they come. He's got the air of a used-car salesman who's landed on hard times. The kitsch finery and feigned elegance of the place makes him uncomfortable. A young woman in a designer suit swans past, nose in the air, hair tossed back.

'*Ja, nee*, I wonder how much a room here costs a night?' Johnny muses aloud as we walk from the steel and glass lift, our feet sinking into the thick carpets. We order tea and scones lathered in cream. 'High tea,' we joke, even though it's only midday.

I switch on my recorder.

———

Johnny's unravelling began three years ago. On 30 September 2008 he drove to Delmas, a small farming town east of Johannesburg. In the car with him were four Thais: Punpitak Chunchom, Kritsada Jangjumrus, Tool Sriton and Sukana Naudea. South Africans are notoriously bad at pronouncing Thai names correctly, so many Thais living in the country simply adopt English names. Punpitak was 'Peter', and Kritsada called himself 'Jacky'. Johnny, who had mastered some broken Thai during a stint diving off the beaches of Phuket, was their fixer and had set up the meeting.

He parked the car, a white Mazda Etude, at *Die Boskroeg* (The Bush Bar), a popular local watering hole outside the town. In the car was $60 000 in cash. The Thais had brought a scale with them. Johnny had been asked to find a seller, and he had been surprisingly lucky. One day, as he was driving from Polokwane to Johannesburg, he saw a man transporting stuffed trophy animals on the back of a bakkie. Johnny flashed his headlights at the man to draw his attention, then waved at him to pull over. He wanted to know where he could get rhino horn and how it all worked.

He asked the man – who turned out to be a professional hunter – if he had any rhino horn for sale. The hunter took Johnny's number and said a friend of his would call him to make arrangements.

In due course the prospective seller contacted Johnny. He was a game farmer in Musina, he said. He would SMS Johnny a photo of the goods. When the image arrived, it showed a few horns propped up against a brick wall. The Thais were excited, Johnny less so. There was something about that wall that reminded him of a government building.

At *Die Boskroeg*, Olivier and Jangjumrus got out of the car and went into the bar. The man who met them was stocky, barely cracked a smile and had a handshake like wrought iron. There was a black man with him, but he said little. Yes, he had the horns with him, the man said. 'Where's the money?' They went outside to the car. Jangjumrus – they called him Jacky or Jap – took the scale out of the boot and weighed the horns. Satisfied, he bent down and pulled a thick roll of US dollar bills out of one of his socks. The money changed hands. The horns were loaded into the boot and Johnny and the Thais took off.

On the gravel road leading from the pub, things happened fast. Cars cut them off, and rough men with police ID pulled them out of the Etude and cuffed them with cable ties. 'I didn't know what went wrong or what we had done wrong,' Johnny tells me. 'I knew they were buying horns, but I didn't know how it worked or that you needed permits. Suddenly I'm sitting in a cage at Delmas police station.'

The seller was also in the police station. But he wasn't behind bars. Johnny called out to him. 'That's not my name,' the man snapped and walked away. He was a cop. Johnny had been stung.

The bust was the first time investigators had heard of the Xaysavang Export-Import Company. It was a nugget of information that would not be forgotten. Johnny and Jacky were separated from the others and taken to the Middelburg police station holding cells. Jacky, Johnny says, smoked dagga in his cell, which he bought from the bored policemen on duty.

On 9 October 2008, Olivier and Jangjumrus were found guilty. Olivier was fined R120 000 or four years' imprisonment, and Jangjumrus R80 000 or four years in 'tjoekie'. It wasn't long before they were out. They had a benefactor with access to seemingly unlimited amounts of cash.

———————

Johnny takes a sip of tea but declines a scone. He sits on a couch, his head cocked to one side. He's deaf in his left ear, the result, he tells me, of a landmine explosion in Angola when was a young *troepie* in the mid-1970s. 'I was in a truck that got hit. I only have about 15 per cent hearing. That's why I talk so loudly. Because I can't hear you properly, I think you can't hear me.'

For years, he says, he has been fascinated by Thailand. He spent some time there, met a Thai *girltjie*, did some diving and a bit of 'piece work'. It was a place where he could escape the drudgery of life in South Africa. He still yearns for it. He's bought himself a computer program that purports to 'make you between 10 per cent and 20 per cent fluent in Thai in 120 hours'.

Lone men of a certain age, like Johnny – he's fifty-four – flock to Southeast Asia. For many of these *farangs*, Thailand offers a certain, illicit allure. The impermissible easily becomes permissible and anything – absolutely anything – can be bought for a few hundred dollars, sometimes less. Some find solace in girls. For others, it's boys or girls-who-are-boys or that little taste of brown sugar or hash or whatever the corner touts are pushing on that particular day.

Driven by a midlife crisis, a desperate bid to escape a desultory existence elsewhere, a desire to revisit a misspent youth or a myriad other reasons, for them, Thailand can be a seductively fickle mistress. Thousands flock each year to the seedy clubs in Bangkok's Patpong Road and their earthly delights or the beaches and bar girls of Phuket and Pattaya.

The place gets under your skin and never really lets go. But easy dreams of hedonism all too easily turn into nightmares. AIDS is widespread. Drugs are readily available. You can see the living dead on the streets with their unkempt hair, skin burnished by the sun and booze, and ragged eyes that have seen too much. Invariably they're clutching at some young thing with no future.

Back in South Africa, Johnny, always something of an outsider, found an acceptance in Johannesburg's tiny Thai expat community. They're a motley lot, numbering only a few thousand. The husbands are often white, middle-aged men; the women young. Some have made it in business or the restaurant trade or the airline industry. Far more are on the fringes: the strippers, hookers and masseuses. Used up in Thailand, they've been trafficked to South Africa to work in strip joints and massage parlours. Many are indentured to pimps and traffickers, who cover their passage to South Africa with a 'loan'. The interest rates are extortionate and designed to keep them in hock.

'She'll have to fuck a hundred guys to get anywhere near paying her way out,' a gangster I once knew leered, gesturing at a Thai woman waiting for clients in a strip club. He was wrong. It would have to be a lot more. 'When Thai women come to South Africa and they stay for a long time, they're not here on holiday. They work in certain places,' Johnny says coyly.

For Johnny, the trouble started with 'K.K.' and a lost passport. One day in 2007, or early 2008 – he can't remember exactly when – he gave a Thai woman a lift to the airport. Her flight was due in two hours. He was on his way home when 'K.K.' called. He explained that he was a Thai Airways manager. The woman Johnny had dropped off had lost her passport. Could Johnny look around in his car? Johnny searched everywhere but found nothing. The woman was booked into a hotel at the airport, and K.K. contacted the Thai embassy on her behalf. The following day, Johnny chanced on the passport. He called K.K., who told him the woman had received temporary travel documents and had already boarded the next flight.

'You sound like a nice guy,' K.K. said. 'Next time you're in Johannesburg, let's get together. I play golf. Join me.' When they did finally meet, it was K.K. who broached the subject of 'business'. He had some friends who spoke little English and didn't know their way around but needed local help. 'I don't know anything about business, but I can help with the talking,' Johnny offered. K.K. had a house in Kempton Park, not far from the airport, and the Thais were staying there.

'These guys were buying lion bones, known as "sets", which they were exporting to Laos. I understood that the bones would be used for making some sort of *muti* ... for use in their culture.'

That's how Johnny first met 'Jacky' and the others.

The clear leader of the group was a man they all called 'Chai'. His real name was Chumlong Lemtongthai. 'He seemed to me to be a powerful individual ... He spent most of his time in Bangkok and visited South Africa for stretches of two to three months at a time.' Chai's boss, Johnny discovered later, was someone called Vixay Keosavang. He was based in Laos and had never travelled to South Africa. Chai often had long video chats with him. One day he called Johnny over to say hello. Johnny saw a 'middle-aged Asian man' on the computer screen. The man greeted him, then resumed his conversation with Chai. They spoke rapidly in Thai and Johnny couldn't follow what they were saying.

Johnny did his bit to help the Thais. 'I assisted with certain aspects of seeking lion sets and would be paid an amount of about US$100 per set that I found and they purchased. This would be paid to me in cash, in rand. Chai would pay for these sets in cash and would only pay [the seller] once the sets had left South Africa, with all the relevant documentation. He would go to the casino near the airport ... and draw the cash from a machine there. Sometimes he would draw hundreds of thousands of rand from the machine.'

They were doing a roaring trade. But they wanted more. And they wanted something far more elusive; something they called 'bamboo'.

––––––––––

A passport may have led Johnny to K.K., but it was by pure chance that he eventually landed in the lap of Paul O'Sullivan. O'Sullivan attracts adjectives like flies. Over the years he's been called an eccentric, a maverick, a vigilante, a crime crusader, a troublemaker, an opportunist and a publicity whore. Some have suggested that he should be South Africa's next police chief. The 'gangsters' he routinely harasses prefer far less complimentary terms, laced with invective.

What O'Sullivan possesses – and it would be churlish to suggest it is merely the luck of the Irish – is an uncanny ability to sniff out big cases. He's obsessive, working leads and a private network of informants for months, sometimes years at a time. Reluctant witnesses are browbeaten into submission. 'I work on them psychologically,' O'Sullivan says with a smile. Invariably his case files make their way to the police and the front pages of newspapers.

'He's an unguided missile,' a senior police official once said to me in frustration after yet another of O'Sullivan's investigations was splashed across the front page of a newspaper. 'The problem is you can't control him, but he gets things done,' the man grudgingly conceded.

'Most of what I do will never make the papers,' O'Sullivan said to me one day when I visited him in his offices at Securitas, the private security company he worked for at the time. 'It's just too small. But then there are those special cases that I make my own,' he added with an impish grin.

O'Sullivan boasts that he learnt his craft from 'the best': Britain's Secret Intelligence Service, MI6. He takes his cases personally – sometimes *too* personally. 'Never piss in an Irishman's beer and expect him to roll over and take it,' he likes to say.

O'Sullivan has a genuine sense of outrage at the rot that has seeped into every level of South African society and has crippled and corrupted the South African Police Service and intelligence services. But often it is his theatrics that grab headlines.

In 2011, after orchestrating the arrest of a Czech fugitive and alleged 'mob boss', Radovan Krejcir – a man allegedly linked to several murders in South Africa and the Czech Republic – O'Sullivan turned up at Krejcir's favourite restaurant. As reporters clustered for soundbites around the table in the Harbour Cafe in Bedfordview, east of Johannesburg, O'Sullivan raised a pint of Guinness and proclaimed: 'Czech mate, Krejcir, you will never sit here enjoying yourself – in fact, you will never sit and eat anywhere in South Africa – again.'

But two weeks later, out on bail, Krejcir was back at his table behind a sheet of bullet-proof glass he had had installed in a paranoid bid to thwart a supposed 'Russian hit team'. '*Saluté*, Paul O'Sullivan,' he said, lifting up a Pilsener Urquell. The hacks lapped it all up, regurgitating it for their readers to enjoy over cornflakes and Rice Krispies.

O'Sullivan made his name through his obsessive pursuit of South Africa's national police commissioner and Interpol president, Jackie Selebi. The Irishman's unstinting six-year investigation of Selebi unravelled a tangled web of organised crime and exposed Selebi's involvement with drug dealer Glenn Agliotti, known to his criminal underworld associates as 'The Land-lord'. In August 2010, Selebi was sentenced to fifteen years' imprisonment for corruption stemming from bribes he had received from Agliotti, a man he famously once described as 'My friend, finish and *klaar*.'

O'Sullivan has paid a heavy price for his dedication to the job, both personally and financially – his marriage crumbled, his family was rushed into hiding in Europe and his considerable savings dwindled to almost nothing. He now lives in a modest face-brick townhouse, and he has worn the same fraying suit for nearly a decade, he likes to say. More often than not, he is pictured wearing the same olive-green and brown tie patterned with images of the Big Five.

––––––––

May 2011

O' Sullivan is in a funk. An abortive late-night raid on Krejcir's Bedfordview home on 22 March has led to excoriating press coverage. I was with him for a while on the night of the raid, sitting at a table outside a News Cafe in Bed-fordview. O'Sullivan, chain-smoking heavily, was co-ordinating snippets of information from sources and passing it on to the police. Krejcir's movements were being tracked via his cellphone, its GPS co-ordinates triangulated and mapped. The signal was static and fixed on his house.

Krejcir was being sought for fraud. The cops also wanted to question him about the previous day's drive-by slaying of his friend, Cape Town underworld boss Cyril Beeka. And there was talk of a 'hit list' hidden somewhere in Krejcir's house.

The police's Directorate of Priority Crimes Investigation, known as the Hawks, were using the South African State Security Agency (SSA) to provide operational support. They no longer trusted the police Crime Intelligence unit, which was in utter disarray, riddled with nepotism and corruption. Hawks investigators had discovered that their phones were being tapped by their own spooks and information supposedly leaked to Krejcir. Then there was the problem of General Joey Mabasa, the former head of police Crime Intelligence in Gauteng, who had an uncomfortably close relationship with Krejcir. Krejcir's wife, Katerina Krejcirova, shared a company directorship with Mabasa's wife.

Later that night, members of the police's Tactical Response Team (TRT) used an armoured vehicle to run down the gates of a house in Kloof Road in Bedfordview. I followed them in as they threw thunderflashes and used battering rams to smash their way through doors and security gates. Then they ran into the back wall. Krejcir's four-storey mansion towered above them in the inky blackness. They had the wrong house. The TRT scaled the wall with ladders and stormed the mansion. They might as well have used the driveway entrance in Kloof Road – it would have caused a lot less damage.

Krejcir was nowhere to be found. His eighteen-year-old son, Denis, and a guest, Miloslav Potiska, were cuffed and taken away. Simon Guidetti, the owner of the house the cops had destroyed, sued for R1.2 million in damages. Denis Krejcir also filed a lawsuit. A general in police Crime Intelligence later claimed, when I spoke to him, that Krejcir had been in his mansion all along, hidden away in a steel-and-concrete safe room. Krejcir handed himself over to police three days later.

O'Sullivan has taken flak over the raid and needs to do some damage control. He is worried about what his kids might read. His reputation, he feels, has taken a knock.

Enter Johnny Olivier.

———————

After the Delmas bust, Johnny had lost heart and cut all ties with Punpitak and the rest. He had been sacked from his job. His boss had not been amused when the Mazda Etude – a company car – had been impounded by the police. Johnny had packed his bags and gone to Durban to look for work. But work was scarce, and he soon found himself back in Johannesburg.

Johnny liked to spend time at the Emperors Palace Casino, near the airport in Johannesburg. He wasn't much of a gambler, but there was something about the place that drew him back time and again. Two years after the Delmas debacle, in June 2010, he bumped into Punpitak and a couple of others at the casino. It wasn't a surprise.

'The boss, Chai, loved going there,' he says. 'He said it relaxed him. He could easily lose R30 000 or R40 000 a night and it would be a joke for him. I told them I'm not interested in their shit with rhinos. But they told me they were now only doing lion bones and asked if I could help them. I was short of cash, so I decided to do what I could … but made it clear I did not want to be involved in anything that might be illegal.'

As Johnny tells it, their assurances won him over. 'Somewhere on the internet, I read that there was nothing illegal about trading in lion bones. The lions are hunted legally and the skins and heads go to the hunters. The rest is left over, and the farmers discovered they could make a buck out of the bones.'

Johnny went to work and later helped his contacts rent a house in Edenvale, not far from the airport, to the east of Johannesburg. It was to become their base of operations.

But Johnny's relationship with his housemates, particularly with Punpitak, was strained. Johnny, a self-professed teetotaller, was offended by their propensity for booze and women. They were a '*klomp dronkgatte*', a bunch of drunkards. Punpitak was also a layabout. He'd spend days in the house, watching DVDs and doing nothing really constructive.

The only one of them that Johnny harboured any real respect for was Chai. Chai spent money like water. 'He's actually a very nice person,' Johnny says. 'Person to person, that is. Outside of animals and wildlife. He can be very giving. Once, he won R43 000 [at] the casino and called up all his friends and took them to dinner at the Ocean Basket.'

Johnny often accompanied Chai on his spending sprees. He remembers a day when Chai picked up a fifty-four-inch Samsung flatscreen television, a Sony sound system with speakers that could blow your socks off, a leather lounge suite and mattresses for the Edenvale house. It was all paid for in cash. 'Chai never had money on him. Peter always carried the cash in a black rucksack. The only time Chai had money on him was when he took R10 000 or R20 000 to go and gamble.' To Johnny, Chai's supply of money seemed 'endless'.

One Sunday, Chai announced 'out of the blue' that he wanted to buy a Hummer. 'I told him the car dealerships were all closed but, no, he wanted a Hummer,' Johnny says. The Thai scoured the internet, until he found one for sale at R230 000. He had made up his mind.

Olivier accompanied two of Chai's minions to Emperors Palace. They had been given a pair of ATM cards. Inside the casino they headed straight for a bank of ATM machines. 'They drew and drew and drew. Every time they got R2 000 out, they folded the bank slip around it and drew again. It took a long time. We got out of there at 6 p.m. with massive packets of cash in our pockets. We were walking like cowboys. *Jirre*, I wish my bank card could do that.'

When they arrived at the seller's house, Chai opened the Hummer's doors, glanced inside and said: 'I'll take it.'

Johnny's contempt for the others, tinged with the inherent racism of many of his generation, was growing. Their incessant partying grated on him. The drinking, whoring and endless karaoke was just too much. 'They drank more than they slept. There were times when I came home and found condoms strewn outside, which they had just chucked out of the windows. Every night it was parties and Thai girls and booze and thunderous music. They used to blow between R3 000 and R4 000 a night on girls. They bought litres of box wine and Jack Daniel's.'

The landlady, an elderly woman, was at her wits' end. Her tenants were a strange lot. She didn't really know what they did for a living. Often they would disappear for days on end and then, on their return, would party until dawn. On one occasion she complained about the appalling stench wafting from the garden.

Johnny knew what it was, but didn't tell her. The men had returned from one of their forays to North West province and had brought back a bloody hunk of meat. It looked like a trunk: long and pink, with grey skin pulled back. But it wasn't a trunk. It was a rhino penis.

The Thais cut it up like you slice salami. They lit a fire in the braai, *moered* it on and sealed it with the heat from the coals. Then they took the charred flesh and spread it out on a grid in the garden to dry in the sun. For a while, one of the men used a branch to chase the flies away. He wasn't very successful. 'The smell was horrific. There were more flies than you would find at a sewage farm,' Johnny says.

The slices remained there, decaying in the heat. The Thais clearly had no idea how to cure meat. The idea, Johnny says, had been to package it with *droëwors* and export it to Thailand. Fortunately they scrapped the plan and buried the penis in the garden.

One particularly raucous party kept the old lady awake until 3 a.m. Her grandchildren were visiting and had been petrified by the noise and the screams. She complained to Johnny, who confronted Punpitak. 'I'd stayed somewhere else that night and come home in the morning. [Punpitak] still had a glass of wine in his hand. They'd been drinking Overmeer and Drostdy-Hof like water, and shot after shot of Jack Daniel's.' Punpitak's breath stank of stale cigarettes and booze. Somewhat predictably, he blamed the noise on the neighbours.

'Peter. Stop! I don't believe you,' Johnny said to him. Punpitak lashed out.

'I thought you were my friend,' he whined, and drunkenly grabbed Johnny by the shirt. There was a scuffle. 'I did a bit of Thai boxing when I was younger,' Johnny says. 'I'm old now, so I knew I must *moer* [him] within three minutes because I can't hold out longer than that. I aimed nicely and headbutted him and there he lay. I don't know if I broke his nose, but there was a lot of blood.

'Another one of them just stood there like Chuck Norris, looking at me. He didn't know a *boertjie* could *bliksem* that hard. I just wanted to show him that we aren't guys who fuck around. We kept the English going for a long time during the Boer War and we'll keep you Thai guys going just as long.' Chai was angry that 'one of his family' had been injured. 'To hell with them,' Johnny thought.

———————

Johnny talked too much. He liked to impress. That's how he got chatting to Jim. It is not his real name. Johnny didn't know it at the time, but Jim is one of Paul O'Sullivan's informants. He's good at sniffing out information. Jim listened attentively to Johnny's ramblings. He didn't like him and thought he was a bit of a whiner, but Jim was good at keeping up appearances. Johnny told him they were buying rhinos. Jim was intrigued.

O'Sullivan, meanwhile, had offered his services to Ed Hern, a former stock-broker who had founded the Krugersdorp Lion and Rhino Nature Reserve in the mid-1980s. Hern had lost rhinos to poachers and was desperate. So desperate, in fact, that he and his daughter, together with a vet, had developed a procedure to 'infuse' the horns of their rhinos with a pink neon dye and a pesticide as a 'deterrent' to poachers. O'Sullivan put out some feelers, but was quickly distracted by the Krejcir case.

After the fall-out with Punpitak, Johnny grew steadily more embittered, and, he claims, increasingly concerned about the legality of the transactions. 'I thought about going to the police, but Chai always said that in South Africa you can do what you want if you have money.'

One of the Thais had been caught by the cops on previous occasions, first for speeding and then for drunk driving. 'He bribed them with seven or eight thousand rand and they let him go. If I went to the cops, they could just pay them off.'

Instead, Johnny approached Jim, who had, by now, told him about his con-nection to O'Sullivan. Johnny gave him sixteen pages of documents, containing a list of five names, farm addresses, identity numbers, and permit after permit for lion carcasses and lion bones. Jim handed everything over to O'Sullivan.

O'Sullivan poked around, but he had his 'hands full with other matters of a transnational criminal-syndicate nature'. It would be months before he took another look at Johnny's file, but the abortive raid on Krejcir's house provided the impetus. O'Sullivan dusted off the documents and asked Jim if he could 'get any further data about the foreign links to lion bone activities'.

Weeks later, Jim called him. He was excited. Johnny wanted to talk.

11 May 2011

Securitas's offices are situated in Wynberg, a bleak industrial zone in Johannesburg's northern suburbs. Surrounded by car dealerships, tow-trucking companies and scrapyards, the area borders on the poverty of Alexandra Township on the one side, and the leafy riches of Sandton on the other.

In a boardroom, Johnny is spilling his guts as O'Sullivan takes notes, his grey-green eyes hard, his questions blunt. Johnny is a gold seam.

His tale is a remarkable one, told quickly with barely a pause for breath. Over the course of two hours, Johnny gives up names, places and dates. He tells O'Sullivan about the lion bones, the rhino horn deals and the pseudo-hunts that gave them access to a steady supply of rhino horn. But his most astonishing claim is that the syndicate used prostitutes – most of them young women trafficked from Thailand to South Africa – as fronts to obtain rhino hunting permits.

Over the next six days, O'Sullivan pulls together 220 pages of documents, including hunting and export permits, email correspondence and invoices from safari operators for rhino 'hunts'. It is all there on a platter. Particularly damaging is an order for fifty sets of white rhino horns: 100 horns in total. The price is R65 000 a kilogram. Fifteen rhinos can be shot a month. The document is addressed to Marnus Steyl, a lion breeder and game farmer in the Free State. There are three email addresses and a cellphone number for Chumlong Lemtongthai.

An image of a cheetah has been used as the backdrop for a crude cut-and-paste letterhead bearing the name: 'Xaysavang Trading Export-Import. Co, Ltd' [sic]. The company's address is in the Lao People's Democratic Republic, or Laos as it is more commonly known. 'Purchasing foreign in South Africa,' it proclaims in broken English.

NEW ORDER PRODUCTS MONTH 15-05-2011, TO 20-08-2011
IMPORT THAILAND I HAVE CITES PERMIT IMPORT THAILAND

1, WHITE RHINO 50 SET, 1 MONTH CAN SHOOT 15 RHINO
YOU DO CITES PERMIT EXPORT OF SOUTH-AFRICA
1,KG X 65,000R CITES PERMIT IMPORT THAI,

2, LION BONES 300 SET, 1 SET 10,000R FOR 10KG IP.ONLY,
CITES PERMIT IMPORT LAOS PDR

––––––––––

In the Michelangelo Hotel, Johnny puts down his cup. His voice is hushed. In the background a man is fiddling with the lounge's TV set. There is a rugby game on.

By mid-2010, the Thais were actively refocusing their efforts on the acquisition of 'bamboo', the term they use to refer to rhino horn. And, they believed, they had found a loophole in the hunting laws that would give them access to an unlimited supply.

The regulations are clear: a hunter can hunt only one rhino a year. But there is no national or centralised permitting system. Efforts to centralise this data has resulted in little more than an Excel spreadsheet, rife with spelling mistakes and errors. Part of the problem is that each province approves and issues its own permits in accordance with provincial wildlife ordinances, which can differ widely from province to province. Where there is a will, there is way, and the permitting officials who vet the hunters and check their credentials prove all too easy to manipulate and corrupt.

Chai is 'very clever', Johnny says. 'He told me that he's been in the wildlife trade for twenty-two years and has done everything from horn to ivory and bones. He is brilliant. If he looks at the horns on a living rhino, he can estimate their weight exactly. For instance, let's say he'd estimate it at about 5.3 kilograms. When the rhino is later shot and the horns taken off, he'll only have been about point five of a kilogram out. He's that accurate.'

Johnny put out feelers and found a hunting outfitter. Juan Pace is the owner of Shangwari Safaris, a business established in 1996. Its website boasts that it operates in six African countries and 'specializes only in dangerous game hunting'. Pace is also a member of PHASA. The Thais said they had

165

heard that Thai citizens could not legally hunt rhinos. Pace said he'd check. The word came back to them: 'It doesn't matter what country you're from, you can shoot.'

———————

Either in August or September 2010, Pace secured the first rhinos to be slaughtered. Chai paid over R1 million in cash for them. As before, the money was drawn from ATM machines at Emperors Palace. Chai felt safe there. By Johnny's reckoning, it would have taken more than 500 withdrawals of R2 000 each – the withdrawal limit of the machines – to get the cash together.

Chai made sure there was a record of the transaction. 'While we were paying Juan,' Johnny said in his statement to O'Sullivan, 'Chai was busy taking pictures with his camera. I know that Chai carries a Sony laptop around with him. If this computer was obtained, I believe investigators would have everything.'

The photographs show Pace and his wife grinning stupidly over a heap of cash piled up on a pink tablecloth in their home. Their two young sons look on.

Johnny said the rhinos were taken to the Leeuwbosch Game Lodge near Stella in North West province, where they were promptly dispatched in a hunt. Hunting records show that Punpitak and Tool Sriton, another of the Thais arrested alongside Johnny in the 2008 buy-bust, shot two rhinos at Leeuwbosch on 10 September 2010.

This is what Johnny told O'Sullivan:

Then the horns were sent to a taxidermist by the name of Savuti
Taxidermy, and he specialises in mounting the horns onto a shield,
thereby turning it into a hunting 'trophy'. This was an important part of
the process, as Savuti would then be able to get a CITES permit for the
trophy and it would be shipped to Laos and the whole thing would be
legal ... [T]he 'trophy' is just a cover for getting the horn out of South
Africa and into Asia.

Once in Asia, it obviously would enter the black market as rhino horn for 'medicinal' purposes. The person allegedly 'hunting' the rhino would never see the animal, or its horn, again, after the 'hunt'.

I do know that the horn eventually goes to a guy by the name of Xaysavang ... From this I would draw the conclusion that Xaysavang is the 'big boss' of the whole operation.

I interviewed the owner of the farm, Dr Deon Engelbrecht, in July 2011. He denied any wrongdoing. 'You can't do canned hunting here, because here you have to go out and look for the rhino. I know they came and hunted a rhino, and then I stopped it. I didn't supply rhinos to them. It was their rhino that they brought here. I had nothing to do with the transaction.'

An invoice, dated 14 November 2010, and sent to Chai by Leeuwbosch Game Lodge and Safaris, records the sale of one 'white rhino bull with 2 horns' at a 'unit price' of R65 000 a kilogram. The horns weighed 7.12 kilograms. Another invoice shows that the syndicate bought twelve female lion carcasses and thirty-two male lion carcasses from Leeuwbosch for R318 000.

Engelbrecht said he no longer owned rhinos because of the 'high risk' of poaching. He lost a rhino to poachers in early 2010 and 'then got rid of the things'. Some time in January or February 2011, permits were issued for a further two rhinos to be hunted on his farm. Both hunters were Vietnamese.

The Thais had had their taste. 'Bamboo' was where the real money lay. Late in 2010, some of the men, including Johnny and Punpitak, travelled to Winburg in the Free State to examine a stash of lion bones.

A sign at the entrance to a farm outside the town promised: 'For all your wildlife needs ... Steyl Brothers – We do it in "Steyl"'.

9

The Killing

16 January 2011

In the shade of a tree on a game farm in North West Province, a white rhino bull has taken shelter from the stupefying heat. It dozes, ears twitching, its massive chest rising and falling in slow rhythm. It is a magnificent beast with long, curved horns.

There's a sharp crack and a puff of rust-red dust erupts from the animal's hide as the first bullet tears into it. A terrible, almost indescribable keening cuts the air, like a baby crying out or a pig being slaughtered. It is a sound you don't easily forget.

The GoPro camera strapped to Marnus Steyl's head records the rhino's desperate struggle to escape. It rolls onto its side, feet thrashing wildly as it battles to stand. A rifle barrel, distorted by the lens, snakes into view. A second shot hits the animal as it staggers forward and away from the source of its pain, kicking up a cloud of dust. Steyl reloads. The rhino – confused, unable to see or smell its killers – turns full circle. A few seconds later, a third shot rings out. The animal charges behind a bush. Five seconds elapse. Harry Claassens, the PH who regularly accompanies Steyl's clients, raises his rifle and fires. The rhino runs a few paces and collapses under the tree. Mewling in agony, it tries to rise up on its haunches, then topples over.

Steyl bends down to pick up a spent cartridge and hands it to the tracker. In the background, a Thai man looks on. The rhino's cries are getting softer now. Steyl tries to reload, then swaps rifles with Claassens. Forty seconds after the fourth shot, Steyl speaks. '*Waar moet ek hom skiet*? (Where must I shoot him?),' he asks Claassens uncertainly, voice hoarse with adrenaline.

The men move closer. About ten to fifteen paces from the animal, they stop. Steyl clumsily shoulders the rifle. He fires quickly. Too quickly. The scope kicks back, cutting him above the eye. The bullet hits the animal in the head. Steyl pauses. The rhino's movements are weaker, its squeals muted. '*Daai een te laag*? (That one too low?),' he asks Claassens. Ten seconds tick by. '*Hy's* gone (He's gone),' Steyl announces.

Steyl ejects the cartridge from the breach, hands it to Claassens and pushes the bolt home. He wipes blood away from his eye. But the rhino isn't dead yet. Blood oozes from flared nostrils. An eye stares glassily into the middle distance. Its right hind leg twitches. Ragged breaths displace scrub and dust near its head.

The men approach their kill to inspect the damage. '*Kyk die eerste skoot, Harry. Die eerste twee. Is hy te laag daar*? (Look at the first shot, Harry. The first two. Is it too low there?)' Steyl asks. Claassens says nothing. They watch the animal die. Steyl removes the camera and appears to hold it in his hand. The camera tilts and focuses on the Thai man. He's standing there, expressionless, his hands at his sides. He's not holding a rifle. Steyl walks away from the rhino. He looks down at the camera, fumbling for the off switch. There's a flash of a striped brown-and-white Jeep golf shirt, blond hair and a ruddy, sunburnt face, puffy from too many braais and booze. Then nothing.

———————

The dusty little Free State *dorp* of Winburg lies just off the N1 highway halfway between Kroonstad and Bloemfontein. It's a shell of a town, grubby and decaying, the roads irreparably potholed. Those who can, escape when they're young and rarely return for more than a fleeting visit.

A dirt road leads away from the R708 near Winburg to Steyl's farm, Klipplaatfontein. Inside enclosures surrounded by double layers of game fencing, lions prowl listlessly in the sun, occasionally feeding off bloody, fly-blown hunks of meat. Corrugated containers, used for game capture and relocation, rust nearby.

Steyl founded a game-capture business here with his brother Nelius in 2001. Next they established Steyl Safaris and Boschrand Lodge, which was 'built to fulfil all the needs a hunter might have'. The Steyl Group website boasts that the brothers are a 'dynamic duo' with a 'passion for animals'. Their ventures are described as 'intertwined ... with the sole purpose of promoting South Africa & South African wildlife, and creating a heritage for future generations'. A gallery of hunting images shows an array of hunters grinning over their kills. Many are lions. In one photograph, Steyl crouches beside the carcass of a male lion. He has his arms around his young son. The boy doesn't smile. The animal's jaws are agape, its left paw is smeared pink with blood.

Steyl made headlines in June 2006 when one of his lions, an eight-year-old male, escaped from the farm. Breathless news reports in *Die Volksblad*, the local Afrikaans newspaper, described how stray lions were terrorising Free State communities. The Free State accounts for the largest number of captive-bred lions in South Africa. It is also a hotbed of 'canned' lion hunts, where caged animals are released, only to be shot weeks, days, and sometimes even minutes or hours, later. In some instances they've been doped to make them easier targets.

There have been other escapes from other farms. The previous month a lion had been tracked down and shot near Winburg after breaking free from a game farm. There were also reports of a lion being sighted near Harrismith in the Eastern Free State. In Winburg, a posse of thirty farmers were marshalled to find Steyl's lion. It had apparently escaped after someone cut the game fence on the farm. Steyl picked up the bill, which ran to about R8 000 a day. It took the men two weeks to capture the errant animal and return it to its cage.

———

On a sweltering summer's day in 2010, Johnny Olivier and Punpitak Chunchom set off on the 300-kilometre drive from Johannesburg to Winburg, bound for Steyl's farm and a barn stinking of death. One of Juan Pace's cronies, a man Johnny knows only as Izak, had seen an advert about Steyl's captive-bred lions in *Landbou Weekblad*, a weekly agricultural magazine. He'd called him up. Steyl had lion bones for sale and was keen to do business.

Steyl had done well from breeding lions and from trophy hunts. But the hunters wanted the heads and pelts of their kills and little else. They'd have them mounted, usually with lifeless glass eyes and teeth bared in a silent snarl. Displayed in a pub, or spread out as a rug on a living-room floor, the dead beasts were the perfect talking point for alcohol-drenched evenings filled with improbable tales of danger and adventure in the African bush. Perhaps the hunters thought they were the next Hemingway or Selous or Percival. Trophies gave those fantasies a semblance of reality.

That left the carcasses, which had little use. Grey, skinless, headless obscenities, spattered with blood, they would be left for the vultures and scavengers to feast on or be hurriedly buried in pits to rot into the soil.

Steyl was a relative latecomer to the lion-bone trade. Other lion breeders in the Free State and North West provinces had been quick to cash in on the growing Asian demand for alternatives to dwindling stocks of tigers, whose bones, flesh, bile, blood, fat, eyes, teeth, claws and whiskers are used in traditional potions, medicines and vile-smelling 'wines'.

In December 2009, the Free State's Department of Environment provoked a furore when it issued permits to a controversial lion breeder by the name of Kobus van der Westhuizen, which effectively licensed him to kill lions and sell their bones. The department unsuccessfully attempted to mollify critics by emphasising that he was only allowed to trade with a dealer in Gauteng and not in China.

Buti Mathebula, the department's head, did little to lessen the ire of conservationists and animal rights activists when he told *Volksblad* journalist Charles Smith: 'Lions in the Free State are not of any value to us from an environmental point of view. They're not roaming free in the wild. If someone wants to hunt lions in the Free State, that's fine. We don't want these lions here. We're better off without lions in the Free State. There are problems with fences. If they escape, they kill people.'

Van der Westhuizen, the owner of the Letsatsi La Africa Wild Animal and Predator Park, was unrepentant. 'Tell the greenies to go to hell and go moan somewhere else,' he said. He seemed to have few qualms whom he would do business with. In fact, in June 2010, he invited Chai and a Vietnamese national, Bach van Lim, to visit the park and watch the FIFA World Cup there.

Werner Boing, a senior official in the Free State department responsible for issuing and enforcing permits, says there is not much he can do to stop the trade, which is not illegal.

Ninety per cent of the animals killed for their bones are lionesses, Boing says. 'As long as the bones have value, I can't tell a farmer that they can't sell them. I don't like it, but I don't have any grounds on which to stop it.' Male lions are rarely put down for their bones. 'There is a big hunting market for male lions, particularly in North West province, where they are issuing an incredible number of permits.'

He confirmed that Van der Westhuizen had originally applied for a permit to put down twenty lions in order to sell their bones. That permit lapsed and another was issued. Ten lions were destroyed. Boing told me that a permit application for a lion to be put down has to include a justification.

'You would have to say why you want to put the lion down. In a lot of cases it is old lionesses that don't have breeding potential. They can't just be shot. Our requirements are that a vet be there [to put the animal down] and a conservation official also be present.'

Official figures for lion-bone exports from South Africa are unreliable and contradictory, made even more so by chaotic attempts to merge statistics from nine provincial departments. In April 2011, the South African Minister of Environmental Affairs, Edna Molewa, said eighty-six permits were issued in 2009 for the export of lion carcasses, and 171 permits for lion skeletons in 2010. All the consignments were destined for Laos. But more detailed figures, released earlier in response to questions posed by the opposition Democratic Alliance (DA), indicate that 142 carcasses and fourteen 'floating bones' were exported in 2009. The figures for 2010 state that 235 carcasses were exported from North West province alone, and 1363 bones from the Free State. In contrast, records held by the CITES secretariat suggest that eighty 'bodies', five skeletons and 250 kilograms of lion bones were shipped from South Africa to Laos in 2009. The CITES figures for 2010 show that 130 skeletons were exported to Laos, along with 586 bones, fifty-four claws, ninety teeth, six skulls and fifty-four trophies.

Why the demand for lion bones? The answer lies in the steady decline of the world's tiger population and an unwavering belief in many Asian countries that the bones are a panacea for a range of ills. The staggering growth of Asia's economic dragons and the increase in disposable income have fuelled the trade.

According to the WWF, the global tiger population is thought to have fallen by over 95 per cent since the turn of the twentieth century, down from 100 000 then to perhaps as few as 3 200 today.

A seminal sixteenth-century Chinese *materia medica* – which still holds currency in traditional Chinese medicinal circles – describes how the bones are used.

> The yellow [bones] from the males are best. Animals shot with arrows should not be used because the poison enters the bones and blood and is harmful to people … The bones should be broken up and the marrow removed. Butter or urine or vinegar is applied, according to the type of prescription, and they are browned over a charcoal fire.

The bones' uses are varied.

> For removing all kinds of evil influences and calming fright. For curing bad ulcers and rat-bite sores. For rheumatic pain [of] the joints and muscles, and muscle cramps. For abdominal pain, typhoid fever, malaria, hydrophobia. Placed on the roof it can keep devils away and so cure nightmares. A bath in tiger bone broth is good for rheumatic swellings of the bones and joints. The shin bones are excellent for treating painfully swollen feet. It is applied with vinegar to the knees. Newborn children should be bathed in it to prevent infection, convulsions, devil possession, scabies and boils, it will then grow up without any sickness. It strengthens the bones, cures chronic dysentery, prolapse of the anus and is taken to dislodge bones which have become stuck in the gullet. The powdered bone is applied to burns and eruptions under the toenail.

———

Steyl appears to have little interest, beyond a certain morbid curiosity, in the medicinal uses of the bones. For him, it is about the money.

As the bakkie, with Izak behind the wheel, jolts along the dirt road to Steyl's farm, Klipplaatfontein, Johnny catches a glimpse of the lions pacing in their enclosures. Back and forth they prowl. Back and forth. Back and forth. Their movements are slow and lethargic, dulled by months or years of captivity. Two lion carcasses, freshly skinned, hang nearby in a container.

Johnny takes an instant dislike to Steyl. He's an 'arrogant, domineering little *bliksem*', '*windgat*' and brashly self-important. Inside a barn, Steyl shows them the lion bones, spread out haphazardly on the floor. The bacterial stench of decay chokes the air.

Punpitak has an eye for this sort of thing. He sifts through the bones, arranging them into sets. After a while, the skeletons begin to take shape. There are twelve sets in all, but there are bones missing and those that are there are small. A thousand rand a kilogram is the going rate. If the skull and feet are still intact, an additional R5 000 is added to the purchase price. The men pay Steyl R60 000, bag the bones and heft them onto the back of the bakkie.

It will be months before they hear from Steyl again. When they do, he has a new business proposition for them to consider.

Johnny takes the call. It's Steyl. 'I've got a bunch of rhinos. Do you want to hunt them?' he asks. Steyl says he recently bought a game farm in North West province. It is called the Aurora Private Nature Reserve. The previous owner's brother-in-law, Harry Claassens, is a registered professional hunter in the province. They have become firm friends.

Johnny is uncertain: 'We don't really do rhinos, we do lion bones. But I'll ask Chai if he's interested.' Chai is more than interested. He can barely contain his excitement. 'Yes,' he yammers. 'Trophies, trophies, trophies!'

The deal is struck. Steyl will supply the rhinos and organise the hunting permits. It shouldn't be too hard. The North West provincial authorities dish out permits like business cards. And they don't ask too many hard questions. Now Steyl needs hunters, and Punpitak knows where to find them.

Green strobe lights cut through the darkness. A mirrorball turns slowly, shards of light illuminating the shadows huddled around the stage. Lady Gaga blares from the speakers. A tattooed dancer gyrates around a steel pole in a gynaecological display of feigned eroticism.

It's 3 p.m. on a Thursday afternoon in Church Street, Pretoria. The bar is starting to fill up with regulars clutching shot glasses, beers and *polisiekoffie*: stiff double brandies and Coke.

Flamingo's is one of Pretoria's more notorious dens of iniquity. In a previous incarnation it was the stomping ground of an infamous Pretoria biker gang. And in 2010, after a torrid night's drinking at the club, Blue Bulls and Super 14 rugby star, Bees Roux, beat a Metro policeman to death. Roux claimed during his trial that the policeman had tried to rob him after stopping him for drunk driving and that he had defended himself. He received a suspended sentence in a plea deal that included paying R750 000 in compensation to the dead man's family.

In August 2011, the club's one-time silent partner, a disgraced safari-company owner, Hugo Ras, was arrested in a police raid on his three-storey home in Magalieskruin in northern Pretoria. During a search, investigators found an unlicensed firearm and large quantities of M99, a powerful anaesthetic that is widely used in game capture and also to dart rhinos. The drug – which is 3 000 times more potent than morphine – is fatal to humans, and its distribution is meant to be strictly controlled.

Police had obtained a warrant on the basis that they wanted to question Ras about the murder of a Russian stripper, Lana Muratava. She had disappeared from Flamingo's late one night in November 2010 and was last seen alive with a man in a white Land Cruiser. Her corpse was discovered days later in a ditch next to a road in Hammanskraal. There were claims that she had been killed with M99, but early tabloid press reports suggested that the back of her skull had been repeatedly bashed in. Other rumours alleged she had been strangled.

Ras was charged, but not for the murder. He and seven others, including three veterinarians, faced provisional charges of contravening the Medicines and Related Substances Control Act over the illegal distribution of M99. One of the men in the dock alongside Ras was Dr Douw Grobler, a veterinarian and former head of game capture at the Kruger National Park. Grobler had made an international name for himself in the 1990s at Kruger, where he was involved in the large-scale relocation of animals, including elephant and rhino. He was fired by the park in 2001 for the unauthorised sale of animals from the park's buffalo-breeding project.

I met Ras outside the Pretoria North Magistrate's Court in April 2012. He was in a chatty mood. The case had been postponed again and charges against five of his co-accused had been dropped. He believed the case was crumbling. He denied any knowledge of Muratava's death. 'The girl was an interpreter for me when I had Russian clients on my farm.' The clients, he says, invariably 'wanted an interpreter and also a girl to fuck. I decided to make a plan and get a girl who interprets and screws. She makes more money and there is one less person in the Land Cruiser when we go out hunting. That is the only fucking connection I had with her. I never touched her. The stories that people think up are like *Isidingo*, *The Wild*, *Sewende Laan* and *Binnelanders* [local television soap operas] all rolled into one.'

It wasn't the first time that Ras had fallen foul of the law. In 2000 and 2001, he was arrested for various contraventions of nature conservation and customs regulations and fined. In 2004, the *Mail & Guardian* newspaper revealed that a bull elephant Ras had purchased from the Kruger National Park had been hunted by a Texan oil magnate within hours of its arrival on a game farm near Rustenburg in North West. Gavin Hulett, a park warden, told the paper that four bull elephants had been sold to Ras on condition that they would not be hunted. Ras claimed the bull was shot after it broke out of camp.

A year later he was back in the news, this time charged with murder after a contractor working on his farm was attacked and killed by a lion. The charge was eventually dropped. The same year, Ras was fined for assault. The day I spoke to him outside court, he boasted about his numerous run-ins with police and the courts, saying the charges rarely stuck.

A group of young Thai women is clustered in a corner of the club, tarted up in short black dresses, lashings of make-up and stiletto heels. They're on display, like so many cattle. A girl called Tanya slugs back a shot of tequila, sneers at the Thais and launches into a racist tirade. 'I don't fucking know where they come from,' she says in Afrikaans. 'They must fuck off. They're irritating, just irritating. They speak loud and they're like fucking kaffirs, man,' she says, using a crude racist slur for black Africans.

She's twenty-six, but her face is hard and old, her eyes like cut glass. She's worked here, in Flamingo's, on-and-off for years. 'Are you a dancer?' I ask.

'No', she says. 'I'm into fucking.'

The Thais are Tanya's competition. Her overtures unsuccessful, Tanya moves on to another table and another potential client. Her place is quickly taken by a twenty-eight-year-old Thai woman with an infectious laugh. She's been in South Africa for three years, she tells me. Her family is poor, from a rural town somewhere. Her father worked in a factory until he couldn't work any more. He's seventy now. Her mother is sixty.

'In my country, people get paid very little. That's why I came here.' A friend had invited her over with promises of money to be made.

'I can do any job,' she says. 'Cooking, cleaning, washing, whatever.'

For a year she worked for a Chinese boss in a factory shop in Nelspruit. The hours were brutal. 'We sold blankets, TVs, T-shirts, anything. I was crying a lot then. When I came to this country, I can say "sorry", nothing else. So I learn English.'

She eventually moved to Johannesburg, and another 'friend' found her a job in a strip club. 'The first time I worked, I didn't want to take my clothes off. I was scared. Someone wrapped a skirt around me and then they pushed me out onto stage. Go make money, go, go, go, they said. A guy gives me R100 or R200 and I say, "Why you give me money?" I didn't understand.'

Now she charges R500 for a lap dance. Just yesterday she made R2 800. She is worried about AIDS and doesn't have sex with clients. 'Only jacuzzi dancing,' she says. 'I only six months working here. When I get enough money, I look for other business. Sometimes the people are like animals. The other day, I dancing back there,' she says, gesturing in the direction of a private room near the bar. 'This crazy guy, he opens his pants and takes it out. I could not believe it … Another guy wants me to sucky-sucky, no condom. It's not safe.'

I leave the table and head for the men's room on my way out. A sign on the wall reads: 'Viagra for sale at reception.'

The Thai women who ply their trade at Flamingo's and other strip clubs and massage parlours scattered around Gauteng are ideal for Punpitak's plan. They're outsiders: isolated and on the fringes of the expatriate community. Most barely speak a word of English. And most have families to support back home. A few thousand rand can go a long way and, for Punpitak, it's a lot cheaper than flying in hunters from Thailand and Vietnam.

He trawls the clubs for candidates, chatting up the women with assurances of money, paid holidays at safari lodges and vague promises of work in tourism. He purports to be a successful businessman and ostentatiously flaunts the trappings of his wealth – thick wads of cash, a giant silver bling-ring on his left hand and, of course, the Hummer.

Johnny Olivier says Punpitak, whom he most frequently refers to by his *farang* name, Peter, is 'the biggest bullshitter I've ever met'.

'Peter went to clubs in Midrand, Rosebank in Johannesburg and Pomona Road. He held a carrot out to the girls: "Do you want to make a quick R5 000? You get to go on holiday, you get R5 000 and all we need is your passport." Any Thai citizen living here trying to make a buck would take an offer like that in the blink of an eye ... Peter would disappear for a night, and the following morning he'd pitch up with copies of two or three Thai girls' passports.'

Punpitak's quest is aided by William, a grotesquely bloated South African pimp who lives with his Thai wife, Mau, on a smallholding in Midrand, halfway between Pretoria and Johannesburg. The couple run a group of Thai 'girls' who work the club scene.

Many of the 'girls' come to South Africa on holiday visas. Weeks after their arrival, fresh paperwork is submitted on their behalf to the Department of Home Affairs in Germiston on Gauteng's East Rand, requesting a change in 'permit status'. A copy of a 'life-partnership agreement' with a South African man and confirmation of employment as a 'part-time beauty therapist' accompanies the forms.

'The reason for my application is that I met Nicholas F… at a party held for a mutual friend,' a letter, purportedly written by one of the women, reads. '[W]e had an instant connection we became friend [*sic*] and eventually decided to live together. He rents a garden flat from his aunt … I have been offered part-time employment. I wish for my visa to be amended to accompanying spouse and extended for the period that I can remain in South Africa and continue to build a future with my life partner and soul mate.'

The paperwork includes a standardised note from 'Nicholas F…' in which he affirms the story, saying he met the young woman at a party after a Thai festival, that they 'have a lot in common' and enjoy the 'same things in life', and that he promises to 'care for all her needs'. The same addresses are used in multiple applications and the same wording appears in some of the supporting documents. But despite the glaring similarities, home affairs officials approve the applications.

Mau, William's wife, quickly becomes an integral part of Punpitak's scheme, convincing women in her wide circle of Thai 'friends' to hand over their passports and go on 'safari'.

Johnny takes on the role of administrator. He scans photocopies of passports and emails them to Steyl, who submits the permit applications. The process runs like clockwork. 'You can tell Peter he can come and hunt, as the permits [have come] through,' Steyl says when he calls back a week or so later.

Data compiled by the South African Department of Environmental Affairs show that the first hunts take place in November 2010. Four hunting permits are issued to Miss Boonta Kongklin, Miss Onsuthee Konsanit, Miss Purichaya Hatthakit and Miss Pecharat Janmeetes respectively. Hunting records released by North West province in response to questions in Parliament indicate that the permits were issued on 12 November 2010. An invoice sent by Steyl on 16 November 2010, and addressed to Mr Vixay Keosavang and Mr Chumlong Lemtongthai of Xaysavang Trading Export-Import in Laos, requests payment of R246 000 ($36 176) for a hunted rhino with horns weighing 4.1 kilograms.

A text message sent on 2 December 2010 from Chumlong to Steyl reads: 'Transfer usd 36,176.00'. Two weeks after the first hunts, the next batch of permits is issued. Once again, the hunters are all Thai women: Miss Jirarak Suwannatrai, Miss Onuma Laechankham, Miss Siriporn Phengjoy and Miss Sawitree Suebthangjai.

The department's records are telling. Between November 2010 and March 2011, at least twenty permits are issued to Thai women to conduct rhino hunts on Steyl's North West farm. Some, like Siriporn Phengjoy, Boonta Kongklin and Sawitree Suebthangjai, are listed on permits issued in both 2010 and 2011. And in every instance, the professional hunter who accompanies the 'clients' is Harry Claassens.

Xaysavang's 'hunters' account for at least thirty of the seventy-three permits issued over an eight-month period in the Dr Ruth Segomotsi Mompati District, where Aurora is situated. Each hunt yields an average of four kilograms of rhino horn – 120 kilograms for thirty hunts. Steyl stands to make R7.2 million. Not bad for Steyl, but even better for Xaysavang, which can expect to make anywhere between $8 million and $10 million on the black market.

Johnny is growing increasingly uncomfortable about the hunts, or so he says. Although Punpitak and the rest of the syndicate initially keep him in the dark about their plans, the pattern quickly becomes apparent.

'It all looked very strange,' Johnny says. 'I'd be told there are rhinos available; the next thing I'd get passports from Peter and I'd send them to Marnus. But it was just girls hunting. If they are hunting trophies, why are the hunters all girls who live here? They probably never see the things again after they've hunted.

'I'm surprised nobody notices. If so many women suddenly start to hunt rhinos, surely somebody will ask questions. Where do they get the money to pay for the hunts? You're talking about hundreds of thousands of rands. Those poor girls will have to lie on their backs for a long time to make that kind of money. But nothing is asked and nothing is done.'

This is how Johnny remembers it. He is sitting in the back of a white Toyota Land Cruiser, sipping a cold drink and wolfing down a sandwich. It's hot as hell and the driver has parked in the shade of a thorn tree. Johnny, as usual, is wearing a pair of Crocs – his favourites. But he doesn't like walking in the veld with them. 'There are these long thorns that go right through the rubber into your foot,' he explains. 'Anyway, I'm not a hunter.' Out there somewhere, Marnus Steyl, Harry Claassens and a tracker are looking for a rhino to kill.

A shot rings out. It must be about 300 metres away. Then another and another. One of Marnus's farmworkers, who is waiting with Johnny and a couple of Thai girls in the Land Cruiser, grins. It must be Marnus doing the shooting, he says. Harry only ever needs one shot. Marnus needs two or three, sometimes more, before the rhino goes down. Earlier, Marnus had asked Johnny if the girls wanted to shoot. They said no. The rifle was too big and they didn't know how to shoot.

Sometimes before a hunt, Harry takes the girls to go and fire off a couple of shots at paper targets. It is a low-calibre rifle, but at least they can say that they fired a weapon of some kind and there will be powder residue on their hands. Not that anyone's likely to check.

The regulations governing hunts are clear: the hunter in whose name the permit has been issued must fire the first shot. If they wound the animal, the PH – in this case, Harry – can finish off the kill. But that rarely happens. Harry is often the lone triggerman. The Thai and Vietnamese women have no interest in killing the animals themselves. They aren't dressed to hunt. They wear sandals and shoes with soles so thin that even the smallest thorn will go straight through them.

There are bursts of static on the radio and a voice that sounds as if it's emanating from a tin can breaks the silence. The rhino is down. They can come. The Land Cruiser bounces through the bush. Farm labourers have already started clearing the brush away from the dead animal's head. A rifle is handed to one of the girls. She poses next to the kill, mugging for the camera.

The photographs take an age. First the girl, then Marnus, then Marnus and the girl, then Harry, then Punpitak all take turns to stand over the carcass, grinning inanely. Johnny poses too. He will later claim the scene repulsed him. 'It's not a nice feeling to see such a big animal lying dead at your feet.' Sometimes, the girls even have to fight back tears, he says.

The horns are removed by Steyl's labourers and sent to a taxidermist to be mounted as trophies on crude wooden shields. It is a regulatory requirement. The heads and skins are dumped and the meat is sold to a butcher.

North West nature conservation officers are usually on hand to record the hunt. Their role is ostensibly to ensure that the hunting permit-holder and the hunter are one and the same and oversee the measuring and weighing of the horn, the process of microchipping it and the signing of the hunting register. The 'pink slip' from the register – a carbon copy of the entry made by the PH – is given to the official for his records.

Usually, they'll also snap a picture of the 'hunter' and her trophy. They are expected to complete a 'daily activity report' recording the details of the hunt. Sometimes they do, sometimes they don't. More often than not their presence is simply to dot the Is, cross the Ts and fill out the paperwork that gives the pseudo-hunt a veneer of legitimacy.

Evidence exists that some of them are not averse to accepting 'gifts' from hunting outfitters or hunters. One of the Thais, for instance, apparently bought a cellphone for a North West official. On another occasion, Johnny sees cash being slipped to a nature conservation officer attending one of the hunts. It looks to be about R400 or R500. 'It looked like it was a normal arrangement,' Johnny says. He isn't doing too badly himself. For shuffling a little paperwork and acting as a go-between, he makes R5 000 for every rhino killed. He calls it 'blood money'.

––––––––––

The stream of passports, CITES export permits and lists of hunters' names flowing through the syndicate's email accounts on Yahoo, Hotmail and Google provides a detailed electronic trail of their activities. One of the accounts is hunting303@gmail.com.

Registered on 18 May 2011, it is used to record correspondence between Chai – using the email address poter.2022@gmail.com – Steyl and North West conservation officials. Chai has always been something of an Apple acolyte, and many of the mails are sent from his iPad and iPhone. He writes little, probably because of his limited English. But the subject lines of his emails provide an insight into the extent of the operation.

20 May 2011

Email from poter.2022@gmail.com to steylgame@mweb.co.za, copied to hunting303@gmail.com

Subject: New passport for shooting

23 May 2011

Email from poter.2022@gmail.com to steylgame@mweb.co.za, copied to hunting303@gmail.com

Subject: 5 Passport for shooting

23 May 2011

Email from poter.2022@gmail.com to steylgame@mweb.co.za, copied to hunting303@gmail.com

Subject: + 2 Passport for shooting

26 May 2011

Email from poter.2022@gmail.com to steylgame@mweb.co.za, copied to hunting303@gmail.com

Subject: 8 passport for shooting

26 May 2011

Email from poter.2022@gmail.com to steylgame@mweb.co.za, copied to hunting303@gmail.com

Subject: 18 names for shooting wait you confirm we can go.

And so they continue.

Attached to the emails are neatly typed lists of names, addresses, and passport and identity numbers for batches of hunters. Invariably, the headers are the same: 'Name for shooting rhino farm Steyl Game.' There are tax invoices too, all issued by Steyl Game in Winburg for amounts ranging from $30 000 to $32 000.

One mail, dated 15 May 2011, is from Johnny to Chai. He's trying to make amends for the punch-up with Punpitak at the Edenvale house.

I had time to calm down and I worked through things. I am sorry about what happened in the past but things like that happens [sic] in all families and friends. I leave things in the past and I forget things that happened in the past and I am looking forward. You have always been good [to] me and I feel I need to do everything I can to help you with your business here in South Africa with no heart [sic] feelings.

So if you want me to assist you in Permits, passports and help with conservation, I will help you were ever [sic] I can like in the old days. I am [a]waiting your response regarding the above and looking forward to work with you as a family.

King Regards
Johnny Olivier.

What Chai doesn't know is that Johnny is already spilling his guts to O'Sullivan. The email is a ruse to get him back into the fold as an informant. Two days later, O' Sullivan presents copies of his report, including Johnny's statement and 222 pages of supporting documentation, to police, the EWT and, most significantly, the South African Revenue Service (SARS).

———————

12 June 2011
Suvarnabhumi International Airport, Bangkok
Chai boards a Thai Airways flight to Johannesburg. It's been six months since he was last in South Africa. He hefts his laptop bag into the overhead luggage bin and takes his seat.

He's not travelling alone. There are five others. They are a motley lot. One or two look like peasants, while the rest could pass for students or backpackers. Hunting permits have been arranged for them in South Africa. Soon another ten rhino horns will be on their way to Thailand and Laos.

The plane taxis along the runway and thunders into the sky. Nine thousand kilometres away in Johannesburg, a cellphone rings. 'He's on his way,' a voice says. 'He'll be at the airport tomorrow – flight 703.'

The SARS men have been waiting patiently for their quarry. Weeks have passed. Six flights have come and gone. But still they wait.

The operation is code-named 'Project Sayam'. It is being run by Charles van Niekerk, an operational specialist in SARS's tax and customs investigations division, and Lindsay Mudaly, a senior investigator.

For the past few weeks, the two have busied themselves checking and rechecking every facet of Paul O'Sullivan's report on the syndicate. From the documents it is clear that Chai is the lynchpin in Xaysavang's South African operations.

In several instances, including the order for fifty 'sets' of rhino horn, he is listed as a director of the company. A 'confirmation letter', apparently signed by Vixay Keosavang in Laos and imprinted with his personalised stamp, describes Chai as the 'manager' in charge of purchasing 'zoo animal(s)' in South Africa. In his statement to O'Sullivan, Johnny Olivier referred to Chai as the 'leader' and the man who 'handled all the cash transactions'.

'He seemed to me to be a powerful individual,' he had told the Irishman.

According to Johnny, Chai has been involved in the 'wildlife business' since his early twenties. He was born in Tak, an agricultural and strategic military region in northern Thailand on the border with Myanmar, in September 1968. Chai owns at least two properties in Thailand, including one in an upmarket gated community in Bangkok, which he shares with his girlfriend, Muy Namsang.

Chai is a collector of sorts: he fancies Rolex watches, Apple gadgets and custom-made Infinity handguns with garish pistol grips. He also has a penchant for Hennessy cognac, Krong Thip 90 cigarettes and Smith & Wesson ammunition. And he loves gambling. It is not uncommon for him to blow R30 000 (about $3 500) a night in a casino. This he does for relaxation. Overpriced cars are another vice. In Thailand he has a white BMW 520d and a sporty metallic-grey Nissan 370Z, which his girlfriend has appropriated. In South Africa, it is the Hummer – a dead brand that even yuppies with money to burn have forsaken.

But there are two key details that emerge from Johnny's statement. The first is that Chai obsessively photographs everything, from the hunts to the pay-offs. Wherever he goes, he takes a camera. Perhaps it is his way of keeping records. The second is the fact that Chai 'always' carries a Sony laptop around with him.

'If this computer was obtained, I believe investigators would have everything,' Johnny had said.

---

13 June 2011

The arrivals terminal at OR Tambo International Airport in Johannesburg is stirring. Red-eyed passengers filter groggily through the airport. Outside, the brittle, black cold of a Highveld winter awaits them.

It is 6.16 a.m. Thai Airways flight 703 touches down early. Inside the airport, Chai takes the lead as the men follow the signs and conveyor belts to the immigration counters. The two SARS investigators are waiting. They bide their time, observing the Thais from a distance. Chai hands his passport to an immigration officer. Partially concealed behind a pillar, one of the SARS men hastily snaps a photograph. Blurred by bad light, movement and nerves, the image shows Chai, dressed in black, with the five Thais clustered close behind him.

Once they have cleared immigration, Chai detours into a duty-free shop near the baggage carousels and emerges with a bottle of Johnnie Walker whisky. The rest collect the bags. They head for the green customs channel – they have nothing to declare. The SARS men are there ahead of them, eyeing their prize – the laptop bag under Chai's arm.

Chai is taken aside and questioned. The laptop is confiscated and sealed in an evidence bag. A cellphone, camera and some documents are also seized. The SARS men have no interest in arresting Chai just yet. They let him go, along with his five companions.

Meanwhile, in the arrivals hall, Punpitak Chunchom and another Thai man, Phichet Thongphai, are spotted by undercover cops. They are waiting patiently for Chai and the others to emerge. The Hummer is parked outside. The cops question the two men. Then, together with SARS investigators, they escort them out of the airport and follow them to the Edenvale house. Chai and his hunting party are left stranded at the airport.

A search of the property turns up another laptop, a pile of documents and a small quantity of lion bones – primarily teeth and claws. Neither Punpitak nor Phichet has a permit for the bones. They are promptly arrested. Two weeks later they will plead guilty to contraventions of environmental legislation, receive fines of R10 000 each and be ordered to leave South Africa.

———

The SARS Computer Forensics Lab is situated in a nondescript corner of a sprawling office block in Sunninghill, Johannesburg. It is the most advanced laboratory of its kind in South Africa. Banks of computer screens line a sterile, climate-controlled room with anti-static flooring. The walls are reinforced with steel, and a steel grid runs through the ceiling. It is designed in such a way that if there is a fire, suppressant gas will be dispersed automatically from vents throughout the laboratory to smother the flames.

Insulated from the network that runs through the rest of the building is a computer server in which case files and evidence collected by the lab's analysts is stored. Biometric fingerprint readers ensure that only the five people authorised to use the laboratory have access to the server room. Next to it is a workshop where computer hard drives are removed from confiscated laptops and desktops before their data is 'imaged'.

Along a wall are a number of hard-shell plastic cases, inside of which is an array of forensic gadgetry, connectors and adaptors that allow the analysts to copy any computer drive and extract data from virtually any mobile phone or tablet. Perhaps the most important tool is a 'write blocker'.

As with the investigation of any crime scene, evidence has to be preserved and then analysed. Here, the crime scene is a hard drive, memory stick, back-up disk or cellphone, and the evidence is in bits and bytes, ones and zeroes. Every time you switch on a computer, data is modified. If you copy files to other drives, key file information such as dates and times can often change. For digital evidence to be accepted in court, it is vital that the original drive is preserved as it was when the suspect last used it. Also, any 'images' of that drive have to be exact, down to the very last digit.

A write blocker does just that. Once a hard drive is removed from a computer, it is plugged into the device and 'imaged' onto another drive. The write blocker prevents any new data from being written to either the original drive or the duplicate image. This ensures that the evidence isn't modified or damaged in any way and remains 'forensically sound'.

It is here that Chai's laptop is sent to be analysed. Johnny was right. The laptop has 'everything' the investigators need: emails, hunting permits, waybills, receipts, video clips, and hundreds of photographs documenting rhino horn, lion bone and ivory transactions. Among them are dozens of images of Thai 'hunters' posing with rhino carcasses, of rhino horns being cut, weighed and crated, of elephant tusks lined up on a tile floor, of neatly arranged sets of lion bones, claws and teeth. There is Punpitak, clutching a bloodied horn, Chai leaning nonchalantly against the hulking mass of a dead rhino or mugging for his computer's webcam with his collection of pistols. There are photos of pay-offs and bundles of cash piled high on tables. There's Chai and Punpitak and the rest of the gang at the casino with the Hummer, and Chai in Thailand in orange Buddhist robes.

———————

Chai is arrested on 9 July 2011, shortly after he returns to Johannesburg with the hunting party. Five rhinos have been shot. There was little the investigators could do to intervene, as the hunting permits were valid. Chai initially pleads guilty to ten counts relating to contraventions of the Customs and Excise Act and admits in a statement that he is a director of Xaysavang Trading, a company that 'engages in the dealing of rhino horn and lion bones, teeth and claws'. He also admits that he instructed 'the export of the rhino horns indicated in the counts to which I pleaded guilty'. Later, when it becomes clear that prosecutors intend to pursue other charges, he withdraws the plea. His lawyer tells the court that his plea was made in the mistaken belief that he would receive a fine and be allowed to return home.

On 4 November 2011, having been lured back to South Africa with the promise of more deals, Punpitak Chunchom is arrested at OR Tambo. Four days later, Marnus Steyl hands himself over to the police. I had spoken to him briefly in July, shortly before publishing a series of articles exposing the syndicate's activities. 'You can write what you want,' he had said over the phone. 'We know our things are in order.'

On 27 March 2012, Tool Sriton is arrested in the parking lot of the Emperors Palace Casino. Finally, on 17 May 2012, Harry Claassens is picked up by police at his farm in North West province. The Thais are kept in custody, the South Africans released on bail.

Harry Claassens becomes a State witness and is indemnified from prosecution. In November 2012, Chumlong Lemtongthai is sentenced to forty years in prison after pleading guilty to smuggling rhino horn trophies out of South Africa for the purposes of trading them on the black market. Charges are controversially withdrawn against Marnus Steyl, Punpitak Chunchom, Tool Sriton and two of Steyl's farm labourers, but could be reinstated. Both Chunchom and Sriton have left South Africa.

---

22 July 2011

I call William. The voice on the phone sounds like it has been steeped in a vat of whisky. Did he and his wife supply Thai strippers to hunt rhinos? I ask. There is a long pause.

'Well, you got me,' he says. Another pause. 'It's a serious allegation and I know everything about it ... My wife did organise women [for them], which is true, but they said they were booking the girls to go with them weekends, you know. They didn't say they were going to take them for rhino hunting.'

He's getting angry. Johnny Olivier, he says, 'is one of the kingpins of the whole fucking set-up. He is the guy who took the girls, took their passports and actually made the permits for the women. And now he is trying to take the blame from him and serve it on somebody else.'

He denies the women are strippers or prostitutes, a claim that seems at odds with his earlier statement that the girls had been 'booked'. 'It was some of my wife's friends, and their husbands and boyfriends didn't even know about it,' William continues. 'They just told them they were taking them sightseeing for a weekend and they'd give them R5 000 each. When the women came back they said they had been convinced to pose for pictures with the rhinos. They didn't do any shooting.

'When I realised what was going on, I told my wife: "You must fucking stop this *kak* and leave these fucking people alone or you'll pick up *kak*."' He claims he reported the matter to the police. 'In October 2010, when this thing started, I reported it to the cops. I can understand Thai and I smelt something was wrong. The cops did *fokol*.'

After my meeting with Johnny at the Michelangelo Towers, I drive to a shopping mall in Midrand, halfway between Johannesburg and Pretoria. William is waiting for me. Two of the 'hunters' want to talk. Outside an Indian restaurant, half a dozen Thai women and their South African husbands and boyfriends are crowded around a table snacking on poppadoms and sambals. William is a bear of a man. He dwarfs his wife, Mau, and the other Thais at the table. One of the hangers-on, a man named Jones, takes the lead in the discussion. They're pissed off with Johnny, he tells me.

'The women,' he says, 'played cards with William's wife every weekend.' She was also friends with Peter, Johnny and Chai. 'Peter said they had bought a *moerse* share in a farm in Botswana and wanted to do something in tourism for Thai people. They'd fly them in to come and look at the animals. But they said they needed Thais to entertain the tourists, make food for them; all those nice things. They said they'd pay the girls R5 000 each for every tour group that came in. Everyone thought it was a great idea. Even my wife wanted to do it,' Jones says.

'They said that because the farm was in Botswana, the women needed to give them copies of their passports so that their visas could be done. When they talked about permits, we thought it was to go over the border. I told my wife it sounds like a smart idea. "You should apply, get your permit sorted and you can also go," I told her.

'It was all about tourism for Thai people. There was nothing about prostitution or rhinos.'

Jones says the first group left in October 2010. A second group followed them a few weeks later. 'Then the girls came back with these photos of rhinos and horns and all those *lekker* things.'

William, who has been listening intently to the conversation, interjects. 'When I saw those pictures, I told Mau I'd kick her dead if she ever sends people again. And I said I don't want those people [the men from Xaysavang] at my place again, because I'd seen what was going on. Those trophies never went to the girls.

'Now I'm hearing my wife and I are involved in human trafficking. It's a *kak* story. Six years ago, I managed a club above Teazers in Midrand. And Johnny probably thought I was still involved with those things. The so-called prostitutes he mentions in his statement always come to my house on Saturdays to sit and play cards with my wife and make Thai food.'

As an afterthought, he adds: 'I always eat out. I don't eat what they make. The girls knew nothing about hunting permits. I also didn't know. I didn't even know about the copies and everything.'

Jones continues: 'William said to me these guys are busy with fucking smuggling. Just stay out of it.'

William calls one of the Thai women closer. Her nickname is Wi, she says hesitantly. She won't tell me her real name and says she fears reprisals from the Thai authorities. She has reason to be afraid. Her face appears in several photographs the SARS investigators lifted from Chai's laptop. In one she poses nonchalantly with a rifle next to the carcass of a rhino. She's wearing jeans, a cap and a T-shirt with an image of a unicorn rearing up. The rifle takes her to her shoulder. She grins at the camera. In others, Steyl stands behind her, his hands on her shoulders.

William's wife moves closer, as does another woman, called Nit, who acts as translator. 'Johnny and Peter tell me we going to take you on holiday to visit farm and go see animal. I never see big farm before.' She only heard the shots, she says. Then she was driven to where the rhino had fallen. 'I see the rhino but I don't know if it is dead or alive. It was the first time I see a real rhino. Before, only on TV in Thailand.'

She was handed the rifle and told to go and stand next to the animal. She remembers the rifle being heavy and difficult to hold. 'I felt sad,' she says. 'Why they kill them, why they kill such a big animal?' But did she smile in the pictures, I ask. She giggles. 'When you take photo, you have to smile,' she answers.

Another woman is ushered forward. She says her name is Wan. 'It was very sad,' she says of the killing. 'I cried. I don't agree with what they did. I think it was wrong to shoot such a big animal.'

Like Wi, she claims she never fired a shot. 'They make me stand there. I carry rifle on my back. It was very heavy. I feel sorry for rhino.'

A phone rings. I can hear William speaking to someone about Johnny. '*Die fokken doos. Ek wil hom dood donder.* (The fucking cunt. I want to beat him to death).' Both Wi and Wan confirm being paid R5 000 each by Johnny. But they deny they're prostitutes or strippers.

'That not true,' Wi says. 'Why they tell story like that? Not all Thai lady that come to work here is like that. I'm very angry. The boyfriends are also not happy.'

As I prepare to leave, William leans over. 'Johnny and Peter did go and get whores. They booked whores in clubs and then they held parties with them and convinced them to go with them.'

———————

The video runs to 25 minutes and 39 seconds. I watch it again and again, looking and listening for details. Play. Pause. Fast forward. Pause. Rewind. There's Chai, grinning and giving a thumbs-up after he adjusts the camera on Marnus's head; the boot tracks in the dust, a black fence line, the whispered words and hand signals, the way they move – Claassens expertly rolling his feet to mute the sound of his boots on the ground; the hands that hold the rifles; the flashes of colour from the men's shirts; the spacing of the shots; the rhino's penetrating cries.

But it is the Thais I watch most closely: Chai in a black windbreaker, a white, striped shirt and jeans, and the other man – the silent shadow trailing Marnus. Hunting records identify him as Nimit Wongprajan of 166 Moo 2,

Vunghenrat Village, Khon Kaen, Thailand, passport number R737660. Wongprajan's nickname is Pisong. He's wearing jeans, white tennis shoes and a charcoal-coloured jacket. A cap is pulled low over his eyes.

18.32: Steyl gestures to Nimit to stay down.

18.48: Harry and Steyl, slightly crouched over, leave the tracker and
    Nimit behind them as they inch forward. Nimit is unarmed.

20.30: Steyl raises, then lowers, a rifle a number of times.

20.58: Steyl fires a shot.

23.57: The rhino lies dying under the tree. Marnus takes off the GoPro
    and hooks it on his belt. The camera focuses on Nimit. He's standing
    in the background, hands empty at his sides.

The bureaucratic details of the hunt are faithfully recorded, the weight of the animal's horns – four kilograms – the unique numbers of the microchips inserted into them and, most importantly, the permit – number O 21980 – issued to Nimit Wongprajan.

But the footage doesn't show Nimit firing a single shot.

Other details later slip into place. Nimit's brother, Nikorn Wongprajan, is an agriculture officer in the flora department at Bangkok's Suvarnabhumi Airport. Nikorn's girlfriend, Arunee Senam, works for a cargo-handling company, Bangkok Flight Services, and according to her Facebook page, is also employed by a logistics firm. Hunting records show that hunting permits were issued to both Nikorn and Arunee for rhinos that were shot at Aurora around the time of Nimit's hunt.

The paper trail from Nimit's 'hunt' – as with most of the others – leads from Steyl to Chai and back again.

In May 2011, Steyl invoices Nimit for R208 000 or $32 000 for the horns. The invoice appears to have been emailed to Chai. Four days later, the money is transferred from a Bangkok bank account held in Chumlong (Chai) Lemtongthai's name to an account at the Bank of Athens in Johannesburg's Bedford Centre.

The beneficiary is Steyl Game CC.

10

Juju and the 'Poacher'

Mike Peega was one of the elite in a military regiment that prides itself on the high failure rate of its selection course. Only about 30 per cent of the candidates survive the bone-crushing, soul-sapping tests of character that Special Forces operators call the 'ultimate challenge'. Most crack under the strain. Some have died. The entry test is gruelling enough: forty push-ups without breaking rhythm, sixty-seven sit-ups in two minutes, a five-kilo-metre run in twenty-four minutes, and forty six-metre 'shuttle runs' in ninety-five seconds.

There is also a battery of psychological and aptitude tests. A hellish six-week pre-selection phase follows in which the candidates are pushed to breaking point six-and-a-half days a week and up to twenty hours a day. The final selection lasts a week and simulates 'the most extreme physically and mentally stressful conditions that could ever possibly be experienced by a human being'. No sleep, no rest, no food. Any infraction or sign of aggression is an instant cause for disqualification.

Peega survived all that and more over the next fifty-one weeks of training. He was sent to 5 Special Forces Regiment in Phalaborwa, a Lowveld town bordering the Kruger National Park, where summer temperatures easily peak at 47 °C. He gained experience in intelligence gathering, as well as urban and rural reconnaissance.

Then, in March 2007, he applied to join the Customs Border Control Unit (CBCU), a division of SARS. A SARS official who had also served in Special Forces vouched for him, and Peega was hired. He signed a secrecy clause and was assigned to the Special Projects Unit, an investigative division within SARS that would later be renamed, euphemistically, the National

Research Group (NRG). Its focus was on South Africa's burgeoning 'illicit economy' – smuggling and trafficking in drugs, abalone, cars, cigarettes, counterfeit goods, rhino horn and ivory – as well as money-laundering and tax-evasion schemes.

Less than two years later, in December 2008, Peega's career would come to a shattering end. In hindsight, perhaps it was to be expected. But nobody could ever have predicted the nature of his disgrace or that it would propel him to the heart of a political scandal involving South Africa's most controversial politician, Julius Malema.

———————

Christmas Eve 2008
Near midnight, on a dark road outside Vaalwater in Limpopo province, Captain Herman Lubbe is looking for poachers. He is in an unmarked police car and driving fast. Behind him, the town's lights fade into the blackness until they're only a muddy, orange glow. It has been a long day and it promises to be an even longer night.

Lubbe, a veteran of the police's Stock Theft Unit, has received a tip-off that a syndicate he's been tracking is on the hunt. The men, he's been told, are in a red Toyota Corolla, registration HDL814NW, and they're driving in the direction of Melkrivier, fifty kilometres north-east of Vaalwater. It will take him until dawn to find them.

At 5 a.m. on Christmas Day, he spots the Toyota leaving Melkrivier. It's maroon, not red, he notes. And the registration begins with HLD, not HDL. There is only one occupant. Lubbe hangs back and trails the vehicle. He suspects the man behind the wheel is the getaway driver and that the rest of the gang has been dropped off at a game farm to look for rhino. The driver will probably wait in Vaalwater until they need him. A police informant is tasked with keeping an eye on the vehicle.

Lubbe's instincts prove to be right. At 11 a.m., the driver takes off. He's in a hurry. Lubbe takes up a position at the entrance to Leseding Township on the Vaalwater/Melkrivier road. The car's description and its registration number are radioed to police units deployed to watch the main access routes around Vaalwater. Lubbe is in luck. The car drives right past him and turns into Leseding. There are four occupants. He bides his time.

A short while later, Lubbe sees the car leaving the township. This time, there are only two occupants. The vehicle is heading in the direction of Bulgerivier. Lubbe radioes ahead: 'Pull them over,' he says.

When he gets there, the Toyota is at the side of the road. The doors are open. A policeman is guarding a suspect. The other occupant, Lubbe hears, high-tailed it the second the car came to a halt. He is barefoot, wearing a blue T-shirt and camo shorts. He won't get far. Lubbe carries out a cursory search of the car. Near the driver's seat, he finds a cellphone and a pair of tennis shoes. In the back is a loaf of bread, three bottles of still water and a two-litre Fanta Orange. He opens the boot.

Inside is a large axe and a .303 hunting rifle fitted with a Bushnell scope. A live round is in the chamber and ten more are in a magazine. There are five soft-nosed .303 rounds, designed to expand on impact. In hunting parlance, they are used to 'maximise the wound channel'. The remaining bullets are all sharp-point ammo, although the tip of one has been cut off, presumably to ensure it fragments when it hits the target.

Then there's the clothing: a camouflage overall and a green windbreaker the suspect says he bought in France, and brown army fatigues, which he claims belongs to the runaway, a man named Washington. Inside the car Lubbe finds a Malawian driver's licence made out to Washington Phiri Kateka. The suspect hands his wallet to Lubbe. There's the usual stuff inside: bank cards, a driver's licence and a bit of change. But there is something else that catches Lubbe's eye. It's an access card used by SARS officials. The name on the card reads 'Michael Peega'.

Lubbe sweats Peega for information, but he denies that he's a poacher. He works for SARS, he says, but is currently operating undercover for SAN-Parks. His handler is someone called Lumbe, who is based in the Kruger National Park. Lubbe doesn't believe him. (Later the 'handler' is identified as Andrew Lumbe, a senior environmental crime investigator at SANParks. He tells police he knows Peega from Phalaborwa, but is adamant that he is not his handler and that Peega is not a SANParks 'CI' – a confidential informant.)

Peega keeps talking. He says that he met Washington in Pretoria and drove with him to Vaalwater, where one of Washington's friends took them to a game farm to shoot rhinos. But they didn't find any rhinos and were on their way home when the police pulled them over. Peega says he dropped two men off in Leseding before they left. They have an AK-47 with them. He can show the cops where it is.

Peega leads them to a tin shack in the township: Number 59B. Police storm inside. A woman is home with her baby. Her name is Sarafina Baloi. Next to her, on the ground, is a black tog bag, and inside it an AK-47, two rounds of ammunition, a hand-axe, a black balaclava and an army jacket. There's also a passport made out in the name of Joshua Elias Baloi. The woman says the bag belongs to Joshua, her brother. Lubbe arrests her and her husband, Joe Mashaba. As they drive away, Sarafina points to a man in the street. 'There's Joshua,' she says. Police confront him. He denies that the bag or the AK belong to him. But his face matches the photograph in the passport. Lubbe takes him in too.

On 26 December, Washington is arrested. He's still barefoot. He tells Lubbe he's from Mozambique. His real name is Washington Hlongwane. It is not long before he confesses. He works for a man called Ignatius, he says. He shoots the rhinos, hacks off the horns and Ignatius buys them. Washington says he uses a .303 rifle, which he's hidden away in Brits near Pretoria. He'll take the cops there.

———

12 January 2009

Police officially inform SARS, in writing, about Peega's arrest. His employers haven't heard from him in weeks, and he had been on leave when he was apprehended. A day later, Peega makes a confession, one that he later claims was extracted from him through torture. Lubbe laboriously fills in the requisite forms. 'Michael Peega states further voluntarily ...' In neat black capitals with a cheap plastic pen, Lubbe writes: 'Who recruited you to be part of the syndicate?' Then Peega's answer: 'Josias recruited me. He asked me to help him shooting rhino. I know Josias from Phalaborwa, where I was a trained as a soldier.'

Gradually the tale unravels. Late in November 2008, 'Josias' (whose surname is not mentioned in the confession) meets Peega at Gold Reef City, a casino and theme park in Johannesburg. He introduces him to Washington and another man with the unlikely name of Gogo, which means 'grandmother' in Zulu. Their target is the Sable Ranch, a high-security game farm and breeding facility twenty kilometres outside Brits.

It is night when they get there. A poacher's moon lights their way through the bush. Washington takes the lead. Gogo carries the hunting rifle, a .303. He's used it before, he says. 'The ammunition is perfect.' Peega is wearing his French camouflage. Washington shows them where to go to find their prey. 'Just wait. The rhino will show up,' he promises. But the rhino don't turn up, and at sunrise they blearily make their way home.

A week later, they try once more, again without success. Peega waits in the road for Washington and Gogo. In the distance, he hears a shot. A short while later the two men scramble into the car. They heard the shot too, they say. It wasn't them.

At this point in the interrogation, Peega contradicts himself. Apparently referring to the first incursion, he tells Lubbe: 'The first time I took a shot at a young rhino. They were three and I tried to shoot the young one for maybe I will get some shots at the other. I think I missed.'

The men aren't deterred by their failures. In December they travel to a new target, in Thabazimbi. Again they enter a game farm at night and walk to a waterhole, where they wait in vain for rhinos. Eventually they give up. Peega hefts the .303 over his shoulder and they hike to another waterhole, where he and Washington fall into fitful sleep. Gogo sets off on his own. It is early morning when Washington and Peega are startled awake by a gunshot. They follow the sound until they find Gogo.

'Gogo told us that he had shot a small rhino ... Washington cut the two horns with an axe. We went out of the farm and was [sic] picked up on the road,' Peega says.

Later that day, in a hotel room in Gold Reef City, the men meet to divide the spoils. Ignatius is also present. He calls himself Igi. He's the intermediary between the poachers and a Chinese man in Cape Town, who flies up to Johannesburg to collect the horns. Igi tells the men that they 'could get better money if we had a bigger rhino horn'. Peega, Washington and Gogo each receive R10 000 for their efforts.

Their next foray takes them into the Kruger National Park. Peega, who accompanies them to Phalaborwa, spends the night carousing with old army buddies. Washington heads off to meet someone he knows can help. Rodgers Mathebula works in the park as a traffic warden. He has an insider's knowledge of its byways and pathways. With Washington in tow, he crosses through the Letaba Ranch to the north of the town and into the Kruger. They spend the night there looking for rhinos, but eventually give up and leave empty-handed in the early hours of the morning.

Vaalwater is next. Peega describes meeting Baloi at a 'tin house' in the 'location'.

'Me and Washington slept in the car until early light. Two persons went with me and Washington in an easterly direction. The one guy told us to stop. Baloi drove the car away. Me, Washington and another guy with [an] AK-47 rifle went into a game farm. I carried the .303 rifle with the telescope. Washington carried the axe.

'We didn't see any rhino and we left. We were picked up by the same Baloi. In Vaalwater we dropped Baloi and the other guy. Me and Washington travelled back in the direction of Thabazimbi. On the way we saw a police car that told us to stop. I was arrested.'

———

16 January 2009

The SAPS announces the arrests. Eleven suspects have been charged 'in connection with the poaching of black and white rhino', national police spokesman Colonel Vish Naidoo says in a statement. They include five Mozambicans, three Chinese nationals, two South Africans and one person of 'unknown nationality'. Two AK-47s, four .303 rifles and R16 000 in cash have been seized. The Chinese suspects are two Cape Town–based 'business-men', Jianwei Wu and Zhongda Yu, and a medical doctor from Bruma Lake in Johannesburg, Wei Guan Hu. The Mozambicans include Joshua and Sarafina Baloi, Joe Mashaba and Washington Hlongwane.

Peega's name is listed, but police say nothing about his links to SARS.

The statement quotes the police's head of detectives, Commissioner Ray Lalla: 'The police members, in close co-operation with SANParks, spent days and nights – even Christmas Day – tracking these suspects and have put their all into ensuring that those responsible for the killing of these beautiful creatures for blood money were brought before the courts.'

Details about the investigation begin to trickle out. Peega's undoing, it turns out, was the arrest of Mathebula, the Kruger traffic warden, on 12 December 2008, two weeks before the ill-fated Vaalwater trip. He'd been picked up after helping two poachers gain access to the park to look for rhinos. He'd dropped them off to conduct a recce near the park's Phalaborwa Gate, with five loaves of bread and eight litres of Coca-Cola to sustain them. Game wardens found the men hiding in the veld a day later and arrested them. They ratted on Mathebula, who, in turn, implicated Washington and Peega. Investigators found a .303 rifle in Mathebula's possession.

After the arrest of Peega, Washington and the others, the police set a trap for the Chinese buyers at Bruma Lake. It is a simple buy-bust operation. Undercover cops lure the men to a meeting. Four rhino horns, weighing twelve kilograms, are sold to the Chinese for R360 000. Surveillance teams capture everything on camera. Police move in and arrest the men. They find a cellphone, which is used to send photographs of rhino horns to prospective dealers in Hong Kong.

On 9 February, Wu pleads guilty to two counts of illegally receiving and possessing rhino horns. He is sentenced to a R20 000 fine or three years' imprisonment. He is given a further five-year suspended sentence and ordered to leave South Africa. The other Chinese are released on bail of R100 000 and R200 000 respectively and warned to appear in court.

Beeld newspaper describes it as the biggest rhino horn case ever brought to book in South Africa. According to the charge sheet, it involves fifty rhino horns worth an estimated R20 million on the local black market.

———

Peega is released on R20 000 bail. He returns to work. SARS removes him from the unit and transfers him to head office in Pretoria pending a disciplinary inquiry. He is still required to report for duty each day, but begins arriving for work later and later. He is given a written warning. It's the final straw.

On 10 February 2009, at 10 a.m., Peega loudly tells colleagues he's going to 'expose' SARS. His angry threats are reported to his managers. A short while later, Peega's boss gets a call from his lawyer, Elise Swanepoel, who suggests that if SARS is prepared to pay Peega a year's salary as severance, he'll go quietly. Failing that, he intends approaching 'the newspapers'. The SARS man is outraged. It is tantamount to extortion. He tells the lawyer that he regards her approaches as 'highly unethical'.

At a meeting with the lawyer later that day, Peega's boss and another manager remind her of the secrecy oath Peega has signed and suggest that he bear the safety of his colleagues – who are investigating organised crime – in mind. Should he carry out his threat, SARS requests that they be given time to put contingency plans in place to protect the operatives Peega plans to betray. Swanepoel is non-committal. She is merely acting on the instructions of her client, she says.

Peega's disciplinary hearing is held over three days and ends on April Fools' Day 2009. Not once during the hearing or his subsequent appeal against his dismissal does he claim that he was part of a 'sting operation' targeting rhino poachers.

Details also begin to emerge of Peega's uncomfortable proximity to senior politicians, most notably former ANCYL president Fikile Mbalula, a member of the ruling party's national executive committee and later a cabinet minister. Peega repeatedly boasted to colleagues that he knew Mbalula from 'days long before I joined SARS'.

On one occasion, in August 2008, Peega was in Durban, along with five colleagues, carrying out investigations into the trafficking of drugs, abalone and pirate DVDs. They were checked in at the Hilton Hotel. One day, in the lobby, Peega 'bumped' into Mbalula. While the other members of the team went to their rooms, Peega lingered behind, huddled in conversation with Mbalula.

Peega seemed to make a habit of running into senior ANC figures. At Durban airport, while standing in a queue at the Avis rental desk, he spotted Tony Yengeni, a controversial ANC national executive committee member and convicted fraudster who was once dubbed the 'Gucci socialist' for his taste in fine clothing and flashy cars. Peega approached Yengeni and they spoke for a bit. He then introduced Yengeni to his colleagues.

During the Durban trip, Peega also arranged a tour of the Hilton Hotel's presidential suite for his colleagues. He boasted that President Jacob Zuma was staying there at the time, but that he had a contact in security personnel who could get them into the rooms.

In June 2009, Peega is unceremoniously dismissed from SARS. But he isn't finished with them yet.

––––––––––

2 *March 2012*

Peega is emphatic. The meeting is off. I'd called him two days earlier, explaining that I wanted to hear his story. He seemed keen to talk and we'd arranged to meet in Soweto.

At 9.02 a.m. on the day of the meeting, my phone buzzes. It is a rambling text message from Peega, reproduced verbatim below:

> Im in a meeting with my family over our meeting and since im still not employed talking to journos wil tarnish my name further so they suggest i cancel all engagements with the media as it has brought enough stress in the past and i might remain unemployable,so to respect their wish i will humbly cancel the meeting so i can concentrate on clearing my name and im aware that this statement will b used against me,tnx.

I push him for more.

> [D]espite al evidence that could not be contested by sars i was still nailed, i've accepted my fate n doin my best to move on, its hard bt im enduring, im sorry i cant be of help again.

I send him another SMS, asking if – as he has claimed – his confession to

Lubbe was coerced. 'Honestly i stil have med reports of what i went thru while tortured ...'

Would he send me the report? I ask. 'Sir im already talkin to u which is against my families wishes,lets nt push it, lets leave it to rest, my loss of everything is enough, no more.'

Peega, it seems, has a lot to hide.

―――――――

In intelligence circles, 'information peddlers' are regarded with contempt. They are the whores of the spook's trade – operating on the fringes, disseminating smears and shopping half-truths that contain just enough fact to give them a modicum of credence. But in the ugly succession battles that have become a hallmark of the ANC under Zuma, peddlers are useful puppets.

In a March 2012 editorial, *Mail & Guardian* editor Nic Dawes observed that if Zuma's tenure as president had taught South Africans anything, it was that power is contested 'not at the ballot box or in the public sphere, but in the spook-haunted corridors of the secret state'. Smears and conspiracies have become the 'universal solvent for scandal'.

In the wake of his dismissal, Peega becomes just such a peddler. He forms a bond with a loose grouping of disgraced SARS and intelligence operatives, some of whom have been dismissed for fraud or resigned their posts in the face of disciplinary hearings. He pesters his former teammates, claiming he is investigating SARS and now works for the presidency. He tries to recruit them as informants and coerce them into providing him with affidavits implicating SARS in a range of illegal activities.

They reject his advances. He becomes abusive and angry. He and – it seems evident – the coterie of spooks surrounding him, try at first to extort money from SARS. Their threats, some of them contained in emails, are explicit. If the Receiver plays ball, they'll keep their mouths shut. If not, they will release a damaging 'dossier' to the press.

Journalists love the word 'dossier'. Not only does it look good in a headline, but it has come to denote something both weighty and secretive. It is not merely a reference to a bundle of documents, but a portent to revelations of deeds both dark and dastardly. A great number of dossiers have been shopped to newspapers in South Africa in recent years. Most have been tendentious, badly written smears.

There was the 2003 dossier which suggested that National Prosecuting Authority head Bulelani Ngcuka – the man who had pursued allegations of corruption levelled against Zuma – had 'most probably' been an apartheid spy, agent RS452. The claims fell apart when the real agent RS452, Vanessa Brereton, confessed. Then, in 2006, came the notorious 'Special Browse Mole Report', created by an investigator in the now-defunct Scorpions investigations unit, which outlined rumours that the Angolan intelligence establishment planned to covertly support Zuma in his bid for the presidency. It, too, was rubbished.

More recently, in 2011, a 'top-secret' dossier emerged after the arrest of disgraced police Crime Intelligence boss Richard Mdluli, which attempted to link the then national police commissioner, Bheki Cele, and senior ANC politicians, including human settlements minister Tokyo Sexwale, to a plot to unseat Zuma.

In November 2009, Peega's dossier is leaked to a newspaper. A journalist shows a copy to SARS. Among the documents is a report that details the activities of a shadowy intelligence unit within SARS, which purportedly targeted key Zuma allies and supporters. It claims that the unit was 'personally' set up by SARS boss Pravin Gordhan, later the Minister of Finance in the Zuma cabinet. Some of the 'revelations' contained in the report read as follows:

> Post Polokwane we were given projects and subjects named as tax offenders, but on close inspection we realised that the concerned targets were JZ [Jacob Zuma] sympathisers or what came to be known as friends of JZ. [S]ubjects of interest were mostly in Gauteng and [Kwa-Zulu-Natal] provinces and internally in SARS especially if perceived to be aligned to JZ. [W]hen the black members objected to the merit and reason for the investigation they would not be paid their allowances or either redirected to more hostile operations but operations still carry on with the exclusion of black foot soldiers …

Operations would involve stealing of mail from residences (dumpster diving), interception of emails, mobile and landlines, extraction of bank statements, installing of tracker systems on vehicles and posing as loitters [sic] around the premises while monitoring movements via hidden cameras even using sound enhancers to listen to the conversation of our targets.

[It is quite evident that SARS was playing a dirty and dangerous game, the issue was WHY are the state resources being abused in such a dirty way? ... Some of us threatened to go public with the units [sic] activities and were threatened with disclosure clauses, all of a sudden approvals of only legitimate cases were made available to us as members and the direction changed to investigating counterfeit and textile industry ... Someone must stop this nonsense otherwise the security of the country is threatened ...]

Peega had clearly been watching too many bad spy movies. The document is littered with references to 'honey traps', 'bugging', 'cryptology', 'covet [sic] tactics' and 'counter-intelligence'. SARS compiles a fourteen-page briefing document on the dossier. Peega's claims are all too easy to refute.

The journalist shelves the story, for now. SARS reports the dossier to police and intelligence agencies. In the weeks and months that follow, various versions of it will crop up again and again.

---

22 February 2010

Julius Malema, president of the African National Congress Youth League, is on the defensive. Damaging details about the sources of his wealth have begun to emerge. The most damning revelations have appeared in both *City Press* and the *Sunday Times*. The newspapers conducted separate investigations, but came to similar conclusions: Malema's opulent lifestyle is being bankrolled by a string of lucrative government contracts.

One Malema-linked company had reportedly benefitted from government tenders worth R140 million over the previous two years. There were also questions about the lavishly appointed R3.6-million house Malema had bought in Sandton in 2009. It would later emerge that he had paid more than half the purchase price in cash. Then there is his unashamed taste for designer clothes, R250 000 Breitling watches, bottles of Moët & Chandon champagne and fast cars. How can he afford it all on a reported salary of just R25 000 a month? Malema has long positioned himself as a 'revolutionary' struggling for the poorest of the poor. The lie is wearing thin.

Malema – who is frequently referred to in newspapers, often mockingly, by his nickname 'Juju' – is the *enfant terrible* of South African politics. His role as kingmaker during the ANC's 2007 Polokwane conference – which marked the end of the Thabo Mbeki era and the beginning of Zuma's ascent to power – cemented his position in the party ... for a while, at least.

In a stagnant newspaper market, editors love him. With every bombastic outburst and every racist, sexist and hypocritical statement, Malema sells papers. His ability to court controversy is unrivalled. For many whites, he is the embodiment of their worst fears and their worst and most racist prejudices of black Africa. It is easy to dismiss him as a buffoonish clown, and many do.

But Malema is shrewder than that. With his brand of pseudo-communist rhetoric, he taps into the very real frustrations and anger of millions of black South Africans living in grinding poverty in appalling conditions that have changed little since the advent of democracy.

When cornered about his lifestyle, Malema resorts to bluster. Rhetoric, not facts, is his retort to criticism. Critics are labelled counter-revolutionaries, colonialists, racists and even – as in one memorable incident involving an unfortunate BBC hack – 'bloody agents'. Once, when I interviewed him, he answered a question he didn't like with an attack. 'Let me tell you, my friend, I defeated you and your apartheid regime and I will conquer you again, once and for all!' He then launched into a tirade against my forefathers, claiming he had 'defeated' them too. (Malema was thirteen when South Africa's first democratic elections were held in 1994.)

At a hastily convened press conference in the lobby of the ANC's head-quarters in Luthuli House, Malema lashes out at the two Sunday newspapers, saying he takes 'serious exception for being audited by media institutions through spreading of lies and rumour ... that I have millions [of rands]. [I]t puts both me and my family in danger as criminals might believe the lies and resort to criminal victimisation against myself and my family with the hope that I have money.'

But he doesn't stop there. The following day, during an interview on state radio station SAfm, Malema drops his bombshell. He and other senior ANC figures loyal to Zuma are the targets of a vicious smear campaign by SARS. He claims he has been given an 'intelligence dossier' to prove it.

> We have got a document of a list of people ... who must be targeted. These people are still called Zuma people.
>
> They [the unnamed intelligence agents who handed him the dossier] found this to be very unacceptable and they thought they needed to alert us. We had to take it to the police to verify it, and so far we are satisfied with the investigation ... The preliminary report shows that this is an authentic document that deserves to be taken seriously. I told the president [Zuma], 'I will give you that report before I take it anywhere else.'
>
> There are still concerted efforts to try and discredit the leadership of the ANC and particularly those who are seen in the frontline in defence of President Zuma. We are dealing with a concoction, a mix masala of a political environment which is polluted, and people who have resorted to dirty tricks.

Malema continues his fight-back campaign on the radio station Metro FM, saying the document had been delivered to his office by 'anonymous fellows' and contains a 'long list of our names. There were instructions to people in SARS to investigate [me] ... deputy police minister Fikile Mbalula and [Zuma's spokesman] Zizi Kodwa'.

That night, on national television, Malema goes further, saying the document was compiled by 'very senior people in SARS, very senior management, some of them in cabinet today'. It is clearly a veiled reference to Gordhan.

SARS hits back. Spokesman Adrian Lackay tells the *Star*: 'SARS has a proud record of integrity and applies the law with fairness, with impartiality and equally to the affairs of all taxpayers.'

In a story headlined: 'Malema Spy Saga Grows – "Hit list" aimed at Zuma backers created by fired SARS man', the newspaper reveals that Peega had approached them with the dossier in 2009. In an interview, he confirms that the document Malema is referring to is his. He maintains that he stands by the contents.

'I'm not backing off. That's why I want SARS to confront me in public to say this document is not authentic. I'm 200 per cent behind it.' Peega says his trial for rhino poaching has been subjected to a number of postponements, adding that he had been part of a sting operation and was not a poacher.

———

In March, ANCYL spokesman Floyd Shivambu ups the ante when he tries to peddle a file containing personal information about the *City Press* journalist Dumisane Lubisi, who co-wrote the Malema exposé, to reporters. It includes illegally obtained information about Lubisi's bank accounts and details of his salary, cars and property. In a statement, Shivambu accuses Lubisi of 'tax fraud, money-laundering and tendering'. Once again it is an ill-founded smear, and nineteen political reporters lodge a formal complaint against Shivambu with the secretary-general of the ANC, citing his efforts to intimidate Lubisi. The Communication Workers Union also wades into the spat, saying it is 'of the view that the conduct of comrade Floyd is a ghost resurrection of Hitler's Nazi Germany propagandist Josef Goebbels'.

Lubisi's next story reveals that 'aggrieved former government employees' are 'spying on "enemies"' of the Youth League and identifies 'one of the key figures in this shadowy business' as Michael Peega.

'Peega is one of the people looking for confidential information about journalists and politicians who are critical of Malema's lifestyle and activity ... Peega and others apparently worked from plush offices of the Youth League's investment company, Lembede Investment Holdings, and had laptops, 3G connections and money available to gather information.' Peega dismisses the allegations as 'bullshit' and says: 'I am currently unemployed and have not collected any intelligence information from anyone.'

A few days later, on 23 March 2010, *Business Day* publishes reports that

Peega once 'moonlighted as a bodyguard' for Mbalula when he was president of the Youth League.

The report cites affidavits lodged with police that outline details of Peega's work for Mbalula. This included driving Mbalula, Malema and Kodwa to a luxury resort in Limpopo, and transporting the trio to the Durban July horse race in KwaZulu-Natal. Peega denied that he had ever worked for the Youth League, and Malema said that while he knew Peega, he did not employ him. Mbalula said he had 'no comment at this stage'.

The following week, police make a shocking announcement. Key evidence in Peega's case, as well as R500 000 and a cellphone that was seized when he was arrested, had been stolen from a locked police safe in the Organised Crime Unit offices.

Over the next eighteen months there will be further revelations about Malema's financial affairs. Then, in July 2011, *City Press* discloses that Malema is the sole trustee of a 'secret family trust'. The newspaper reports that the trust, named after Malema's five-year-old son, 'may explain how he has been bankrolling his lavish lifestyle'. 'Thousands of rands' are paid into the trust account on a regular basis, unnamed sources are quoted as saying. Later it emerges that in 2010 alone, more than R3 million was deposited into the trust.

Malema calls yet another press conference. He says it is 'nobody's business' where his money comes from. He is not answerable to the media, he says. 'I'm answerable to law enforcement agencies. If SARS comes it is absolutely no problem. I will give them an answer. If the Hawks come, I'll give them an answer.'

Amid a growing chorus of calls for the taxman to investigate Malema's financial affairs, SARS spokesman Adrian Lackay says that the revenue service will consider doing so and that various allegations about the sources of Malema's wealth amounted to 'suspicious activity reports', which, by law, have to be investigated.

———

22 August 2011

'Poaching dockets go missing', screams the front-page headline of the *Star*.

'The rhino-poaching dockets against the man who penned ANC Youth League president Julius Malema's explosive "intelligence" document last year appear to have vanished.

'The *Star* understands that the National Prosecuting Authority has started an urgent investigation into their disappearance, while the man at the centre of the charges – Michael Peega – continues with his life …

'On 6 August 2009, the case was assigned to a warrant officer at the Polokwane Organised Crime Unit … But no further entries are recorded on CAS, the police's filing system.' The case itself is withdrawn.

'There was a rumour the dockets had been sold,' the state prosecutor handling the case, Advocate Ansie Venter, tells me. 'That was my fear too, but they were never sold.' The investigating officer handling the case had resigned from the police, she says. The files were eventually found among a pile of other documents in a cupboard in his office. The exhibits stolen from the police safe have never been recovered. At the time of writing, the case against Peega had been placed back on the court roll and was set to proceed.

In May 2012, I give Malema a call on his cellphone. It has been a month since the ANC finally upheld a decision to expel him from the party. He had been accused of 'sowing division' within its ranks and bringing the party into disrepute. SARS has hit him with a reported R10-million tax bill. He tells *City Press* that his detractors have 'unleashed all state agencies against me because they want to silence me'. He seems a little less combative than I remember. I ask him about his relationship with Peega.

'I never received any information from him,' Malema claims. I suggest that Peega is the most likely source for the 'intelligence dossier'.

'You can try any trick, you will never succeed with me,' Malema responds. It is a familiar retort. He continues: 'I knew him as helping Mr Mbalula, but never got anything from him. I don't know this man. I don't know what he does. I have no background on him, he never worked for me, he never gave me that information.'

There's a pause. Then he adds: 'Maybe he gave the information to other people and they gave it to me. I don't know.'

11

Poacher's Moon

Two mounds of earth under the dead limbs of a marula tree mark the spot where Dario Zitha and his friend, Maqombisi Mongwe, are buried. Spiny branches of sekelbos cover the graves as protection from scavengers. Strewn among the branches are some of the dead men's possessions: Dario's toothbrush, a used tube of Colgate toothpaste and a blue rucksack; Maqombisi's empty wallet, a battered ashtray, and pieces of green, pink and blue chalk. A few compact discs – among them a compilation of Irish country music – glint in the sun. Scratches criss-cross the surfaces.

Dario, the eldest of five brothers, was thirty-eight when he died. He was his family's 'breadwinner' and a father of three. Maqombisi was in his mid-thirties, also married, also described as a 'breadwinner'. He loved music, they say.

A dirt road leads from the graveyard to Canhane, the tiny village south of Lake Massingir in Mozambique's Gaza Province, where the two men spent their lives. The villagers say they left for 'the bush' one day in September 2011. A week later they were returned home in cheap pine coffins with rope handles. The men saw the pale corpses – drained of blood – and the gaping wounds left by the high-velocity bullets that had torn through them. Dario's youngest brother, Batista, twenty-three, who had accompanied them, was under police guard in a South African hospital. He had been shot in the legs.

A brief statement, issued on 9 September 2011 by the corporate communications department of SANParks, provides a terse record of their deaths. 'A joint operation consisting of … SANParks rangers and the South African National Defence Force, yesterday at [Houtboschrand], Kruger National Park, resulted in a shoot-out which led to two suspected poachers being fatally wounded and the third wounded – under police guard in hospital [*sic*]. A member of the SANDF also sustained wounds to the leg and is currently receiving medical attention and is in a stable condition. Two rifles, an AK-47 and a .416 hunting rifle, were discovered at the scene. Investigations are currently under way.'

Rey Thakhuli, the SANParks general manager for 'media, events and stakeholder relations', is quoted in a news report as saying that 'a sweep of the area revealed no animal carcasses or injured animals'.

———

In the shade of another tree, her legs folded under her on a grass mat, Dario's mother, Amelia Makuvela, works at a makeshift loom with perforated stones serving as weights to stretch the threads. A white headscarf covers her hair. Her blouse is spotless, but frayed with age and torn at the back. Her home – a hut made of rough-hewn wood and plastered with orange mud – is situated a short distance away.

Nearby is a modern construction with ornate burglar bars, lace curtains, a *stoep*, and grey, unfinished cement walls. It stands apart from most of the other wood, mud and thatch homes that are typical of the village. A motorcycle covered with plastic sheeting and a grubby red windbreaker leans against a wall. It is the house Dario was building when he died. His widow lives there now, with their two young sons. Dario's daughter has been sent to South Africa to stay with relatives.

Mrs Makuvela doesn't smile. She's reluctant to discuss her sons with strangers. Dario's brother, Albert, dressed in a green workman's overall, takes a seat in the dirt beside her. His sister, Lurdes, sits on her mother's left. The visitors are given white plastic chairs to sit on. The village headman's son makes the introductions. In the background, a bored young boy in a torn blue T-shirt and shorts hacks at bushes with a rusted metal bar. A cock crows. Another answers in the distance. Chickens scratch listlessly in the dust. A village cur, ribs showing through skin and fur, ambles past. Two young girls carrying muddy plastic buckets of water stop for a moment and stare at the strangers.

What happened to Dario? Why was he killed? The family is in denial and talks of 'rumours'. Nobody wants to speak ill of the dead. Albert answers. 'There are rumours that he was killed by rangers in South Africa, that he was poaching ... but I don't know if that's true. I was staying in South Africa when he died. I think he was on his way to look for a job in South Africa.

'When the body came back, it was covered, but you could still look at the face. He had a big wound in the back of his head and a smaller one in front. The head was completely open at the back. He was also shot in the groin and chest. His one arm looked like it had been chopped where it was shot.'

He claims that police in South Africa did not investigate the circumstances of the shooting. No post-mortem was conducted. No inquest was held. (Police records show that an inquest docket was opened on that date in connection with an incident in Houtboschrand, but, oddly, its status is classed as 'undetected', meaning there was insufficient evidence to proceed with an investigation. The dead are identified as Mozambican, but their names are listed as 'unknown'.)

Perhaps Dario was simply crossing the park to find work or to visit him in Johannesburg, Albert speculates. Nobody knows. 'Once you cross the border, whether you have a firearm or not, whether you're a poacher or not, they will shoot you. No warning.'

Mrs Makuvela seems less certain of her eldest son's innocence. She refuses to talk about him. Later, when Albert shows me a photograph of Dario and passes it to her, she shakes her head and refuses to take it.

'My worry now is for the young boy,' she says. 'Batista is very young and he doesn't know anything. His brother [Dario] took him with him to Kruger and put him where he is now. Batista was shot in the legs and taken to hospital by police.'

She travelled to the South African town of Komatipoort for Batista's trial. Her eyes redden with tears as she speaks. In court, 'the man who caught them was called'.

'He said they saw the footprints where they crossed the border and followed them. They found the three men where they were sleeping. One of them woke up and shouted, "Let's run." They started running and the rangers shot them. The young boy [Batista] wasn't carrying anything, but next to him on the ground they found an axe. They also found two firearms with the others, but only one was a danger.'

Were the brothers poaching? Like Albert, she speaks of 'rumours'. 'The rumours say they went to Kruger to go poaching. I don't know why they were really there. [Batista] won't explain it to me now.'

Months later, I discover from police that Batista had been convicted on poaching-related charges and sentenced to twelve months' imprisonment or a fine of R5 000. A further three-year jail term was conditionally suspended for five years.

The residents of Canhane and the surrounding villages view the Kruger National Park – which lies about thirty kilometres to the west – as a dangerous obstacle. It stands between them and the promise of jobs and money in South Africa. Passports are difficult and expensive to obtain. The wheels of Mozambique's corrupt bureaucracy turn at a snail's pace unless they are greased with cash. For many – particularly those eking out a living below the breadline – there is little choice but to risk the predators, rangers and soldiers. For them, the promised rewards outweigh the risks. Every year people leave for the bush and vanish. Some drown, others are taken by animals. Dozens – some say hundreds – are killed by lions and crocodiles. There are whispered stories of a man-eating pride that lies in wait at full moon to pick off stragglers.

Albert, who found work as a builder in Soweto, near Johannesburg, used to brave the myriad invisible pathways through the bush, but now he is one of the lucky ones – he has a passport. 'It is difficult to get work here in Canhane. There are no jobs. You have to go to South Africa to earn money. There are also no jobs in Kruger for us, so we just pass through. There is no benefit from Kruger for us here. Inside Kruger there are dangerous animals. Sometimes we meet lions on our way, but we take the risk because we can't survive here. Life is very hard in the village and we don't have money to feed our families. But we know that if we can just cross the border and pass the animals, we can find a job in South Africa and support, clothe and feed [our families].'

The treacherous journey through the Kruger offers many a stark choice: why risk being torn apart by animals or arrested or shot simply to earn a pittance in Johannesburg when you can take the same risks for a much greater reward? In a good month, Albert earns R3 000. By contrast, a rhino poacher can pocket anything between R15 000 and R80 000 for a set of horns. For young men like Dario and Maqombisi, the temptation must be overwhelming.

At least two other poachers lie buried under the marula and mopane trees in Canhane's cemetery. And locals say a dozen more from the town of Massingir and the surrounding villages have been shot and killed in the Kruger over the past two years. Many have been arrested. The names of some of the dead are recorded in the files at the police station situated inside Kruger's main camp, Skukuza. Nearly half a dozen are from Massingir: Valoyi Mongwe – killed near the Houtboschrand ranger camp on 16 August 2011; 'Joao' – shot dead, also near Houtboschrand, on 22 November 2011; Humino Chico, Christo Jose and Jerson Chauke – shot and killed in the Nwanetsi area on 11 March 2012.

Yet there appears to be no shortage of takers prepared to risk everything for a few kilograms of rhino horn. The money-men, who come from Maputo or from Chokwe, a district capital to the south-east, with their promises of guns and cash, don't have to look far for recruits. It is here, in villages like Canhane, that the war on rhino poachers is being lost.

———

A few kilometres south of the Mozambican border, two hulking shapes lie motionless in the veld. It is windless and oddly silent but for the angry buzzing of flies. The stench is unbearable. The vultures have been here, the familiar white lines of their excrement streaking the hides of the two carcasses. It is a rhino cow and her calf. The horns are gone. Only tattered flesh remains. A piece of white bone, picked clean by scavengers, juts obscenely from one of the calf's hind legs. Perhaps the calf was killed as it harried the poachers hacking away at its mother's head. More likely, it was killed for what little horn it did have.

The area around the carcasses has been cordoned off with yellow police tape. Square flaps of skin have been cut into the animals' sides and peeled back to reveal ribcages, mangled intestines and a seething mass of maggots. The bullets that killed the rhinos have been removed to be compared with others, and samples of tissue have been sent for DNA analysis. If the horns are ever recovered, a match will be crucial to obtain a conviction.

Investigators have scoured the ground for clues: spent shell casings, cigarette butts, plastic wrappers, footprints, tracks, bloodstains – any scraps of evidence that will lead them to the killers. Air support is called in. Rangers, soldiers, police and trackers fan out. It is a race to stop the poachers before they make the safety of Mozambique.

'The line of poachers to our border is never going to end,' Ken Maggs, the head of SANParks's environmental crime investigations unit, says bluntly. 'Not only is the price of horn going up exponentially, but given the unemployment levels in Mozambique and South Africa, there is no limit to the number of people who are going to come across.'

Maggs has worked in South Africa's national parks for the past twenty-five years. He knows more about poachers and their methods than most other investigators in South Africa. It was Maggs who warned in 1994 that 'sufficient evidence exists to indicate that an intensified onslaught on the elephant and rhino populations is imminent'.

Maggs is fifty-seven, with close-cropped hair that is rapidly turning white and an intensity of expression that gives him a passing resemblance to a younger, fitter Dennis Hopper. He rarely allows himself to be photographed. 'I, for one, stay out of the limelight,' he says. 'This is a serious business and there are serious risks.' People who have dealt with Maggs describe him as dedicated, efficient, shrewd, manipulative and adept at navigating the fickle political currents of SANParks. He can also be refreshingly frank, which is probably why his employers don't allow him to speak to the media too often. In my case, it took several months of emails and phone calls before the SANParks spin doctors grudgingly acceded to an interview. Maggs seemed surprised that they had.

He took over command of Kruger's anti-poaching unit in 1994. It was a one-man operation based at Skukuza with the huge task of co-ordinating anti-poaching operations and intelligence gathering. Over the next decade, the unit gradually grew in size, eventually expanding operations to the Eastern and Western Cape, Gauteng and Mpumalanga.

The bulk of the unit's work is centred around the Kruger. The park is immense – the size of the state of Israel. Maggs uses the United States–Mexican border, and the vast amounts of money, resources and manpower that the US government has poured into stopping thousands of illegal immigrants from slipping through the 'rat holes' in the fence line, as an example. Despite this, they keep coming.

'People say we should put up a big fence. Look at the US–Mexican border. Are they getting on top of it? We have a fairly remote 400-kilometre border with Mozambique. A fence is not going to stop anyone. If there's a will, there's a way. All a fence is going to do is give you a feeling of false security.'

It is a view that environmental officials initially didn't heed. In January 2012, environment minister Edna Molewa announced that talks were taking place with the Department of Public Works about repairing and electrifying a 150-kilometre strip of border fence between the Kruger and Mozambique. It would cost between R250 million and R400 million to erect and a further R100 million a year to maintain.

The plan was controversial for another reason. The original fence – a remnant of apartheid – had been erected in 1975. It had carried a lethal 3 300-volt, one-amp current and was responsible for more deaths over a three-year period than the Berlin Wall in its twenty-eight-year history. Official SADF statistics suggested that eighty-nine people had died on the fence between August 1986 and August 1989. In reality, the numbers were probably closer to 200 a year.

The fence was switched over to 'non-lethal alarm mode' in 1990. In 2002, sections were torn down to allow for the creation of the Great Limpopo Transfrontier Park, which straddles the South African, Mozambican and Zimbabwean borders. Molewa's officials were careful to stress that if the fence was to be electrified again it would carry a non-lethal current and would serve mainly as an 'early warning system'.

Three months later, Molewa finally conceded that the fence would be 'too expensive and difficult' to maintain. The plan was scrapped. Instead, the department would explore the creation of 'buffer zones' between the park and Mozambique.

I ask Maggs about the deaths of suspected poachers in the Kruger. 'Last year, we killed twenty-one people,' he says matter-of-factly. 'This year, it is about seven so far. Shooting people doesn't solve the problem at all. But you have to be aggressive.'

It is a view shared by Bruce Leslie, a senior special-operations ranger in the park. 'Unfortunately people will die because of the nature of war,' he says. 'But I suppose the brutality of it actually is being lost on me at the moment. I think to survive the emotional side of things, one gets hardened. It is like seeing dead poachers now. I've seen enough this year not to worry about them any more.'

Maggs bridles at suggestions that Kruger is implementing an unofficial 'shoot-to-kill' policy and that immigrants trying to make their way across the park are being caught in the crossfire.

'All of the guys shot in the park have been in armed conflict. We can't just go and shoot somebody for the sake of shooting somebody. We are bound by laws, whereas the poachers are bound by no rules. A poacher can come in, see one of my guys and kill him. If he gets away with it, he gets away with it. These are armed aggressors coming across our border. Nobody asked a Mozambican to come across.

'At any one time there are ten to fifteen groups of poachers operating in the park in different areas, all armed with a multitude of weapons. They can come in a group of five, armed with three weapons, and engage the rangers who – funnily enough – also have families and also live in communities and will be as sorely missed by their families and communities as the poachers are by theirs. We've had hundreds of thousands of people crossing the border from Mozambique into Kruger, and there is certainly no trend of us going out of our way to shoot people. The refugees who come through the park don't come through armed. So if you're coming through with an AK-47, what exactly is it that you're wanting to do?'

At the time of my trip to Mozambique, five months into 2012, the Kruger had lost 127 of the 210 rhino recorded to have been poached in South Africa so far that year. In 2011, 252 rhino were killed in the park – more than half of the 448 rhinos poached that year. Figures for the previous year are similarly disturbing: 146 of the 333 rhinos killed for their horns were poached in Kruger.

'This is where the war is being fought,' Maggs says. 'This is where you can physically see it, where all the stats are generated. This is where you have people, armed to the teeth like Rambo, and the reaction teams fighting poachers.' He calls it the 'glamour side', a good-versus-evil struggle that makes for easy heroes and simplistic headlines. But of equal importance, he says, is the silent war, the 'longer-term, undercover and infiltration operations that are far removed from the poacher with a gun in Kruger'.

'We need to be working aggressively at every level,' Maggs says. 'You can't put all your resources into one thing and then neglect the others. You can't expect to win the war if you're only fighting on one level. Environmental crime, like the trade in abalone, elephant ivory and rhino horn, has become a lot more organised. Five years ago, if you were a poacher and you had a bit of understanding that there was a possible market for rhino horn, you would shoot a rhino and sit on the horn until you could sell it. The longer you sat on it and tried to sell it, the more likely it was that you would be detected and intercepted.

'Today there are really large amounts of money driving the trade and the conduits are very slick. If a rhino is shot at 4 a.m. in Kruger, the horns are in Gauteng or across the border by late morning ... The criminals will always be one step ahead, because they are not governed by any rules other than to secure what they need to get and secure the money they require.'

Maggs, who says he remains an 'eternal optimist', claims that 'this war will be won by a few highly dedicated, highly motivated individuals'.

'I know they're out there, because I work with them every day. They are determined to make a difference and there are no hidden agendas.'

But despite these efforts, the clumsy attempts of the official spin doctors to control the flow of information about the poaching crisis has created a perception, rightly or wrongly, that hidden agendas do, indeed, exist. As the poaching situation has worsened, SANParks officials – many of whom once spoke openly to journalists – were muzzled. The spin doctors became the gatekeepers.

In March 2012, SANParks abruptly announced that 'all matters relating to rhino poaching' would now be dealt with by the Department of Environmental Affairs. The move was justified on the basis that rhino poaching was a national crisis and not limited to areas controlled by parks authorities.

Gareth Morgan, the opposition Democratic Alliance's shadow minister for environmental affairs, said at the time that this would only create 'unnecessary suspicion'. It did.

Pelham Jones, chairman of the Private Rhino Owners' Association, was quoted in a news report complaining that even prior to the SANParks announcement, there had been 'almost extreme secrecy' surrounding rhino poaching statistics. During parliamentary hearings into the crisis, held in January 2012, Jones said statistics, including information on successful prosecutions, seemed to be 'some kind of state secret' and, despite the fact that rhino poaching was a matter of 'huge international interest', SANParks and the Department of Environmental Affairs were 'not media friendly'. And when it came to their flagship, the Kruger, they were particularly obstructive.

This contempt isn't limited to journalists. During the parliamentary hearings, a senior SANParks official abruptly upped and left the meeting, without excusing himself, in order to avoid missing his flight. The chairman, ANC MP Johnny de Lange, was enraged. 'I take great exception! Now I just have to sit here with egg on my face like a fool 'cause he just walks out of my meeting. Maybe I'm old-fashioned, but there [are] just basic rules of decency. Everyone in this room has [used] their private money to get here ... He must know that I won't be very supportive of any performance bonuses for him ... or any promotions for him.'

SANParks seems to pride itself on its ability to spin the media, even setting corporate 'targets' to measure its success. Its 2011 annual report, for example, lists a series of contentious issues that had made headlines during the financial year. Among them, environmental concerns around controversial plans to build two luxury hotels in Kruger, an 'experimental research fire' in the park in which one rhino was killed and others severely burnt, the mugging of tourists in Cape Town's Table Mountain National Park, accusations of mismanagement and, predictably, the rhino crisis.

The report notes that 'SANParks's handling of these issues resulted in potentially contentious issues receiv[ing] neutral rather than negative media coverage'. As a result, SANParks claimed, it enjoyed '96% neutral/balanced to positive media reporting'. Negative coverage – which was influenced by 'reports on the "alarming" escalation of rhino poaching', the experimental fire and accusations of mismanagement of the Table Mountain National Park – consequently fell well 'within the corporate target of below 10%'.

Both SANParks and the Department of Environmental Affairs appear to have found that the arrests of 'suspected rhino poachers' are a sure-fire way of obtaining 'extreme positive to positive' media coverage. And so, month after month, the figures are trotted out: so many rhinos killed, so many 'suspected' poachers arrested.

A typical statement – this one issued in May 2012 – reads: 'The Kruger National Park lost a disturbing total of 127 rhinos since January 2012. Encouragingly, the number of arrests continues to rise, with arrests for 2012 now totalling 128.'

It's followed with the usual tepid assurances that government views the poaching of 'this national treasure' in a 'very serious light' and that it 'continues to prioritise our fight'. Significantly, these press releases don't refer to the number of successful prosecutions.

There is a good reason for this. South Africa's conviction rates in relation to arrests are notoriously low. Prosecutors have wide discretion to decide which cases have 'reasonable prospects for success' and should be pursued. Jean Redpath, a noted crime and justice researcher, uses an example of a year in which the National Prosecuting Authority received 517 000 case dockets from police. Only 74 000, or 14 per cent of those cases were ultimately prosecuted. The NPA declined to prosecute in more than 300 00 cases (60 per cent) and referred a further 130 000 back to police for further investigation. The NPA, however, routinely boasts conviction rates in excess of 80 per cent. In the case of rhino crimes, it laid claim in August 2012 to an 83 per cent conviction rate. But it is a meaningless figure. The number of successful prosecutions is not measured, as expected, against the number of arrests reported annually. All it does is reflect successes in cases finalised in court in a given year. For instance, the NPA reported that between February

2011 and March 2012, twenty-eight rhino cases were finalised. The 83 per cent conviction rate relates only to those twenty-eight cases, some of which had been dragging on for years through the courts. Bear in mind that 573 people were arrested for rhino-related crimes between January 2010 and July 2012.

A recent US study concluded bluntly that 'any system which pays attention to conviction rates, as opposed to the number of convictions, is liable to abuse'. It argued that a prosecutor with one successful prosecution could boast a '100 per cent conviction rate'.

The battle for access to information that goes beyond the official press releases and statistics is a tedious one. Questions are often ignored or go unanswered for weeks, and sometimes months, at a time, with no explanation as to the delay. In one instance, a simple, uncomplicated query I sent to the department – which required nothing more than a single-line response – took twenty days to be answered. Attempts to gain access to the Kruger National Park to report from the front lines of the 'rhino war' are repeatedly rebuffed. The stories of Maggs and his men have gone largely untold. 'Unfortunately our rangers are not allowed to speak to the media,' is a standard refrain from SANParks.

The only concessions to this rule have been rare, scripted media junkets during which reporters from various newspapers and television and radio stations are flown to the Kruger, taken on a stage-managed tour of a 'rhino crime scene', introduced to a hand-picked group of rangers and given briefings by senior parks officials. It is a textbook public relations exercise: get the hacks in, keep them busy, give them a story and get them out. It is designed to impress. And in most cases it does.

The secrecy around the statistics has led to widespread speculation that the numbers are being manipulated. So far, there is no hard evidence of this, but neither the department nor SANParks has done much to alleviate the rumours. SANParks spin doctors, in particular, are notorious for their defensiveness and arrogance.

In June 2012, for example, I sent Rey Thakhuli, the SANParks spokesman, an email asking him about the discovery of eight rhino carcasses in the Kruger on 16 April that year. The discovery had not been reported in the media and

SANParks had not issued a press release about it, despite the unusually large number. I wanted to know why.

His response was astonishing. He excoriated me for making 'wild statements'. 'The allegations you are making leaves a bitter taste in one's mouth … [I]t tells me that your research is not up to scratch.' He claimed that the only incident in which eight carcasses had been found that year was in January. 'I request that you thoroughly check your facts before making this kind of unfounded and baseless allegation … I see this as a slap ón our face [sic].'

I had checked my facts. The source of my information was a written reply, by the Minister of Environmental Affairs, to questions posed to her in Parliament by the DA. And the original data used to formulate her response – which gave a detailed daily breakdown of the number of carcasses discovered in the Kruger between January and June – had come from SANParks.

I wrote back to Thakhuli and asked him if he was suggesting that the minister was making 'wild' statements. He ignored the email and later referred all further inquiries to the minister.

A week later, Thakhuli sent me a muted email conceding that eight carcasses had indeed been discovered in the Kruger and recorded on the SANParks computer system on 16 April. They had been found in various parts of the park, he said. Four were 'fresh' and four were 'old'. He offered no explanation as to why the media was not informed about the incident, saying only, 'We give weekly updates on statistics and these were given as well.'

For their part, the spokesmen argue that 'reckless' and 'sensationalist' reporting is to blame for the worsening media relations. 'There are too many reporters out there who behave more like environmental activists than journalists,' one spokesman confided. 'And they are not interested in how difficult it is to source some of the information they are looking for. They just want it immediately.'

Sonja Meintjes, head of biodiversity enforcement in the Department of Environmental Affairs, says there are journalists who will 'set you up to make a fool of you. Then we're in trouble. We could lose our jobs.'

Maggs, however, agrees that the public relations battle has been badly handled. 'Absolutely, yeah,' he says. 'Where we've had the opportunity to take people to the coalface and show them what is being done, they've come away suitably shocked, impressively shocked that there are guys out there who are so committed, passionate and dedicated.'

But this image of 'passionate and dedicated' game rangers committed to the fight was sorely tested in February 2012, when close to half the rangers employed by Kruger went on strike. They were reportedly demanding salary and allowance increases of between 78 and 1200 per cent. The strike dragged on for three long months. It was a cynical ploy, capitalising on the rhino crisis. 'It was unheard of,' Maggs says.

Tourists visiting the Kruger were threatened. Staff members who dared to go to work were intimidated. Insiders I spoke to were scathing. Many rangers, they said, particularly those who had been in the park for a number of years, had 'got too comfortable. They're *slapgat*, badly disciplined, don't want to work and don't won't to go out into the bush.' They were a drain on morale.

Frequently, in the course of my research, I heard tales of field rangers flagrantly ignoring orders or going on patrol armed with camping chairs and brightly coloured gas cookers. They'd heat the food on gas stoves, ignoring the fact that the smells and smoke were a dead giveaway to the men they were supposedly hunting. They refused to work overtime. And they would camp close to roadways so that they could quickly head home the moment their shifts ended.

Maggs, who argues that there 'is no better substitute to stopping a poacher than a well-motivated, well-equipped field ranger operating on foot', says, 'It would be crazy for me to sit here and tell you the strike had no effect. If you take away your ears and eyes in the bush for any length of time … it is going to have an impact on detection and reaction.'

During the strike and its immediate aftermath, SANParks steadfastly refused to release figures of the number of rhinos lost. It was only in June 2012, with the minister's release of detailed poaching statistics for Kruger, that the impact became clear. Of the 149 rhinos lost between January and June, 102 were killed during the strike.

Maggs admits that there is some residual damage to levels of trust between park management and rangers. 'You can't one day be up to your armpits in anti-poaching, with a rifle, gun and knives, lying in 40 °C temperatures in the bush and the next day be toyi-toying outside a gate, interfering with tourists and kicking cars, and then expect the trust relationship to build.'

And then there's corruption. 'At the prices being paid for rhino horn, corruption will permeate everything,' Maggs says. 'It is in the police, it's in the army, it's in the park personnel, and we don't believe for one moment that we're exempt. We'll fight it where we can, but we must understand that it will be there. What is important is how you deal with it when you find it. Do you put it under the covers? Where we've discovered corruption, we've acted and will continue to act.'

In February 2012, two field guides, a ranger and a traffic officer were arrested in the Kruger in connection with a poaching incident in which two rhino were killed.

The following month, a former policeman, 'Big Joe' Nyalunga, was arrested in the town of Hazyview in Mpumalanga. Four rhino horns and a quantity of dagga (marijuana) were seized. The horns are believed to have been poached near the Pretoriuskop section of the Kruger. Seven Mozambicans with ties to Nyalunga were also arrested. A search of three properties owned by Nyalunga, and one he rented, led police to more than sixty hunting knives and pangas – some still bloodied – night-sight equipment, silencers for .375 and .458 hunting rifles, stolen laptops and television sets, and an electronic money-counter. Two steel trunks found in one of the houses were broken open. Inside police discovered more than R5 million in cash. A camera belonging to Nyalunga was also recovered. On it were photographs that appeared to show a terrified, handcuffed man being tortured. The man's identity is not known and police fear he may be dead.

At the time of his arrest, Nyalunga was out on bail pending his appearance in a money-laundering case. It stemmed from his arrest in December 2011 after he was stopped by police on the N4 highway near Middelburg. Three million rand in cash was found in the boot of his Range Rover, a vehicle he had bought six months before and which cost R640 000. Nyalunga had paid for it in cash.

Inside the Range Rover, police forensics experts found traces of animal material, later identified through DNA analysis as having originated from a white rhino. As a policeman, Nyalunga had been stationed at Komatipoort, a border town just south of the Kruger. He had abruptly resigned in 2009 and left under a cloud after becoming the subject of investigations into a criminal syndicate that smuggled cigarettes and stolen cars across the Mozambican border. In 2010 he was linked to the murder of a man who was beaten to death in Hazyview. The body was eventually recovered from the Inyaka Dam near Bosbokrand. The corpse's feet had been bound together with a length of wire and weighted down with a rock.

For his bail hearing in May 2012, Nyalunga was taken to court in an armoured police personnel carrier, surrounded by a phalanx of riot cops armed with R5 rifles. 'We received information from a reliable source that Nyalunga might attempt to escape,' the police investigating officer, Swys Vermaak, told the magistrate. Nyalunga had also tried to smuggle a cellphone into his cell, Vermaak said, and police investigating him were warned that he planned to have them killed.

Says Maggs: 'Increasingly you're seeing armed robbers, cash-in-transit gangs, car hijackers and ATM bombers shifting towards rhino poaching. It's lucrative and the risks are a lot less. If, for instance, you carry out a cash-in-transit robbery, going there with fourteen or fifteen people all armed with AK-47s and assorted firepower, there is a good chance you'll run into the police's special task force and get the hell shot out of you.'

He's right. The crackdown, particularly on cash-in-transit robberies, has been bloody and ruthlessly efficient. A few years ago, I remember rushing to the scene of a failed heist near the Carousel Casino in North West. At the time, the crimes were a dime a dozen. The papers were filled with horrific tales of security guards being executed, blown up or burnt alive by gangs determined to breach the armoured doors of the cash vans.

In this instance, the gunmen drove into a trap. Someone had ratted. The police task force laid an ambush and sealed off the road minutes before the heist was due to take place. A cash van became a Trojan horse. Seconds after the gang made their move, they were met by a hail of bullets. A police helicopter appeared in the sky.

Within minutes, the crackle of semi-automatic rifle-fire ceased. The carnage was spread out over a kilometre. A dozen bullet-riddled bodies, splashed with blood, and torn bits of flesh lay scattered over the road and in nearby mealie fields. Spent cartridge casings littered the ground. Grey, dead fingers clutched at the triggers of AK-47 assault rifles. Some had been mown down as they ran. In the weeks and months that followed, more gangs were ambushed and intercepted. Rarely was anyone ever taken alive.

'So, given the risks, is it worth it?' Maggs asks. 'Now they don't even have to get their feet wet. If they arrange for someone to go out and shoot a rhino and bring them the horn, they're going make hundreds of thousands of rands. The only thing they'll have to do illegally is buy the horn from a local group of poachers, transport it and sell it. It is low risk and, even if they get caught, with some of the sentences being meted out, it's not really a deterrent. Some of the guys we've arrested have had millions of rands in their possession. How do you fight that kind of money?'

And despite various efforts, including the much-vaunted deployment of South African Defence Force soldiers in March 2011 as part of 'Operation Corona', little seems to be stemming the tide. Maggs concedes that operations targeting poachers cannot be sustained indefinitely.

'I don't think we're going to have an option,' he says. 'We must possibly be looking at supplying the demand legally. How we are going to do that needs to be addressed. We will need to fully understand the dynamics of trade and the demand.'

'But,' he cautions, 'supplying rhino horn won't solve our problems overnight, because there are such powerful syndicates and individuals involved. Do you think they'll just give up?'

———————

It's just after two on a Sunday afternoon in Massingir in southern Mozambique. Ice-cold 2M beers in brown bottles are being served under the thatched roof of an open-air shebeen on the town's main road. The man sitting opposite me in the purple tracksuit is drunk out of his mind and extolling the virtues of the porridge they make in his home village. Occasionally, manic giggles interrupt his slurred monologue. He gives me a high five, his eyes unfocused and rolling in his head.

Next to the drunk man, Jonas Mongwe shoots me a gap-toothed grin. 'He works across the road at the police station,' he says. 'He's the head of police intelligence in Massingir.' Mongwe laughs. The purple spy nods emphatically and gives me another high five. Mongwe leans closer and gestures at a man draped over a wooden railing, fondling a young woman. 'That one ... he does poaching. He knows all about the product. Maybe he'll talk to you.' He calls out to the man, clearly an acquaintance, and explains what we want. There's laughter.

'I'm too drunk to talk,' the man says, and continues to paw his girlfriend. An old gent in his Sunday best – a neat black suit, brown shoes and a fedora – glances disapprovingly at him. Then the old man looks quickly away, orders a Coke and leaves, walking down the street past Mongwe's shiny new Toyota Hilux. It's a double-cab, worth about R300 000, probably more, depending on the extras. I notice it is registered in Mpumalanga province in South Africa.

They say Mongwe is dangerous. There are whispers about his underworld connections, but nothing anyone can prove. Perhaps it's just idle gossip. He says he's a businessman. He's likeable, oozes charm and has an air of quiet authority. In Massingir and the villages around it, everyone seems to know him. Some respect him, others clearly fear him. Mongwe runs a spaza shop and a taxi business. He knows the byways through Kruger well. He's walked them himself. He knows the poachers too. His cousin was one. Now he lies rotting in the grave alongside Dario Zitha.

'Once you kill a rhino, you get rich,' he says. 'But, at the same time, you die early. I've seen many people die ... The bosses come from Maputo and they recruit here in the villages, especially among the youth. They say: "We have the money, we have the weapons." And the youth have a hunger to get rich. The line is endless. They won't stop. If they [the rangers and army in Kruger] kill Jonas, you can give money to another guy to go in. People are dying, but daily people are going in.'

From Pafuri in the north to Massingir and the towns of Sabie, Magude and Moamba in the south lies the 'corridor' separating Mozambique from South Africa and Kruger, Mongwe explains. It is along this 'corridor' that the money-men come looking for recruits. 'The people who are dying are from these rural areas. If someone says, "Let's go and poach," they are going to get thousands and thousands of rands. People get involved so easily … I don't think it will stop. They can put up a fence or do whatever patrols they want, but if there is a market, people will kill the rhino and people will die.'

How much can a poacher make? 'A kilo of rhino horn, if I'm not mistaken, is about 400 000 *metacais* (R120 000 or $14 500). There are three steps in the market: the rural area, Chokwe, and then Maputo. The prices differ from [those who sell] in Chokwe [to those who sell] in Maputo.'

Sometimes the poachers come into Mongwe's shop and he listens to them talking. Or late at night, he'll be approached by someone wanting him to take them to Chokwe urgently. 'If you come to me urgently at night, I know. I'm short of money, so why not? If you promise to pay me a good price, I'll take you. If I say no, you will go to other people and they'll take you. I'll lose business. I know I'm taking a risk, but money is bread and butter.'

———————

Zachariah bites his lip nervously, eyes flicking from side to side. He's agreed to talk after some persuading from Mongwe. But it is clear he doesn't want to be here, in the Mozambican bush along a little-travelled dirt road, talking to outsiders. Not far away is the *Rio Olifantes*, or Elephants River, which runs between Mozambique and South Africa. Distant hills mark the beginning of the Kruger National Park and the point where it dovetails with Mozambique's *Parque Nacional do Limpopo*.

Zachariah, Mongwe says, was a bit-player in a gang of poachers. Now he catches fish for a living. He's illiterate and poor. The tennis shoes he's wearing are cracked and worn. His tracksuit pants are threadbare and filthy. Mongwe translates as he speaks. 'It's because I'm poor that I got involved in poaching. I wake up at home with my wife and we just look at each other. There is no bread, there is nothing. I'm the first-born in my family and the breadwinner. I'm looking after my brothers and sisters for school. I have to buy them food, clothes, everything. In the end, instead of stealing a goat from a neighbour, it is better to take the risk of going to the bush to hunt.

'I first found work in Maputo and I worked very hard, but my master didn't pay me as agreed, so I left and came down here to see what I could do.'

In Massingir, he got to know a group of poachers. One day they invited him to join them in the bush. 'I carried the food and water. Many times when they went into Kruger, I would stay in [the] camp to do the cooking and the others would go in to get the product. I didn't shoot. They shot it [rhino] in the head.'

On one occasion, the men sent him to find water. As he made his way through the bushes, he saw something moving. He inched closer, then stopped in his tracks. It was a rhino. It was the first time he'd seen one. 'I saw it, but I was afraid to go near it. I went back and told the bosses, and they said I must stay behind. Finally they came back with the product. They left me and said that if the police come, I must not tell them where they are going.

'It is an emotional thing because there is the hope that if you can kill the animal and get the product out, you will get a lot of money. Then we can pay school fees, food and household costs. But there is also the disadvantage that because you will eventually finish the money, you will have to go back again to the bush.'

Will he return? 'No, I won't go back because the risk is too high. The promise of money is there, but so is the danger.' These days, he says, he makes a living from the fish he catches. But across the river where he casts his nets lies Kruger and the promise of real money. Mongwe believes Zachariah may still be helping poachers.

'I don't think he is telling the truth,' Mongwe says. 'There have been fishermen killed going into Kruger. In some cases, the poachers use the fishermen to get across the river into Kruger.'

Zachariah's story shifts and changes. He's clearly nervous, and at times I wonder if he isn't just telling us what he thinks we want to hear. Asked about the poaching and his feelings about the killings, Zachariah says he feels bad. 'That animal is a meaningful animal. Even now it has big value. Behind the rhino there is money. On the money we use daily (the 20 *metacais* note, worth about R6.00 or 70 US cents) there is a picture of a rhino, which means the money is there. So if we continue killing, it is not good.

'The government must take some blame, because they don't create jobs for the people or protect the animals properly. They put that animal on the money, which means it has value and it needs good protection.'

———————

That night, a rust-red poacher's moon rises into the darkness – the largest full moon of the year. As it ascends, the colour bleeds away until only a silvery glow remains. Pale light filters through the bushes and the thorn trees. Out there, somewhere in the shadows, silent groups of poachers are heading south. And across the border in the Kruger, the game rangers, soldiers and cops are lying in wait.

Four days later, the stinking remains of two rhino carcasses are found near the park's Crocodile Bridge gate. The horns have been hacked off. The rangers pick up the trail: broken blades of grass, scuff marks in the sand, flattened scrub, crushed plants. Police and soldiers are deployed. Hours later, there is the crackle of gunfire and a man lies dead. Two others are taken away, their hands cable-tied behind their backs. Four horns, a hunting rifle and an axe are found.

The number of rhinos killed in the Kruger now stands at 130. And another corpse is consigned to a cheap pine coffin and a dusty grave.

12

Hard Knocks

Thando (not his real name) pokes gingerly at the contents of the sweating refuse bag. A cloud of fat green-and-blue flies, disturbed from their feast, buzz angrily into the air. The choking stench of decay sucks the air out of his lungs and he stifles a retch. His hands are double-wrapped in plastic shopping bags. He reaches deeper into the refuse bag, sifting through the grey ooze. The maggots and heat have done their work. Whatever is in there no longer has any discernible form. It was probably a dog, Thando laughs, screwing up his nostrils. He scoops out a handful of rot and smears it on the horn propped up against a tree. Later he'll bury it and wait for a buyer.

Thando is a smuggler, hustler and two-bit con man. He'll try anything as long as there is money to be made. These days, cigarettes are his thing – boxes and boxes of them bought on the cheap in Zimbabwe and trafficked illegally across the Limpopo River into South Africa. He sells them in Pretoria, charging up to three times what he paid for them in Zimbabwe, less expenses doled out to couriers and, most importantly, to the transporters with their souped-up cars. It is a risky enterprise, made more so by the currents, crocodiles, wild animals and the 'guma-guma' – the notorious thugs who lurk in the no-man's-land separating the two countries.

————

The Musina cops are shit-scared of the guma-guma. The more enterprising gangsters control smuggling networks that ply the highways and byways across the border. They'll move anything from cigarettes and gold to ivory and rhino horn. They smuggle people, too, exacting heavy tolls for safe passage from those unlucky enough to stray into their path. Often, they rape, rob and kill.

The *Médecins Sans Frontières* clinic in Musina is a refuge for the battered survivors, many of them illegal immigrants too terrified to go to the police. Every year the clinic treats hundreds of people who have been raped and robbed. In a recent year, it recorded 253 rape cases. For the same period, the total number of sexual crimes reported to the Musina police was only ninety-six. At least half the cases seen by the clinic involve incidents of 'compelled rape'. Men are forced by the guma-guma to rape their wives, girlfriends, sisters, cousins, mothers, grandmothers or total strangers. It amuses the thugs. A woman who works at the clinic told me that many more women are probably raped but never seek help. 'The women who come to us tell us about others in their group who were beaten and raped, people we never see. So the figures are probably a lot higher.'

Nobody knows how many human bones – bleached white by the sun – are scattered among the scrub, baobabs and fever trees in that strip of no-man's-land. For those who survive the river crossing and the gauntlet of guma-gumas, the Norex security fence – a jagged 260-kilometre steel scar that stretches from Pontdrif to the northern Kruger Park border with Zimbabwe – poses little hindrance. Coke cans, bright-green Sprite bottles and vivid strips of cloth, left behind by smugglers and traffickers, serve as markers for a myriad escape routes. Discarded cellphone airtime vouchers and cigarette butts dot the ground, along with countless dusty footprints.

Along the length of the fence line, barbed silver entrails spill inwards and outwards where the fence has been slashed, cut, trampled, burrowed under or prised apart. Just a hundred metres from the army base under Beitbridge, the link between South Africa and Zimbabwe, is a gaping hole that a troop of thieving baboons uses as a thoroughfare.

From 2000, as Zimbabwe's economy worsened and the violence meted out by police and supporters of Robert Mugabe escalated, so did the number of refugees and illegals crossing the border. By 2006, year-on-year inflation in the country exceeded 1000 per cent. Activists for the opposition Movement for Democratic Change were regularly beaten by police. Many were tortured. Some were killed.

As the 2008 elections drew closer, people flooded south to escape the violence, terrified of what might happen next. Along the border fence, journalists – me among them – waited for the battered, broken and bloodied refugees. We'd call out to the furtive shapes in the undergrowth, assuring them that it was safe to come across, that we weren't the cops. Occasionally, someone would emerge from the bushes. They'd hesitate, uncertain whether to trust us. Then they'd make the final dash, crawling under the barbed wire and through the fence to the waiting microphones, notebooks, cameras and questions.

The images were powerful and rammed home the brutality of what was happening in Zimbabwe. Men with broken bones and faces swollen from beatings, women with their clothes ripped and bloodied. Even the children didn't escape unscathed. We helped where we could, but we still felt like vultures.

Some mornings, if you drove along the fence early enough, you could see the clean-up crews in no-man's-land making useless attempts at patching the holes. They would hoard the scattered clothes and shoes the refugees had abandoned in their haste to escape Mugabe and the guma-guma. If you found the right vantage point, you could catch glimpses of the guma-guma gangs in the distance as they crossed over dead ground and vanished into the thickets and thorn trees. Some could be seen above us, moving around on the underside of the bridge.

On one occasion, I raised my camera to photograph one of them as he clambered up onto the bridge. He saw me and turned, fumbling for something behind him, then lifted his arm. It took me a second to realise he was holding a pistol. I ducked. When I looked again, he had disappeared among the struts and support beams.

The Zimbabwean crisis created a myriad new business opportunities for those ruthless enough to seize them. It was a boom time for smugglers. A Musina panel-beater is said to have bought thirty pickup trucks and hired drivers. Every day they would drive along the fence line and the farm roads picking up refugees coming from Zimbabwe. They charged R200 a head to take them to safety, away from the soldiers and the cops. The business wasn't much of a secret, but the police did nothing to stop it.

Over time, as conditions in Zimbabwe gradually stabilised, the flood of refugees slowed. But the smugglers continued to ply their trade. I remember peering through a pair of powerful binoculars as half a dozen distant figures waded across the river from Zimbabwe. On the South African shoreline, they stopped to catch their breath and wait for the stragglers. Piled up on the bank were what looked like boxes: probably cigarettes sealed in plastic or wrapped up inside black refuse bags. It was hard to tell.

Three of the figures were still in the river, up to their necks in water. As they slowly made their way across, I traced the river's curve to a sandbank 500 metres further down, out of sight from the figures in the water. Lined up on its shore, baking in the sun, were the unmistakable shapes of a dozen crocodiles. That day, they seemed content to laze in the heat.

Hennie Erwee, a local criminal lawyer, says 'cigarettes and cars' are the smugglers' mainstay. 'The real money lies with the corruption at the bridge. The guys who smuggle the containers through the border – I hear they make about R6 million per container. Then they pay the bribes: 150 000 for a cop, another 150k to a customs guy. Let's say the guy brings through ten containers a month, then that cop and that customs guy stand to make 1.5 million each. They're never going to say anything. Every year new cops and customs guys come here and try to start from scratch and clean it up. But within three months, they've also been bought off ...'

'There's a lot of money involved,' Erwee says. 'Be careful, they'll fucking take you out.'

———————

It is September 2011. I'm back in the town to look for a rhino poacher. Rodgers Mukwena – the former teacher I'd come across during my investigations into Johan Roos in 2010 – is rumoured to have fled here to join his wife. His notoriety in Zimbabwe's south-eastern lowveld has grown since then. Linked to numerous incidents of zebra and rhino poaching, he has somehow always escaped prosecution. I am hoping to find him and, perhaps, persuade him to talk to me. It is a gamble and probably a futile exercise, but it is worth a shot. You never know what you'll find. But first I need a way in.

I'm not alone on this trip. Travelling with me is Godknows Nare, a Zimbabwean ex-con. He'd come to South Africa in the mid-1990s, been arrested during a bungled armed robbery and spent the next decade in jail. In prison, he dabbled in journalism. 'Jail,' he says, 'was a college, where I studied to be a better person.'

His release coincided with Zimbabwe's collapse. It was an ideal time for someone who had the skills and the access to find work as a 'fixer'. Local and international television networks and correspondents were clamouring for stories about Zimbabwe. Godknows, somewhat to his surprise, discovered that not only did he have a knack for the job, but that he quickly became invaluable. Everyone from the BBC and Al Jazeera to the *New York Times* eventually came knocking at his door. He won awards. They nicknamed him the 'Mayor of Musina'. Godknows knows the town like the back of his hand and has an uncanny ability to tap into its underbelly.

Nare takes me to meet Thando. He might know where Mukwena is. Thando also has an intriguing sideline. Nare has arranged for him to show it to me. Thando rents a room in the township and I'm told he changes addresses as often he changes phone numbers. He spends a lot of time in the bush, bringing out shipments of cigarettes. Each shipment is escorted by armed groups of men known as *impis*. It is common for rival gangs to waylay consignments. There have been shoot-outs. The human mules that carry the contraband in duffel bags and sacks need protection.

Each man carries two boxes. Sometimes there are up to twenty of them in a group. The couriers are paid R200 a head. A box contains about fifty 'bricks' of cigarettes. Each brick consists of ten packs of twenties. A box costs about R1150 in Zimbabwe, and sells for R3000 in South Africa. It is a lucrative business, and a dangerous one.

'People get killed,' Thando says matter-of-factly. 'It's just like drugs. Even soldiers have killed each other in the bush over cigarettes.' But if there is blood to be spilt, it won't be his. He has his 'guys', and they have their guns. 'Me, I can't be killed, bra,' he says. 'I'm hard-core. Killing is another story. You can come to kill me, but you can be killed yourself.'

Thando is contemptuous of law enforcement. 'This is South Africa. You can bribe anyone and everybody, as long as there is money. Money talks. As long as I'm sorted here in South Africa, I don't fuckin' care.' He boasts that he has cops and ambulance drivers on his payroll. 'Musina is fucked up, man. I've been using a police van and an ambulance here for smuggling. You pay the driver and then he goes off with the cargo.' He laughs and mimics the sound of a siren. 'Wee! Wee! Wee! Wee!'

The people who make the real money here in the township – in Nancefield and Freedom Park – are into cigarettes, he says. There's the guy with the black Hummer parked outside his house. He's a player – a dangerous one at that. Then there are the men with the Audi A4s, BMWs and 'Tony Yengenis' (the nickname for Mercedes-Benzes, derived from the name of a corrupt ANC politician). 'All the nice cars you see are from cigarettes.'

Although Thando comes from Zimbabwe, he's lived in South Africa for years. He worked as an electrician, and then later as a cook in the kitchen of a private boarding school. He always dreamt of making real money. He wants to move more shipments of cigarettes more often. 'At the moment, I'm only doing it once or twice a month.'

What about rhino horn? 'There are people who do that here,' he says. Two of them live nearby, but there is bad blood between Thando and them and it is unlikely they'll talk. There are others on the farms along the border he can introduce me to. What about Mukwena? I ask. Thando has heard the name. He'll see what he can find out. But first he wants to show me something. It is his 'special thing'.

We drive into town. Our first stop is Al-Noor Motor Spares, then Copperpot Body Parts. Thando ticks off a list: Bodyfilla, Q-Bond, Superglue, Gum-Gum exhaust paste and sandpaper. It comes to R270 and change. Back in Freedom Park, we follow a series of rutted dirt roads to the edge of the township. Finally Thando tells me to stop at a run-down shack. A battered blue bakkie with rusted axles and no tyres is parked outside. The fresh skin from the head of a cow and a skull lie drying in the sun on a discarded grey foam mattress. 'You can leave your car here. It's safe,' Thando assures me. The few people who are around stoically ignore us. A hill surmounted with radio masts lies ahead of us.

I follow Thando as he hikes up to what he calls his 'private place'. The only sign that other people have been here are empty beer bottles and spent condoms discarded in the bush after fumbled, hurried couplings. The only sound is of our feet crunching on the scrub. The temperature is climbing rapidly to a scorching 37 °C, and it is not even summer yet. Near an ancient baobab, Thando sets down his tools and supplies, packed in a cereal box. He reads out the slogan on the side: 'So delicious, so nutritious, so good for you.'

First Thando makes a conical frame out of wire coat hangers. He then inserts a 500-millilitre plastic bottle filled with water and sand into its centre. After soaking a cardboard box in water, he tears it into strips and mashes it up before cramming it into the frame around the bottle. Then he adds the tip of a cow horn to the point of the 'item'.

Once that is done, he coats on Bodyfilla, waits for it to dry and begins sanding. Then he smears on black layers of Gum-Gum. When it dries, which it does rapidly in the sun, it turns grey. The final touches include a band of horsehair and pieces of cow bone, which he breaks up with a rock and pastes to the base with Q-Bond and superglue. The whole process takes five hours.

Finally, he hands me the finished product and announces with a chuckle: 'People want rhino horn. I make them rhino horn.' Thando's sideline is a con. It is known as a 'knock'. And Thando knocks them hard. He preys on people's avarice. It amuses him.

'I charge a lot of bucks,' he says. 'It depends on how badly they want it. The last one I sold for R15 000, another for R25 000. These people like things. They like rhino horns, so now I make them so that they can get them faster.' By the time the victims of the scam realise they have been duped, Thando is gone.

'I'm saving rhinos,' he says. 'The cops can't arrest me for doing this because I'm trying to prevent animals from being killed.' Later, he admits to smuggling the 'real thing' from Zimbabwe. The bad blood with the two local poachers stems from a rhino horn deal that he hijacked.

He had agreed to act as a middleman in a sale, as the poachers wanted to keep their distance. Thando met the buyer and showed him the horn. 'The guys had wanted R50 000.' Instead, he and the buyer cut a private deal. 'I sold it to him it for R25 000. He was very happy.' Thando pocketed the cash and returned to the poachers with a replica horn, claiming that the man had backed out of the arrangement. They weren't fooled for long.

'They could see it was a fake, *mos*. They know the stuff they deal in. They couldn't believe what I'd done. They knew that I'd robbed them. But there was nothing they could do about it. Now they don't trust me any more.'

I tell him I'm suprised they didn't kill him. 'They're scared of me,' he says, then adds: 'If they want to play with guns, they must come …'

The only people Thando seems to fear are the Chinese. 'I've seen them on TV. Those people, they can *mos* fight and jump. They say a child of five years old in China already knows karate. Have you heard that? Me, I favour some-one pointing a gun at me than being killed like that. The [Chinese] break your bones and you go to hospital and lie there and suffer till you die. It is not like a gun. With a gun, it's just "bang!" and it's game over.'

––––––––––

In daylight, Thando's fakes wouldn't easily pass muster. But he has other tricks up his sleeve. He takes the 'item' to a dumpsite littered with cow bones, rotting animal parts and bags of refuse. There he scrounges for a dead dog or cat and rubs the worm-eaten flesh on the horn before burying it in a plastic bag. 'The temperature in the bag keeps it rotting and smelling like shit,' he says. Only when he finds a buyer will he dig it up again.

For the con to work, the deal must go down at night. Normally, Thando arranges to meet the 'mark' near the taxi rank in Musina. The last one he 'knocked' was a Nigerian; before that, a businessman from Nelspruit. 'A rich man,' he says. 'He told me he knows how to test if the item is real. Then he put the tip in his mouth – the cow horn – and bit it. He thought by tasting it he could tell if it was real. He bought it anyway.'

Thando makes sure the meeting takes place in an area where police fre-quently patrol. Their presence aids the 'knock'. Often Thando will hang back and just let the mark sit there alone in his car, waiting and waiting. He knows that with each passing cop van, the buyer's fear is heightened. When he's let them sweat for a bit, he makes his move.

The deal is done quickly. Thando slides into the car. The buyer usually asks to inspect the horn, and Thando obligingly whips opens the plastic packet. The stench in the confined space is overpowering. 'Eish! When I open that item, they don't want to check it too long. They just want to get out of there, away from the smell and the cops. They can see it's a horn, so they just say, "fine, fine, fine", and hand over the bucks. Then I'm gone.'

Sometimes, Thando has another surprise in store for his clients. He arranges for one of his cop friends to trail the mark and arrest him on suspicion of smuggling rhino horn. He's thrown in jail, the 'horn' is returned to Thando and the cop gets his cut.

'Sometimes, after they have been arrested and released, they will even come back for more. They think because they were arrested, they got the real thing.'

He grins.

––––––––––

Thando thinks his scam is unique. It isn't. From Africa to India to Asia, fakes abound. In Vietnam, horn is often cut into small slabs, weighing between 80 and 100 grams, before it is sold. In this form, it is often impossible to tell the difference between a rhino horn and a water-buffalo horn. It is a common ploy. There are indications that a large percentage of what passes for rhino horn in the medicinal markets of Hanoi and Ho Chi Minh City is actually fabricated from buffalo horn. In the 1980s in India, cow horns were mounted on cement bases and 'suitably coated to pass off as a genuine rhino horn'. The horns of saiga antelopes have also been used.

In 1983, researchers were shown six fakes in Zambia made from resin, cow hair and cow dung. Other fakes were carved from stone or moulded in plastic. Fakes made from buffalo horns and cow bones were reportedly commonplace in the 1980s and 1990s. A 1995 report compiled by TRAFFIC, the trade-monitoring network, describes how a buffalo horn 'is shaped and then the basal surface of a rhinoceros horn imitated by using wax or other resinous substances'.

According to the report:

In many cases it is very difficult to distinguish real horn from manufac-
tured imitations, but examination of the base very carefully is often the

best way of doing so. Real rhinoceros horn has many minute canaliculi-like channels that dot the base creating a pitted surface. It is very difficult to reproduce these on fakes. The most interesting fakes and usually the ones resembling real horn most closely are those using bamboo root. The roots of certain kinds of bamboos are dug out and carved in the form of a rhinoceros horn. They are then dipped in oil and hung in the sun for many days until the correct colour is attained ... Bamboo has a porous base which lends itself to the creation of a simulated rhinoceros horn base ... In most cases, the fakes succeed in being passed off as real ones, and ... fetch prices commensurate with rhinoceros horn prices.

More recently, there is evidence of fakes being sold on the internet through auction sites and online classified adverts. The prices, which are substantially lower than black-market rhino horn prices, usually give them away. In 2010 and 2011, reports surfaced in India of reproductions being sold in the state of Assam in the north-east of the country. According to one article, the fakes are 'crafted out of wood or dry bamboo root' and then 'smeared with the flesh of some common animals, like frogs, to give the smell'.

'It is believed that rhino horns are identified by their distinctive odour.'

In January 2011, police in Thimphu – the capital of the Himalayan kingdom of Bhutan – arrested a man who was trying to pass off a fake horn. The suspect confessed, saying he had bought it in India for the equivalent of about US$14. He also admitted to selling another fake to an unwitting buyer for about US$7 000. He was charged with fraud or, as the newspaper colourfully described it, 'deceiving and cheating'.

In March 2012, South African police discovered two 'still-bleeding rhino horns' after bumper-bashing in Bedfordview in eastern Johannesburg. Four men were arrested. One of them was wearing a SANParks uniform. The motorist who had crashed into them told Metro police that he had noticed them behaving 'suspiciously', trying to conceal a large cooler bag behind a tree shortly after the accident.

When police opened the bag, they found the 'bleeding' horns. Tests later confirmed that the horns were fake and carved out of wood. That same week, a clerk employed in the police forensics laboratory appeared in the Pretoria District Court, charged with stealing several rhino horns from a lab safe and replacing them with plaster of Paris fakes.

In Zimbabwe, a senior civil servant employed by the country's mining ministry was arrested in early 2012 after police searched his car and discovered what looked like a rhino horn. Hamandishe Chinyengetere – the ministry's human resources director – spent the night in jail. Zimbabwe parks officials inspected the horn and concluded it was a cow horn. Chinyengetere was released without charge. A police spokesman told reporters no offence had been committed.

———

Days go by before I hear from Thando again. He's been 'to the bush', he says. There are no leads on Mukwena. The man is a ghost. Pehaps he's left Musina. Nobody seems to know. Thando asks me to fetch him in the township. Godknows and I meet him at 11 a.m. and we drive towards Beitbridge. Just before the border, we turn left past a long line of trucks waiting to cross into Zimbabwe. Customs' computer systems are down and there are massive delays.

The road curves and dips and we're at the fence. We turn left again, away from the army base and the bridge looming up above us, and follow the fence. I count the holes. There must be one every fifty or 100 metres. We drive past one of the army's lookout posts. A soldier emerges into the sun, stretching and rubbing his gelatinous belly. His shirt's off and he's yawning as if he's only just woken up. We drive on for an hour or more.

Finally we stop on the outskirts of a farm. Not far from the road are the box-shaped houses of the farm workers. Thando goes inside to find a friend. He's away for a long time. Godknows fills me in. The man we're about to meet is one of the transporters. His name is Moshe. His uncle had a reputation in the area – everyone knew him. 'He was known as Rich. He killed lots of people. He used to rob people out in the bush. If they had cigarettes, he'd take them and kill them. One day someone decided to get rid of him. They drove into him with a car and then rode over the body to make sure he was dead.'

Eventually, Thando wanders back to the car with Moshe, who's clutching a quart of beer in a brown bottle. Moshe knows some of the poachers operating in Zimbabwe. He can take us to meet one – his brother-in-law. As we drive, Moshe, sitting behind me, talks about smuggling and the cigarette trade.

'The police escort the cigarettes in their vans. If you've got ten boxes, which you'll sell for R30 000, then you give the cop R5 000 to take [the boxes] in his van away from the border. Then you have to get a guy to transport [the boxes], and that costs.'

Moshe is starting to brag now. He likes American action movies and it's beginning to show. 'We move at night,' he says. 'I like to use an Audi A4. You have to speed. We use fake number plates, sometimes Zim plates. We don't stop for cops. Even if there's a roadblock, we don't stop. We make as if we're slowing down and then, when they come close, we give it petrol.' He boasts that he's done the 460-kilometre trip to Pretoria in under three hours.

We stop at another run-down housing compound on a farm near the fence line. Steve, Moshe's brother-in-law, lives here. He comes out to meet us. He looks ill and complains of chest pains. He says he recently quit smoking. Steve claims to have gone hunting for rhinos only days before, somewhere in southern Zimbabwe. He won't tell me where.

'It was too difficult. We couldn't find any, and it was dangerous because of the rangers. The guys [poachers] who shoot stay in Beitbridge [on the Zimbabwean side of the border]. I used to assist them to get it [rhino horns] across the river and then someone would take it to Johannesburg. It was the real thing. I checked it myself.' He claims not to know the identity of the buyer.

'Some of the people that kill those things, they don't even use guns. They use poison. They put it in the water or inside cabbage and leave it there for the rhinos. They once asked me to go and buy that poison. I went to the shop, but when I go there they wanted letters saying I could buy it.'

The poison he's talking about is aldicarb. In the townships, they call it 'two-step' because, once you've ingested it, so the story goes, you will be dead in the time it takes you to walk two steps.

Aldicarb is the active ingredient in two commercially available poisons: Temik and Sanacarb. The small black granules that make up the poison resemble poppy seeds. Its distribution is meant to be strictly regulated, but it is readily available on the black market. Packets are often sold by informal traders at taxi ranks and spaza shops. It is frequently used as 'rat poison'. House robbers favour it as a means of killing any dogs on a property before they break in. It is also often used in suicides.

There may be some credence to Steve's story. While the poisoning of rhinos is rare, there have been cases. In 2005, five rhinos were found dead at the Nwanedi Nature Reserve in Limpopo. The horns of one of them had been hacked off. Police said at the time they believed a waterhole had been laced with Temik. Dozens of other animals had also been killed.

Then, five years later, Richard Holtzhausen, the operational manager of Wildlife Ranching South Africa, an organisation established to represent the interests of game farmers, released details of another incident. Fourteen cabbages, cut in half and 'sprinkled with blue crystals, smaller than the size of ground peppercorns', had been found in the vicinity of rhino middens on a game farm in Mookgophong. The rhinos were just a hundred metres away when the cabbages were found. None of the rhinos died.

And in Zimbabwe, there were reports that self-proclaimed 'war veterans', who had seized land in the Chiredzi District, were poisoning game and rhinos. A local resident, Nelson Maponga, told a reporter: 'The poachers are placing poisoned cabbages at animal drinking points so that when the animals come for water, they will also eat them. They will track them until they die, then take the horns off … Most of them are working as poaching agents for South African–based rhino horn dealers.'

We drop Thando off in the township near the dumpsite. He wants to check on his horn. He's heard about a buyer who is prepared to pay 'big bucks' for rhino horn. Over the past six or seven years, he says he's made ten to fifteen horns. People have come to Musina from all over the country in search of rhino horns. And they'll keep coming.

'It's all a game, bra,' he says. 'Sometimes you win. Sometimes you lose. It is all just a game …'

16 January 2012

On the outskirts of Pretoria, Colonel Karel Swanepoel is driving back to the office from a crime scene when he spots a lone figure crossing an open stretch of veld. The man is carrying a black plastic refuse bag in his left hand. It seems heavy, perhaps a little too heavy. Swanepoel, the commander of the Kameeldrift police station in Pretoria, slows the car to a crawl. After twenty years on the force, he trusts his instincts.

The man approaches the road, walking fast along a footpath. As he nears Swanepoel's car, he suddenly lurches forward into a run. The cop floors the accelerator. The runner rounds a tree, dumps the bag and keeps running. He doesn't get far. Seconds later, Swanepoel cuts him off and arrests him. The reason for the 100-metre dash soon becomes evident. Inside the bag are three rhino horns. They're still 'fresh', clearly the result of recent kills. One barely qualifies as a 'horn'. It is probably that of a calf.

At the police station, the suspect is booked. A photograph is taken. His fingerprints are recorded. Someone scrawls a case number and a name on the cover of a brown docket-folder: 'Kameeldrift CAS 71/01/2012 ... Rodgers Mukwena'. The 'game' has finally caught up with the 'Teacher'.

The Veterinary Genetics Laboratory at the Onderstepoort campus of Pretoria University is situated on the second floor of a cold, echoing old building. The doors leading into the lab are fitted with electronic locks and keypads. Large padlocked chest freezers guard police evidence bags and samples of rhino horn. There's also a 'cupboard full of weapons', ranging from knives and axes to pangas (machetes) and even chainsaws.

It is here that samples from the three horns are sent for analysis. Holes are drilled into them and the filings are collected in plastic containers and bagged. Normally, 20 milligrams is the smallest sample size that can be used to map the DNA of an individual animal. However, the lab has previously managed to extract DNA profiles from microscopic fragments of horn vacuumed up from the carpet of a car.

'We only deal with samples. We don't keep any horns here,' says Dr Cindy Harper, who heads up the laboratory. 'It is such a valuable commodity now that it is extremely dangerous, so the horns are kept in stockpiles [that] are either managed by the police or SANParks.' DNA profiles of rhinos killed by poachers and horns recovered by police are recorded, along with a growing inventory of live animals, on a computer database dubbed the Rhino DNA Index System, or RhoDIS. It is loosely modelled on CODIS, the US Federal Bureau of Investigation's mammoth Combined DNA Index System, which stores roughly 10 million DNA profiles.

Harper's laboratory uses a set of twenty-five DNA markers and an additional 'sex marker' to sequence the unique 'DNA fingerprint' of an animal. By contrast, the FBI's CODIS database uses only thirteen genetic markers to generate individual DNA profiles. Because rhino populations are so small, they are likely to be inbred, and therefore more markers have to be used to make an individual identification.

Until fairly recently, scientists believed it was impossible to obtain nuclear DNA – the type of DNA used to make individual identifications – from rhino horn. That changed in 2007. A wildlife forensics conference held at Onderstepoort became the catalyst for a research project to determine a means of 'individually identifying rhinos from their horns'. It was conducted in conjunction with the TRACE Wildlife Forensics Network, an international NGO established to promote the use of forensic science in wildlife crime investigations. The timing was fortuitous. The following year, rhino-poaching incidents in South Africa would increase sixfold.

'Everyone thought it couldn't be done, because it was commonly believed that rhino horn was just a clump of hardened hair,' Harper explains. 'But if you look at the actual structure of rhino horn, it's not hair at all. Rhino horn does not contain a bony core. It is made up of cells that grow out from the surface of the skin of the nose. The cell tubules harden and connect together with a matrix of calcium and melanin. It is keratinised or hardened, a bit like a horse's hoof. And where there are cells, you can find nuclear DNA.'

The first case in which DNA profiles were used successfully to link smuggled horns to a specific rhino occurred not in South Africa, but in the United Kingdom. A Lancashire antique dealer, Donald Allison, was stopped at Manchester Airport on 30 June 2009 shortly before he was due to board a flight to Beijing. He was carrying what at first appeared to be a bronze sculpture of a bird perched on a log. On closer inspection, border agents discovered that it was made of fibreglass and resin. Inside the log were two rhino horns wrapped in cling film and tape.

Samples from the horns were sent via the TRACE network to Harper's team. Investigators had also put out a request to British and Irish museums for information on recent rhino deaths. The Colchester Zoo quickly responded. A white rhino bull, unfittingly named Simba, had been euthanised after falling seriously ill that April. For thirty years it had been one of the zoo's star attractions. The carcass had been incinerated, but blood samples from medical evaluations had been stored. A DNA profile was extracted. It matched the horns. Later, Essex police established that the rhino's entire head had been stolen from the abattoir where it was sent to be burnt. It was sold to Allison for £400. He was subsequently jailed for twelve months.

The second test case made legal history in South Africa. A Vietnamese security guard named Xuan Hoang was arrested at OR Tambo International Airport in Johannesburg in March 2010 after seven rhino horns weighing sixteen kilograms were found in his luggage. Samples were sent to Harper's laboratory for analysis and matched to a poaching incident a few days before Hoang's arrest. Hoang was sentenced to ten years in jail. The case set a new legal precedent, as the fact that the horns could be tied to a specific poaching incident played a significant role in the magistrate's decision.

Harper says that she and her team have 'no idea about the background to the investigations' in which they conduct DNA analysis. 'I prefer it that way. I get the stuff in and I run it completely blind. I have absolutely no involvement with the rest of the investigation. The big issue is the chain of custody, how the evidence is collected, how it reaches us and how that is recorded. DNA evidence is rarely questioned by the courts – it is the evidence chain that is normally attacked by the defence. We supply DNA collection kits and have done a lot of training.'

The laboratory employs only a handful of staff and for years has operated on a shoestring budget. By July 2012, the RhoDIS database contained 5 000 individual rhino DNA profiles. According to Harper, the number of poaching cases in which DNA analysis is now being requested is increasing. 'Theoretically, you can do the analysis in a day. But if you've got a backlog and only a certain number of staff, it gets longer and longer.'

In April 2012, environment minister Edna Molewa gazetted new 'norms and standards', which require the collection of samples of horns and blood in DNA kits whenever live rhino are darted to be translocated or treated. These samples are then to be handed over to the Veterinary Genetics Laboratory for profiling. Arguably the only true forensic 'science', DNA analysis is now an indispensable tool in South Africa's fight against rhino poaching. Efforts are also under way to expand the reach of the database to other African, Asian and European countries.

'As an investigation tool, it's brilliant,' says Colonel Johan Jooste, head of the endangered species section at the Hawks and an executive member of the Interpol Wildlife Crime Working Group. 'Without a doubt, it is one of the best tools we have.'

———————

It had been months since I'd heard anything about Mukwena. The last sighting of him had been in the Bubye Valley Conservancy in Zimbabwe on 27 December 2011, two days after a rhino had been shot dead by poachers. He had been seen driving a Toyota TownAce minibus that had once belonged to Nobby Mlilo, a key poaching middleman from Mpande. Mlilo – an ex-soldier – had been shot dead by Zimbabwean police four months earlier while trying to poach rhinos in the Chipinge Safari area, 236 kilometres east of Masvingo. Mukwena, it seemed, had inherited or taken over the vehicle, which was believed to contain a secret compartment underneath the spare wheel for smuggling rifles. It would be the last sighting of him for a while.

The arrest of a Zimbabwean poacher by a watchful police-station commander made headlines in a number of South African newspapers. But the reports didn't name the suspect and there were no journalists in court when the case was first called. The story was quickly forgotten. It was only by chance that I spotted the docket on the desk of a policeman two weeks later and recognised the name of the man I had tried to find in Zimbabwe and Musina.

----

6 February 2012

Three weeks after Rodgers Mukwena's arrest, Harper calls Captain Charmaine Swart, the investigating officer, with the DNA results from the horn samples. It is a match. The horns are from a cow and calf that were poached in the Dinaka Game Reserve, a privately owned game farm in the Waterberg Mountains 230 kilometres north of Johannesburg. The incident had occurred two weeks before Mukwena's arrest.

Confronted with this information, Mukwena initially agrees to co-operate with the cops. Under police escort, he is taken to Dinaka to formally 'point out' the crime scene and walk investigators through the details of the crime. He denies killing the calf, blaming it on an accomplice who, he claims, shot it to stop it 'bothering' them while they cut off the cow's horns. He names the henchman as Never Ndlovu, the same man who had accompanied Hardlife Nkomo and Life Mbedzi on their ill-fated 2009 incursion into Bubye. Ndlovu was arrested four months after that incident, but had been released on bail and disappeared before he could be sentenced. At the time of writing, there was still a warrant out for him in Zimbabwe and a R5 000 reward for any information leading to his arrest.

Two days after the 'pointing out', Captain Swart receives a call on her cellphone from a man calling himself 'Mike'. He claims to be Rodgers Mukwena's brother and says he would like to discuss the case with her and the possibility of arranging bail for Rodgers. The matter is out of her hands, Swart says. Mike makes Swart an offer: he'll pay her R13 000 if she can 'make a plan' to lose the docket and arrange for Rodgers to 'escape' on the way to his next court appearance. Swart thinks it over, then tells Mike to call her back in a few days to discuss the details. They eventually agree to a meeting at a Wimpy fast-food restaurant in Pretoria North. The rendezvous is set for 11 a.m. on 15 February, two days before Mukwena is due back in court.

Mike is waiting for Swart at the Wimpy when she arrives. She had called him earlier and told him what she would be wearing. He nods in recognition as she pushes her way through the glass doors. They take a seat in one of the red booths and order coffee. 'Is everything organised?' Mike asks. 'Yes,' Swart says. One of her colleagues will be taking Rodgers to court and will 'let him go and make it seem like he escaped'.

'Rodgers must never be seen again,' she adds. Mike agrees, saying he plans to take him to the Zimbabwe border. He'll need Rodgers's passport and driver's licence. Mike says he's willing to pay a further R2 000 if Swart can get them to him before the escape. She agrees, then hands Mike an envelope. The docket is inside it, she says. Mike gives her the money. It is in denominations of R100 and R200.

'Do you want to count it?' he asks.

'No, it's fine. I trust you,' Swart replies and slips the money into her handbag. She stands up. Seconds later, on her signal, a police back-up team surrounds Mike. The documents in the envelope are blank. The money, less R170 of Swart's own cash, which she had declared before the operation commenced, is counted out in front of Mike. It adds up to R13 000, as promised.

Mike's identity document gives his name as Mokibelo Michael Mokoena, a variation on Mukwena. He's forty-two and lives in Shoshanguve. Like the man he says is his brother, he's a teacher and works at a junior secondary school.

On 22 November 2012, Rodgers Mukwena was sentenced to ten years' imprisonment after pleading guilty to charges of illegal possession of rhino horn. The case against Mike was still pending at the time of going to print.

13

The Embassy

23 April 2008

Tommy Tuan is trapped. Spread out on a bed in Room 122 at the Road Lodge in Kimberley are wads of cash. Thick bundles of hundred-rand bills held together with rubber bands. One million two hundred and eighty thousand rand plus change. There's also a duffel bag and ten rhino horns weighing just over twenty kilos. Hidden under an armchair, where he can't reach it, is a 6.35mm pistol. It is compact, light and – unless you know what you're doing – more likely to hurt someone or piss them off than kill them. Outside, in the parking lot, is a grey Honda Accord with red diplomatic licence plates. But between Tommy and the door are three cops.

———

Tommy's real name is Nguyen Thien Tuan. It is a tongue-curdling mouthful for most South Africans, so he uses Tommy instead. He's thirty-three, owns a jewellery business in Port Elizabeth – a coastal city in the Eastern Cape – and lives in a modest townhouse complex with his wife, Tran Thu Hien. They're planning to buy a place of their own soon. They came to South Africa from Vietnam two years ago. In July 2006, Tommy bought a business and renamed it Tuan's Designer Jewellers. He rented shop 41 at the Walker Drive Shopping Centre.

Business seemed good. Tommy even sponsored a horse race at Arlington Race Course in February 2008: the Tuan's Designer Jewellers Maiden Juvenile Plate – a 1000-metre race for two-year-olds. A horse called Major Domo was the first across the line. Triumphant Surge came in second and Run Wolf Run, third.

But the jewellery business has another purpose. It is a front. Tommy buys and sells rhino horns. In 2008, single horns can still be traded quite legally within South Africa's borders as long as you have the necessary permits. The real problem arises when you want to export them. That's illegal. Only hunting trophies can be exported legally. But Tommy has friends at the Vietnamese embassy in Pretoria, and they have a 'diplomatic bag'. The 'bag' itself can take on many forms, from an envelope to a parcel, or a suitcase to a shipping container. Whatever shape it takes, it is immune from search and seizure as long as it is correctly marked.

The demand for rhino horn in Vietnam is growing at an unprecedented rate. Tommy and others like him are scouring the length and breadth of South Africa for horns. As long as the price is right, many game farmers are happy to part with rhino horns. Usually it is the 'loose stock' they've accumulated over the years as a result of natural mortalities. Nobody pays much heed to the permits and paperwork.

But these endeavours have not gone unnoticed. The politicians are muttering about a crackdown. There are concerns, too, that legal trade within South Africa is being used to launder horns from animals killed by poachers. A ban on internal domestic trade is looking increasingly likely. Time is running out, and so is Tommy's luck.

———————

Tommy is a relative newcomer to the trade, one of a growing number of Vietnamese smugglers who are aggressively pursuing a share of the burgeoning market for rhino horn. The Vietnamese community in South Africa is small. Only about seventy Vietnamese nationals are said to have been given permanent residency status in the country, and a number of them have been linked to the illegal trade in rhino horn. According to the wildlife trade-monitoring network TRAFFIC, several Vietnamese students who had registered for courses at South African universities have been arrested in recent years trying to smuggle rhino horn out of the country. But there are others operating on the fringes, remnants of the 'old school' that dominated smuggling networks – particularly of ivory and abalone – in the 1990s and early 2000s.

Charles Lee, as he calls himself, is one of them. I have been told that Lee was shopping around for horn. Someone had given me his name, number and an introduction, so I called him up to arrange a meeting. As far as he is concerned, I am the middleman in a transaction that can potentially net him a small fortune. We agree to meet at the News Cafe in Bedfordview, ironically the same place as I had waited with Paul O'Sullivan for police to make a move on Radovan Krejcir.

Lee arrives late, sweating and bustling with apologies and good humour. He takes a seat and calls out to the waitress: 'Hello, my girlfriend. Cappuccino!' Then he produces a box of cigarettes and lights the first of many smokes.

He tells me he is originally from Taiwan, but studied in the US in the late 1980s, then found work as a translator on a luxury cruise liner. He was twenty-five when he arrived in Cape Town in 1990. He had a contract with the cruise company, but was soon augmenting his rather paltry income with a black-market currency racket. His English came in handy too.

'I would do people favours. That's how I made my money. I helped one Chinese business set up a company. There were lots of jobs for me. I helped people with port control, customs, the police, even the mafia businessmen. I had a good time in Cape Town. There were good women – not just one woman – and nice seafood.'

Lee's activities gradually expanded. By 1993 and 1994, he says, he was 'exporting tons of shark fins' from South Africa. According to Peter Gastrow, a special advisor to the Ministry of Safety and Security in the mid-1990s, Chinese criminal gangs and triad societies were heavily involved at the time in exporting large quantities of dried shark fins from Cape Town via Johannesburg to Hong Kong and 'other destinations in Southeast Asia'.

In a research paper, published in 2001 by the Institute for Security Studies, Gastrow wrote that police investigations in 1992 and 1993 'confirmed for the first time that individuals linked to at least three different triad societies were actively involved and that their illegal activities were much broader than the trade in shark fins ... With the assistance of the Hong Kong Police, with whom informal contacts had been established, police established that individuals operating from Cape Town were members of the Hong Kong–based 14K triad, and the Wo Shing Wo triad. The Taiwanese-linked criminal group active in Cape Town was referred to as the "Table Mountain Gang" at that stage. Police soon discovered that members of these triad societies were also operating in the Johannesburg/Pretoria area, as well as in every harbour city in South Africa.'

I ask Lee about the triads. 'I don't get involved with this mafia thing,' he claims. 'Sometimes the mafia comes to me to ask for help as a translator. I do a lot of interpreting in the courts, so I get a lot of knowledge by helping people here and there. These Chinese [gangsters] cannot speak proper English when they come to South Africa. We just do business with them. We don't want to get involved in that violent stuff. We have our own businesses and our own lives.

'We are not afraid of those kinds of rubbish. They're small-time. The real leader won't bother to come here. I met one of the big shots once, but you cannot tell he is one of the mafia leaders. He's a businessman. You don't see him shouting and turning over tables like Michael Corleone in the movies. He just gives orders.'

Lee says he enjoyed the coast for a time, but soon found that 'living in Cape Town is like being in the Stone Age'.

'To make business, you need to be in Johannesburg. But living in Joburg, you feel like you are living in a jungle. It is totally overwhelming. All my friends have been robbed or hijacked. If you drive a nice car, be careful. That's why I use a taxi. My car is in a garage in Polokwane. I leave it there. I'm low profile.'

If it isn't the criminals robbing you, it is the police, he says. 'People get arrested without a warrant. When the cops see a Chinese, they see an ATM. All the police want are bribes. Every month from the 25th to the 5th, they go for the Chinese.'

'Except here,' he adds, nodding in the direction of the police station across the road from our table. 'The police here get good salaries and if you make a donation to them, they are happy.'

The conversation drifts back to business. Lee – who tells me he is there on behalf of 'a friend' – wants to know the price I can offer him. 'Eighty-five thousand a kilo,' I thumb-suck. I know I am pushing my luck. But I want to test him. The going rate from pseudo-hunts is about R65 000 a kilo.

'Eighty-five is too high,' he says. 'My friend knows the value. I don't want to waste your time. Perhaps 60 000 …?'

I tell him I'll think it over. But first I want to know more about his 'friend'. Who am I in 'business' with exactly?

'You don't have to think twice,' Lee replies. 'We are simply business people. We plan well. We start with a few pieces, maybe 100 pieces or fifty pieces. Money is not an issue.'

His friend has a wide range of 'commodity' interests in South Africa, Mozambique and Ghana. 'My friend is one of the biggest buyers. He wants tons of horn. But if the connection isn't secure, he doesn't want to get involved. My friend has traded horn before in another country, not here. The shipment will go through two or three different countries before it is moved out. That way everything is clean. There is no trace. You can feel secure. You are dealing with professionals.'

I tell Lee that the man I 'represent' has access to a relatively large stockpile of horn. But it is illegal to sell it and illegal to buy it. How can we pull off the deal?

'Look, your friend is sitting on a cash mountain, a gold mountain. But he is crying for money. The solution is simple. We arrange a place for the pickup, we collect the goods and your friend announces that it was stolen. Nobody will blame him and he'll get his money.'

I ask Lee about the uses of rhino horn. 'The number-one use is for blood circulation. There are also rumours that it helps a person who has contracted cancer to live longer. But it doesn't really cure the disease. It just helps the rich people to extend their life, enough time to write the will.' He laughs.

We finish our coffees. Before we part company, Lee warns me not to mention the 'product' by name over the phone. 'Call it something else. Let's call it "lady head". And when you're ready, let us know. You can take us to the place, we can make sure there is no GPS [tracker] in the shipment and we can take it from there. If you are happy, we can do more business.'

---

23 April 2008

Tommy arrives in Kimberley after dark and hours late for the meeting with the seller. He goes straight to the Road Lodge and checks into a room. He isn't alone. He's brought along a friend to look after the money and act as the bagman during the deal. Tommy calls the seller and asks him to come to the hotel. The man agrees. He asks Tommy if he'll mind if the owner of the horn comes along too. Tommy doesn't. They meet in the parking lot. Tommy tells the men he has brought R1.4 million in cash, but he doesn't have it with him. He insists on doing the transaction at the Road Lodge and not at another hotel, as originally planned. He doesn't know the town well and doesn't want to drive around. He confides that he is scared to go anywhere else, because it could be a 'police trap'. The men relent. To avoid any misunderstandings about the legality of the deal, they warn Tommy that they don't have permits for the horns. It won't be necessary, he says.

An hour later, they are back. One of the men carries a heavy duffel bag over his shoulder. Tommy is waiting for them in the lobby and guides them up the stairs to his room on the first floor. They lock the door, shut the windows and close the curtains. There is an electronic scale on a table. Tommy switches it on and begins weighing the horns. On the bed, an ashtray slowly smoulders, filling up with cigarette butts, blackened and burnt to the quick. Tommy jots down the weights in red ink on a scrap of paper. Some of the horns still have ragged pieces of nasal cartilage attached to the bases. The final tally is 20.559 kilograms. Tommy subtracts 200 grams to factor in the unwanted cartilage. At R63 000 a kilo, it comes to a total of R1 282 617. They round the figure off to R1 280 million.

Tommy places a call on his cellphone. A few minutes later, someone raps on the door. Knock. Pause. Knock-knock. Pause. Knock. Satisfied, Tommy unlocks it. A pair of white takkies flashes into view and disappears. Tommy reaches into the corridor, picks up a black carry-bag and returns to the room. He locks the door, then heaves the bag onto the bed and begins unpacking the cash. He is so absorbed in his task that he doesn't notice one of the men press the green dial button on his cellphone. Somewhere outside, another cellphone rings briefly and then stops.

There's a hard knock at the door. Tommy goes to see who it is. But the seller is already in front of him, pulling on the handle, and then another man pushes his way into the room. He's saying something. About being a police-man. Tommy freezes. Then the disbelief and shock kick in.

Tommy's wrists are cuffed. The money on the bed is photographed, packed into two large plastic evidence bags, and numbered. Someone finds the pistol, six rounds of 6.35mm ammo and a single 9mm round. Once the room has been searched, Tommy is taken away. The bagman has vanished.

In the hotel parking lot, police find and impound the Honda. Earlier in the day, everyone involved in the operation had been briefed to keep an eye out for it. Under no circumstances, they were told, should Tommy be allowed to transfer the horns to the car. The vehicle's registration number is D BBB 127D: 'D' for 'diplomatic'. The registered owner is Pham Cong Dung, the political counsellor at the Vietnamese embassy. Next to the ambassador, he is the most senior Vietnamese diplomat in South Africa.

––––––––––

For some time now, the embassy in Brooklyn, Pretoria, has been a thorn in the flesh of the cops investigating the illegal rhino horn trade. Two years before Tommy Tuan's arrest, police had uncovered evidence that the embassy's eco-nomic attaché, Nguyen Khanh Toan, was using his diplomatic immunity and the diplomatic bag to smuggle rhino horns out of South Africa. There was little they could do about it other than complain. South Africa's Department of Foreign Affairs wrote a nasty letter to their Vietnamese counterparts and Nguyen was recalled to Vietnam.

That same year, in Hanoi, a corruption scandal involving a senior Viet-namese bureaucrat, Nguyen Van Lam, led to further damaging revelations of high-level involvement in the rhino horn trade. Lam – the deputy head of the Vietnamese 'Government Office' – had reportedly 'admitted shortcom-ings' in accepting 'cash gifts' from state agencies three years earlier. He was forced to resign. The bribes had come to light years earlier after Lam forgot a suitcase at Hanoi Airport in 2003. Security staff opened the case and found ten envelopes inside it, stuffed with cash. Lam's explanation was startling. He said most of the cash was from 'friends and colleagues' who wanted him to buy 'rhino horns' for them.

In South Africa, increasing numbers of Vietnamese couriers and middle-men were appearing in court on charges of smuggling rhino horn. Most of them were either unable or unwilling to speak English and, as a result, the courts were heavily reliant on the Vietnamese embassy for referrals to qualified interpreters. Tommy's brother – as it so happened – was one these 'preferred' translators.

It wasn't long before police investigators found evidence directly impli-cating some of the interpreters in the illicit trade. In one instance, police at the Kempton Park Organised Crime Unit obtained a photograph of a man posing next to the carcass of a rhino, a rifle in hand. A detective instantly recognised him as one of the interpreters in the trial of a courier who had been arrested at OR Tambo International Airport with rhino horn stuffed in his bag.

———————

Two days after Tommy's arrest, police receive a letter from Dung. He wants his car back. He has an explanation. 'On 23rd April 2008, Mr. Nguyen Thien Tuan, aquaintance [sic] of my relative Nguyen Anh Bao, dropped in my res-idence and said that his car was out of order, and asked Mr. Bao to borrow the car. Then he took my car and went away until yesterday, 24th April when I was informed that my car was catched [sic] by police in Kemberley [sic]. I assure hereby that I know nothing about Mr. Tuan's doing neither the borrowing of the car and would like to get my car back for use as soon as possible.' The Department of Foreign Affairs leans on the cops. Four days later, Nguyen Anh Bao, armed with a letter from Dung, collects the Honda in Kimberley.

But Dung's stated ignorance will be challenged seven months later. On 17 November 2008, the environmental television programme 50/50 airs grainy surveillance footage of a Vietnamese embassy official receiving a number of rhino horns from a known trafficker. The horns are transferred from the boot of a car that has stopped in the street outside the embassy. Dung's Honda is parked nearby. The recipient of the horns is later identified as Vu Moc Anh, the embassy's first secretary.

This time, the embassy reacts. The ambassador, Tran Duy Thi, tells Vietnam's *Tuôi Tre* newspaper that 'so far Ms. Moc Anh is insisting she was just helping people'. She denies any involvement in rhino horn smuggling and claims she only 'helped transfer' the horns. 'Ms. Moc Anh said she had received a call at noon offering to sell her rhino horns, but she declined,' the ambassador tells the journalist. 'Some time later she received calls from two Vietnamese asking her to help by "having a look at the horns".' According to the ambassador, Anh told him she 'came out [of the embassy] to have a look and help handle the horns for them'.

The newspaper also tracks down Dung and asks him about his car, which, unusually, was parked in the street outside the embassy during the transaction. Normally it would be parked inside the embassy walls. 'The car is registered under my name,' he admits, 'but I was not the one to use it on that day.'

In the days that follow, Ambassador Thi condemns the incident. 'This is a highly reprehensible act ... stemming from pure greed. This is not just a private act; it is one that has a repercussion on the embassy and the image of Vietnam itself.' He claims that staff at the embassy had been 'repeatedly cautioned not to engage in such activity'. On 20 November, Vietnam's foreign ministry announces that Anh has been recalled to 'clarify the affair'. Some time later, Dung also leaves South Africa.

The South African government says nothing, opting to sit on the fence and engage in 'quiet diplomacy'. A senior official in the Department of Environmental Affairs, Magdel Boshoff, is given the uncomfortable task of relaying the message.

'At this stage we will not request ... an investigation. We don't want to prejudice diplomatic relations with Vietnam,' she tells *50/50*.

The story soon fades from the newspapers. But questions remain about Anh. There are unconfirmed reports that she has been posted to another African country, possibly Mozambique. In March 2012, in response to questions from the Wildlife Conservation Society, Vietnam's foreign affairs ministry says there is 'no evidence of Moc Anh's involvement in rhino horn dealing in both Vietnam and South Africa'. It says it accepts Anh's version that she was filmed while 'helping a rhino horn dealer review his papers' and 'was not involved in the deal'.

Tommy is released on bail. His case drags on for nearly two years. In February 2009, the then Minister of Environmental Affairs, Marthinus van Schalkwyk, announces a moratorium on the trade in rhino horns and products within South Africa. Two months later, according to TRAFFIC, Tommy is seen making 'several trips' to game ranches near Vryburg in North West province. Later, local residents find him alongside a road claiming to have been the victim of an attempted car hijacking and the theft of 'large sums of money'. He hurriedly leaves the scene a short while afterwards and never files a report with the police. It is widely believed that Tommy may have got himself caught up in a rhino horn deal 'gone wrong'. In May 2009, Tommy and his wife, Tran Thu Hien, obtain permits to hunt two white rhinos in KwaZulu-Natal. In January the following year, the couple obtains two more permits, to hunt rhinos in the Free State. The address they provide in their applications is on a main thoroughfare in Hanoi, not Port Elizabeth.

Eventually Tommy is found guilty of illegal possession of rhino horn. In March 2010, he is fined R200 000 or two years' imprisonment. The magistrate suspends a portion of the sentence for a period of five years on provision that Tommy not be convicted of a similar offence. The cash from the hotel room is forfeited to the State. Tommy opts to pay the fine. Not long afterwards, he returns to Vietnam. His wife remains behind in South Africa.

In January 2011, she and a twenty-two-year-old man, Phuong Huynh Phat, are arrested at Wonderboom Airport near Pretoria. Four rhino horns worth about R400 000 are found in their possession. Police had been tipped off ahead of their arrival and were waiting when they landed in a private helicopter. The chopper belongs to Dawie Groenewald, the notorious game farmer and safari operator from Limpopo.

Both Hien and Phat are adamant that they participated in legal hunts on Groenewald's farm, but later Phat pleads guilty to illegally possessing and conveying two horns. He is fined R100 000 and given a suspended sentence of four years' imprisonment. The horns and a piece of rhino skin are forfeited to the State. Interestingly, Phat may have hunted another rhino in Limpopo a year before his arrest. In January 2010, records show that a hunting permit had been issued to a 'Huynphat Phuong' by Limpopo provincial authorities. At the time of writing, Hien continues to fight the case and maintains her innocence.

In September 2011, a court order is granted giving the State the power to seize Tommy's assets as proceeds of crime. These include a Mercedes-Benz E500, a Toyota Hilux and a R1.8-million house he bought in a quiet suburban street in Port Elizabeth in 2009.

———————

30 June 2010

Xuan Hoang cuts a pathetic figure in the dock of the Kempton Park Regional Court. His eyes are dark smudges, his shoulders bent. Grubby clothes hang on a painfully thin frame. Somewhere below him a cell door slams shut and the sound reverberates up the stairs from the holding cells to the dock. He winces. Around him, there is a babble of conversation. Fragments of Afrikaans, Sotho and English – none of which he understands. To his right sits the Vietnamese interpreter. He's bored, fiddling with his Blackberry.

Hoang is twenty-nine and married with two children. He works as a security guard in Hanoi and earns about $100 a month – easy cannon fodder for a syndicate willing to pay him ten times that amount to collect a package in South Africa.

On 29 March 2010, Hoang jetted into OR Tambo International Airport in Johannesburg – the first time he had ever flown on an aeroplane. He had been told that someone would be waiting for him with a suitcase. His instructions were to collect the bag and take the next flight out. He did as he had been told.

As Hoang cleared immigration on his way to board the outward flight, he was stopped by customs agents and taken aside for his luggage to be searched. Packed in the suitcase were seven rhino horns weighing just over sixteen kilograms. Hoang was arrested. He told his interrogators that he never opened the bag and had no idea what was inside it.

In court, Hoang pleads guilty to charges of fraud and illegal possession of rhino horn. Mario Scholtz, a veteran wildlife investigator, formerly with the police's Endangered Species Protection Unit and now with Environmental

Crime Investigations at SANParks, is called to testify in aggravation of sentence. So far in 2010, Scholtz tells the court, South Africa has lost rhinos worth R40.6 million. Horn is being bought in South Africa at R55 000 a kilo and sold on the black market in Vietnam for nearly three times that. An example should be set.

Hoang's lawyer asks the court for mercy. His client was only a courier, he says, a poor man with a family that depends on him. The presiding magistrate, a man with the suitably regal name of Prince Manyathi, is unmoved. His court catches the bulk of the smuggling cases detected at OR Tambo, a few minutes' drive away. There has been a dramatic growth in the numbers of rhino horns being intercepted. But the syndicates keep learning and adapting. They're an inventive lot. Horns are cut up to mask their shapes, after which they are sometimes divided up into different suitcases. Others are hidden inside moulds and plaster statues. In some cases, real horns are concealed inside fake ones.

But with each seizure the customs officials are growing more adept at finding the contraband. They now know what to look for on the X-ray-machine monitors. And the EWT, with the help of police and prosecutors, has conducted extensive training sessions on species identification, legislation, crime-scene management and court proceedings. If they're still unsure, there's always the old ten-rand test that they were shown in the days when specialist training wasn't available. 'If you don't know what you're looking at,' one instructor taught them, 'take a ten-rand note out of your wallet and look at the picture of the rhino on the front. That's the shape of the horn. That is what you should be seeing.'

They're aided by newly trained sniffer dogs that have been imprinted to smell out rhino horns. (Customs officers prefer to refer to their animals as detector dogs. 'It's not like they have a cold or a runny nose,' one told me indignantly.) The syndicates go to extraordinary lengths to hide the stench of decay. Horns are wrapped in foil or cling wrap. Toothpaste or shampoo is smeared inside the suitcases. Even naphthalene balls have been used. It may fool humans, but it doesn't fool the dogs.

Manyathi clears his throat. The fact that Hoang may only have been a courier is not an extenuating factor, he says. 'Fines are clearly not a deterrent ... You travelled to South Africa knowing that you were going to do something illegal. The purpose was self-enrichment, without any consideration for what the damage would be.' He sentences Hoang to ten years' imprisonment, without the option of a fine.

The severity of the sentence is unprecedented. For years, stiff fines and suspended prison terms have been the norm. To the syndicates they're little more than a costly inconvenience; an added business expense that can be recouped on later shipments.

A year later, two more couriers unfortunate enough to stumble into Manyathi's court are slapped with prison sentences of twelve and eight years respectively. Duc Manh Chu and Nguyen Phi Hung had been arrested at OR Tambo thirty minutes before the opening ceremony of the FIFA World Cup on 11 June 2010. They had hoped that customs officials would be distracted by the spectacle playing out on television. They were wrong. The X-ray-scanner operators sounded the alarm. Twelve rhino horns were found stuffed in Chu's luggage. A further six horns were found in Hung's bags.

Manyathi is clearly unimpressed. 'I don't one day want to have to show my grandchildren pictures of rhinos because all the live animals have been killed by greedy people,' he says in his judgment. Chu gets the maximum sentence: ten years for the illegal possession of the horns. Manyathi tacks on an additional two years for fraud. There is no option of a fine. Hung gets six years on the illegal-possession charge – effectively one year for each horn – and two years for fraud. Both men later appeal their sentences ... without success.

14

Shopping for Rhino Horn in Hanoi

December 2011, Northern Vietnam

Mrs Dung's smile is bright and birdlike. 'I have just what you're looking for,' she says, leading the way to the back of the shop. Shelves cluttered with ceramic vases, plates, tea sets, cups, bowls, spoons and serving dishes line the room. 'I sell many of these,' she tells me, scratching around in the darkness and dust of a corner shelf. 'Last year I sold 800 to the army. In total, I think I sold about 1800. Quite a few went to clients outside Vietnam ...'

'Here,' she says, dusting something off. 'Sixteen dollars for the big one. Eight dollars for the small.' She hands me two rather unremarkable-looking dishes, one inside the other. Both have been glazed a dark aquamarine. 'You can touch inside if your hands are clean,' she nods. The bases of the dishes are white and rough. They feel unfinished, with raised nodules like fine sandpaper. A shallow lip protrudes outwards.

'These are what you use to make the medicine,' Mrs Dung says. 'You grind a little bit of the horn off on the bottom in hot water and drink it. It is good for many treatments. For the first stage of cancer, it is very good. The second stage ... Well, there is nothing much you can do.' Neatly painted in white on the side of the larger dish is an image of an African rhino. One of its feet is raised and its head is down. It looks to me as if it is running.

————

The village of Bat Trang is situated on the polluted banks of the Red River, thirteen kilometres from the centre of the Vietnamese capital, Hanoi. It is

264

famed for its pottery and ceramics and has been for several hundred years. The old traditions still thrive here, but these days the villagers derive much of their income from producing cheap knock-offs of Chinese blue-and-white porcelain. It is a monotonous parade of writhing Chinese dragons, impossibly picturesque mountain villages, crystal streams and ancient woods. I read somewhere that the villagers export ceramics worth about $40 million every year. As I wander the streets, I stumble upon the occasional oddity – a ceramic Smurf, an American eagle, a clay tiger, a crocodile, a buxom porcelain woman in an orange bikini, two wrestlers, and even an ancient Chinese figure wearing a pair of seventies shades.

There is a wet sheen on the roads where they have been hosed down to dampen the fine grey dust from the pottery works. Narrow alleyways lead from the main streets to a hidden network of workshops, spinning potters' wheels and fiery kilns. The air is thick with the loamy smell of wet clay. There is also a tantalising scent of spring onions, ginger, cloves, pepper and cilantro. It is lunch time, and the potters and shopkeepers are all tucking into steaming bowls of *pho bo*, the delectable beef noodle broth that is practically Vietnam's staple dish.

———————

Two words and a photograph in a tiny sports shop in central Hanoi led me to Bat Trang. Little more than a hole in the wall with a metal shutter, the shop sold tennis rackets, squash rackets and fake Nike socks. A wheeled display cabinet stood at the entrance. Two pamphlets had been stuck up against the glass. One advocated the benefits of a brand of racket strings. The other promoted a ceramic dish. Below the latter was a slogan in Vietnamese that I couldn't understand, but three words stood out. *Sừng tê giác* – rhino horns. The pamphlet, as I would later discover, was an advert for a 'high-quality rhino horn grinding dish'. On the back of it was an image of a black rhino in a green field.

And there was an address and a telephone number in Bat Trang.

———————

Adverts for rhino horn grinding-dishes abound on Vietnamese websites, online social networks and discussion forums. A typical advert, which had received 7720 hits and nearly 300 responses by the time I viewed it, recommended the use of rhino horn for more than seventy medical conditions, ranging from heat stroke and high fevers to delirium, convulsions, 'hysteria', encephalitis, infections and poisoning. Somewhat surprisingly – given that the use of rhino horn as an aphrodisiac has long been discounted as the sensationalist invention of the Western media – the advert noted that it could also be used to treat impotence.

There were detailed instructions on its use. Pour a little hot water into the grinding-dish, grasp the horn and, using circular movements, rub it against the roughened base of the dish. As fragments of horn mix with the water, it should turn a milky white. The smell it gives off is slightly acrid.

'Drink 0.5 to 1 grams a day,' the advert advises. 'The horn can be used on its own or with other medicines for the purpose of healing.' Prospective customers are warned against buying 'low-quality dishes', which may contain 'impurities and toxic chemicals'. The base of a 'quality dish' should be white and 'feel a bit rough' in contrast to a substandard dish, which invariably has a yellow, uneven base and 'loses its roughness after first use'. In Vietnam there has been a steady, resurgent interest in traditional medicine in recent decades. Scattered across the country today are roughly fifty institutes and hospitals where traditional medicine is practised. Most state hospitals have departments of traditional medicine, and about 9000 health centres are licensed to practise it.

A comprehensive pharmacopoeia – published in Vietnam as recently as 2006 – suggests that rhino horn is 'effective in treating ailments like high fever, delirium, convulsions and headaches'. Four grams can supposedly treat a drug overdose. And a mixture of burnt rhino horn powder, water, aloe, nuts and radish seeds will cure cholera, the authors claim. Rhino horn, the book continues, should ideally be 'harvested by splitting the thick skin from around the nose bone and carefully scraping the hard membrane at the base of the horn'.

'Good quality horns are coloured black, polished, without cracks and have ... a sweet smell ... Rhino horns taste a bit salty, bitter and sour.' When ingested, the authors claim, it targets the heart, liver and lungs, temperature, calms the mind and reduces pain. It should n< pregnant women or in cases where fever is relatively low. It is also ..... , considered a strong aphrodisiac', the entry states.

The latter claim is supported by a 2012 TRAFFIC report that describes evidence of a 'rhino wine' being marketed as a performance enhancer to 'improve the sexual prowess of men'. Known locally as *tuu giac*, it is used exclusively by wealthy consumers, and can apparently be made from any rhino derivative, including blood, dried dung, a penis or fragments of horn mixed with a strong rice wine. This, according to TRAFFIC, seems to parallel developments in the tiger bone trade. Increasingly, tiger bones, which have traditionally been used in the treatment of arthritis, are being marketed in tiger wine concoctions as a sex tonic.

According to the pharmacopoeia, skin from a rhino's groin and armpits 'can be used to help strengthen our health to prevent disease'. The skin is 'processed by removing fur, membrane and grease from the skin, exposing it to the sun during the day and drying it by fire at night for 100 days, soaking it in wine for a month, then exposing it to the sun or drying by fire'. Before it can be used medicinally, it is 'soaked in ash water for seven nights, washed and steamed until it is well-cooked' and then 'eaten every day'.

The chapter concludes with a note to readers. The rhino population, it states, is in rapid decline worldwide. 'It has become an extremely precious species at risk of extinction and included in the Red Book of many countries ... They are now protected by strict and comprehensive legislation and scientists are studying methods to cut their horns to protect them from hunting.'

Whether rhino horn has medical properties or not is largely irrelevant. In Southeast Asia, many people still believe that it does, and that belief will not be easily swayed, even with overwhelming scientific evidence to the contrary.

The horn has been used in traditional medicines for at least 2 000 years. It is used in various herbal remedies and compounds to break a range of ailments, primarily for its supposed antipyretic or fever-reducing qualities.

The handful of published scientific studies that has been conducted into the purported medical benefits of rhino horn have demonstrated little. In

1990, researchers at the Chinese University of Hong Kong found that extracts of both rhino horn and buffalo horn demonstrated 'significant antipyretic action' in rats, but only at massively high doses, far higher than would be used by a human patient. Seven years later, scientists at the University of the Witwatersrand in Johannesburg came to the contrary view. They dismissed the claims as a 'myth' after carrying out experiments which, they wrote, 'unequivocally' proved that rhino horn administered to rabbits had absolutely no fever-reducing qualities.

———

Mrs Dung is in an expansive mood. 'You use very little water in the dish because otherwise it dilutes the horn too much,' she tells me. 'I use it for back pain and arthritis. It is also very good for the blood.' Where did she buy it? 'I got a little bit of horn from a soldier. It was very expensive. About 10 million dong [roughly $500]. But you can use it many times. Sometimes people sell tiny bottles of horn scrapings for 1 million dong. If you can buy a whole horn, it is good for the whole life of the family. But only rich families can afford it.'

She warns me about shopping for rhino horn in the traditional medicine streets of Hanoi's Old Quarter. 'Sometimes they sell you fakes. Buffalo horn, especially. It is never guaranteed that you are getting the right thing. If you buy it from a soldier, you are guaranteed.'

The Vietnamese army's links to wildlife trafficking and environmental crimes have long been a subject of speculation. A 2011 report by the London-based EIA exposed the 'pivotal role' of the Vietnamese military in the illicit timber trade between Laos and Vietnam. Dr Scott Roberton, who heads up the international Wildlife Conservation Society's Vietnam office, says there have been 'anecdotal reports over the years of army vehicles being used to transport wildlife, army officers colluding with traffickers to facilitate cross-border trade in wildlife and other goods and, of course, the army hunting wildlife'.

Mrs Dung says the soldier who sold her the rhino horn also bought a large number of grinding dishes for the men in his unit. 'They are my main customers. Sometimes they give the dishes as a special gift. The army [is] in the forest near the Laos border and Cambodia border and there are a lot of animals there. Elephants, tigers, bears ... So they bring back medicine from the animals for the family or as a special protection.'

And then there is China. 'A few years ago in China they had a lot of horn, but now they don't any more. At the time they didn't have the proper pure dishes like we have, so they came to buy here. I remember, a few years ago I sold a thousand to the Chinese.'

As I pay for the two dishes, Mrs Dung says, 'I know that in your country – in Africa – there are a lot of horns. Perhaps we can do business?'

———————

A block away from Mrs Dung's shop is the address I'd jotted down earlier outside the Hanoi racket store. A large blue and yellow signboard above the doorway reads in English: '*Thien Duc Porcelain Ceramic – To make contract porcelain ceramic for your demand*'. Inside the shop, neat rows of statues and vases – some exquisitely beautiful, others chintzy and kitsch – fill a long room bathed in cold, fluorescent light.

The shop's owner is a man called Cong. His wife's name is Lan. Unlike Mrs Dung, she seems reluctant, even unsettled by my questions. Tran, my interpreter, asks them about the advert. Cong, a toothpick dangling from his mouth, mutters something and his wife scurries wordlessly to the back of the shop. She returns a while later with a rustle of cellophane. In her hands is a blue box covered with a fine layer of brownish dust. Inside it is a white porcelain dish adorned with a simple ideogram and a cobalt lotus flower. Unfortunately, the design is ruined by the inclusion of the shop's name, telephone number and a '100%' quality guarantee. The price for the dish is 1 million dong (about $50). Not cheap in a country where the average monthly wage ranges between $100 and $185.

'The product is different here than in other shops,' Cong says. 'Better quality and a higher price, so we only sell about 200 or 300 a year. We have some foreign customers, but many local.' The toothpick twitches. 'We make the very best quality. We use special pigments and we make them by hand.

We use only pure Japanese clay and German gas ovens. The dishes are baked first at 700 °C, then at 1400 °C. They are sterilised of all toxic substances.'

He's warming to the subject now. A tea set is drawn nearer and he gestures for us to sit. In a large glass jar is his 'special' mix of herbal tea. 'Normally I don't enjoy tea,' he says, 'because it is bitter and I can't sleep well. But this tea, I can drink every day. It is very good for health.' He tells me his wife's name means 'orchid'. 'Mine – Cong – means "power",' he laughs. 'So, you want to buy rhino horn?' he asks.

'No, but I'm interested in its uses.'

'It is very expensive ...'

'I know.'

'One gram will cost you between 1 and 3 million dong [between $50 and $150]. The tip of the horn is the most expensive. It is also higher quality and you can use less for the same results.' He leans closer. 'I have some at home that I use.'

'Ah, what for?'

Cong laughs. He mimes swigging something from a glass and then clutches his head and rolls his eyes. 'Sometimes I drink a little too much. It is good for the head if you have a lot of alcohol.'

'Really? You mean you use it for hangovers?'

'Yes, it is the very best treatment.'

He pours another cup of tea. 'You have many rhino horns where you come from, no? Here is my card. Contact me if you'd like to sell, but only for personal use.'

————

For a quarter of a century, from 1949 to 1976, Hong Kong dominated the rhino horn trade. More than 40 per cent of East Africa's declared exports ended up there. Esmond Bradley Martin, arguably the world's leading expert on the trade, believes that Hong Kong served primarily as a way station and that its importers were not involved in the 'processing of rhino horn or hide for medicinal purposes'.

Instead the horns were sold directly to pharmaceutical firms or re-exported to mainland China, Macao, Taiwan, Singapore, Japan, South Korea, Malaysia and Indonesia'.

The Middle Eastern oil boom of the 1970s and the 1977 CITES trade ban saw Yemen supplant Hong Kong as the primary destination for shipments of horn. Between 1970 and 1977, Yemen recorded receiving 22.5 tons, which, Martin wrote, represents the death of 7800 rhinos. The horn was used to make the handles of *jambiyas*, the ornate daggers that young men were traditionally given to mark their coming of age. By 2000, the trade in Yemen had faded, due largely to the availability of cheaper substitutes like water-buffalo horns, wood and plastic, a growing move away from traditional dress, and increasing levels of political and economic instability that followed September 11, 2001.

In Asia, Taiwan was a significant end-user and exporter, trading directly with apartheid South Africa, which supplied it with at least half a ton of horn between 1978 and 1985. It also sourced large quantities from Hong Kong, recording imports totalling nearly three tons between 1966 and 1985, when imports and exports were officially banned. But the government did little to enforce the ban, and trade – particularly in Asian horn and white rhino horn from South Africa – continued to thrive for much of the 1980s and early 1990s.

Piet Lategan, the former police colonel who headed up South Africa's Endangered Species Protection Unit for nearly a decade, remembers rhino horn being openly sold in Dihua Street in Taipei's Old Quarter. 'If you asked someone how much it cost, they would ask you straight up, "Are you buying, selling or investigating?"' he laughs.

Internal trade was banned on the island in 1989. A register of rhino horn stockpiles, compiled in 1990, lists 1.4 tons of horn held by 410 registrants. But a subsequent survey showed that there were 1800 pharmacies in Taiwan that all stocked rhino horn and suggested that the sizes of stockpiles were probably closer to between four and nine tons. Martin and his wife Chryssee observed in a 1991 article published in the conservation journal *Oryx* that 'Taiwanese self-made millionaires are notorious for their conspicuous consumption of rare and exotic wildlife, and the Chinese traditional adage that animals exist primarily for exploitation is nowhere more pronounced than on this island'.

At the heart of the trade, though, lay China. For at least 2 000 years, rhino horn has been an integral component in traditional Chinese medicine (TCM). Since the eighth century, China has been a major importer of rhino horn, first from Asia and later, via Arab traders, from Africa. During the Tang Dynasty – China's 'golden age', which lasted for nearly 300 years from 618AD – historians recorded the existence of vast numbers of rhinoceroses along the Yangtze River. They were said to be so numerous that 'hunting expeditions would round them up by the scores, or even a hundred or more at a time'. By the mid-nineteenth century, China's rhinos were all extinct.

In the 1950s, under Chairman Mao Zedong, the country saw a dramatic revival in TCM practice. Specialist research institutes and colleges flourished and, at Mao's behest, there was a determined push to integrate Eastern and Western medical practices. In the late 1960s and 1970s, during the excesses of the 'Cultural Revolution', thousands of peasants were trained as primary health-care workers. They became known as the 'barefoot doctors'. Their training was designed to give them a basic grounding in hygiene, first aid, and traditional and Western medicines.

Writing in 1982, Martin said that 'one consequence of the resurgence of traditional practice has been a significant increase in demand for rhino horn in China'. Between 1949 and 1976, China directly imported 13 per cent of East Africa's declared exports. Little is known about the stocks it imported from other countries or entrepôts like Hong Kong and Taiwan.

In the mid-1970s, anywhere between two and four tons of rhino horn a year was going to China. Between 1982 and 1986, long after the imposition of the CITES trade ban, China imported at least ten tons of horn. Much of it is believed to have come from Hong Kong, Macau, Taiwan and North Yemen, with smaller quantities smuggled in from Singapore and Thailand.

In 1988, the Chinese CITES management authority ordered that all medicine factories and import and export companies register their stocks of horn. The final tally came to nearly ten tons. The China National Corporation of Traditional and Herbal Medicine in Beijing had the largest stockpile at just over 3.4 tons, followed closely by the Guangdong Drug Corporation with 1.5 tons. It was estimated at the time that between 600 kilograms and 700 kilograms of horn was used annually in medicines.

Martin wrote that if demand continued at that rate, there would be sufficient stocks for fifteen years – enough horn to last the Chinese market until 2003.

———————

Vietnam's emergence as the leading destination for rhino horn in the world – beginning in 2003 – took South African authorities and conservationists by surprise. For years, the focus had been on China's black market.

In May 1993, the People's Republic had announced a blanket prohibition on the sale, purchase, importation, exportation and possession of rhino horn. Traders were given six months to dispose of their remaining stock, including medicines. Rhino horn was also deleted from the country's voluminous, state-sanctioned pharmacopoeia.

Surveys conducted by TRAFFIC in 1994, 1995 and 1996 found that while a worrying residual black market remained, China had made a 'substantial effort to implement the ban ... The results of these surveys could indicate that China has been highly successful in implementing the domestic ban on trade in rhinoceros horn ...'

The benefits seemed to extend to southern Africa, where poaching levels remained consistently low between 1994 and 2000. The beginnings of the current crisis can be traced to 2002. Twenty-five rhinos were poached in South Africa that year, sharply up from six the previous year. A decade later, 448 rhino would be poached in a single year.

Vietnam's first forays into the rhino horn market were detected in 2003, when the earliest pseudo-hunts took place in South Africa. By 2010, the Vietnamese accounted for as many as 70 per cent of all 'legal' rhino hunts. Oddly, Chinese involvement in hunts seems to have been relatively low. Records compiled by South Africa's Department of Environmental Affairs show that, since 2007, Chinese nationals have only acquired and exported twenty rhino trophies. But questions persist about the extent of China's links to the trade, and there has been some speculation that Vietnamese syndicates may be acting as proxies for Chinese interests. But there are few recorded seizures of horns passing through Vietnam's northern borders with China. In December 2009, a man was arrested by Chinese authorities after he crossed the border with two rhino horns he had bought from a Vietnamese dealer for $63 000.

Then, in April 2011, a truck passing into Guangxi Province from Vietnam was stopped and inspected by border guards. More than 700 elephant tusks and thirty-two ivory bracelets, weighing a total of two tons, were discovered. It was one of the largest ivory seizures ever in China. Inside the truck was a single rhino horn. TRAFFIC has previously identified Vietnam as a 'backdoor' transit route for ivory to China, but believes the same is not true for rhino horn.

Vietnam's dominance of the trade has been fuelled by its rapid economic growth, increases in disposable income, deficient law enforcement and, perhaps most significantly, a resurgent belief in the horn's curative properties, fuelled in part by a cancer myth.

The origins of the urban legend can be traced to about 2006. On the streets of Hanoi and Ho Chi Minh City, a story slowly began circulating. With every telling, the tale evolved. Soon it went viral. The story went something like this: A senior Vietnamese Communist Party official – possibly a government minister or even a retired prime minister, depending on who you cared to listen to – had been diagnosed with cancer. Some said it was cancer of the liver, others of the stomach and lungs. The official was at death's door. Doctors said there was no hope. Then a traditional healer was consulted. Regular doses of rhino horn, drunk with water or alcohol, were prescribed. Within a matter of weeks or months, the patient had made a miraculous recovery.

Like many urban legends, the story had the power to convince. In a short time, possibly egged on by the syndicates that were trying to flog their product, it gained relatively widespread acceptance. The wildlife NGO, Education for Nature–Vietnam (ENV), which set out to investigate its veracity, later concluded that the story was 'most likely the result of artful journalism'.

Nevertheless, it would have far-reaching consequences. Within two years, rhino poaching figures sky-rocketed. In 2007, thirteen rhino were poached in South Africa. The following year, the figure rose to eighty-three, and it continued to rise every year after that: 122 in 2009, 333 in 2010 and 448 in 2011.

Zimbabwe was also hit hard, losing a record 126 rhinos in 2008. Elsewhere in Africa, the West African black rhino was officially declared extinct in late 2011. And there were dire warnings that the northern white rhino, a subspecies once found in Uganda, Chad, Sudan, the Central African Republic and the Democratic Republic of Congo, was on the brink of extinction. Only seven survived – all of them in captivity.

The ramifications would be felt in Vietnam, too. During the decades of war and afterwards there had been no recorded sightings of Javan rhinos in Vietnam. The animal was believed to have disappeared from mainland Southeast Asia.

Back in 1988, a Xtieng tribesman had shot and killed a rhino cow in an area that would later become part of the Cat Tien National Park. The following year, world-renowned biologist, George Schaller, led an expedition deep into the forests. Footprints and dung samples confirmed that at least ten, and possibly fifteen, rhinos lived hidden in the dense undergrowth. Camera traps later recorded the only images of them ever seen.

'That the animal outlived the [Vietnam] war and the destruction wrought on its habitat by bombardment and defoliation is proof of a remarkable ability to survive,' zoologist Charles Santiapillai marvelled in the journal *Pachyderm*, four years after the rediscovery. But, he cautioned, 'Given the high price rhino horn fetches in the international market, the Javan rhino is worth more dead than alive to those Chinese middlemen in Ho Chi Minh City who trade in rhino horn.'

He was wrong in one respect. Its value would be to Vietnamese middlemen.

In October 2011, WWF-Vietnam country director Tran Thi Minh Hien called a press conference. 'The last Javan rhino in Vietnam has gone,' he announced. 'It is painful that despite significant investment in the Vietnamese rhino population, conservation efforts failed to save this unique animal. Vietnam has lost part of its natural heritage.' A subspecies that was once endemic to Southeast Asia was extinct. There are now officially no rhinos left in Vietnam.

The skeletal remains were discovered in Cat Tien National Park in southern Vietnam in April 2010. Six months earlier, WWF researchers and park officials had embarked on a survey to determine how many, if any, Javan rhinos still existed there. Twenty-two dung samples were collected for analysis.

The 6 500-hectare 'rhino core area' – where traces of two rhinos had been found during an earlier study – was surveyed three times. Tests on the dung samples revealed that they all belonged to a lone rhino cow. Of the second rhino – last detected in 2006 – there was no sign. Then, on 29 April 2010, local villagers stumbled upon the carcass. It had been shot in the leg, probably in late 2009 or early 2010, and the horn had been removed. Samples of skin and teeth were taken and sent to Queen's University in Canada for analysis. The results confirmed what the researchers had dreaded.

It was a tragic end to a subspecies that had somehow survived the devastation of the Vietnam War – the bombings, napalm and Agent Orange – only to fall to a poacher's rifle.

————

To gain some understanding of why an urban legend about a politician, rhino horn and a cure for cancer would gain the traction that it did, I visited one of Vietnam's few specialist cancer hospitals. Vietnam has a population of about 89 million people – the thirteenth most populous country in the world. Every year, according to the World Health Organization, up to 200 000 people are diagnosed with the disease, and there are between 75 000 and 100 000 deaths. But only about five major government hospitals are properly equipped to treat cancer sufferers. And, between them, they only have enough beds to accommodate 20 per cent of the crushing demand.

The Vietnam National Cancer Institute – better known as 'K Hospital' – is situated in the heart of Hanoi in an attractive French-colonial building with green shutters and neo-classical arches. A pediment with Roman lettering recalls the hospital's Gallic heritage: *Institvt Dv Radivm De L'Indochine*. Its doors first opened in the 1920s, and it shows. Dark wooden card-catalogues line the main hallways. Slides of tissue samples are packed in ancient wooden trays piled up next to modern microscopes. Some of the equipment is still marked 'Made in the USSR'. There are rooms that don't appear to have changed much since the fifties and sixties. The luckier chemotherapy patients receive their treatment reclining in split-leather armchairs that spill foam through the cracks.

Every day, a swarm of scooters and motorbikes surrounds the hospital. Hundreds of patients crowd a courtyard. The wait is interminable. The relief when a patient's name or number is called out over a tiny loudspeaker mounted on a pole is almost palpable. Some days as many as 700 or 1000 people will push their way into the hospital. Doctors can average up to 100 patients a day. Many of them are from small rural villages and towns, and have scraped together what little they have to seek treatment. Often it is too late.

The wards in Vietnam's cancer hospitals are hopelessly overcrowded. It is not uncommon to find three, even four people sharing a bed and a few more sleeping underneath it. In 2011, the hospital's children's ward was reported to have twenty-five beds for sixty-six patients. Beds are only for those who can afford them. The poor have to sleep on the floor or curled up on mats in the corridors and stairwells. Some sleep on the streets.

Rampant corruption affects almost every aspect of Vietnam's tangled bureaucracy. And it extends to the heart of the country's state hospitals, where underpaid doctors, nurses and administrators readily supplement their income with bribes. Their willingness to accept these supposed 'tokens of thanks' is unsurprising. A doctor with ten years' experience earns a salary equivalent to about $200 a month. A chief nurse with fifteen years' experience will probably earn $175 a month.

Patients know that to get proper treatment, a 'tip' is often required. Usually it is cash, sometimes the offer of an 'opportunity' to a medical doctor or nurse. The latter can involve anything from discounts in a shop owned by the patient's family to enrolling a doctor's children in expensive schools or arranging the purchase of an apartment for them at a greatly reduced 'corporate price'. The practice is commonly referred to as *tê nan phong bì* or 'envelope evil'.

A detailed survey published in September 2011 by corruption watchdog Transparency International found that large 'envelope payments' frequently accompanied operations where there was a 'high chance of mortality'. The amount paid was usually based on the gravity of the illness.

Tran, my interpreter and guide through the hospital, is fatalistic. 'The rich people get treatment outside Vietnam. If you are seriously sick in Vietnam and you can't go to Thailand or Singapore, then you have to accept to die. A lot of people who go to Hanoi and Saigon for treatment are in the final stages and it is too late, because in the local areas they don't have medical facilities. More and more people are getting cancer. There is a lot of pollution in Vietnam today. There are factories poisoning the water with chemicals. In the countryside the soil is polluted and it affects the food. People smoke a lot of cheap cigarettes. And there are chemicals like Agent Orange, which poisoned the soil during the war.'

'It is a harrowing experience for patients,' says Dr Scott Roberton, the Wildlife Conservation Society country rep. 'In Vietnam, if you are diagnosed with cancer, you are going to die, and that's how the doctors approach it. For them, there's no point in trying to treat someone with cancer, and they make no effort to try and protect patients from infection. Often it is the untreated, opportunistic infections that kill them and not the cancer.'

Roberton has lived in Hanoi for more than a decade. His wife is Vietnamese. 'My brother-in-law died of cancer and for eighteen months we went with him through hospitals here, in China and in Singapore. It opened so many doors. It was like being in another world and it helped me gain an understanding of the real challenges we face in tackling the use of rhino horn, tiger bones, bear bile and other animal parts. Radiation therapy makes you ill, so people here don't trust it. This is faith-based medicine. The traditions have existed for thousands of years. People believe in them. You can't dispel the myth of rhino horn's curative properties with Western science, because it works like a placebo. And there's such an interest here in alternative remedies. Patients will try everything and, if they can afford it, they will try rhino horn. It doesn't matter if there is anything real behind it or not.'

In a hospital in China where his brother-in-law, like many other financially well-off Vietnamese, went for treatment, Roberton was astonished at what he saw. 'People openly showed us their rhino horns, although there were quite a lot of fakes. There was a Taiwanese bloke, a famous architect, and someone had gifted him an adult stuffed tiger. You'd walk into this big fancy hospital room and there was this tiger, which was meant to give him strength in his fight.' There were similar scenes in Singapore in a hospital popular with Vietnamese patients. In the oncology ward, 'every single Vietnamese person had rhino horn', Roberton says.

Medical doctors in state hospitals often promote the use of rhino horn to their patients. 'I've tried everything, including rhino horn powder every day,' a businessman in his eighties told the news agency AFP in May 2012. 'Now the doctors have told me I'm in a stable condition. I have lots of money, I am old [and] I just love to live. I have no reason not to spend money on buying the expensive rhino horns and drinking its powder if it helps me.'

At 'K Hospital' there is a thriving department of traditional medicine, where I was told that medical staff regularly encouraged patients to use rhino horn in conjunction with standard cancer treatments. And a doctor at Bach Mai hospital – Hanoi's largest – has been secretly filmed in his office grinding up rhino horn in one of the Bat Trang dishes and sharing the mixture with a visitor.

'I use this every day,' the doctor can be heard saying. 'Look at me. Can you believe I'm sixty? The more the better, I say.'

———

Cong's claim to have used rhino horn to help ameliorate the after-effects of too much rice wine seemed scarcely credible, at first. But the further I travelled, the more frequently I heard the story. And in the months that followed, there was increasing evidence of a disturbing shift in the Vietnamese consumer market.

It has been dubbed the 'Ferrari factor'.

'The new rich want luxury goods that are rare, exotic and expensive as indicators of their success,' says Doug Hendrie, an advisor to ENV. 'These values, in addition to the fact that rhino horn is supposed to be good for you, may be driving the surge here in Vietnam.'

Popular Vietnamese websites, including one linked to an official government newspaper, carry articles touting rhino horn's supposed ability to 'improve concentration and cure hangovers'. 'Rhino horn with wine is the alcoholic drink of millionaires,' proclaims an article on the website viet-bao.com. Another describes rhino horn as 'like a luxury car'.

Vietnam's *nouveau riche* are monied, trendy and ostentatious. It is not uncommon to see a bright yellow Ferrari or a Porsche lumbering cautiously through the chaotic crowds of bicycles and scooters in Hanoi's Old Quarter.

Designer labels and stores crowd the air-conditioned frenzy of the Vincom Towers shopping mall in the centre of the city: Prada, Valentino, Hugo Boss, Givenchy, Armani, Pierre Cardin, Dr. Martens and Longines. There's even an Ecko Unltd store with its distinctive red-and-black rhino logo. The centre-piece of the shop is a plastic rhino. But unlike in South Africa – where the company has put up giant billboards cashing in on the poaching crisis – not a word of protest is evident here.

In Vietnam, rhino horn has been elevated to a status symbol. It is hugely expensive and, theoretically, illegal. Those with money want it, not only for its perceived health benefits, but also because it has such an illicit appeal. Displaying a horn on a shelf or a table is both an overt statement of wealth and one of untouchability. There are stories of businessmen and govern-ment officials drinking brandy from carved rhino horn cups or whole horns being displayed in homes on the altars that families use to pay respect to their ancestors.

Nguyen Huong Giang is one of the new wealthy. The twenty-four-year-old lives in a modern high-rise with wooden floors and expensive furnish-ings. She carries an iPhone and wears tastefully extravagant jewellery. In March 2012, she openly discussed her use of rhino horn in an interview with an Associated Press stringer, Mike Ives. Unlike many others, she had no qualms about being identified and was clearly unconcerned about possible repercussions. She even agreed to be photographed preparing a rhino horn elixir.

'Nguyen Huong Giang loves to party,' Ives later wrote, 'but loathes hang-overs, so she ends her whiskey benders by tossing back shots of rhino horn ground with water on a special ceramic plate. Her father gave her the 10-cen-timetre brown horn as a gift, claiming it cures everything from headaches to cancer. Vietnam has become so obsessed with the fingernail-like substance that it now sells for more than cocaine.

'"I don't know how much it costs," said Giang, twenty-four, after showing off the horn in her high-rise apartment overlooking the capital, Hanoi. "I only know it's very expensive…" [S]he estimates her horn will last another ten to fifteen years. But once her stash is depleted, there may not be any rhinos left on earth to satisfy her craving.'

Vietnam is one of Asia's 'rising dragons', a 'communist capitalist playground' that has a seen a dramatic economic transformation in recent decades. On the surface, it is a country reborn – one that has defied the odds and prevailed despite decades of war, the loss of Soviet financial support and a series of crippling economic crises. It has been hailed as a model of economic liberalisation. The country's first stock exchange was opened in 2000, and seven years later it joined the World Trade Organization (WTO).

Prior to the 2008 global recession, Vietnam had been averaging a remarkable 7 per cent annual growth in its gross domestic product. And, until it finally hit a wall of financial instability brought on by a combination of high inflation, large trade deficits and a weak currency, it was one of Asia's fastest-growing economies.

But Vietnam is also a country in the grip of a paranoid and authoritarian political regime that seems determined to cling to power. Bill Hayton, a BBC reporter and producer who was expelled from the country for his reporting, has described Vietnam as a place where 'the trappings of freedom are apparent on every street, but from the economy to the media, the Communist Party is determined to remain the sole source of authority'.

Their presence is felt from the flags outside shops to the phalanxes of green-uniformed soldiers and the tinny loudspeakers on street corners that once warned of air raids and now continue to pump out party messages and propaganda. State-owned enterprises still dominate the economy and account for 40 per cent of the total GDP. In the pages of the newspapers there are reports of crackdowns on government opponents.

A few days after my arrival, *Viet Nam News*, the English-language daily, carried an article about a seventy-one-year-old Buddhist activist, Nguyen Van Lia, who had been sentenced to five years' imprisonment. His crime: 'Abusing democratic freedoms to infringe upon the interests of the state'. It was not an unusual occurrence. Dozens of other dissidents have received similar jail terms for opaque crimes like distributing 'anti-state' leaflets or collaborating with 'reactionary' groups.

Vietnam's spectacular economic growth has come at a price. The impact on the country's environment has been devastating. Hayton – in his book *Vietnam: Rising Dragon* – refers to the 'dogmatic Marxist-derived belief that the environment is just another resource to be used up in the service of humanity'. Scott Roberton says Vietnam's economic model is, at its heart, driven by a desire 'to make money, no matter what the cost'.

Increasing affluence has led to a growing demand for rare meats and exotic animals to be eaten or used in traditional medicines. Across Vietnam, restaurants advertising *dac san* or 'speciality dishes' abound. Anything from pangolins and civets to snakes, monitor lizards, turtles and deer can be served up. The rarer the animal, the more its flesh is prized. Newspapers have carried lurid tales about the new rich and their wild parties with 'processions of supercars and sexy music shows by long-legged girls' at which 'the meat of endangered animals such as anteater, deer, muntjac, bear and snakes' is consumed.

Surveys conducted in Hanoi in 2007 and Ho Chi Minh City in 2011 reveal disturbing trends where 'affluent and highly educated people are more likely to use wild animal products than those with less money and education'. Businessmen and government officials are the most profligate, dining out and treating guests to an array of exotic dishes as a means of enhancing their status.

In Vietnam, the greatest threat to wildlife is human consumption. Estimates suggest that up to 4500 tons of wild fauna, excluding fish and insects, are used each year as food, medicines and ornaments. Law enforcement efforts have a negligible impact, intercepting between 2 and 5 per cent of the illegal wildlife trade. According to the Hanoi survey, many people found that the consumption of wildlife was 'appealing despite, or even because of, [its] illegality'. Disconcertingly, the survey found that 'non-consumers [of wildlife] will potentially become consumers if their standard of living and disposable income increases'.

In May 2011, wildlife inspectors conducted a raid on a restaurant run by the matriarchal 'kingpin' of a wildlife trafficking ring in Da Lat, a popular tourist destination in southern Vietnam. Minutes after they left, the woman, Mrs Tu Loan – a matronly sixty-year-old – was back in business and offering to sell rhino horn to an undercover journalist from *Thanh Nien* news.

'One hundred million [$5 000] for 100 grams. No bargain,' she reportedly said. 'I just want to help you. Let me ask a friend of mine to bring the rhino horn here. I used to trade in it, but it has become scarce in the past three years.' The director of the local forest protection department, Tran Thanh Binh, later told the reporter that Loan was the 'most infamous wildlife king-pin … in Da Lat' and 'any rhino horn [sold in her restaurant] must have been sourced from her, not anyone else'.

Investigations by Roberton and his colleagues at the Wildlife Conservation Society turned up evidence that she ran a zoo in addition to the restaurant and allegedly used it to 'launder protected species'. The raid was not the first. In August 2010, officials confiscated 300 kilograms of illegal game meat from her restaurant. But despite the raids and mounting evidence, Tu Loan remained in business and untouchable.

You only need to travel to Ha Long Bay, probably one of the most spectacu-larly beautiful places in the world, to see the damage wrought by rampant development, crass commercialism and uncontrolled tourism. A UNESCO World Heritage site, it consists of hundreds of limestone islets and pillars ris-ing dramatically out of the South China Sea. The bay, with its hundreds of fake Chinese-style junks and cruise boats, attracts close to 2 million tourists a year.

But it is dying. Mangrove forests that once lined the shores and protected the bay by filtering out the soil and pollutants being carried into the sea by rivers and streams have long been stripped. In their place is the ugly concrete of Ha Long City. Just north of Ha Long Bay is Cam Pha, the heart of Viet-nam's coal-mining industry. Coal dust blights the sea. The sludge has become so thick, it can be mined. The tourist boats leak diesel into the water. You can smell it on the sea air as you drift between the islands and see the oily iridescence on the water's surface.

The cruise lines all boast that their boats are fitted with septic tanks. Many of them are, but few are equipped to process the raw waste, and the onshore facilities are inadequate. The result, as Hayton bluntly puts it, is that 'the shit of a million and a half boat passengers a year [now closer to two million] is being dumped directly into Ha Long Bay'.

About a thousand people live in four traditional floating villages shel-tered by massive limestone karst pillars. Once upon a time, the waters teemed with fish. But years of overfishing, some of it involving the use of poison, explosives and electric current, has decimated the fish stocks. Most of the fishermen living there now eke out a living from whatever fish they can farm in polluted net pens and from tourism.

Vietnam is a signatory to more international environmental conventions and agreements than most other Southeast Asian countries. But in reality, this has more to do with projecting a favourable image of the country, and saving face, than protecting the environment.

In September 2011, South Africa and Vietnam held bilateral talks in Johannesburg. A media release announced that the countries had 'agreed on a process towards the finalisition [*sic*] of [a] Memorandum of Understanding (MOU) to collaborate among others on natural resource management, wildlife protection and law enforcement'. At a press conference – in which the Vietnamese delegation had grudgingly agreed to participate – I asked Ha Cong Tuan, the then deputy director of Vietnam's forestry administration, about the persistent myth that rhino horn could cure cancer and rumours that its use had been endorsed by a senior Vietnamese government official.

His response was telling. 'I can publicly declare that it is a rumour in Vietnam,' he said through an interpreter. 'Me, myself personally, and others as well, hear that rhino horn can cure cancer. Personally I don't believe in that statement or rumour and we already requested that a medical research institution ... verify if rhino horn can cure cancer and make [the findings] public'.

'You have to look at comments like that within the Vietnam political context,' says a leading conservationist who works in Vietnam, but doesn't want to be named. 'People will often say something in a meeting by beginning with the statement: "In my opinion ..." In effect that allows them to say anything they want with absolutely no accountability. If the person is ever questioned about the statement, he can simply say: "I made it clear that I was speaking in my personal capacity." It is something that is very common in the government workshops we do. Often, I have to step in and tell an official that I don't want to hear their personal opinion and that they are there representing their department and I'd like them to speak on behalf of the department. Usually they then have nothing to say.'

Tuan, who subsequently became Vietnam's Deputy Minister of Agriculture and Rural Development, concluded his response with assurances that Vietnam has 'laws and regulations in compliance with CITES', and that 'we are well aware of the importance of biodiversity conservation'. He added that Vietnam's own 'rhino population is very small, nearly extinguished ... We are making our best effort to conserve wildlife,' he said. The following month came the announcement that Vietnam's last Javan rhino was dead.

Tuan made no mention of the fact that Vietnam had been censured by CITES for non-compliance on three recent occasions. Nor did he address the fact that the country's wildlife legislation is widely regarded as contradictory, riddled with loopholes and poorly implemented. Enforcement agencies are notoriously corrupt, and there is growing evidence that customs agents seize shipments of contraband wildlife not because they are illegal, but because they can make money out of them.

Significantly, the view of animals and plants as commodities that exist to be exploited permeates the country's conservation laws and regulations. Legislation governing trade in protected species refers specifically to animals that have 'scientific, environmental or high economic value'.

In effect, to qualify for regulatory protection, an animal or plant must have a quantifiable value. If it has no value – even if it is incredibly rare or endangered – it has little, if any, legislative protection.

Fines imposed for wildlife crime also have virtually no deterrent effect. The enforcers regard the penalties they impose as income generators. The criminal syndicates see them as little more than an irksome business expense – a tax on stupidity for those caught and unable to bribe their way out of trouble.

The port of Haiphong, for instance, saw a series of massive ivory seizures between early 2009 and 2011. The most spectacular occurred in May 2010, when twenty-two tons of ivory was seized from a container that had been shipped from Malaysia. The ivory was being stored in a warehouse. Customs officials began agitating to sell it, and eventually Vietnam approached CITES for clarity. They were told in no uncertain terms that the ivory could not be sold. By then, some of it had already disappeared, supposedly 'eaten by rats'.

Since then, ivory seizures at Haiphong have ground to a halt. 'Essentially the customs people have taken a decision that if they can't make money out of stopping the trade, why should they bother stopping it,' a conservationist familiar with the matter told me.

At the time of writing, nearly a year after the talks in Johannesburg, the MOU – little more than a formalised 'gentleman's agreement' – had yet to be signed. But there were persistent mutterings that the signing was imminent. Somewhat disingenuously, the Department of Environmental Affairs' deputy director-general, Fundisile Mketeni, claimed in May 2012 that the signing was merely a 'ceremonial thing' and that 'we [South Africa and Vietnam] are already working together'.

I asked Sonja Meintjes, the department's deputy director for biodiversity compliance, about the delay and whether the document was worth the paper it was written on. She claimed a draft agreement was currently being reviewed by the Vietnamese. But why had it taken so long to finalise? 'Well, remember that they must translate everything into Vietnamese,' she said. And she argued, despite Vietnam's history of flagrantly ignoring environmental agreements, that the document would give South Africa a 'platform of engagement'.

'If it is on the table, we can say: "Listen, the presidents or ministers or whoever agreed on this co-operation. Let's co-operate."'

South Africa's reliance on a diplomatic agreement, which Vietnam was clearly so reluctant to sign, seems naive. Vietnam, today, is without doubt the world's leading destination and consumer of rhino horn. The rot that has allowed the illicit trade to flourish extends deep into the Vietnamese government and officialdom. There is no political will there to end the trade. Arrests and seizures at Vietnam's ports occur rarely, if at all. And Vietnamese diplomats still appear to be involved in the trade despite the scandals in South Africa.

'Vietnam doesn't have any rhinos,' a conservationist in Hanoi said to me one day. 'As far as people here are concerned, why should Vietnam worry about another country's natural resources when it can barely look after its own environment?'

15

The Kingpin

14 December 2011, The Lao People's Democratic Republic
The Xaysavang Hotel is easy to miss. A nondescript, $10-a-night flophouse in the small town of Paksan in central Laos, it is situated in a dusty side street that ends in a checkpoint 300 metres further on. Beyond a boom is a slipway leading down to the edge of the Mekong River and the ferry boats that regularly ply the crossing between Laos and Thailand.

A sign outside the hotel advertises beer and karaoke. Stunted palm trees line a driveway leading to a concrete courtyard and a series of cheap clapboard rooms. In a corner is a tacky green-and-gold Buddhist shrine with votive offerings of Pepsi and bottled water that have been left to evaporate in the heat.

By 10 a.m. the truckers, traders and prostitutes that usually frequent the hotel are long gone. We park our car inside the hotel grounds and get out. The door to what appears to be the reception is locked. The interpreter I'd hired for the trip – a sickly hotel desk-clerk with a passable grasp of English – calls out. Nothing. It is oppressively quiet.

I wander across to a carport, where three cars are covered in a thick layer of dust. They seem oddly out of place: a Mercedes-Benz import from the United Arab Emirates, a new-model Mini Cooper and a Toyota Land Cruiser. The tyres are flat.

Finally a man emerges from behind one of the rooms. He's the caretaker, he says. 'We're looking for Vixay Keosavang,' my interpreter tells him. The man shakes his head. The 'boss' isn't here today. Perhaps we should try his house. It is just a short distance away. He gives us the address and a phone number.

'Whose cars are those?' I ask as we turn to leave. 'They're the boss's,' he says, and grins.

———————

I first saw the name in May 2011, in a file of CITES permits and export paper-work for the Xaysavang Trading Export-Import Company. Among the papers were waybills and permits listing a Mr Vixay Keosavang of No. 174 Ban Anousonxay Rd, Paksan district, Bolikhamxay Province, Laos, as the con-signee or importer of at least thirteen lion carcasses and various white rhino trophies. There were three invoices for a total amount of R981 600 (about $120 000), addressed for Vixay's attention at Xaysavang Trading. The invoices reflected the sale of three trophies – six rhino horns – priced at R60 000 a kilogram. Their combined weight was 16.36 kilograms.

Over the course of several months I accumulated nearly 400 pages of documents, in addition to hundreds of photographs, detailing Xaysavang Trading's business dealings. In all, Vixay's name occurs just sixteen times. For the most part he remains a shadow, a distant puppet master manipulating the strings but never dirtying his own hands.

Few South Africans have ever heard of Laos, so much so that a lawyer representing two Xaysavang employees noted their place of employment in an affidavit as the 'Vichai Company ... a company registered in Louse [sic] and operating out of Louse [sic]'.

An early report by investigator Paul O'Sullivan, summing up his inquiries into the company, refers to 'intelligence [which] indicated that [Chumlong] Lemtongthai', a key Thai figure who was arrested in July 2011, 'is No. 2 in the syndicate and that the No. 1 is a Vietnamese resident, by the name of Vixay Keosavang, or Vixay Xaysavang, with (assumed to be Thai) passport no. S0044894'.

Johnny Olivier – the South African fixer who blew the whistle on the syn-dicate – referred to Vixay as the 'big boss' of the operation in his statements, and claimed that he was briefly introduced to him by Chumlong during an internet video chat.

The first public mention of Vixay's name in connection with Xaysavang's operations, as far as I have been able to ascertain, was in an October 2007 edition of Vietnam's *Tien Phong* newspaper. In one of a series of investigative reports examining the illegal primate trade between Laos and Vietnam, a Vietnamese journalist, Huong Quoc Dung, described meeting Vixay at the Xaysavang Hotel in Paksan.

Dung had unearthed a set of CITES documents, including a permit, which had allowed Xaysavang to export more than 80 000 wild animals to Vietnam, among them 7 000 monkeys, 13 000 snakes and 60 000 turtles. The monkeys went to Trung Viet, a Vietnamese company that reportedly shipped thousands of supposedly 'captive-bred' animals to the United States. The company also had links to a controversial Miami-based clearing house that imported monkeys from around the world and sold them off to animal research laboratories.

Dung's investigations suggested that the CITES documents had been forged to conceal the real origins of the animals and cover up the fact that they were not 'captive bred' but had been caught in the wild. When the Vietnamese journalist confronted him, Vixay claimed ignorance, saying he knew nothing about the shipments or the documents. He also denied that Xaysavang had ever exported wild-caught animals to Vietnam or any other country.

The interview did shed some light on the company's dealings with Vietnamese and Chinese businesses. Vixay told Dung 'there are very many Vietnamese companies dealing with us in ... timber import and export and consumer products'.

Laos's timber industry – which sees an estimated 90 000 hectares of forest cut down each year to meet a growing demand for raw materials from neighbouring countries – is notoriously corrupt. The London-based EIA says 'flagrant violation of Lao law is the norm' in a timber industry driven by 'powerful vested interests profiting from the illicit trade in logs from Laos to Vietnam'.

Vixay also told Dung that he had partnered with a Chinese businessman, whom he identified only as 'Mr Chen', in a primate-breeding venture on a 22-hectare farm just outside Paksan. The animals, predominantly long-tailed macaques, would be bred for export to China. Mr Chen had invested $1 million in the project, he said. The initial contract was for ten years, ending in 2016. He claimed that in a little over a year since 2006, 300 macaques had been bred on the farm.

'Our plan is to breed 10 000 individuals,' he said. Within five years the farm would descend into a horror show.

―――――――

Laos is one of Southeast Asia's poorest nations and one of the world's few remaining one-party communist states. Since 1975 it has been led by the Lao People's Revolutionary Party (LPRP). No other political parties are tolerated, and the Laotian constitution refers to the LPRP as the 'leading nucleus' of the political system. Corruption and cronyism are rife. The international corruption watchdog, Transparency International, routinely lists the country near the bottom of its annual Corruption Perceptions Index.

Since the collapse of the Soviet Union, its long-time benefactor, Laos has struggled to find its feet among Asia's rapidly rising dragons. Today the country remains heavily dependent on foreign aid. Economic reforms have been slow. Laos applied to join the WTO in 1997, but it has taken more than fifteen years for its membership to become a reality. In 2011, a stock market was opened in the capital Vientiane in the hope of attracting foreign investment. But 80 per cent of the country's 6.5 million people still eke out a living from subsistence agriculture. And only about 5 per cent of the land is considered arable.

In part, this is due to the fact that Laos has the dubious distinction of being the most heavily bombed country in history. A deadly harvest of cluster bombs and unexploded munitions still litters the countryside nearly forty years after the end of America's 'secret war' there. From 1964 until 1973, B52 bombers saturated the forests and fields along the length of Laos's border with Vietnam. Their target was the Ho Chi Minh trail, a 1 600-kilometre-long spider's web of jungle paths and mountain paths that criss-crossed the Laotian and Cambodian borders and served as a key supply route for the North Vietnamese in their war against the south and its US allies.

The statistics are staggering. Bombers flew 580 344 sorties, dropping 2.4 million tons of bombs, more than all the bombs dropped on Germany and Japan combined during World War II. Cluster bombs sprayed 260 million 'bomblets', slightly smaller than tennis balls, across the countryside. It is estimated that 80 million of them didn't explode on impact. Every year 300 people on average – many of them children – continue to be killed or maimed. The decade-long bombing campaign cost the US $2 million a day (about $17 million in today's currency). In the seventeen years since 1995, the US government has provided a little over $59 million to fund projects aimed at removing unexploded ordnance.

The Vietnam War, and the French Indochina War before it, left another legacy: a complex network of smuggling routes running between Laos and the five countries that share its borders: Myanmar (previously known as Burma), China, Cambodia, Thailand and Vietnam. Historically, the mountains and forests on Laos's north-west frontier formed part of the infamous 'Golden Triangle', a vast region of opium production that straddled borders with Thailand and Myanmar.

In the 19th century, demand for opium in China grew to insatiable heights. It was driven by unscrupulous British, American and European traders, who traded opium grown in Bengal and India in exchange for silks, teas and other Chinese goods. By the 1900s, it was said that a third of China's population was addicted to opium.

This mass addiction prompted rapid expansion of opium cultivation. To meet the demand, traders from China's Yunnan province, just north of Laos, also extended their operations into the Golden Triangle. Fields of lilac poppies flourished in the highlands and inaccessible jungle-covered mountains. Opium production became the 'mainstay' commercial crop for Laos's Hmong hill tribes. Eventually, in the 1940s, the French cornered the trade. Between 1946 and 1954, during the French Indochina War, cash-strapped French intelligence agencies seized control of opium traffic and used the profits to finance covert operations in the region.

In a ground-breaking book, *The Politics of Heroin in Southeast Asia*, a US historian, Alfred W. McCoy, wrote that by 1951, the French 'controlled most of the opium trade from the mountain poppy fields to the urban smoking dens'. Insiders dubbed it 'Operation X'. According to McCoy, this clandestine opium traffic produced 'a legacy of Corsican narcotics syndicates and corrupted French intelligence officers', many of whom would later become 'key figures in the international narcotics trade'.

The CIA's subsequent secret war was also dogged by allegations that its Laotian operations were funded with the proceeds of heroin trafficking. Many of the claims centred on Air America, a passenger and cargo airline that was covertly owned and operated by the agency in Laos. Its motto was 'Anything, Anywhere, Anytime, Professionally'. In addition to flying spies, soldiers, diplomats, civilians and casualties all over Southeast Asia, the airline provided key logistical support to CIA-backed Hmong guerillas. As for drugs, the agency has consistently denied any 'knowing' involvement in the trade. A recently declassified 'secret history', published by the agency's Centre for the Study of Intelligence, does concede that 'narcotics production [in Laos] continued in sometimes uncomfortably close proximity to the irregular [Hmong] forces managed by the CIA'.

There were no laws in Laos prohibiting the trade in opium and heroin until 1971, and personal use of the drug was legal up to 1996. Until a government crackdown in the late 1990s, Laos remained the third largest producer of opium poppies in the world. Since 1998, however, the amount of agricultural land that was used for opium production is reported to have fallen by 98 per cent. An aggressive anti-drugs campaign, fuelled by the government's desire to increase its international credibility, saw the poppy fields systematically eradicated. But the smuggling routes remained, old networks that now carried new 'products': timber, people, animals, ivory and, sometimes, rhino horn.

The ground floor of the Joma Bakery next to the Benoni Cafe in the heart of the Vientiane's tourist quarter is packed with expats and travellers gulping down lattes, turkey sandwiches, smoked salmon bagels, tuna melts and salads. At a table upstairs a man is showing me photographs of brutalised pangolins; bundles of them trussed up in blue nylon sacks.

Also known as scaly anteaters, they are today among the most threatened animals in the world. There is massive consumer demand for them in China and, to a lesser degree, Vietnam. In restaurants, their flesh is sold as a delicacy. Despite the fact that there is no scientific evidence to support the claim, the blood and scales are said to be imbued with medical properties that promote weight loss, enhance lactation in pregnant women and, like rhino horn, supposedly cure cancer.

They are killed to order in restaurants. The animals are knocked unconscious and their throats are slit to drain the blood. Then, sometimes still half alive, they are thrown into a pot of boiling water to remove the scales before being chopped into small pieces, which are braised and added to soups and a variety of other dishes.

The photographs show sacks of pangolins crammed into a rusted cage on the back of a Toyota. Shot on a cellphone camera, the images were taken in a village somewhere near Route 8, one of the highways linking Laos and Vietnam. On the side of the vehicle is a circular blue-and-white company emblem featuring stylised images of snow-capped mountains, forests, a highway, the Mekong River and the Thai-Lao Friendship Bridge that spans it. Two trucks, a cargo ship and aircraft complete the logo. Lettering in Lao and English reads: 'Xaysavang Trading Import-Export Co., LTD'.

The man seated across from me has agreed to meet me on condition that I not disclose his identity. 'I've got a family,' he says, by way of explanation after taking his seat. 'I've got to be careful.' As it is, he's taking some risk talking to an unaccredited foreign journalist. The Laotian government doesn't much like prying outsiders and exercises an authoritarian control over local media. All newspapers, television and radio stations are state-owned and run. Foreign journalists who obtain official accreditation to report in the country usually find themselves accompanied everywhere they go by 'minders' from the government's state security agencies.

Crimes such as 'distorting' LPRP party policies, 'spreading false rumours' and 'slandering the state' are punishable with imprisonment. In 2003, two European journalists and their translator were arrested on trumped-up murder charges after travelling to central Laos to report on conflict between the Hmong and the communist regime. (A low-level Hmong rebellion has been simmering since 1975.) The journalists were detained after being caught up in a shoot-out in which Laotian troops killed a Hmong village security guard. After a summary trial lasting only two-and-half hours, the three men were each sentenced to fifteen years in jail. Laos later bowed to international pressure and released them. Two Hmong tribesmen who had helped them were not so lucky. A decade later, they remain in prison.

Conditions in Laotian jails are said to be appalling. Released prisoners have told of inmates shackled together in leg irons, forced to sleep on concrete floors in cells stinking of human excrement. They are routinely starved and beaten. In its 2012 annual report, Amnesty International reported that three demonstrators who were arrested in October 1999 for attempting to stage a peaceful protest against the government were still being held in jail despite having completed their ten-year prison sentences. Activists claim that a network of brutal secret prisons exists where dissidents, among them Hmong rebels, are held.

I caught a glimpse of one such prison from a boat on the Mekong River. It was set in a jungle clearing, guarded on one side by the river and on the other by green hills and dense, almost impregnable forest. Two long barracks were flanked by watchtowers manned by silhouetted figures armed with rifles. The boatman steered a wide berth away from the bank that the prison stood on and cut across the current.

'It is a bad place,' the boatman said.

Upstairs at the Joma Bakery, a man takes a seat within earshot of our table. He slouches with his back against a wall and then promptly dozes off. Or appears to. My contact looks uncomfortable. His voice drops to a whisper as he glances across at the interloper, whose eyes are hidden by sunglasses. Finally, he suggests that we move. 'I don't know who he is,' he whispers, 'but it could be someone trying to listen to us.'

Once we're settled in another room and another corner, he tells me about a shipment that was stopped by a customs officer at Vientiane airport on 9 May 2004. There were 400 pangolins weighing about 600 kilograms packed in crates. Twenty of them were already dead. The cargo was bound for Vietnam en route to China and was accompanied by CITES permits and documentation, which may have been forged. The shipment was detained for several hours and then, inexplicably, someone ordered that it be released. This was done after a tax of $6 a kilogram had been levied. The customs officer who had stopped the cargo was later reprimanded. The name on the export manifest was Xaysavang Trading.

Documents I received from another source shed even further light on the extent of Xaysavang's wildlife-trafficking operations. One is a sales contract between Xaysavang Trading, represented by its 'director', Vixay Keosavang, and a Vietnamese import-export company called ThaisonFC, JSC. In terms of the agreement, which was signed in March 2009, Xaysavang would provide the Vietnamese with 100 000 live animals, including 40 000 rat snakes, 20 000 monocellate cobras, 10 000 king cobras, 20 000 water monitors and 20 000 endangered yellow-headed temple turtles – all of which are considered delicacies in parts of Asia. Xaysavang stood to make $860 000 from the deal (about R6.9 million). The shipments would be delivered in tranches over the next eight months through several Vietnamese land borders, ports and airports.

A certificate of origin issued to Xaysavang Trading by the Bolikhamxay Provincial Chamber of Industry and Commerce in Paksan on 16 March 2009 shows that 2 000 yellow-headed temple turtles, weighing about 10 tons, were to be shipped by truck from Laos to Vietnam. Vixay's business card lists him as the deputy chairman of the Bolikhamxay Chamber of Industry and Commerce.

From other documents it would appear that Vietnam may not have been the final destination. In an earlier transaction, ThaisonFC, JSC, received a shipment of 2 000 live yellow-headed temple turtles from Laos and re-exported them to the Quang Da Seafoods Trading Company in China's Guangxi province.

———————

Xaysavang Trading was formally registered in Laos on 8 August 2008 with reported start-up capital of just over $1.6 million. The enterprise registration certificate lists Vixay Keosavang as the sole director.

It remains unclear when exactly the company expanded its business operations to southern Africa. The whistleblower, Johnny Olivier, remembers meeting Punpitak Chunchom, Vixay's 'man in South Africa', and some of the Thais working for Xaysavang, in mid- to late-2008. At the time, the main focus of their enterprise was the purchase of lion bones. Records obtained by Gareth Morgan, a DA Member of Parliament, showed that five South African game farmers and taxidermists shipped at least 327 lion carcasses or skeletons to Xaysavang in Laos between 2009 and 2010.

The first time the company appears to have been implicated by name in illegal activities in Africa is in a press statement released by the Kenya Wildlife Service (KWS) on 27 July 2009. It recorded that KWS, together with Kenyan customs, had seized 280 kilograms of 'raw elephant ivory' and two un-mounted rhino horn 'trophies' weighing eighteen kilograms. The estimated value was $1 million.

The consignment, which had originated in Mozambique, was 'illegally destined to Laos'. According to the statement, 'The captured trophies were registered in the name of Xaysavang Trading Export Import Company Limited and destined to Paxsan District-Bolikhamxay Vientiane-Laos.' KWS head Julius Kipng'etich commented that 'since Mozambique has no rhinos and elephants, we suspect the trophies were illegally poached from neighbouring countries and transported to Maputo by road'.

Waybills issued by Mozambique Airlines in Maputo show that other consignments were routed from there to Johannesburg, and then on to Hong Kong, Bangkok and, finally, Vientiane. On 25 November 2010, 435 kilograms of cargo was shipped from Mozambique. The contents were listed on the waybill as 'personal effects'. The shipment, which was addressed to Xaysavang Trading in Laos, arrived in Bangkok on 6 January 2011, and was detained and searched by Thai customs officials. Inside two pallets they found sixty-nine elephant tusks and four pieces of ivory worth an estimated $320 000 (about R2.6 million).

———

The farm on the outskirts of Paksan is run-down and neglected. Dozens of macaques clamour for attention in filthy, rusted cages. Some appear to have escaped and run wild around the wire pens, scaling the sides and looking in at the macaques that are still caged. There is little food. They are housed fifteen to twenty in a pen. Many of the animals are ill and painfully thin, their hair falling out in clumps. There are rumours that Xaysavang is in trouble; that Mr Chen and the Chinese have pulled out and that the monkeys are being left to starve to death.

In late 2011, an undercover team from the British Union for the Abolition of Vivisection (BUAV) – a British-based NGO that campaigns to stop animals from being used in scientific experiments – counted 575 macaques in pens on the farm. They found that many of the animals were starving to death. 'Some were dead in their pens.'

A man, who claimed to be the owner but is not named in the BUAV report, told them he did not have money to feed the monkeys, but in the same breath claimed that he was opening a 'zoo' and had been granted a government licence to do so. 'I'm opening a new farm which is bigger than this one,' he said.

———

In July 2012, the WWF released a 'wildlife crime scorecard' assessing levels of CITES compliance and enforcement in twenty-three countries that are central to the international wildlife trade. Laos, Vietnam and Mozambique were the worst performers. Vietnam was the top destination for rhino horn from South Africa. Laos and Mozambique had failed utterly in enforcing the international ban on trade in ivory, the 'scorecard' found, citing a recent survey in Vientiane that found 2 500 items of ivory at twenty-four retail shops.

'While much of Laos's illegal ivory was said by traders to derive from Laos's Asian elephants, there have been seizures of African ivory en route to Laos in Thailand and Kenya,' the WWF report noted. 'Laos itself has never reported an ivory seizure.'

In a clear reference to Xaysavang, although it did not name the company, the report raised concerns about the trade in rhino horn trophies and lion bones from South Africa to Laos and Vietnam. 'While the end-use of the lion bones is not known, it is likely that they are feeding into illegal internal markets for tiger bone medicine. Laos and Viet Nam should clearly enforce prohibitions against the use of captive big cats to supply internal and international trade.'

————————

Vixay Keosavang first came to the attention of Thai police nearly a decade ago. A 2003 Thai crime intelligence report on key figures in the illegal wildlife trade lists him by name and includes details of numerous wildlife transactions in which he was allegedly involved. Tons of animals were routed to buyers in China, the report states. It also suggests ties between Vixay and a Malaysian wildlife dealer. Information contained in the report about Vixay himself is sketchy and suggests that he may have at one stage been a police officer in Vietnam.

A far more detailed profile emerges in information from Vietnamese sources. Vixay was born in 1958 in Xiangkhouang Province in north-eastern Laos. During the CIA's decade-long 'secret war', it would gain the unenviable distinction of being the most bombed province in the most bombed country in the world.

In the late 1970s, Vixay was conscripted into the Lao People's Army. Reports suggest he was discharged in 1993. There is some speculation that he still has ties with Laotian military intelligence structures. There are also suggestions that he held a senior position in a powerful state-run company with interests in construction and international trade.

His political links seem to have taken shape in the early 1990s, when he was reportedly appointed as secretary to the chairman of the Bolikhamxay provincial assembly. Over the next ten years he worked in various positions within the provincial government, heading its 'foreign co-operation division' and later serving as deputy director of the province's Department of Trade. His business card lists him as vice-president of both the Laos national swimming and boxing committees.

Vixay reportedly told Huong Quoc Dung, the Vietnamese journalist, that he had been 'assigned by leaders' in 2002 to run Xaysavang Trading. He did not name the 'leaders' and would give no explanation for the strange 'assignment'.

In his house is said to be a collection of photographs showing him posing with senior Laotian government ministers, including the Minister of Trade, and the Minister of Planning and Investment. Perhaps most troubling of all is a report which states that Vixay accompanied the Laotian deputy prime minister, Bouasone Bouphavanh (later the country's prime minister for four years), on an official visit to Vietnam in 2004.

It seems clear that Vixay's background as a senior government official and his carefully cultivated ties to powerful Laotian and, possibly, Vietnamese politicians ensure that he can continue his dealings without fear of arrest or prosecution. Steven Galster, who heads up the Bangkok-based Freeland Foundation, which investigates wildlife crime and human trafficking in the region, describes Vixay as 'the Mr Big in Laos'.

'He seems so well protected and we haven't met any law enforcement officers in Laos who are able, or willing, to take this on.'

Vixay's home is just over a kilometre from the hotel. Its location hints at his influence. To reach it, we drive north, away from the river, past the offices of the Ministry of Justice, the People's Court of Bolikhamxay Province and a local bank. We turn left into a street that leads to the Bolikhamxay planning and investment department. In the centre of the block is a sprawling building that houses the main provincial administration offices. Diagonally opposite it is a bright yellow, red and blue sign and the name Xaysavang Trading Export-Import. A Laotian flag flutters in the breeze. An ornate green-and-gold fence fronts the property. By Laos's impoverished standards, the house is a mansion, although one that has seen better days. It is an odd-shaped construction with three second-floor balconies that look as if they have been randomly pasted onto the side of the building. The roof is a zigzag of red tiles, the garden unkempt and the grass overgrown.

The main gate is unlocked, but the front door is shut and there is no sign of Vixay. I dial his cellphone number. A male voice answers, but before I can say much, he cuts me off. 'No English,' he says. I hand the phone to the interpreter. I had decided it would be best to keep my story vague. The interpreter has been briefed to tell Vixay that I have travelled to Laos from Africa and would very much like to meet him to discuss business. Given that I didn't have official press credentials, I had decided I would only broach the subject once I met him.

Vixay is in Vientiane, the interpreter tells me. We had probably passed him on the road. He is tied up in meetings in the capital, he says, but will have time to meet in a few days. He asks that I send him a fax with a formal request.

Before I travelled to Laos, I'd only ever seen one photograph of Vixay. It was affixed to a copy of the 2008 company registration form. Formal and sterile, it told me very little. It showed a man with neatly combed black hair, plump cheeks and full lips in a neat black suit with a red tie.

Later I was shown digital footage that had been secretly filmed with a hidden camera in the office of Vixay's house in Paksan. The footage was blurred and unsteady but, for a few moments, Vixay was clearly identifiable. He looked a little older than in the photograph, but there was no doubting that it was the same man. The camera panned. On the wall behind Vixay was a buffalo trophy. To his left was a photograph of him and his wife, both dressed in white, probably on their wedding day, mounted in a gilt, baroque frame. It was propped up on a table flanked on one side by a heavy wooden chair with dragons for armrests and, on the other, by a grey, steel filing cabinet.

The investigator who had obtained the footage remarked after I watched it: 'Imagine what stories that filing cabinet could tell.'

I never did meet Vixay. The first meeting was postponed, then the next. When I pressed him, he did what any wildlife trafficking kingpin in Laos would do. He called the police. Eventually I sent him a fax with a list of questions about Xaysavang's activities. He didn't answer them. When the interpreter called him, he grew angry. He denied any involvement in trafficking rhino horn and lion bones, and insisted that his business was legally conducted 'on behalf of the Laotian government'. When the interpreter called him again, he was threatened with arrest. My fax had been given to the police, he was told. They were investigating. I was warned to leave. Later I heard that someone had been asking questions about me at the hotel I had stayed at in Vientiane. But by then I was in Hong Kong, on my way back to South Africa.

It was a frustrating end to my search for the kingpin. But, in a way, it was also a reminder of how untouchable the crime bosses who drive the rhino horn trade really are.

In South Africa, arrests for rhino-related crimes have almost doubled. Police are beginning to chip away at some of the Vietnamese syndicates, and a number of high-level figures and key contact men in South Africa have been arrested. But more than 80 per cent of arrests continue to be those of poachers – low-level hired guns from impoverished villages in Mozambique, South Africa, Zambia and Zimbabwe. They are cannon fodder, easily replaced. The remaining 20 per cent of those arrested are middlemen, couriers and local exporters. Their arrests are more disruptive. But eventually someone else always steps into the breach.

Within months of the arrests of Vixay's alleged lieutenants, Chumlong Lemtongthai and Punpitak Chunchom, there were indications that another Thai national had arrived in South Africa to co-ordinate Xaysavang's shipments. The company suspended efforts to export rhino horn trophies, but the flow of lion bones continued unabated.

Vixay, however, seems not to have given up on his quest for supplies of horn. A short time after my return home, an undercover investigator recorded Vixay bragging that he had 'many customers' for rhino horn in Vietnam. He claimed the Laos government had given him a 'quota' to trade in ivory, horn and tiger bones. And he said he would be prepared to pay many thousands of dollars for a kilogram of rhino horn.

It is surely only a matter of time before someone steps forward to claim the bounty.

Glossary

BAKKIE – pickup truck

BLIKSEM (N) – scoundrel

BLIKSEM (V) – beat (someone) up

BOERTJIE – diminutive of Afrikaans word for farmer

BOSSIES – literally bush-mad or crazy. Often used in reference to soldiers suffering from post-traumatic stress disorder

BRAAIVLEIS – barbecue where meat is grilled over an open fire

DIE BOSKROEG – The Bush Bar

DOOS – vulg. cunt

DORP – small town

DROËWORS – dried sausage

FARANG – generic Thai word for a Westerner

FINISH AND KLAAR – South African expression meaning 'that's an end to it'

FLOSSIE – Hercules C130 military transport plane

FOKOL – none; nothing; often translated as fuck-all by English-speaking South Africans

GIRLTJIE – derog. diminutive

IMPI – usually refers to an armed band of Zulu warriors involved in urban or rural conflict

IMPIMPI – rat, informer, traitor

JIRRE – exclamation of astonishment/horror/dismay. Derived from the Afrikaans word *Here*, which means God

JISSUS – exclamation of astonishment/horror/dismay/irritation. Derived from Jesus

KAK – shit, rubbish

KAPLYN – the cut-line: the narrow strip of no-man's-land cleared of bush that served as a buffer between Angola and Namibia

KLOMP DRONKGATTE – a bunch of drunkards

KOPPIES – hills

LEKKER – South African word widely used by various language-speakers to mean very nice/good or pleasant

MOERED – vulg. beat up

MOERSE – vulg. tremendous/big/massive

MOS – just

MUTI – traditional medicine

OKES – guys

OUENS – guys

PLAT – literally flat; down to earth

POLISIEKOFFIE – literally police coffee. Refers to a popular drink mix of Coca-Cola and brandy

ROOI GEVAAR – the red peril or communist threat

SLAPGAT – slapdash

STOEP – veranda

TERRS – terrorists

TJOEKIE – jail

TROMMELS – metal trunk

TROEPIE – a diminutive reference to a foot soldier. From the word 'troop'

WOEP-WAP – onomatopoeiac word for the sound a knife makes

WINDGAT (ADJ.) – vulg. windbag, braggart

Abbreviations and Acronyms

ANC African National Congress

ANCYL ANC Youth League

ATF Bureau of Alcohol, Tobacco and Firearms

BBC British Broadcasting Corporation

BCCI Bank of Credit and Commerce International

BUAV British Union for the Abolition of Vivisection

CBCU Customs Border Control Unit

CI confidential informant

CI Crime Intelligence (of the South African Police Service)

CIO Central Intelligence Organisation (Zimbabwe)

CITES Convention on International Trade in Endangered Species of Wild Fauna and Flora

CODIS Combined DNA Index System

CSI Chief of Staff Intelligence (South African Defence Force)

DA Democratic Alliance

EIA Environmental Investigation Agency

ENV Education for Nature–Vietnam

ESPU Endangered Species Protection Unit

EWT Endangered Wildlife Trust

FBI Federal Bureau of Investigation

FNLA Front National de Libération de l'Angola (National Liberation Front of Angola)

IFAW International Fund for Animal Welfare

ISCOR Iron and Steel Corporation

IUEF International University Exchange Fund

KWS Kenya Wildlife Service
LPRP Lao People's Revolutionary Party
MDC Movement for Democratic Change
MI Military Intelligence
MOU Memorandum of Understanding
MPLA Movimento Popular de Libertação de Angola (People's Movement for the Liberation of Angola)
NPA National Prosecuting Authority
NPB Natal Parks Board
NRG National Research Group
NUSAS National Union of South African Students
PAIIC Pan African Industrial Investment Corporation
PH professional hunter
PHASA Professional Hunters' Association of South Africa
PIDE Policia Internacional e de Defesa do Estado (Portuguese International and State Defence Police)
RAR Rhodesian African Rifles
RENAMO Resistência Nacional Moçambicana (Mozambican National Resistance Movement)
REF Rhino and Elephant Foundation
RhoDIS Rhino DNA Index System
Rhodesian SAS Rhodesian Special Air Service
SADF South African Defence Force (post-1994 it has been known as the SANDF – South African National Defence Force)
SAHA South African History Archive
SANF South African Nature Foundation
SANParks South African National Parks
SAPS South African Police Service
SARS South African Revenue Service
SAS Special Air Service (British)
SCI Safari Club International
SSA State Security Agency
SWAPO South West Africa People's Organisation
SWAPOL Namibian Police (originally South West African Police)

TCM traditional Chinese medicine

TOPS Threatened or Protected Species regulations

TRT Tactical Response Team

UNITA União Nacional para a Independência Total de Angola (National Union for the Total Independence of Angola)

USFWS US Fish and Wildlife Service

WHO World Health Organization

WTO World Trade Organization

WWF World Wide Fund for Nature (prior to 1986 it was known as the World Wildlife Fund)

ZANU-PF Zimbabwe African National Union–Patriotic Front

Zimparks Zimbabwe Parks and Wildlife Management Authority

ZRP Zimbabwe Republic Police

Acknowledgements

This book is the result of a more than two-year-long investigation into the criminal underworld of rhino horn trafficking. It is a book that could not have been written without the selflessness and sacrifice of those closest to me, the unforgettable kindness of strangers, and the invaluable contributions of many people who have encouraged and helped me along the way.

I am incredibly fortunate to have the close circle of friends that I have, some of whom played a more direct role in this book than others, but I am grateful to all of them for their support in the long months that it took to produce.

Two of the finest investigative journalists I know, Jacques Pauw and Sam Rogers, were unstinting in their support. Jacques, my former editor and colleague at Media24, believed in this story from the very beginning and encouraged me to pursue it. His advice, guidance and insights into the often rocky road of writing a book were indispensable. As were his lunches.

Geoffrey York and Erin Conway-Smith were voices of sanity amidst the chaos. This book would have been much poorer without Geoffrey's keen eye, his astute reading of the manuscript, and his numerous suggestions, comments and edits. I am indebted.

No journalist should be without a lawyer like Willem de Klerk. One of the finest media lawyers working in South Africa today, he is someone whose judgement, candour and guts I have come to respect.

Thanks also to Robb Northey, Julia de Bruyn and Tim Hopwood. And I should not forget Bea, my constant writing companion and 'co-author', who sat on the windowsill, watched me write and sometimes dozed off as I droned on about the book.

Killing for Profit took me on a journey across southern Africa and Southeast Asia. In Zimbabwe, I am particularly thankful to Blondie Leathem, Natasha Anderson and Norman English. In Vietnam, to Scott Roberton. There are a number of other people who aided me in South Africa, Zimbabwe, Laos and Thailand – sometimes at great risk to themselves – whose identities have to be protected. They know who they are.

Stephen Ellis, a scholar and journalist of the old school, completed my collection of Operation Lock documents and graciously shared his unparalleled knowledge and insights of the operation and the SADF's involvement in the smuggling of ivory and rhino horn.

My gratitude to Judge Mark Kumleben, whose work shed so much light on a dark chapter in our history, for allowing someone he'd never met to borrow the only copy he has of his invaluable 1996 report.

Karl Ammann and Steve Galster – two inspirational wildlife investigators – added immeasurably to my knowledge of the trade and the operations of Southeast Asian syndicates.

I was privileged to share the road with several journalists and filmmakers. Special thanks to my most frequent travelling companions, friends and fellow troublemakers: Phillip Hattingh, Pierre van Heerden and Kyle Hattingh. Your generosity and kindness can never fully be repaid.

My appreciation to Peter Gwin, who travelled a path similar to mine and readily shared insights and ideas. He also memorably introduced me to the Dead Guy at one of Washington D.C.'s best-kept secrets.

I'm particularly grateful to Kelly Buzby. Also to Karen Schoonbee – an incredible researcher and journalist – whose contribution to this book was invaluable. Thanks, too, to Russell MacLaughlin for introducing me to the 'invisible highway' and the people on it.

Many thanks to Clifford Bestall, Jonah Hull, Chris Everson and Sebastian Dunn, Charles Moore, Braam Malherbe, Godknows Nare and Melusi Ngwenya.

I am proud to have worked with several Media24 colleagues who have done exceptional reporting on rhino crimes and whose work and support have aided this book: Wolfram Zwecker, Buks Viljoen, Elise Tempelhoff, Marietie Louw-Carstens and Hanti Otto. Thanks also to my former editor in the Media24 investigations unit, Andrew Trench, who suggested that there might be a book in my rhino investigations. Also Ingrid Pepler and the editors who published the stories, Tim du Plessis, Peet Kruger, Ferial Haffajee and Yvonne Beyers.

Many people went out of their way and gave of their time to answer persistent questions and aid my broader understanding of an extremely complex issue. In particular – though not in any particular order – I would like to thank Ian Player, Jan Breytenbach, Des Burman, Johan Jooste, Joanie Spies, Ansie Venter, Marilé van Heerden, Tom Milliken, Jo Shaw, Rynette Coetzee, Gareth Morgan, Rhishja Cota-Larson, Ken Maggs, Mario Scholtz, Bud Cockroft, Hendrik and Elise Daffue, Charmaine Swart, Charles van Niekerk, Adrian Lackay, Kirsty Brebner, Sonja Meintjes, Magdel Boshoff, Olga Kumalo, Albi Modise, Johnny Olivier, Michael 't Sas-Rolfes, John Hume, Dawie and Sariette Groenewald, Hennie Erwee, Chris van Wyk, Adri Kitshoff, David Newton, Piet Lategan, Selomie Maritz, Ed and Lorinda Hern, Ruben de Kock and the Lemmer and Zitha families.

Pulling together a book is a collaborative effort. Many thanks to Kirsten van Jaarsveld, who painstakingly transcribed the recordings of a large number of my interviews. I am also indebted to the team at Zebra Press: publisher Marlene Fryer, who took a chance on a little-known writer; my editor, Ronel Richter-Herbert, who patiently coaxed this book into being amidst a flurry of missed deadlines; and Jane Housdon for her diligent proofreading, advice and insights.

The costs of research and travel for this book were partly covered by a grant from the Taco Kuiper Fund for Investigative Journalism, administered by the Valley Trust and the Wits Journalism Programme. My thanks to Margaret Renn, Anton Harber and Brigitte Read.

Writing a book is a selfish exercise. You cut yourself off, and hole yourself up in a room with your laptop, files and thoughts. The walls are soon plastered with torn-out notes, press cuttings, snippets of 'vital' information, ideas, stats and increasingly complex spider diagrams mapping out chapters. For months, everything but the book is ignored. You grow a scraggly beard. Simple daily chores go undone. You become increasingly obsessive and irritable when anything other than the book intrudes. Your friends start to make jokes about Boo Radley and Howard Hughes. As weeks turn to months, the process takes a toll, particularly on those you love.

This book could not have been written without the immense selflessness and support of my partner, Trish. More than anyone, she deserves praise. She didn't baulk when I decided to resign from my job to write it – she allowed me to live a dream, even at times when the deadline pressures made it seem more like a nightmare. She gave far more than I deserved and I am eternally grateful.

My father Robert and my mother Anita gave me a love of history, story-telling and writing, and encouraged my single-minded pursuit of a career in journalism, even though it sometimes worried them. Sadly my mother is not here to see this.

Nor is Marléne Burger – an indomitable journalist who took me under her wing all those years ago. I miss you both.

JULIAN RADEMEYER
JOHANNESBURG
SEPTEMBER 2012

References

BOOKS

Adams, Douglas, and Mark Carwardine. *Last Chance to See*. London: Random House, 2011

Adams, Jonathan S., and Thomas O. McShane. *The Myth of Wild Africa: Conservation Without Illusion*. Berkeley: University of California Press, 1997

Ahern Jr, Thomas L. *Undercover Armies – CIA and Surrogate Warfare in Laos*. Center for the Study of Intelligence, Central Intelligence Agency, 2006

Barlow, Eeben. *Executive Outcomes: Against All Odds*. Alberton: Galago Books, 2007

Basson, Adriaan. *Finish & Klaar: Selebi's Fall from Interpol to the Underworld*. Cape Town: Tafelberg, 2010

Bonner, Raymond. *At the Hand of Man: Peril and Hope for Africa's Wildlife*. New York: Knopf, 1993

Breytenbach, Jan. *Eden's Exiles: One Soldier's Fight for Paradise*. Cape Town: Queillerie, 1997

Brown, Robin. *Blood Ivory: The Massacre of the African Elephant*. Stroud: History Press, 2008

Burger, Marléne, and Chandré Gould. *Secrets and Lies: Wouter Basson and South Africa's Chemical and Biological Warfare Programme*. Cape Town: Zebra Press, 2002

Capstick, Peter H. *Death in the Dark Continent*. New York: St. Martin's Press, 1989
———. *Death in the Long Grass*. New York: St. Martin's Press, 1978

Davies, Ben, and Jane Goodall. *Black Market: Inside the Endangered Species Trade in Asia*. San Rafael: Earth Aware Editions, 2005

Dennison, André, and J.R.T. Wood. *The War Diaries of André Dennison*. Gibraltar: Ashanti, 1989

Duffy, Rosaleen. *Killing for Conservation: Wildlife Policy in Zimbabwe*. Oxford: International African Institute, 2000

Ellis, Richard. *Tiger Bone & Rhino Horn: The Destruction of Wildlife for Traditional Chinese Medicine.* Washington D.C.: Island Press, 2005

Endangered Wildlife Trust. *Endangered Wildlife Trust Rhino Security Booklet.* 2011

Fahn, James. *A Land on Fire: The Environmental Consequences of the Southeast Asian Boom.* New York: Basic Books, 2004

Gargan, Edward A. *The River's Tale: A Year on the Mekong.* New York: Vintage Books, 2003

Gibson, Clark C. *Politicians and Poachers: The Political Economy of Wildlife Policy in Africa.* Cambridge: Cambridge University Press, 1999

Godwin, Peter. *Mukiwa: A White Boy in Africa.* London: Pan Macmillan, 1996

Guggisberg, C.A.W. *S.O.S. Rhino.* London: Deutsch, 1966

Hayton, Bill. *Vietnam: Rising Dragon.* New Haven: Yale University Press, 2011

Herne, Brian. *White Hunters: The Golden Age of African Safaris.* New York: Henry Holt and Company, 2001

Hodgson, Barbara. *Opium: A Portrait of the Heavenly Demon.* Vancouver: Douglas & McIntyre, 2004

Kennedy, Michael. *Soldier 'I' – The Story of an SAS Hero.* Oxford: Osprey Publishing, 2011

Kentridge, Matthew. *An Unofficial War: Inside the Conflict in Pietermaritzburg.* Cape Town: David Philip, 1990

Maier, Karl. *Angola: Promises and Lies.* London: Serif, 2007

Martin, Esmond Bradley, and Chryssee Martin. *Run, Rhino, Run.* London: Chatto & Windus, 1982

Matloff, Judith. *Fragments of a Forgotten War.* London: Penguin Books, 1997

McCoy, Alfred W. *The Politics of Heroin in Southeast Asia.* New York: Harper Colophon Books, 1973

Mishra, Hemanta. *The Soul of the Rhino.* Guildford: Globe Pequot Press, 2008

Nortje, Piet. *32 Battalion: The Inside Story of South Africa's Elite Fighting Unit.* Cape Town: Zebra Press, 2006

Owen-Smith, Garth. *An Arid Eden: A Personal Account of Conservation in the Kaokoveld.* Cape Town: Jonathan Ball Publishers, 2012

Pauw, Jacques. *In the Heart of the Whore: The Story of Apartheid's Death Squads.* Johannesburg: Southern Book Publishers, 1991

———. *Into the Heart of Darkness: Confessions of Apartheid's Assassins.* Johannesburg: Jonathan Ball Publishers, 1997

Pickover, Michelè. *Animal Rights in South Africa.* Cape Town: Juta and Company Ltd, 2005

Player, Ian. *The White Rhino Saga.* New York: Stein and Day, 1973

Potgieter, De Wet. *Contraband: South Africa and the International Trade in Ivory and Rhino Horn.* Cape Town: Queillerie, 1995

———. *Total Onslaught: Apartheid's Dirty Tricks Exposed.* Cape Town: Zebra Press, 2007

Pyle, Richard, and Horst Faas. *Lost Over Laos: A True Story of Tragedy, Mystery and Friendship.* Cambridge MA: Da Capo Press, 2004

Read, Tom. *Freefall.* London: Little, Brown and Company, 1998

Reeve, Rosalind. *Policing International Trade in Endangered Species: The CITES Treaty and Compliance.* London: Earthscan, 2002

Roosevelt, Theodore. *African Game Trails: An Account of the African Wanderings of an American Hunter-Naturalist.* New York: St. Martin's Press, 1988

Ross, Hamish, and Fred Marafono. *From SAS to Blood Diamond Wars.* Barnsley: Pen & Sword Military, 2011

Selous, Frederick Courteney. *A Hunter's Wanderings in Africa: Being a Narrative of Nine Years Spent Amongst the Game of the Far Interior of South Africa.* Alberton: Galago, 2006

Smith, Ian Douglas. *The Great Betrayal: The Memoirs of Ian Douglas Smith.* London: John Blake Publishing Ltd, 1997

Stiff, Peter. *Cry Zimbabwe: Independence – Twenty Years On.* Alberton: Galago, 2004

———. *The Silent War: South African Recce Operations 1969–1994.* Alberton: Galago, 2001

———. *Warfare by Other Means: South Africa in the 1980s and 1990s.* Alberton: Galago 2001

Studwell, Joe. *Asian Godfathers: Money and Power in Hong Kong and South East Asia.* London: Profile Books, 2010

Tiley, Sian. *Mapungubwe: South Africa's Crown Jewels.* Cape Town: Sunbird Publishing, 2004

't Sas-Rolfes, Michael. *Rhinos: Conservation, Economics and Trade-Offs.* London: Institute of Economic Affairs Environment Unit, 1995

Wels, Harry. *Private Wildlife Conservation in Zimbabwe: Joint Ventures and Reciprocity.* Leiden: BRILL, 2003

Wilkins, Ivor, and Hans Strydom. *The Super-Afrikaners.* Johannesburg: Jonathan Ball, 1980

JOURNAL, NEWSPAPER AND MAGAZINE ARTICLES

Addley, Esther. 'Into the abyss'. *The Guardian*, 11 January 2002

AFP. 'Vietnam to recall diplomat filmed taking rhino horn'. Agence France-Presse, 19 November 2008

AIM. 'Mozambique: Rhino horns and abalone seized at Maputo airport'.
Agência de informação de Moçambique, 31 May 2012

———. 'Mozambique: Thailand seizes ivory smuggled from country'. Agência
de informação de Moçambique, 6 January 2011

Ammann, Karl. 'The Vietnamese and rhino horn – a dealer speaks'. Swara, 2011

An Dien. 'Rhino remains on death row', Thanh Nien Daily, 23 September 2011

Anon. 'Aansoek om uitlewering'. Beeld, 14 August 1990

———. 'Cancer keeps rising throughout Vietnam'. VietNamNetBridge,
11 October 2010

———. 'Da Lat wildlife kingpin untouchable'. Thanh Nien News, 6 May 2011

———. 'Illegal rhino horn trade: the Vietnamese connection'.
Savingrhinos.org, 16 August 2010

———. 'John C. Lukman Jr obituary'. The Hartford Courant, 27 July 2007

———. 'Operation Jumbo divides S. Africa's animal groups', ENS, 12 January 1999

———. 'Oud-soldaat maak 'n kinkel in ivoor-kabel'. Beeld, 30 August 1995

———. 'Plan to legalize rhino horn trade prompts concerns'. African Eye News
Service, 5 April 2012

———. 'Shoot to kill'. Newsweek, 12 January 2006

———. 'Star witness in South African rhino horn syndicate case unwilling to
testify due to threats against family'. Savingrhinos.org, 12 October, 2010

———. 'Viëtnamese in SA hof oor renosterhorings'. Beeld, 2 February 2011

Armstrong, Sue. 'South African Army behind ivory trade'. New Scientist,
27 January 1996

Badprop, Angola. 'Lana, rus in vrede'. Sondag, 6 February 2011

———. 'Wie is die man in die wit 4×4?' Sondag, 14 February 2011

Bailey, Candice. 'Poaching dockets vanish'. The Star, 22 August 2011

Barton, Cat. 'Vietnam's "cancer-cure" horn habit threatens rhino population'.
Agence France-Presse, 8 May 2012

Basson, Adriaan, and Piet Rampedi . 'Malema's Secret Fund'. City Press,
24 July 2011

———. 'Julius Malema: Mister Cash', City Press, 31 July 2011

Beech, Hannah, and Alex Perry. 'Killing fields: Africa's rhinos under threat'.
Time, 13 June 2011

Beresford, David. 'Illegal lion hunting cases top 130'. Mail & Guardian,
15 August 1997

Bhattacharya, Shaoni. 'Gene detectives track the rhino killers'. New Scientist,
17 November 2010

Blair, David. 'Zimbabwe's great white survivor'. The Telegraph, 11 June 2005

Borrell, Brendan. 'Hunters paying $150,000 to kill an endangered rhino may save the species'. *Bloomberg*, 9 December 2010

Brooke, James. 'CIA Said to Send Weapons Via Zaire to Angola Rebels'. *New York Times*, 1 February 1987

Brown, Karima. 'Fired SARS man "moonlighted for Mbalula"'. *Business Day*, 23 March 2010

Brown, Paul. 'Web of African intrigue'. *The Guardian*, 2 March 1992

———. 'WWF paid for helicopter used to kill poachers'. *The Guardian*, 4 September 1990

But, Paul Pui-Hay, et al. 'Ethnopharmacology of rhinoceros horn. II: Antipyretic effects of prescriptions containing rhinoceros horn or water buffalo horn'. *Journal of Ethnopharmacology*, May/June 1991

Butland, Peter de Villiers. 'PHASA president's opinion'. *African Indaba*, 2009

Carnie, Tony. 'Tracking down the "Boere Rhino Mafia"'. *The Mercury*, 8 June 2010

———. '"It is big-time crime with easy money"'. *The Mercury*, 8 June 2010

———. 'How police tracked down the "Boere Rhino Mafia"'. *The Mercury*, 9 June 2010

Chengetai, Zvauya. 'Zimbabwean security forces accused of poaching'. Associated Press, 11 February 2010

Conway-Smith, Erin. 'Can China help save the rhinos?' *Global Post*, 29 February 2012

Cumming, David. 'Zimbabwe and the conservation of black rhino'. *The Zimbabwe Science News*, May/June 1987

Dawes, Nic. 'Spooks at play in succession politics'. *Mail & Guardian*, 16 March 2012

De Beer, Linda. 'Moordklag laat vaar nadat leeu 'n werker se nek breek'. *Beeld*, 8 November 2007

———. 'Moordklag teen boer nadat leeu werker se lewe eis'. *Beeld*, 18 October 2006

De Swardt, Wilhelm. '328000 kg ivoor uitgesmokkel'. *Beeld*, 18 January 1996

———. 'SAW het jare lank ivoor gesmokkel – Magnus Malan en ander hoës was ingelig'. *Beeld*, 18 January 1996

Drury, Rebecca. 'Hungry for success: Urban consumer demand for wild animal products in Vietnam'. *Conservation and Society*, 2011

———. 'Reducing urban demand for wild animals in Vietnam: Examining the potential of wildlife farming as a conservation tool'. *Conservation Letters*, 2009

Dunham, Kevin. 'Ages of black rhinos killed by drought and poaching in Zimbabwe'. *Pachyderm*, 1985

Du Plessis, Charl. '"Rhino syndicate targets lions"'. *The Times*, 7 November 2011

Eckholm, Erik. 'Poachers and protectors wage war over rhinos'. *New York Times*, 6 May 1986

Ellis, Stephen. 'De lange arm van het wereld natuur fonds'. *De Volksrant*, 24 August 1991

———. 'Of Elephants and Men: Politics and Nature Conservation in South Africa'. *Journal of Southern African Studies*, 1994

———. 'Prince paid thousands into wildlife sting'. *The Independent*, 8 January 1991

Eveleth, Ann. 'Rhino horns for trap go missing'. *Weekly Mail*, 22 September 1995

Fuller, Thomas. 'Notorious Golden Triangle loses sway in the opium trade'. *New York Times*, 11 September 2007

Galster, Steven R. 'The trail leads to South Africa'. *The Nation*, 15 February 1993

Golembeski, Dean. 'Rhino horn smugglers arrested, ring cracked'. *Schenectady Gazette*, 7 November 1988

Groenewald, Yolandi. 'Vietnam embassy in rhino row'. *Mail & Guardian*, 14 November 2008

Gwin, Peter. 'Rhino wars'. *National Geographic*, March 2012

Insight Team. 'How the woman at no. 27 ran spy network for arms firm'. *The Sunday Times*, 28 September 2003

Karimakwenda, Tererai. 'ZANU-PF officials implicated in illegal trophy hunting scams'. SW Radio Africa, 14 September 2005

Karmel, Terese. 'Undercover federal agent getting help from public'. 5 December 1986

Keppler, Virginia. 'Jagter vas'. *Sondag*, 8 August 2011

Kreig, Andrew. 'Suit seeks release of CIA data'. *The Hartford Courant*, 16 December 1976

Lamprecht, Deon. 'Só Het Unita Olifante Uitgewis – Breytenbach'. *Beeld*, 9 September 1995

———. 'Weermag "het olifante laat jag" – oud-lid van spesiale magte sê tande is oor Zambezi gebring'. *Beeld*, 30 August 1995

Lategan, Piet. '"Cream poachers" are greatest threat to Africa's wildlife'. *Mail & Guardian*, 2 April 1999

Louw-Carstens, Marietie. 'Wildboer in tronk oor 30 horings'. *Beeld*, 7 March 2012

Louw-Carstens, Marietie, and Julian Rademeyer. 'G'n bewyse hy stroop renoster'. *Beeld*, 19 April 2011

Lubisi, Dumisane. 'Malema's dodgy spy'. *City Press*, 21 March 2010

———. 'Who is Michael Peega?' *City Press*, 21 March 2010

Lukman, John. 'Africa: our outrage has been selective'. *Hartford Courant*,
29 June 1985

Macleod, Fiona. 'Jumbo-sized toothache'. *Mail & Guardian*, 12 February 1999
———. 'Vets charged for illegal use of tranquillisers'. *Mail & Guardian*,
2 March 2012

Magnus, Liela. 'Jagter eis ná "lasterlike" e-pos'. *Beeld*, 30 August 2005

Mahony, Edmund. 'Man gets 8 months in wildlife smuggling'. *The Hartford Courant*, 17 July 1992

Malone, Andrew. 'How Chelsy Davy's father, Chinese gangsters and a ruthless Mugabe henchman are linked by a vile trade that's driving the black rhino to extinction'. *Daily Mail*, 1 August 2009

Martin, Esmond Bradley. 'Africa's rhino horn trade from 1970 to 1985: An economic explanation'. *Kenya Past and Present*, 1992

Masland, Tom. 'Ivory smugglers become fair game'. *Chicago Tribune*,
12 March 1989

Miller, Susan Katz. 'Stuffed leopard gives smugglers' game away'. *New Scientist*, 1992

Momberg, Eleanor. 'Poachers play dirty to get what they want'. *Sunday Independent*, 19 July 2009

Monare, Moshoeshoe. 'Malema and the spy papers'. *The Star*, 24 February 2010
———. 'Malema spy saga grows'. *The Star*, 24 February 2010

Netsianda, Mashudu. 'Suspected poacher shot dead near Beitbridge'.
Zoutpansberger, 21 August 2009

Nguyen Ba Duc, Dang The Can, Doan Huu Nghi, and Pham Hoang Anh. 'Vietnam National Cancer Institute: A history of its development'.
Asian Pacific Journal of Cancer Prevention, 2001

Otto, Hanti. 'Horings weg uit polisiekluis'. *Beeld*, 29 February 2012

Pappin, Sarah. 'Rhino crimes: are the right people going to jail?' Savingrhinos.
org, 10 February 2012

Pearce, Fred. 'Rhino rescue plan decimates Asian antelopes'. *New Scientist*,
12 February 2003

Pelser, Willem. 'Horings: Chinees gevonnis, 2 op borg vrygelaat'. *Beeld*,
10 February 2009

Peta, Basildon. 'Chelsy Davy's father faces inquiry into business deals'.
The Independent, 21 April 2006

Pitman, Dick, and Glenn Tatham. 'Rhino poaching , Zimbabwe'. *Pachyderm*, 1985

Politieke Redaksie. 'Oud-offisier aan Amerika uitgelewer oor wapens'.
18 May 1992

319

Potgieter, De Wet. 'Call girl murder mystery'. *The New Age*, 27 April 2012

———. 'Noted vet held on rhino poaching charges'. *The New Age*, 24 November 2011

Rademeyer, Julian. '50 te veel laat hom praat'. *Beeld*, 5 August 2011

———. 'Bloedspoor na die Ooste'. *Beeld*, 22 July 2011

———. 'Boertjie takes on rhino gang'. *The Witness*, 6 August, 2011

———. '"BOOM" sê SMS op foon'. *Beeld*, 9 July 2010

———. 'Die prys van 'n gratis vakansie'. *Beeld*, 1 February 2011

———. 'Horings: baie klagte'. *Beeld*, 1 October 2011

———. 'Hunter fined over rhino poaching'. *News24.com*, 19 January 2011

———. ''n Winchester-geweer, 'n plaasaanval en die "mafia"'. *Beeld*, 9 July 2010

———. '"Renosterbende" by Edenvale-huis vas'. *Rapport*, 10 July 2011

———. 'Sex workers used to "hunt" rhino'. *News24.com*, 7 July 2011

———. 'Sindikaat huur vroue om te "jag"'. *Beeld*, 22 July 2011

———. 'Stropery: vrou sê sy huil by karkas'. *Beeld*, 25 July 2011

———. 'Thai woman "cried" next to shot rhino'. *News24.com*, 25 July 2011

———. The Vietnamese connection'. *The Witness*, 22 January 2011

———. 'Wildlife trafficking trail leads to SA safari man'. *News24.com*, 21 July 2011

———. 'Zim-renosters uit SA gestroop'. *Beeld*, 9 July 2010

Rademeyer, Julian, and Marietie Louw-Carstens. 'Stropery: wildbaas ook vas'. *Beeld*, 22 September 2010

Reeve, Rosalind, and Stephen Ellis. 'An insider's account of the South African security forces' role in the ivory trade'. *Journal of Contemporary African Studies*, 1995

Reilly, Ted. 'Black rhino return to Swaziland'. *Rhino and Elephant Foundation Journal*, 1990

Ricciuti, Edward R. 'Guns 'n rhinos'. *Wildlife Conservation*, January/February 1992

Rice, Andy. 'Paul O'Sullivan: "And now I'm also going after Thabo Mbeki"'. *Daily Maverick*, 6 July 2010

Scheepers, Marlise. 'Leeu geskiet wat werker doodklap'. *Beeld*, 27 August 2005

Seanego, Karabo. 'Hunter link to stripper's death?' *Pretoria News*, 8 August 2011

Sheppard Jr, Nathaniel. 'U.S. arrests 3 in rhino-horn, rifle smuggling'. *Chicago Tribune*, 7 November 1988

Smith, Charles. 'Anger over lion bone sales'. *News24.com*, 10 December 2009

Sole, Sam. 'Mike Peega: the man behind the dossier'. *Mail & Guardian*, 26 February 2010

Sparmann, Anke. 'Bad medicine'. *Geo*, 2011

Staff Reporter. 'Canning Kruger's elephants'. *Mail & Guardian*, 9 July 2004

———. 'Lion-baiting on Parks Board man's farm'. *Mail & Guardian*,
30 May 1997

Swart, Freek. 'SA man gedeporteer ná straf in VSA'. *Beeld*, 24 July 1992

———. 'Suid-Afrikaner beken skuld in VSA op smokkel-klagte: hy het
doeane-dokumente vervals, AK 47-gewere ingesmokkel'. *Beeld*, 21 May 1992

Swart, Lucia. 'Leeu breek man se nek met enkele pootveeg'. *Beeld*, 24 August 2005

Tatham, Glenn. 'The rhino conservation strategy in the Zambezi Valley code
named Operation Stronghold'. *The Zimbabwe Science News*, 1988

Tatham, G.H., and R.D. Taylor. 'The conservation and protection of the black
rhinoceros *Diceros bicornis* in Zimbabwe'. *Koedoe*, 1989

Thornton, Steve. 'Letters to green left weekly'. *Green Left Weekly*, 14 May 2003

Thornycroft, Peta. 'Dad had no links to poachers, says Chelsy'. *The Telegraph*,
9 August 2009

Van der Walt, Sarel. 'Magnus erken ivoor is namens UNITA verkoop'. *Beeld*,
19 January 1996

Van der Westhuizen, Christi. 'Die onbekende sy van gevreesde bosvegter
Breytenbach'. *Beeld*, 4 December 1997

———. 'Smokkelaars "word beskerm"; nog ondersoeke nodig', *Beeld*
4 December 1997

———. 'Storie van IFAW-skenking wek agterdog'. *Beeld*, 10 April 1999

Van der Westhuizen, Fantie. 'Regter Kumleben kyk na SA betrokkenheid by die
smokkel van ivoor'. *Beeld*, 7 October 1994

Van Rooyen, Fanie. 'Jagter kry borg om met "groter saak" te help'. *Beeld*,
9 August 2011

Van Schie, Kristen. 'Charges against alleged poacher dropped'. *Star*,
12 October 2010

Van Wyk, Johan. '120 renosterhorings was bestem vir Taiwan – nekslag vir
4 smokkelaars'. *Beeld*, 29 September 1990

Vigne, Richard. 'How economic theory applies to poaching'. *Star* (Nairobi),
31 May 2012

Viljoen, Buks. 'Foto's wys glo marteling'. *Beeld*, 15 June 2012

———. '"Vry maak hy polisie dood"'. *Beeld*, 30 March 2012

Vollers, Maryanne. 'A war to save the black rhino'. *Time*, 7 September 1987

———. 'The rhino wars: Zimbabwe is shooting poachers who menace the rare
black rhino'. *Sports Illustrated*, 2 March 1987

Watts, Jonathan. '"Noah's Ark" of 5000 rare animals found floating off the coast
of China'. *The Guardian*, 26 May 2007

Wellman, Peter. 'Elite Zimbabwe squad wages war to save endangered black
    rhino'. Associated Press, 22 November 1987
Western, David, and Lucy Vigne. 'The status of rhinos in Africa'. *Newsletter of
    the African Elephant and Rhino*, 1984
Zwecker, Wolfram. 'Vyf in hof oor renosters'. *Beeld*, 5 June 2012
———. 'Wildboer in hof'. *Beeld*, 10 November 2011

REPORTS AND PRESS RELEASES

'CITES CoP15 Inf. 32: Illegal killing of rhinoceros in South Africa'. Conference
    of the Parties to CITES, Doha, Qatar, 3–25 March 2010
Bodasing, Ashish, and Teresa Mulliken. 'South Africa's wildlife trade at the
    crossroads'. TRAFFIC East/Southern Africa Report, 1996
Brook, Sarah, Peter van Coeverden de Groot, Simon Mahood, and Barney
    Long. 'Extinction of the Javan rhinoceros (*Rhinoceros sondaicus*) from
    Vietnam'. WWF Report, 2011
'BUAV field investigation report: The trade in *Macaca fascicularis* in Laos'.
    British Union for the Abolition of Vivisection, November 2011
'Bulletin of seizures and prosecutions: March 1997–April 2011'. TRAFFIC
    International, 2011
Carroll, Thea, and Magdel Boshoff. 'Guidelines for the implementation of
    threatened or protected species (TOPS) regulations and the issuance of
    TOPS permits in terms of the National Environmental Management:
    Biodiversity Act (Act 10 of 2004)'. NEMBA, 2007
'Conspicuous consumption of rhino horn'. News from the Frontline, Education
    for Nature Vietnam, May 2012
De Alessi, Michael. 'Private conservation and black rhinos in Zimbabwe:
    The Savé Valley and Bubiana conservancy'. CEI, 1999
'Department of Interior news release'. US Fish and Wildlife Service,
    18 May 1992
Do Thi Thanh Huyen, Bui Huu Manh, et al. 'Consumption of wild animal
    products in Ho Chi Minh City'. WAR, 2011
Drury, Rebecca. 'Identifying and understanding consumers of wild animal
    products in Hanoi, Vietnam'. University College London, 2009
Du Toit, Raoul. 'Management of black rhino in Zimbabwean conservancies'.
    Proceedings of a symposium on rhinos as game ranch animals,
    Onderstepoort, Republic of South Africa, September 1994
Ferreira, Antoinette. 'The National Environmental Management: Biodiversity
    Act No. 10 of 2004 and the TOPS regulations'. NEMBA, 2009

'Inadequate protection causes Javan rhino extinction in Vietnam'. Press release, WWF, 25 October 2011

Jooste, Johan. 'Presentation on the rhinoceros threat'. Directorate for Priority Crime Investigation, 2012

'Journalists and translator released'. Committee to Protect Journalists, 2003

Klingel, Hans. 'Survey of African rhinoceros'. December 1979

Knight, Mike, and Richard Emslie. 'Rhino conservation strategy'. SADC Rhino Management Group, 2011

Kumleben, Justice M.E. 'Commission of inquiry into the alleged smuggling of and illegal trade in ivory and rhinoceros horn in South Africa'. The Commission, 1996

Laburn, Helen P., and Duncan Mitchell. 'Extracts of rhinoceros horn are not antipyretic in rabbits'. University of the Witwatersrand: Freund Publishing House, 1997

'Laos: Opium survey 2004'. United Nations Office on Drugs and Crime, 2004

'Laotian court sentences journalists and their translator to 15 years in prison'. Committee to Protect Journalists, 2003

Leathem, Blondie. '1984: The start of the rhino war and Operation Stronghold'. Unpublished

Milliken, Tom, and Jo Shaw. 'The South Africa–Vietnam rhino horn trade nexus.' TRAFFIC International, 2012

Milliken, Tom, K. Nowell, and J.B. Thomsen. 'The decline of the black rhino in Zimbabwe'. TRAFFIC International, 1993

Mills, J.A. 'Rhinoceros horn and tiger bone in China'. TRAFFIC International, 1997

'More than 1 tonne of ivory and rhino horns seized in Thailand'. TRAFFIC International, 25 February 2011

Nowell, Kristin. 'Wildlife crime scorecard'. WWF, 2012

Nowell, Kristin, Wei-Lien Chyi, and Chia-Jai Pei. 'The horns of the dilemma: The market for rhino horn in Taiwan'. TRAFFIC International, 1992

'Perspectives on dehorning and legalised trade in rhino horn as tools to combat rhino poaching'. Endangered Wildlife Trust, 2011

Razafindrakoto, Mireille, François Roubaud, and Matthieu Salomon. 'Global corruption barometer 2010: Vietnam country analysis'. Transparency International, 2011

Redpath, Jean. 'Failing to prosecute? Assessing the state of the National Prosecuting Authority in South Africa'. ISS, 2012

Reeve, Rosalind. 'The CITES treaty and compliance: Progress or jeopardy?'
  Chatham House Briefing Paper, 2004
———. 'Wildlife trade, sanctions and compliance: Lessons from the CITES
  regime'. International Affairs, 2006
'South African National Parks annual report'. SANParks, 2010/11
'Staff paper prepared for the Steyn Commission on alleged dangerous activities
  of SADF components'. Steyn Commission of Inquiry, December 1992
'S v. Meiring and Another' (1992) 4 All SA 120 (W), *All South African Law
  Reports*
Tran Thi Thu Ha, et al. 'Towards a transparent and quality healthcare system'.
  Transparency International, 2011
't Sas-Rolfes, Michael. 'Saving African rhinos: A market success story'. PERC,
  2011
———. 'The rhino poaching crisis: A market analysis'. PERC, 2012
'Under siege: Rhinoceroses in South Africa'. Animal Rights Africa, 2009
US Embassy Harare. 'Environmental impact of current crises on Zimbabwe's
  wildlife'. Diplomatic Cable, 25 July 2003
———. 'Land reform threatens wildlife'. Diplomatic Cable, 20 April 2004
———. 'Poaching of wildlife is rampant in Zimbabwe'. Diplomatic Cable,
  21 May 2002
———. 'Save Valley: Struggling to hold on'. Diplomatic Cable, 17 December 2004
———. 'ZANU-PF governor forcing himself on Amcit-owned conservancy'.
  Diplomatic Cable, 29 May 2009
Venkataraman, Bina. 'A matter of attitude: The consumption of wild animal
  products in Hanoi, Vietnam'. TRAFFIC Southeast Asia, 2007
'Vietnamese citizen gets 10 years' imprisonment for illegal possession of rhino
  horn'. Endangered Wildlife Trust, 1 July 2010

FREQUENTLY USED WEBSITES
CITES: www.cites.org
Rhino Economics: www.rhino-economics.com
Rhino Resource Center: www.rhinoresourcecenter.com
Saving Rhinos: www.savingrhinos.org
TRAFFIC: www.traffic.org

FILM
Martin, Andrew (director). *Rhino under Threat*. Documentary film. UNTV/
  CITES, 2012

Index